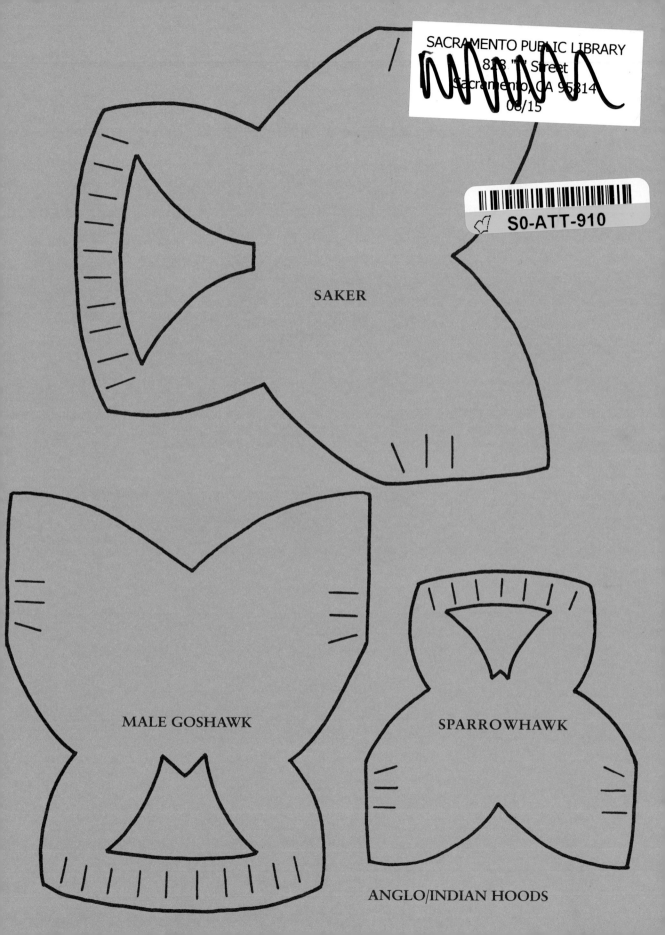

SAKER

MALE GOSHAWK

SPARROWHAWK

ANGLO/INDIAN HOODS

Falconry and Hawking

Falconry and Hawking

Phillip Glasier

BATSFORD

First published in the United Kingdom in 1978 by

Batsford
1 Gower Street
London WC1E 6HD

An imprint of Pavilion Books Company Ltd

ISBN: 9 780713 484076

A CIP catalogue record for this book is available from the British Library.

10 9 8
20 19 18 17 16 15 14

Reproduction by Anorax Imaging Ltd, Leeds
Printed and bound by 1010 Printing International Ltd, China

This book can be ordered direct from the publisher at the website:
www.pavilionbooks.com, or try your local bookshop

Distributed in the United States and Canada by Sterling Publishing Co., Inc.
1166 Avenue of the Americas, 17th floor, New York, NY 10036, USA

Contents

Acknowledgments

My thanks are due to the following people who have helped me in the
preparation of this book:

Greg Simpson, M.R.C.V.S., who contributed the new chapter on Health and Disease.
Mary Btowning, Paul Bevan, John Haywood and Dinah Glasier for the line drawings.
Selwyn Cox, for photographs 45–54 in the chapter on hooding, and for the lure-swinging sequence
nos. 78–99. (The remainder of the photographs were taken by the author.)
Professor Gunilla Åkerström-Hougen for bringing to my notice the mosaics at the Villa of the
Falconer, and for permission to reproduce a picture from her book on the subject.
The Moorland Gallery, who kindly permitted the reproduction of the paintings by George Lodge and
provided the transparencies. Copyright is reserved on all the G.E. Lodge illustrations used in this book.
Tom Cullen, Nicholas Fox, Tony Howell-Jones, Marrin Jones, Charlotte Moore and Egon Muller, and
the whole of my family.

Note on Measurement
Although exact metric equivalents have been given throughout
the text, in practice one can work to rounded-up figures.

Preface

'How lucky you are,' I am frequently told, 'to have learnt falconry from an expert like Captain Knight.' Of course, I was indeed very lucky to have had such an experienced and successful falconer as my uncle to teach me, for it is not easy to learn so practical a sport from books alone.

Many books have been written on falconry, and it is therefore only after a considerable amount of persuasion that I have decided to add to their number. I am still convinced that it is better to have someone to teach you than to rely on books alone. It was because of this conviction that, when I started the Falconry Centre in 1967 at Newent in Gloucestershire, I had the idea of running courses in falconry for beginners. At that time I anticipated a mere handful of people each year, but this estimate was soon proved wrong. Also I had expected that my pupils would be mainly teenage boys, but found myself teaching would-be falconers of all ages, both sexes and from all walks of life.

Now, after some years, during which I have taught several hundred people on courses, I feel considerably more competent to write a book on the subject. However well one may know a job, one soon realises that teaching it is very different from simply doing it oneself. When one is showing people how to do a thing, one can make them do it themselves and then immediately correct their mistakes or give additional advice. But writing about it is far more difficult. Every little detail is important to the beginner.

To cover every aspect of falconry in a course lasting only twelve days is obviously impossible. It means condensing and concentrating on the essentials only, in order to give the beginner enough information to enable him to go away and train his own bird. I hope this book will serve as a reminder to ex-coursers of the many things dealt with during their course. But I would like to think that it goes further than this, and that it would be possible for someone with absolutely no previous knowledge of falconry to train a hawk successfully from this book alone, without any recourse to outside aid.

Obviously not all falconers are likely to agree with everything I have written – that would be quite impossible. Also, the falconry scene is constantly changing, particularly where health and disease are concerned. New drugs and better ways of doing things are constantly being discovered.

To the beginner I would say: do seriously consider all that the keeping of a hawk entails, before you get one. A bird is not a toy to be cast aside, or a gun which can be left in a cupboard until you feel like getting it out again. Nor can you leave it in the care of an inexperienced person while you are away. It is a great responsibility which must not be taken lightly, though falconry is not so difficult as some would have you believe. If you have patience and perseverance you will overcome the many frustrations and obstacles that you will encounter. Then, as Bert says (in his *Treatise of Hawkes and Hawking*, 1619), 'Youre hawke will be a moste sweete satisfaction'.

To train one's own bird, fly it free, and see it come back to one is indeed a 'sweete satisfaction'; to own a bird for some years, flying it as often as possible and hunting with it successfully, is yet more satisfying. To breed your bird, and then do all this, is the best of all. If this book can be of help in achieving any of these ends then it will have served its purpose.

Preface to Third Edition

This seems to be the third preface I shall have done. So if we are not very careful we shall have to alter the title to 'Prefaces' instead of **Falconry and Hawking**.

Naturally, I have re-read my copy of the book and I don't think there's a great deal that needs altering. Knowing how much publishers hate altering anything once it's in print, I think it would be better if we left it all as it is. However, things do change. New ideas come about, and new ideas are really what we need to bring the book up to date. I have divided these additions into two.

New idea one is a completely new chapter on Health and Disease by Greg Simpson M.R.C.V.S., who is a raptor specialist.

New idea two is about keeping trained birds of prey not tied up, but loose in an aviary. This is something that I have been doing for some years now, and it has a great many advantages. At one time we could never have done this because a bird taken from the wild tends to smash itself about, as it has no 'wire' sense. Now that we are breeding so many birds of prey in captivity – and so few are being taken from the wild – a great many of these aviary-bred birds already have 'wire' sense.

The great advantages are that the bird cannot get tangled because it is not tied up and it is at liberty to move around and sit in the sun or in the shade or under shelter if it is raining. (You will probably find that a great many birds enjoy sitting in the rain.) The type of aviary you build is entirely up to you. I have been using 'weld-mesh' – sometimes known as 'twill weld' – and if a bird still tends to crash about I sometimes put in an inner lining of plastic of a fine but very pliable mesh.

In practice birds do not seem to damage themselves. Although, when you first see them clinging to the inside of the aviary, you may well wonder why they do not break valuable flight feathers or damage their ceres. Obviously you must provide shelter of some kind, bearing in mind the great changes that occur in the weather. A bird needs to be able to get out of the wind and, if it likes, away from hot sun or anything else that it may dislike. Beware of frost. Birds can very easily get frost-bitten feet. Personally I like to have an indoor· compartment for bad weather.

It is advisable to have an extra door – with enough space for it to be closed before the main door is opened. If snow is expected, it is best to make the door open outwards – as snow can build up on the inside and prevent it being opened. I also like to have an easy means of getting the bath in and out of the aviary, so that it can be cleaned and refilled without too much disturbance.

Obviously, the design of perches will require careful thought. I advise consulting Greg Simpson's new Health and Disease chapter. Greg has considerable expertise in avoiding 'Bumble Foot' and gives sound advice on the best type of perch.

Birds kept loose in aviaries – both hawks and falcons – stay remarkably tame and are soon accustomed to the idea of being picked up and weighed etc. My old Harris' Hawk would fly out of the aviary into my weighing room without being asked once she got the idea. Having been weighed, she would fly into my car and sit there waiting for me. I never tied her up in the car if we were only going matter of a mile or so, but for long distances I used to tie her up as a safety precaution. Members of the public, seeing a bird in a car, tend to gawp and possibly try and make her move – and all sorts of silly things.

I very rarely put Jesse on her. She wore Aylmeri all the time – together with bells and a device for attaching the electronic transmitter. How much easier falconry has become with the introduction of these devices! But I would like to point out that a transmitter will not persuade a bird to come back to you out of a tree. That will depend on how well you have trained her. I have kept both Harris' Hawks and Peregrines and a Gyr loose in aviaries successfully. Falconer friends of mine have had equal success with short-wings. I have found this method a great improvement on having birds tied by leash and swivel, and thereby greatly limited in their movements.

1 An Historical Outline

In many people's minds the word 'falconry' conjures up a rather stylised, romantic picture of colourful parties of knights and ladies, setting forth on prancing steeds from moated castles, for a day's hawking in the mediaeval countryside. But few people have more than a rather hazy idea of what falconry is really all about. Briefly, it is the art of hunting with trained birds of prey, and although nowadays in the West it is considered more or less entirely as a sporting activity, this was not its original purpose when it began. Almost certainly, the first person to train a hawk did so because he saw in it an efficient means of catching food for himself. (There are still falconers in North Korea who make a living simply by selling the game that their birds have caught.)

The mediaeval picture of falconry is certainly true, as far as it goes; falconry was indeed popular among the European landed gentry during the Middle Ages. But it was confined neither to the upper classes, nor to this particular period of history alone. There had been falconers in Europe since at least Saxon times (and in the East, for a great deal longer), and the sport was to flourish for many centuries thereafter, until various circumstances combined to bring about its gradual decline from the Restoration period onwards.

No one knows when or where falconry first began, and although various theories have been advanced at one time or another to show that it originated in China, Persia, Central Asia and so forth, there is very little concrete evidence to support any of them, and so none can be said to be very convincing. Although the Japanese writer Akizato Rito, in his *Topography of the Province Kawatsi* (1801–1808) states that falcons were among the presents given to Chinese princes during the Hia dynasty (supposed to have begun in 2205 B.C.) this in no way proves that these were falconry birds, or even that falconry was known at that early date. According to Harting (*Bibliotheca Accipitraria*, 1891) a bas-relief depicting a falconer was discovered in the ruins of Khorsabad in Mesopotamia by Sir Henry Layard, during the last century, and this was supposed to date from about 1700 B.C. If the dating was accurate, this certainly shows that falconry is a very ancient practice indeed, but we are still no nearer to knowing its actual origins.

Documentary evidence to show that it was being practised in Central Asia around 400 B.C. is found in the writings of Ctesias (the court physician to the Shah Artaxerxes Mnemon) and the Greek writer Aelian; according to Ctesias,

1 Mosaic from the Villa of the Falconer at Argos, *c.*500 AD.

falconry was not known in Persia at this date. Aristotle (384–322 B.C.) wrote of hawking in Thrace, and Pliny also mentioned it in his *Natural History* some centuries later; but these descriptions seem to me to be not of falconry as we know it, but of something more akin to 'daring' larks (see chapter 2 under the section on the hobby). 'In the district of Thrace . . . men and hawks have a kind of partnership for fowling. The men put up birds from woods and reed-beds and the hawks, flying overhead, drive them down again' (Pliny). The birds would then be netted, and 'the fowlers share the spoils with the hawks'.

The earliest documentary evidence of real falconry seems to come from Japan, where it is recorded that trained goshawks were brought there from China in the 47th year of the reign of the Empress Jingu (A.D. 244). Apparently their training was not maintained, and the sport seems to have been abandoned for some hundred years or so. During the reign of the Emperor Nintoku, round about A.D. 355, the sport finally caught on in Japan. In the chronicle *Nihonshoki* it is recorded that a strange bird was caught and presented to the Emperor, and that a Korean at the court recognized the species (it was probably a goshawk). He was charged with training it, and he put jesses on it and belled its tail, and in the autumn of that year caught pheasants with it in the fields of Mozu (near present-day Osaka). This would certainly imply that at that date falconry was better known in Korea than in Japan. (E.W. Jameson, *The Hawking of Japan*,

1962.) After this, the Emperor set up a hawking establishment, and two centuries later a dog-keeper was installed, to train dogs to hunt with the hawks. From then on falconry became very popular in Japan – so much so, that during the Middle Ages hawking parties assumed enormous proportions, and did great damage to crops by trampling over them in search of game. Hawking had to be banned in the vicinity of Buddhist temples, since instances occurred of goshawks pursuing their quarry into temples and killing in sight of the outraged priests.

It is interesting to note that from this period comes what must be one of the very first records of a woman falconer. Apparently a celebrated Chinese falconer visited Japan, and his methods were so much admired that the Japanese were loath to let him depart again. So they enticed him to stay by encouraging him to marry a young lady selected from a large number of court beauties. The daughter of this marriage, Akemihikari, herself became an eminent falconer, and when she married a certain Minamo Masayori, her father handed over to her the secrets of his art. Through her, his method of training birds became extremely popular, and was known as the Masayori Method (Jameson).

In 1966 Professor John Lane of Long Island University sent me a translation of a curious Japanese regulation of 1487, entitled 'A Prohibition against the Feeding of Turtles, Tortoises and Snakes to Falcons', which runs as follows:

> It is forbidden to feed turtles, tortoises and snakes to falcons . . . Those who do not go in fear of this prohibition will find it difficult to escape divine wrath. Henceforth and hereafter, according to this strict injunction, when there are those who keep falcons in (accommodations) which are smaller than bird coops, or are unable to raise them with bird and animal [meat] alone, they will not be permitted to own falcons. If there are those who still violate this prohibition and still seek out turtles, if they are *samurai*, they will have their stipend lands confiscated; if they have no investiture, then they shall be banished. As for the common people, as soon as they are discovered and reported, they shall be summarily detained, and, in accordance with the circumstances, will be executed and their corpses exposed. So We have ordered. Thus, a matter for the 'Wall Writing'.

During this time, falconry was spreading westwards. Quite how and when it reached Europe is, once again, unknown. One of the earliest known pieces of evidence of falconry in Europe is a floor mosaic, representing a falconry scene, in the Roman 'Villa of the Falconer' at Argos in Greece. This has been dated at circa A.D. 500.

Certainly falconry was being practised in England by Saxon times, since between A.D. 733 and 750 Aethelbald, King of Mercia, was sent a hawk and two falcons by Boniface, Archbishop of Mayence (see 'The Date of the Ruthwell and Bewcastle Crosses' by A.S. Cook, Carlisle Public Library, L.4137). By 821 the sport had become so popular that the monks of Abingdon

2 Goshawk, from *The Mirror of Hawks* by Kawanabe, *c.*1880.

had to petition King Kenulph of Mercia for a charter to restrain over-enthusiastic falconers from tramping over their crops at harvest-time (a parallel with Japan, in fact). We know from the writings of William of Malmesbury, the Anglo-Norman chronicler, that Athelstan and Edward the Confessor were both fond of hawking, while on the Bayeux Tapestry Harold and Comte Guy de Ponthieu are depicted with hawks on fist. It was common practice to take hawks and hounds on campaigns, so that the knights could have some relaxation between battles. Froissart tells us that Edward III took no less than 30 falconers with him when he invaded France. After all, as late as the Peninsular Wars we find Wellington including a pack of foxhounds in his entourage.

By the twelfth century people had begun to write about falconry in Turkish, Spanish and Arabic. The Emperor Barbarossa was a hawking enthusiast, and his grandson, the Emperor Frederick II of Germany, wrote a vast treatise on the subject (*De Arte Venandi cum Avibus*, circa 1247) which has been translated into English and German in this century. Also in Germany, the first printed book on falconry appeared in 1472.

Falconry became part of a mediaeval education, and so the list of famous people who were interested in the sport seems almost endless. This is not to say that the rich and influential were the only people to hunt with hawks; doubtless there were many people among the yeoman classes who flew goshawks and sparrowhawks in order to catch food. But at this period of history the life of the poorer classes went largely unchronicled, and so we naturally know more of the pursuits of royalty and the aristocracy.

Most of the mediaeval kings and nobles took an interest in the sport, and in many courts the office of Royal Falconer was created. In the laws of Howel Dha (circa A.D. 900) we find that the Penhebogyd, or master of the hawks, was only fourth in rank and dignity from the king himself. He sat in the fourth place of honour at the royal table (though he was not allowed to drink more than three times at a meal, for fear he should neglect his hawks through drunkenness). After a particularly successful day's hawking, the king was obliged, by law and custom, to rise and receive the Penhebogyd as he entered the hall.

Various species of hawks and falcons were highly prized, and the people who could afford it went to considerable lengths to get hold of them. They were also considered desirable gifts between kings and princes; King John used to send to Ireland for his hawks, but is also reported as greatly enjoying crane-hawking with a cast of gyrs presented to him by the King of Norway. Edward II also received hawks from Norway.

From very early on, trained birds of prey were considered extremely valuable assets, and there are many instances of ransoms, fines and rents being paid wholly or in part with hawks. Ossian, writing in the third century, refers to the offer of 100 managed horses, 100 foreign captives and 100 hawks as forming part of a settlement following a peace treaty. As late as 1764 the Dukes of Atholl were granted the feudal tenancy of the Isle of Man, for a 'rent' of two white gyrfalcons, to be paid to each succeeding monarch at his coronation. Correspondingly, the penalties for stealing hawks were severe. In the reign of Edward III the theft of a trained bird was punishable with death. A statute of Henry VII decreed that anyone convicted of stealing a hawk from a nest on another man's property should be imprisoned for a year and a day. Perhaps one of the most bizarre punishments for theft was a Burgundian law, which stipulated that the thief, if caught, should have six ounces of flesh torn from his breast by the bird he had stolen. There is also a story that a mediaeval Bishop of Ely, whose hawk was stolen from the cloisters while he was preaching, secured its return by re-ascending the pulpit and threatening to excommunicate the anonymous thief.

At the beginning of the sixteenth century, Cortes, the Spanish *conquistador*, arrived in Mexico, where he found that the Aztec king, Montezuma, maintained an establishment of trained birds of prey used for hunting. This is the first known record of hawking in the Americas.

In Britain, falconry continued in popularity during Tudor times; indeed it is interesting to think that history might have taken a very different turn, had not

Edmund Mundy, one of the royal falconers, rescued Henry VIII from a dyke into which he fell while hawking at Hitchin in Hertfordshire, when his hawking pole broke under his weight. In 1537 the Royal Mews, which since the time of Richard II had occupied the site of what is now Trafalgar Square, was converted into stabling for the king's horses. (It is probably from this date that the word 'mews' – derived from the French *muer*, to moult – began to be used to denote stabling, rather than a specific place for the keeping of hawks.)

During the reign of Elizabeth I, Sir Ralph Sadler, Her Majesty's Falconer, was entrusted with guarding Mary Queen of Scots, whom Elizabeth had imprisoned at Tutbury Castle. Sir Ralph incurred royal displeasure because he allowed his unfortunate prisoner to accompany him on short hawking expeditions in the neighbourhood of the castle. It appears that Mary loved hawking, and possibly Elizabeth's anger was generated as much by spite against her captive as by fears for her own security. Poor Mary is reported as having said to Sir Ralph that she thought herself 'in better grace with Her Majesty'.

James I, like Henry VIII some years before him, legislated against the use of guns, crossbows and longbows to kill game, but he made an exception in the case of hawk-owners, who were allowed to shoot 'Haile shot in Hand guns or Birding peeces at Crow, Chough, Pie, Ringdove, Jey or smaller birds for Hawkes' meate only'. James himself was a keen falconer, and in the Calendar of State Papers (Domestic) for 1611 there is an entry which runs: 'Twelve falcons are come from Denmark for the King; and six for Lord Hay, of which the King has taken two, and hopes he will not be angry'. (We may suppose Lord Hay had very little choice in the matter!)

The sporting side of falconry must have suffered a set-back during the Commonwealth (1649–1660), though probably some people still used hawks to hunt for food. But with the Restoration of the monarchy it came back into fashion once more. In 1662 Samuel Pepys saw the arrival of the Russian Ambassador in London, and described the numerous attendants in his train bringing hawks on their fists as gifts to Charles II. The King was pleased to accept the birds, and took two or three of them upon his fist, on which he wore a gold-embroidered glove specially presented him for the purpose. It is more than probable that the beautiful and ornate hawking bags and gloves which have survived the centuries were in fact ceremonial trappings for just such state occasions. They would have been of little use in the field, where they would soon have been spoilt in the course of normal wear and tear. One of the finest examples, an Elizabethan bag with matching glove and lure, is now in the Burrell Collection in Glasgow.

Falconry continued to be practised in Britain and the rest of Europe after the Restoration, and still had its royal devotees both in Britain and abroad. James II conferred the office of Hereditary Grand Falconer on the Dukes of St Albans in 1688 (an office which has survived, though latterly simply as a sinecure, until the present day). The Russian royal family, who had been keenly interested in the sport and had employed a Grand Falconer since 1550, continued to support

3 Etching by Hollar,
from Francis Barlow's
*Severall Wayes of
Hunting, Hawking and
Fishing according to the
English Manner* (1671).

falconry (apparently the Empress Catherine was extremely fond of flying merlins). But circumstances were combining to bring about its decline. Chief among these was the development of accurate sporting guns, coupled with the enclosure of land (which throughout the eighteenth century and the first half of the nineteenth century gradually encroached upon what had previously been good hawking country). Also, once reigning monarchs ceased to take an interest in falconry, it lost a good deal of ground in the fashionable world.

One cannot help feeling that in many cases where people feel it necessary to band together into clubs for the furtherance of a particular field sport, this is an indication that the sport itself is losing favour as a popular pastime. It takes on the air of something a little quaint and archaic – a museum piece to be carefully preserved, rather than a practical proposition. By 1792 British falconers had formed the High Ash Club in Norfolk, first under the presidency of Lord Orford, and later under that of Colonel Wilson (who afterwards became Lord Berners). This club continued into the 1830s, when it was disbanded. In 1838, Ernest Clough Newcombe founded the Loo Hawking Club in Holland. This counted among its members many of the European aristocracy, and was presided over by Prince Alexander of the Netherlands. One has only to look at the list of members for the year 1840, and to consider the high cost of the subscription (not less than 100 florins per annum) to see that falconry, like many other things with 'scarcity value', was fast becoming the preserve of the rich and titled classes, and less and less accessible to the common man. A rather élitist attitude was setting in.

When the Loo Club was dissolved in 1853, the Old Hawking Club was formed in England, and continued until 1927. (This was the last hawking club in this country to have professional falconers, club hawks and a headquarters of its own.) During the life of the Old Hawking Club, in 1871, the Barnet Committee 'for developing the resources of the Alexandra Park as a noble playground of four hundred acres' tried to revive public interest in the sport. Prizes were offered for the best essays on falconry submitted to the Committee. This effort seems to have come to nothing, apart from the collection of essays.

In 1927 the British Falconers' Club was founded by some of the members of the recently-dissolved Old Hawking Club, and from this date the face of falconry altered. Gone were the days of the old professional falconers, and most of these had to turn to some other way of earning a living. The new club consisted entirely of amateurs, training and flying their own birds. Very few members could now afford the time to keep large falcons in proper flying condition; and this meant that whereas formerly the peregrine had taken pride of place in British falconry, it was now superseded by the goshawk, which did not require so much daily exercise to keep it fit.

In Britain there has always been a continuous falconry tradition, although in some other European countries it died out completely for a time, and has only comparatively recently been re-established. There has now been an upsurge of interest in the sport, and falconry clubs have come into being in many countries; France, Germany, Austria, Holland, Spain, and Italy all have various associations. One of the most active European clubs must surely be the Deutscher Falkenorden, founded in the 1920s. Falconry also has its supporters in the United States and in Canada, where clubs have successfully been formed. It is also gaining popularity in New Zealand, Zimbabwe, Mexico and South America. Some useful addresses can be found in Appendix 1.

Of course it is very encouraging that people are once more taking an interest in falconry, but the very fact that they are has brought its own problems. It is now very much harder to procure wild birds for falconry than it was formerly. The decline in the wild raptor population has alarmed conservationists (and falconers) all over the world; indeed, in some quarters pressure is being brought to bear to stop any more birds at all being taken from the wild. Deeper thought and understanding on the part of falconers and conservationists is required, and a better spirit of co-operation between them. As I shall explain in the final chapter of this book, captive breeding of birds of prey could very largely solve the problems of supply and demand as far as falconers are concerned, and could also be used to help re-instate species in the wild in places where they have become scarce.

There are those who enjoy simply watching and studying birds of prey in the wild; there are also those who have the satisfaction and thrill of flying hawks that they have trained themselves. Both should work together, so that future generations will also be able to experience the same pleasures.

2 The Birds Themselves

In the fifteenth-century *Boke of St Albans* on hawking, hunting and cote-armour appears a famous and oft-quoted list of the birds of prey allotted to various ranks of mediaeval society for their use. The *Boke of St Albans* is the earliest printed English work (though not the first treatise) dealing with falconry. Its authorship is attributed by many to Dame Juliana Barnes (or Berners), although J.E. Harting, in his *Essays on Sport and Natural History*, seems to prove fairly conclusively that she did not in fact write it. The list runs as follows:

Emperor	The Eagle, Vulture and Merloun
King	The Ger Falcon and the Tercel of the Ger Falcon
Prince	The Falcon Gentle and the Tercel Gentle
Duke	The Falcon of the Loch
Earl	The Falcon Peregrine
Baron	The Bustard
Knight	The Sacre and the Sacret
Esquire	The Lanere and the Laneret
Lady	The Marlyon
Young Man	The Hobby
Yeoman	The Goshawk
Poor Man	The Jercel
Priest	The Sparrow hawk
Holy Water Clerk	The Musket
Knave or Servant	The Kestrel

Certainly parts of this list do not make much sense from a falconer's point of view. Eagles and vultures are of little use for falconry, and the same applies, as we shall see, to hobbies and kestrels. The bustard is not a bird of prey at all, and even if one accepts this as being a mis-spelling of 'buzzard' or even the French word *busard* (a harrier) it would still appear that the barons were rather poorly served. Also it seems highly unlikely that there were really any hard and fast rules restricting the use of certain species to certain ranks – after all, in the list itself we find the peregrine (under three different names) allotted to princes, dukes and earls.

What in fact probably happened then was very like what happens today. Only those who are fortunate enough to own land and to have plenty of spare time can afford to fly the more impressive and dramatic birds. The less fortunate must content themselves with something rather less spectacular – which is not to say that they will not get a great deal of enjoyment out of it. So, before you start dreaming of flying a magnificent white gyrfalcon at wild geese, come down to earth. Look at the sort of country that you are going to be able to fly over, see what quarry is there, and work out just how many daylight hours you will be able to devote each day to training and flying your bird. Far too many falconers today are trying to fly the wrong birds for their particular circumstances. They would do far better and have much more fun if they had the right kind of bird, even if it were not so glamorous as they could wish. But some only seem to be able to learn the hard way, while others never seem to learn at all.

Obviously not all birds of prey are suitable for falconry purposes. Vultures, kites, owls and those species which hunt insects, very small mammals, reptiles and so forth, are going to provide neither food for man nor an exciting flight. Out of the several hundred different species in the world, comparatively few are of interest to falconers.

So let us take the birds most suitable for the sport, family by family and species by species. We shall be concentrating on the falconry, rather than the ornithological, aspect of these birds. Anyone wishing for more ornithological detail would be well advised to consult a work such as Brown and Amadon's *Eagles, Hawks and Falcons of the World*. This covers all birds of prey except owls, and gives detailed information on the areas where they are to be found in the wild, both during and outside the breeding season. I should however like to add one word of warning here; at times ornithologists use measurements of wing and tail length in distinguishing between various subspecies. This may be suitable for many kinds of birds, but in the case of birds of prey the length of wing and tail feathers decreases with each successive moult, so that unless the actual age of each individual bird is known, such measurements can be rather misleading. (For instance, the tail of a female goshawk may well shorten by as much as 1.9 cm (¾ in.) after its first moult.) I have purposely not given weights of the species mentioned. Between subspecies, and indeed between individuals of the same subspecies, there can be enormous differences in weight. The 'flying weight' of trained birds will be dealt with in due course.

Falcons

Falcons are long-winged, dark-eyed birds with, as a rule, comparatively short tails. Some members of the falcon family, namely the kestrels, have special methods of hunting, hovering and then dropping, rather than stooping, on their prey; but most falcons generally kill by stooping from a height and trying to knock down their quarry with the talons of the hind toes as they go past. They will also sometimes bind to their prey in mid-air, and, occasionally, strike it with the clenched foot.

For purposes of instruction I have divided the falcons into two groups – large falcons (i.e. those over 1 lb in weight) and small falcons (those under 1 lb in weight).

Large falcons are flown in two ways: either 'out of the hood' at rooks, crows, gulls and so forth, or, for game hawking, 'waiting-on'. A falcon flown out of the hood at birds either just rising or on passage must first climb above them. She usually does this by 'ringing' – that is, by climbing into the wind, and then circling and coming down, with the wind behind her, to get up more speed. She repeats this manoeuvre until she gets above her quarry. The quarry manoeuvres in the same way, to try to keep above the falcon and so prevent her from stooping. Once the falcon gains the ascendancy the quarry will turn down-wind to the nearest cover. An exciting series of stoops should follow, until either the falcon succeeds in knocking down or binding to the quarry, or she is defeated by its reaching cover. Obviously this type of hawking requires very open country indeed, since if cover is close at hand the quarry will go straight into it and there will be no ringing flights.

A falcon flown at game is trained to climb up first and wait-on overhead, and not until she is well up and has ceased to climb are the birds flushed. This type of flying produces very long stoops, as an experienced falcon will sometimes be as much as 400 to 600 feet up. Judging the height of a falcon from the ground is very difficult and, like fishermen's tales, all too often exaggerated.

Gyr *(Falco rusticolus)*   (alternative spellings: jer, ger)   male: jerkin

Gyrs are the largest of the falcons and are to be found in a sub-arctic belt stretching right round the earth. *Polarfalke*, the German name, well indicates their distribution.

At one time they were divided by ornithologists into three: the Norwegian Gyr, the Icelandic, and the Greenland. In adult plumage those from Norway were supposedly a dark grey, those from Iceland a lighter grey, and those from Greenland white with black markings. It has now been realized that one cannot divide them either by colour or by geographical distribution. The late G.E. Lodge, whose painting of raptors is unsurpassed, once showed me 72 study skins of gyrs and invited me to put them into groups. It was quite impossible. They merged from black through all the varying shades of grey and brown to white. One bird even had one side of one type and the other side another. Now at last ornithologists have decided they shall just be gyrs.

They are extremely fast, a lot faster than either a saker or a peregrine. A falcon as large and as fast as a gyr really requires a large and fast quarry to stretch its powers of flight to the utmost. Geese have often been suggested as the right quarry for gyrs and I understand that a trained gyr in North America has taken Canadian geese. Certainly remains of geese are sometimes to be found in their eyries but one should remember that geese nest in the same area as the gyr: there will be young geese that are not yet strong on the wing and adult geese in eclipse that are unable to fly, and these would be easy prey. Ravens and great Black-back gulls might make another possible quarry, though protected in Britain. But from my experience of flying peregrines at gulls the larger the gull the easier it is to catch provided its size does not put the falcon off. In fact I have once caught a great black-back with a peregrine, an eyass falcon.

Gyrs have a reputation of not waiting-on well but of raking away and only succeeding by their superior speed. In the wild gyrs take quite a lot of ground quarry, hares, lemmings, etc. However, flying a falcon at ground game would be a very dreary proceeding.

Leonard Potter, who was professional falconer to the late Guy Blaine, once told me his trained gyr would fly up to wild geese but refuse to tackle them. It would be very difficult in Britain to obtain daily flights at geese and there would be no easy, inexperienced young geese to encourage a young gyr to start with, for by the time the wild geese have migrated from their nesting grounds to the north of Scotland they will be very strong on the wing.

In former times gyrs were given as rich presents from one monarch to another and Sir Thomas Monson, falconer to James I, is said to have expended a thousand pounds before he succeeded in training a cast (two birds) to take kites in fair flight. The larger part of this vast sum would have been spent in fitting out and sending expeditions to trap the birds. Kites were very common in Britain in those days and would be a very elusive quarry. The well known picture by Joseph Wolfe of two gyr falcons on a kite is very strange. The gyrs are far too small in proportion to the kite. The kite in the picture is a red kite but it is not clear whether the commoner kite in Britain in the Middle Ages was the red or the black kite.

In 1845 the Duke of Leeds sent John Pells, his falconer, to Iceland to take gyrs. Eight of these birds were presented to the Loo Hawking Club in Holland. The Club falconers were very experienced professionals but little success attended their efforts to make these gyrs into good heron hawks and after many tries they discontinued the attempt in favour of passage peregrines.

Since writing the first edition of this book I have seen gyrs flown in America at duck. The country was ideal and the two gyrs I saw fly both got up to a good height but tended to swing around in very large circles; they were rarely nicely placed and then only by accident. However when the duck was flushed the gyr, although a long way off, rapidly overtook it and since all the local water was frozen the duck had no hope of gaining cover. But the speed of the falcon was certainly impressive. I would have wanted a more disciplined bird myself but the results were undoubtedly satisfactory. Doubtless some gyrs would be more obedient than others and since the birds I saw fly satisfied their owners they probably saw no reason to change. But unless the falcon is placed correctly over the quarry that dramatic stoop, almost vertical, just does not happen and one is left with a very fast descent at a shallow angle ending usually in a stern chase. But none of these flights really tested the gyrs to their utmost and a peregrine would have been just as satisfactory in the circumstances.

Thanks to the new Wildlife and Countryside Act in Britain I have been unable to import a mate for my jerkin and have been forced to cross-breed. So it does not look as though I will ever have the opportunity to fulfill a lifetime ambition: to fly a pure-bred gyr myself.

They are most beautiful birds and until one has had one on the fist one does not realize how big they are. They become very friendly birds when well manned and are quite playful. But, like a Rolls-Royce, they are a long way from most falconers' reach.

I would like to see more flights before feeling able to judge them fairly. North America is certainly, in places, an ideal country in which to fly them and such birds as spruce grouse make a better quarry than anything we could fly at in Britain.

Saker *(Falco cherrug)*   male: sakret

Sakers are fairly widely distributed throughout central Europe and Asia, in an area bounded by Austria in the west and, in the east, by Tibet and Manchuria. In winter they migrate to North Africa, northern India and southern China. The very large *Falco cherrug altaicus*, from the mountains of central Asia, was long thought to be a type of gyrfalcon, but is now classified as a saker.

Sakers are often called desert falcons, perhaps because they tend to winter in desert areas, and possibly also because they are very popular birds with Arab falconers, who fly them in the desert at houbara (MacQueen's bustard) and sometimes at desert hares. In England, sakers are flown at rooks and crows, and sometimes at game. Doubtless in the desert they give good flights at houbara; but there is no quarry in Britain which acts in the same way as houbara, and all the sakers that I have seen flown in England have usually been very disappointing, frequently refusing to fly at any bird which was prepared to take to the air. Most of their successes arc from a great distance at flocks of rooks just getting up from the ground, taking the rooks more by surprise than by hard flying. Occasionally sakers have an on day and go well, but I have found them to be moody, unreliable and easily lost. (This last may possibly be due to their migratory habits.) Flown at game, they tend to act like gyrs, rarely mounting well or waiting-on in good style. Compared with peregrines, I consider them third-rate.

They do, however, have their admirers, and nowadays, when birds are difficult to obtain, they are obviously not to be despised. It is quite possible that there is more suitable quarry for sakers in America, where, in many parts, the country is more like their natural habitat and might well hold more suitable quarry than that found in England.

Peregrine *(Falco peregrinus)*   male: tiercel, tassel, tercel

There are some 18 subspecies of peregrine listed now, and these subspecies are widely spread about the world.

4 Sakret.

5 Immature peregrine.

Peregrines are flown at a vast variety of quarry – rooks, crows, gulls, magpies, duck, partridge, grouse, black-cock, ptarmigan, woodcock, snipe and, rarely, pheasants. In other countries they are flown at many other species. Generally speaking they dislike taking mammals, though a falcon of mine once picked up a hill leveret whilst grouse-hawking, carried it for some hundred yards or so and then dropped it, the leveret running away apparently unharmed.

There may be more beautiful birds than the peregrine – taita falcons, aplomado falcons and others – but for performance of the very highest quality, the peregrine leaves all the others far behind. Her most valuable trait is undoubtedly her persistence. I know of no other falcon which has this virtue to so great a degree. One of my peregrines once chased a gull for over 19 minutes by the wrist-watch. Although the distance covered from start to finish was not much over half a mile, the actual mileage flown must have been very considerable indeed. It was an aerobatic display of the highest order, and a fine example of the difference that lies between shooting and falconry, since the fact that the quarry escaped did, if anything, enhance the flight.

In former times, when peregrines were flown at herons and kites, a cast of falcons was used, since one bird alone would have difficulty in catching so elusive a quarry. In the past I have caught herons with a single peregrine, and on one occasion a falcon of mine outflew a buzzard. She bound to it high in the air and the two birds came tumbling down together, but she wisely released

24

it some 50 feet above the ground. Nowadays one cannot fly peregrines at herons or kites, since both these species are protected, but a cast is still essential for flying at magpies, as I shall explain later.

Prairie falcon *(Falco mexicanus)*   male: tiercel

Although strictly speaking the male should not be called a tiercel, it is now fairly common practice to do so.

The prairie falcon is found over a large area of the central and western United States, from Mexico and California northwards to the southern part of British Columbia.

This American falcon is one that I have not had as much opportunity to fly as I should have liked, but what I have seen of it I admire very much indeed, and I would place it as my second choice to a peregrine, and certainly far and away above a saker. However, the opinions of American and British falconers are somewhat conflicting, varying from high praise to the other extreme. Prairie falcons appear to fly in a very similar way to peregrines, although in the wild they do undoubtedly take a lot of ground game. The ones I have flown stooped hard and were no problem in any way. In Britain one would fly them at the same type of quarry as a peregrine.

I have seen two prairies flown by an experienced American falconer. We were flying at Alamosa in Colorado and although it was very late in the year there was a large field of oats still uncut. With the aid of a Brittany Spaniel we found a point and the better of the two falcons was cast off. She mounted well and to a very good height, and although not quite as disciplined as I would have desired she didn't stray too far out from the dog. She took a hen pheasant extremely well knocking it down very hard. Later I saw her flown again and was very impressed with her. The second bird was very much a beginner and so one could not judge her performance fairly. She tried but was badly placed and had no chance of succeeding. One falconer told me that prairies often hit their quarry with a clenched foot rather than using the back talons – a difficult thing to prove. There are no rooks in America, but crows, magpies and gulls, together with game birds, must provide ample quarry. Some American falconers have flown them at jack-rabbits (animals similar to our brown hare). Personally I dislike intensely the idea of flying any falcon at large mammals, as this would require stoop after stoop before the bird could be expected to hold its quarry successfully. There are reports of some prairies becoming bad-tempered, particularly after several season's flying, but whether this applies simply to individuals or is a general characteristic of the species, I cannot say.

Lugger *(Falco jugger)*   (alternative spelling: laggar)

Luggers come from India, Pakistan and possibly parts of Afghanistan and Turkestan. Large numbers of them have been imported into Britain recently. They are extremely useful birds to demonstrate flying to a lure, but as far as

6 Prairie Falcon.

7 Lugger.

hunting in Britain is concerned there is very little quarry that they are capable of catching. I have caught young rooks, old rooks deep in the moult, starlings and moorhens with luggers, but in general they lack persistence and kill more by surprising their quarry than by really hard work. This is not altogether unexpected, since in the wild state they prey on lizards, young or weak birds, insects and carrion. However, I think they make a useful contribution to falconry, since they can teach a beginner how to swing a lure and, being fairly tough in constitution, are able to stand up to a certain amount of mishandling and the mistakes in feeding which beginners are almost bound to make.

If flown off the fist at moorhens, like short-winged hawks, luggers can provide a certain amount of sport. The males often appear to be quite fast, and they can be trained to wait-on. Quail would make an ideal quarry for them, and possibly a cast of luggers might do well at magpies, given the right sort of country. I think that luggers might well have more hunting potential in America than they do in Britain.

Lanner *(Falco biarmicus)*   male: lanneret
Lanners are found throughout most of Africa and in the coastal ranges to the north of the Mediterranean. They are charming little falcons and are easy to train. They will wait-on well, but lack the weight and speed of a peregrine when flown at game. Early in the season they are capable of taking partridges, but

later on, when the wind is likely to be blowing harder, they are not able to come to terms with an experienced old partridge anything like as easily as a peregrine. Once again it is, I feel, a matter of not having the right type of quarry in Britain for lanners to show their best. Flown in a cast they would, I am sure, be very good at magpies, wherever one could find such birds in open country. (Parts of Ireland and Spain are ideal for this type of flight.) Several of the lannerets I have flown were surprisingly good at spotting larks, pipits and other small birds that put into cover, and invariably caught them on the ground. Both haggard and passage lanners are slightly easier to train than peregrines of the same age, but are no easier than eyass peregrines.

A great number of lanners have been brought into Britain in recent years, but the percentage of these birds that have turned out to be really good performers has been very low indeed. Of course this may well be due to their trainers, rather than to the birds themselves; nevertheless I find them disappointing for hunting in this country. If we had some of the larger species of quail, as in America, I am sure lanners would make a good showing at them. Like luggers, they make good demonstration birds to a lure, and are a good stepping-stone for the falconer who is eventually going to be able to fly peregrInes.

There are, of course, many other large falcons which have not been dealt with specifically. They are unlikely to be met with in Britain, but falconers who go abroad may come across some of them and be able to try them out. It is always worth while studying the type of quarry on which birds of prey feed in their natural habitat. A great deal can be learnt from this; but it should be borne in mind that although birds obviously do well in their own native countries, they may sometimes fail to come up to expectations elsewhere, where the available quarry may appear similar, but is in fact hardier and stronger.

There is one quarry that I have not yet mentioned, and which may well seem ideal because it is in plentiful supply and is not very popular among farmers – namely, pigeons. You might, now and then, catch the occasional wood-pigeon with some of the short-winged hawks, but if you try to catch pigeons with falcons, at any rate in Britain, you will not only find it almost impossible, but you will also almost certainly lose your falcon.

This takes a bit of explaining. Wild falcons kill pigeons fairly often, but then they do not have a falconer with them to advertise their presence, so they are able to get quite close before the pigeon realises what is happening. No pigeons will sit on the ground while your trained falcon climbs up to a good height – they will get up and fly off as soon as they see you approaching. If you try flying at pigeons out of the hood as they get up, your falcon will have neither the advantage of surprise nor of height. So a chase will develop, and the falcon may well be led a very long way before the quarry either dives into cover, beats the falcon in the air, or (and this rarely happens) is caught. In any case your falcon will end up a long way away from you, very probably out of sight. Even

8 Merlin.

if she starts to return she may well be sidetracked on her way back and start to chase something else, and the whole thing will end, as likely as not, in disaster.

Suppose that you are out game-hawking; your dog is on a point, your falcon is waiting-on nicely, and then suddenly a pigeon flies past. If you have been in the habit of encouraging your bird to go after pigeons, she will leave you and your party of onlookers and will chase off after it, making for much embarrassment and bad language on your part. So please, forget pigeons. In over 40 years I have caught only three.

All the falcons I have mentioned so far are what I call, for want of a better term, the larger falcons. The only reason I have separated them from the smaller ones is that, with the exception of luggers flown from the fist, they all require three conditions to be fulfilled if they are to be flown successfully. Firstly, one must have really large stretches of open country to fly over; secondly, there must be plenty of quarry; and thirdly, the falconer must have a minimum of three to four consecutive months' holiday for flying his birds. To ignore any one of these requirements is bound to end in so low a standard of flying that the whole pursuit becomes a waste of time. (This may sound a very pompous and dogmatic statement, but it is quite true, and any really experienced falconer will, I am sure, agree.)

The smaller falcons – hobbies, kestrels, merlins and so on – I have placed in a different category, since they do not require anything like such vast stretches of open country; neither are they so demanding of time and money if they are to be flown satisfactorily.

Merlin *(Falco columbarius)*   male: jack

The merlin is found in Norway, Sweden, Finland and northern and eastern Russia, also throughout the British Isles (with the exception of the south-east corner). There are also three species of merlin in North America, and an Icelandic subspecies is occasionally seen in Britain. European merlins winter in North Africa, and the American species have been known to migrate as far south as Colombia.

Merlins are the smallest of the British falcons. Lacking as they do size and weight, they can hardly be expected to be as dramatic in flight as peregrines, but they are delightful little birds and, in their own way, most exciting. The only worthwhile quarry for merlins is the lark. This is a protected species, but a special licence may be granted to falconers for a limited number to be taken. The season for larks is very short – from the beginning of August to about the middle or end of September – after this the larks are too good on the wing for the average merlin.

It is not worth keeping merlins over the winter, for several reasons. Very often they fail to survive in captivity. There is nothing much that you can fly at which will provide exciting, high flights. If you do winter a merlin and moult it out, then you will be lucky indeed if its performance is anything like as good the next season. Quite why this is so, no one seems to know. Years ago I read this about merlins, and was somewhat sceptical, so I kept a merlin over the winter and flew it a second season. It was so hopeless that I finally gave up. It would chase and kill anything that was not too hard to get, but it would not go up. So I returned it to the wild. I think that what probably happens with merlins is that with age comes wisdom, for I have never seen a wild merlin flying very high. It does not need to, because its method of hunting is different from that of a trained bird. There is no climbing up, ringing or anything of that kind. Wild merlins make very short stoops, always keeping close to the quarry and never allowing it a chance to gain height.

In former days merlins were known as 'Ladies' hawks', doubtless because of their small size and docile temperament. Both Mary Queen of Scots and the Empress Catherine of Russia delighted in flying these charming birds.

Hobby *(Falco subbuteo)*   male: robin

Hobbies occur almost all over Europe and in a large part of Asia. Although the hobby is considered to be only a summer visitor to Britain (and that only in the southern part of England) I have in fact seen them just north of Inverness and also nesting not far from Liverpool, and indeed I have seen hobbies in this country in every month of the year. (Once, when a goshawk of mine was flying at a rabbit near Andover in Hampshire, she was 'buzzed' by a wild hobby. This was in late December.)

Hobbies are said to have been used for falconry in the Middle Ages, and also for 'daring' larks. 'Daring' was a method of trapping larks – the sight of a trained hobby overhead was supposed to keep the larks on the ground, so that nets could be pulled over them. But although wild hobbies during the breeding season catch small birds in order to feed their young, they are normally mainly insectivorous. This accounts for the lack of success many good falconers have had with trained hobbies. My own hobby would ignore the lure and fly around catching craneflies and eating them on the wing, utterly oblivious of any small birds, although she could easily have caught them had she wished. Certainly hobbies are very fast falcons and, being so small, are very quick on the turn. When necessary they can catch such agile fliers as swallows, swifts and martins, as I myself have seen. But they are completely unsuitable for falconry and, as they do no harm either to game or on farms, such delightful little birds are best left alone.

Red-headed merlin (or red-headed falcon) *(Falco chicquera)*

The Indian race of red-headed merlin *(Falco chicquera)* is distributed through-out the whole of the sub-continent. An African subspecies, *Falco chicquera ruficollis*, occurs in a wide belt stretching across the continent from Sierra Leone eastwards to Ethiopia, and in East Africa as far south as the Zambesi. South of this point it is replaced by another subspecies, *Falco c. horsbrughi.*

These pretty little birds can be treated in much the same way as our European merlins. Like them, they are best when flown as eyasses at larks, when they

9 Wild Hobby at nest.

will put up a creditable performance, equal at least to that of a moderately good European merlin. But eyass red-headed merlins are not easy to come by in this country, although it is to be hoped that this situation may alter in the future, as more and more birds of prey are bred in captivity. The older passage and haggard birds seem reluctant to fly high, but can be used in the same way as sparrowhawks, for flying at blackbirds and starlings along hedgerows, since they are far more inclined than their European counterparts to dive into cover in pursuit of quarry. (Incidentally, a licence is required before you can fly at blackbirds in Britain.) Red-headed merlins tend to be rather delicate in our northern winters, and will require considerably more care than, say, a tough old buzzard – but this, after all, applies to all small falcons and hawks.

Kestrel *(Falco tinnunculus)*
Since kestrels prey mainly on mice, voles and insects and, occasionally, small birds caught more by accident than by design, they can hardly be called falconers' birds in the true sense. They hunt by hovering, sometimes for quite long periods, while they scan the ground below for their quarry. By hovering I mean that they can remain stationary in still air by wing fanning. In an up-current of air or a breeze many birds such as buzzards, eagles and harriers can hang in one place simply by flying forward at the same speed as they are being blown backwards, but this is not hovering.

The majority of falconry books advise beginners to start with a kestrel. The authors presumably have reasons for this which appear good to them, or they would not give such advice. I think they feel that kestrels are common and reasonably easy to obtain, and that the beginner will learn a lot from them. Some of this is true, but I am afraid I still disagree that kestrels are good birds for beginners. When the would-be falconer has, probably after much frustration and many mistakes, finally got his kestrel flying loose, he will want to hunt with it. (After all, this is what falconry is all about – hunting with a trained bird.) But few trained kestrels will hover. Even if they do, one can hardly get excited when they slowly drop down on a beetle or a worm, or at best a mouse – and the results will not be appreciated in the larder. Also, kestrels are very small birds, weighing only a few ounces. The smaller a bird is, the smaller is the margin for error in feeding it. Far too many kestrels are unwittingly killed by beginners who do not realise this. So for these two reasons I am not in favour of kestrels as beginners' birds. However, under the present laws you may well find that your first bird will have to be a kestrel.

There are three other disadvantages in having a kestrel as your first bird. If you start off with one, with the idea of graduating later to a larger bird, such as a goshawk, you will find the transition from one bird to another very alarming. Also, kestrels are not, when trained, particularly energetic birds. The beginner may well have seen other falcons such as lanners, luggers and merlins, all stooping well to a swung lure, and will consequently have been fired with enthusiasm. But once he has trained his kestrel he will find its performance to the lure very disappointing. Few kestrels will put in more than two or three stoops without going off and sitting on the nearest fence-post or tree, and try as he will the beginner cannot get his bird to act like the other falcons he has seen. In due course, disappointed both by the poor performance at the swung lure and at quarry, he will want something better. This will mean, if he is sensible and wants to avoid being 'over-hawked', that he will no longer wish to keep the kestrel. Many books will tell him that this is the time to turn it back to the wild. Although this is not impossible, it is by no means as easy as it sounds, particularly in autumn or early winter. A great many kestrels are killed because their owners just release them and leave them to fend for themselves. Because the birds do not know how to hunt they soon die of starvation. 'Hacking back' to the wild, as it is called, is dealt with in chapter 18, and beginners who have reached the stage of no longer wanting their kestrels, and who wish to release them, should read this chapter.

Unfortunately there is no 'easy' quarry for falcons that are unfit, and so it is essential that they are exercised daily. Since the average person in Britain rarely sees his home by daylight from Monday to Friday during the winter months, he has little chance to exercise his birds at that time of year. So for the majority of people falcons are unsuitable – but hawks and their like can provide a great deal of sport.

10 Kestrel.

Hawks *(Accipitridae)*

Whereas open country is an absolute essential for flying falcons, hawks can be flown in almost any type of country, open or enclosed. This is because they have a different method of hunting. On the whole they are 'sprinters' rather than 'milers' and are amazingly quick off the mark. Their short wings give them great initial power at take-off and enable them to pass through branches easily, and their long tails give them good steering and good brakes. They rarely stoop from a height like falcons, although on occasion they may do so. More often they either 'still-hunt' from trees, waiting patiently for something to come their way, or they fly low through the woods and along hedgerows, frequently flipping over a hedge in the hopes of taking their prey by surprise. The great advantage of hawks to the austringer (an old name for a trainer of hawks – probably from the French *autoursier* meaning a trainer of short-winged hawks) is that they can remain idle all week and yet still put up a reasonable performance at week-ends, provided that they are not expected to take the more difficult types of quarry. (Obviously a hawk that can be flown daily will be a very much better performer because it is fitter.) In fact, hawks are what I call 'commuters' birds'.

Goshawk *(Accipiter gentilis)*   male: tiercel goshawk
Various species of goshawk are found throughout much of the northern hemisphere, in Europe, Asia and America. (Their presence in north-east Persia, Afghanistan, the north-west frontier area of India, and North Korea, seems to have been overlooked by Brown and Amadon.)

For many years goshawks have been the mainstay of falconry for those people unable to afford the time and money to fly falcons. They were known in mediaeval times as the 'Cook's bird', since they provided so much food for human consumption. Goshawks will take an enormous variety of prey, both in the trained and wild states, but they are generally flown at pheasants, partridges, duck, hares, rabbits, squirrels and moorhens. Trained goshawks have also been known to take grouse, peacock, coots, rails; various members of the crow family such as jays, magpies, rooks, bluejays and crows; guinea-fowl, francolin and many other species including quite small birds; and stoats, weasels and rats.

Goshawks vary a great deal in size and colour – the more northerly the race, the bigger they tend to be. They were once common in Great Britain, but became extinct as a breeding species towards the end of the nineteenth century. Now they are once again establishing a small foothold in parts of the country; this is almost certainly due to breeding among falconers' lost birds. If allowed to multiply they could prove to be of considerable use in forestry land, where they would help to keep down the squirrel population, and also on farm land where they would kill wood-pigeons. But wherever pheasants are reared and preserved for shooting, it is unlikely that the bird protection laws will be of much use to goshawks, I fear.

Sparrowhawk *(Accipiter nisus)*   male: musket

Sparrowhawks occur all over Europe and Asia in much the same range as the goshawk, but Accipiter nisus is not found at all in North America. Although now rarer than they used to be in Britain, sparrowhawks are nothing like as scarce as many ornithologists seem to believe. Where their habitat has remained unchanged they are still quite common, but they are not seen a great deal, and unless you are really good at bird identification it is easy to think there are no sparrowhawks around. Where hedges have been grubbed up and fields made bigger, both nesting sites and food have gone, and of course sparrowhawks no longer frequent such areas. For instance, there are now very few in East Anglia, where many miles of hedges have disappeared since the War.

Sparrowhawks are often accused of taking birds that they could never hope to hold unless the prey were already wounded or ill. Some keepers think sparrowhawks can take full-grown cock pheasants seven or eight times their own weight. This is in fact totally impossible. But a good *trained* female sparrowhawk will take quite large birds. This may appear to be a complete denial of what I have just said, but the operative word here is 'trained'. A trained bird has only to grab and hold her quarry long enough for the falconer to go in and assist her. The wild sparrowhawk has no one to help, and soon learns that it is no use trying to catch something that it will fail to hold and which may well give it a rough time into the bargain. Although appearances may be to the contrary, the smaller birds are harder to catch than the larger

11 Immature Goshawk.

12 Immature Musket (male Sparrowhawk).

35

ones, and it is at starlings and blackbirds (as I have mentioned earlier, you must get a special dispensation to fly at blackbirds) that the sparrowhawk shows its skill, rather than at teal, partridges or moorhen. For the really competent falconer, sparrowhawks are excellent. You will find far more flights for them in a given area than you will for your gos, although your larder will not of course gain so much.

The sparrowhawk is the very last bird for a beginner. It is not only extremely hard to tame but, like a kestrel, is so small that the margin for error in feeding is very small indeed. I could never advise a beginner to try one unless he had a very experienced falconer to help him.

There are many species of sparrowhawk throughout the world, and doubtless most of them could make good falconers' birds. Some so-called sparrowhawks are not, to my mind, sparrowhawks at all, but goshawks. (Perhaps I should say that this is a falconer's view and not that of an ornithologist.) As I see it the difference is fairly simple. True sparrowhawks have the breast feathers horizontally barred in both juvenile and adult plumage, whereas goshawks have vertical stripes in their first year which change to bars after the first moult. Sparrowhawks have a very much longer middle toe than goshawks, size for size. These two factors also combine, in my experience, with a marked difference in temperament, sparrowhawks being far more difficult to man (i.e. to tame) than goshawks.

Goshawks and sparrowhawks are the only two species of hawk indigenous to Britain.

Cooper's hawk *(Accipiter cooperii)*

Cooper's hawk is found in southern Canada, all over the United States and in north-west Mexico. It migrates in winter to South America.

Cooper's hawks are very much easier to train than sparrowhawks. They are slightly bigger, which makes it easier to judge how much to feed them, and they certainly have a more equable temperament. An eyass male that I owned was flying loose after ten days – one would be very hard put to it to train a sparrowhawk in so short a time. My personal opinion is that Cooper's hawks are slightly slower in flight than sparrowhawks, but the relative speed of birds is a very difficult thing to judge by eye. One can fly them at almost the same quarry as sparrowhawks, with the addition of mammals, such as water voles and small rabbits, which sparrowhawks are reluctant to take. I hope that we shall be able to breed this species in captivity in the future, as they are extremely useful birds for falconry.*

---

* Both Cooper's hawks and Sharp-skinned hawks vary in average size. The western birds tending to be larger than those from the eastern states. American falconers maintain that the larger Cooper's hawks will take cotton-tails and even jack-rabbits but require the falconer to assist.

13 Cooper's Hawk
(immature plumage).

Sharp-shinned hawk *(Accipiter striatus)*

I have never trained or seen a sharp-shinned hawk flown, but from all accounts they are the nearest thing to a European sparrowhawk that American falconers are likely to come by, though they do not appear to be quite so persistent at quarry. Their extremely small size would indicate that they are in no way birds suitable for beginners and, as with a musket, I would hesitate even to attempt to fly the male. Although they will not provide you with food for yourself, where game is scarce sharp-shinned hawks should give you more flights and more sport than the larger short-winged hawks.

Both sharp-shinned hawks and Cooper's hawks in immature plumage have vertical stripes on the breast, like goshawks.

Shikra *(Accipiter badius)*

Shikras range all over Asia from the southern edge of the Caspian Sea, through the southern part of the USSR to China, Indo-China and Formosa. *Accipiter badius badius*, the shikra most commonly used for falconry, comes from southern India and Ceylon. Larger subspecies are found in the rest of India. There are also two African subspecies, *Accipiter badius sphenurus* and *Accipiter badius polyzonoides*, which have a distribution rather similar to that of the two African subspecies of red-headed merlin.

The Latin name formerly used for the shikra, *Micrastur badius*, was in many ways very apt, since it is in fact a miniature goshawk (*Astur* being the old name for the goshawk). It is an easy bird to man, and seems generally tougher than the sparrowhawk, despite its small size; but it is undoubtedly slower and is best either flown out of trees or thrown from the hand in the style of Indian falconers. Shikras are certainly capable of giving a fair degree of sport against sparrows, and Mr Mavrogordato used to catch small rats with one of his shikras. Colonel Delmé-Radcliffe, in his *Notes on the Falconidae used in Falconry in India* (1871), remarks that shikras 'are not the sort of bird any English gentleman would bother himself with'. From the foregoing one may deduce that they are not particularly exciting birds to fly – nevertheless I feel that they should not be entirely despised. Since the native falconers in India take quail with shikras, it is possible that they might well be of use to some of the North American falconers.

Many other species of hawk are found throughout the world, some of which would doubtless be quite suitable for falconry – for instance, the white and grey goshawks (*Accipiter novaehollandiae*) of Australia and the large Black sparrowhawk (*Accipiter melanoleucus*) of Africa, to name but three. Some species have already been tried out by falconers, with varying degrees of success, and no doubt others will be experimented with in the future.

14 Shikra.

Buzzards

There are a great many species of buzzard spread about the world, very few of which have been used for falconry. In fact it is only comparatively recently that any of them have been tried at all. The fact that they are much bigger and tougher than, say, kestrels, and are also capable of catching a certain amount of quarry (though rarely the most difficult, such as pheasants or partridges) makes them ideal birds for beginners.

Common buzzard *(Buteo buteo)*
These birds are widely distributed throughout the palearctic regions of the world.

Common buzzards, if taken as eyasses, can be trained to take such quarry as squirrels, moorhens and even full-grown rabbits, although a considerable amount of persuasion may be needed to achieve this. Older birds (i.e. passage and haggards) require a great deal more persuasion, since they have already learnt in the wild that there are easier livings to be made either by still-hunting from dead trees, telegraph poles, hayricks and the like, or by hanging in the wind and dropping down on small quarry rather in the same way that kestrels do. Buzzards should be flown in the same way as goshawks, off the fist or out of trees, and one season with a buzzard will help a beginner a great deal if he is thinking of moving on to a goshawk. Generally speaking, buzzards tend to

15 Common Buzzard.

be much slower in flight than the short-winged hawks, and lack persistence at quarry. On the credit side, however, they are far less easy to lose than hawks, since they rarely spot quarry at a distance and so are less inclined to go off hunting on their own account.

Red-tailed buzzard *(Buteo jamaicensis)*

In North America this bird is known as the Red-tailed hawk, but as the genus *Buteo* covers all the members of the buzzard family, we are using the name 'buzzard' here to avoid confusion with the short-winged hawks, *Accipiters*. Another type of Red-tailed buzzard *(Buteo ventralis)* is classified by de Schaunsee as rufous-tailed hawk, which does to a certain extent make matters clearer, but, since it is a *Buteo*, it would be clearer still to call it the rufous-tailed buzzard.

Buteo jamaicensis is found in the West Indies and parts of Central America, and is widely distributed throughout the United States and the southern half of Canada.

The Red-tailed buzzard is a considerably better hunting bird than the European common buzzard, and big females are quite capable of taking brown hares. At feathered game such as pheasants, partridges and duck they lack both speed and persistence, and do not begin to come up to the standard of a goshawk, although flown out of a tree they can catch pheasants that rise directly below them. In this country the main quarry for Red-tailed buzzards is rabbits, moorhens and grey squirrels.

Ferruginous buzzard *(Buteo regalis)*

(In North America this bird is sometimes called the Ferruginous rough-legged hawk, since its feet are feathered down to the toes.) The Ferruginous buzzard is found in the north-west United States, and in southern Canada.

I have not as yet had an opportunity to fly one of these birds, though I was fortunate enough to be given a pair and have since bred ten young birds from them. At first sight a ferruginous does not appear much bigger than a Red-tailed buzzard, but one of my females in high condition weighs over two kilograms (over five pounds), and Giles Greenfield tells me that wild ferruginous in America frequently take jack-rabbits. These birds can be trained to wait-on, and are now finding favour with some of the American falconers. They certainly look very promising, and it will be interesting to see how they perform in Britain.

Harris' hawk *(Parabuteo unicinctus)*

The entire genus *Parabuteo* is composed of only three species, of which Harris' hawk, *Parabuteo unicinctus harrisi*, is the one most likely to be met with in falconry. Sometimes also known as the Bay-winged hawk, Harris' hawk was named by Audubon after a friend of his.

16 Red-tailed Buzzard.

17 Harris' Hawk.

Harris' hawks are comparatively new on the falconry scene in Britain, and I must admit that the first time I saw one I thought very little of it. Rather an ugly bird, I thought. However I got two pairs and have never regretted doing so. They tend to be smaller and lighter in weight than red-tails though since, like the red-tail, their range is pretty large, there is a great deal of variation in size. But on the whole the red-tail is a larger bird. But size is by no means everything and Harris' hawks are remarkably easy to train. You would have to be a very very stupid falconer to fail with a Harris. I did once have a male bird that was very anti-field sports when I had him. In fact, after a brief holiday in Scotland one year when he refused to chase anything whatsoever I passed him on to someone who had more time to spare and in due course he came to realize what he was meant to do.

They really are fabulous birds. They take all the anxiety out of hawking. They will put up with almost anything or anyone. I have flown a Harris with a field of 15 people and a strange dog, and eight of the onlookers were screaming, uncontrolled children. The average accipiter would have flown away into the next county and one would not have blamed it. It would be very difficult to find a bird not only more suitable for a beginner but also for anyone who just has little time to spare for his hawking and even less to keep a bird nicely manned. They will follow like a dog; in fact I flew my present Harris one day for our local Laird and a few weeks later he sent his head-keeper to see her fly as he thought the hawk better disciplined and more obedient than the keeper's dogs. You must

42

not expect any of the Buteo family (Harrises are Para-Buteos) to be as efficient as an accipiter. But Harrises will provide a great deal of sport, though they are hard put to take a large brown hare (though hill hares up to 6½ lbs are certainly possible); and unless game birds get up very close they will soon outdistance your Harris. But one takes the odd pheasant, the occasional partridge, and so on.

To add to their advantages, they can very easily be flown during the hawking season and bred from in the off season.

I have never bothered to hood any of my Harrises though there are times when a bird that will accept a hood is useful. I prefer to make them get accustomed to everything that comes along. Mine will sit in the car and travel happily for hours at a time, putting up with gawping petrol-station attendants and dear old ladies who want to know what sort of a parrot I've got and, of course, the question that everyone asks when you tell them you fly her – 'Does it always come back to you?' To which the answer is, I'm afraid, 'Well it wouldn't be here now if it didn't.' My old female Harris 'Islay' now no longer is tied up to a bow-perch but is left loose in her aviary all the time or in her mews in extremely bad weather. This is a great joy as I know she gets more exercise like this and can choose to sit under cover or not, high up or low down, in the rain (which she frequently does) or out of it.

Harrises will fly well in a team with others of their kind. And I have yet to see them fight over a kill. I am told that five of them have been flown together without any disasters, though that hardly seems fair to the quarry.

It would be hard to lose a Harris' except when it kills out of sight and hearing. Most of them, if they fail to kill, will come back looking for you. That really is a delightful trait and means the falconer need hardly ever even break into a trot let alone have to run. I have become a Harris fan in my old age. But you do not have to wait till then to enjoy flying one.

Hawk-eagles

On the whole these birds are very similar in shape and size to goshawks, but are less energetic, tending to do a great deal of still-hunting in the wild. Hodgson's hawk-eagle (*Spizaetus nipalensis*) was, and still is, used in Japan, where it is flown at hares and at raccoon dogs, which are small fox-like animals whose head markings resemble those of a raccoon. Brown and Amadon call this bird, together with Blyth's hawk-eagle (*Spizaetus alboniger*), the Mountain hawk-eagle. I prefer to retain the old names to avoid confusion.

I myself have flown the Changeable hawk-eagle (*Spizaetus cirrhatus*) at rabbits and moorhens with success, and on occasions have taken pheasants. I have also seen Blyth's hawk-eagle and Wallace's hawk-eagle (*Spizaetus nanus*) flown briefly at similar quarry, with reasonable results. The African hawk-eagle (*Hieratus fasciatus spilogaster*) has been flown very successfully in

South Africa and Zimbabwe, and also in Britain, at the same quarry. (Brown and Amadon classify spilogaster as a subspecies of Bonelli's eagle, *Hieratus fasciatus fasciatus*, though to my mind the two are very dissimilar and live in quite different habitats in the wild.)

There are many other species of hawk-eagle, perhaps the most beautiful being the South American Ornate hawk-eagle (*Spizaetus ornatus*), which has, I believe, been used by some American falconers – with what results I do not know. Another South American hawk-eagle, the Tyrant or Black hawk-eagle (*Spizaetus tyrannus*) is very similar to a goshawk. As far as I know it has never been used for falconry, but it would be interesting to try it out. The very large and handsome African Crowned hawk-eagle (*Stephanoaetus coronatus*) is far too big and powerful a bird for falconry.

Unless we are able to breed more of these birds in captivity, falconers in Britain are unlikely to be able to obtain many hawk-eagles in the future, mainly due to the fact that they come from parts of the world where Newcastle disease is considered to be prevalent, so that permits to import them are unlikely to be granted.

Eagles

In the wild, eagles are magnificent to watch, whether they are just soaring effortlessly around or actually hunting. Once when I was out stalking hinds I saw a large covey of grouse coming downhill over the snow, twisting and turning in the wind. Behind them came a golden eagle. When I first spotted her she was a long way behind the grouse, but her speed was quite amazing and she was rapidly overhauling them. They came over our heads, paying us no attention. A few seconds later we heard the rush of the eagle's wings as she shot past. The stalker and I turned and watched her overtake the grouse with the greatest ease. We saw a massive foot stretch out and take one of them, and then they all passed out of sight behind the hill. It was a most impressive and thrilling moment – the sort of thing one sees once in a lifetime and never forgets. The whole scene has remained etched in my mind ever since.

In the trained state eagles simply do not perform like this. Although I have trained and flown several golden eagles (*Aquila chrysaetos*) and assisted my uncle, the late Captain C.W.R. Knight, M.C., F.R.P.S., in training and flying African Crowned hawk-eagles, Martial eagles (*Polemaetus bellicosus*) and the American bald eagle (*Haliaeetus leucocephalus*), there is no doubt in my mind that all of these big eagles are better not used for falconry. If one could persuade a golden eagle to wait-on, which might be possible, then this would indeed be worthwhile. But flown as they usually are, off the fist or out of trees, eagles are hardly worth watching. They are so big and heavy that it takes them a very long time to get up speed, and in the same type of flight any good goshawk would far outstrip them. The only eagle I would consider for falconry at all is Bonelli's eagle, which in the past has been trained and flown at rabbits and

18, 19, 20, 21 Harris' Hawk in flight. With a bit of wind, or even quite a lot, my Harris will sail out from a hillside and wait on at quite considerable heights at times, 200 feet up is not unusual.

22 Harris' Hawk coming to the fist.

23 Hodgson's Hawk Eagle.

hares. However it has not proved particularly good at game birds, despite the fact that in the wild Bonelli's eagles certainly take hill partridges.

This, then, concludes the list of the birds you are most likely to come across which in my experience are, or could be, suitable for falconry. In my opinion most beginners would be better off with a short-winged hawk or a buzzard, rather than any of the large falcons. If enough merlins could be bred in captivity in the future, these would make ideal summer holiday birds for them, and they would then receive some of the best of both worlds. The time taken and, in Britain, the costs involved in flying any of the large falcons properly mean that only a handful of falconers in Britain fly them as they should be flown. In America and other parts of the world where the game laws are entirely different it is another matter.

3 Training in Brief

One of the questions that crops up time and time again is: 'Doesn't falconry take up an immense amount of time? It must take ages to train a bird. Do you really sit up all night with your birds?' The answer is 'No'. However, if you want to take up falconry you should realise that a certain amount of time *must* be spent *every* day with your bird. You are responsible for its welfare and you cannot go off for a few days and leave someone else to look after it. You can do this with dogs or cats, since most people are quite capable of seeing they are looked after properly. But looking after a bird of prey requires specialised knowledge, which very few people have. So please, consider this very carefully. Once you have the bird there can be no question of becoming bored with it or neglecting it. If you think this might happen then do not on any account take up falconry.

Obviously a beginner takes longer to train a bird than an experienced falconer does. This chapter is intended to show the beginner what to expect in training and what exactly is involved. Training can be divided into four stages, which overlap and run concurrently at times but which are still separate entities.

Stage one is 'manning', or making the bird tame and used to human beings. All wild animals are usually afraid of man and their one idea is to avoid him as much as possible. (Very few will attack humans unless they have young to protect or are cornered.) So a newly-caught bird of prey must first of all be induced to get over its fear before it can be expected to come to you or to hunt for you.

Stage two is training the bird to come to you, first on a line and then loose. Unless your bird is obedient and comes when called, it is going to be as useless for work as a disobedient dog. Initially, training of any animal is based on the reward system: you reward a puppy with a biscuit if it comes when called, a horse gets a lump of sugar. A bird of prey is rewarded with raw meat. In due course the animals I have mentioned will form some sort of attachment to you which has nothing whatever to do with food. A dog will be pleased to see you regardless of whether you give it food or not. The same applies to hawks and falcons. I have a falcon that will follow me if I go for a walk, without my showing her food at any time. The difference between training animals and birds is that on the whole animals are far more intelligent, and will therefore automatically be obedient, after a time, without the constant stimulus of being offered a reward. But a hunting bird is obviously not going to hunt if it is not hungry, and if it does not want the reward you offer, it is not going to be obedient. Therefore keenness plays a certain part in the training of birds of prey, and feeding and condition are most important.

Stage three is getting the bird fit. During the first two stages it is not flying very much and its muscles become flabby. Until you have got it fit you cannot expect it to hunt successfully.

Stage four is the consummation of the first three stages – hunting.

E = Easy D = Difficult	1 Manning	2 Training	3 Fitness	4 Hunting
Falcons	E	E	E	D
Hawks	D	E	E	E
Buzzards	E	E	E	E/D
Hawk Eagles and Eagles	All these take a long time, especially in Stage Three.			

Now let us take the different groups of birds that we have talked about in the previous chapter, and see how each type tends to react to these four stages of training. If you compare the falcons with the hawks you will see that stages one and four are reversed. Because hawks are difficult to man, many beginners get to the point where they feel that their bird is never going to become tame, and they give up the whole thing in despair and probably take up some more vicious sport like croquet. Those who start with a falcon go roaring ahead, with very few problems, until they reach stage four, when they find that their tame, obedient falcon just will not chase anything. They in their turn give up, thinking that there must be some secret that has been carefully kept hidden from them.

Buzzards are comparatively easy in all four stages except the last, in which I classify them as 'medium'. They vary a great deal. Some learn to hunt very quickly, but others can drive one almost to distraction before they get the idea.

The eagles and hawk-eagles all take a longer time to train, simply because they are larger and therefore their powers of fasting are greater. So it will take longer for them to appreciate the rewards you give them.

By and large most birds will conform to this general pattern, but you must remember that you are dealing with living creatures, each of which is an individual in its own right, and therefore you must expect individual variations in behaviour. The time taken to train a bird depends on the expertise of the falconer and the character of the individual bird. An experienced falconer can train a bird, from the time he starts handling it to the time it is flying free, amazingly quickly. A merlin will take about five days to train, a kestrel six or seven days, a peregrine eight to ten. Goshawks take two to three weeks and sparrowhawks four to six weeks. But inexperienced falconers and beginners will of course take longer to train their birds.

I find that many old falconers like to make beginners think that there is a certain amount of mystique attached to falconry, along with various carefully guarded craft secrets. This is not true. If there are any secrets in falconry, which in fact there are not, then this is the one to pay attention to: the earlier you get your bird flying and fit, the easier the whole thing becomes. The big step for all beginners is deciding when they dare fly their bird loose. This is where the main delay occurs, and it is very understandable.

Every falconer has his own methods of training. Basically the rules are the same. If you intend to learn falconry from books then keep to one book and, therefore, one method of training throughout. There is hardly any book that does not have something in it worth reading, and certainly most books are interesting, even when out of date. The real problem for the beginner is to know what still applies and what has been superseded by something better. Perhaps it is better to read the old falconry books after you have trained a hawk rather than before.

People talk about good and bad hawks. I do not believe there is any such thing as a 'bad' hawk in the wild – if there were it would soon die. But there are many falconers who do not get the best out of their birds. Of course some birds are faster than others, some are better at footing, and so on. But both wild and trained hawks learn from experience, and it stands to reason that the more flying a bird does, the more competent it becomes. A freshly-caught bird comes to you with a clean sheet, and what you teach it thereafter is your responsibility. It is considerably easier to prevent a bird from getting into bad habits than to cure it once it has acquired them.

Falconry is very demanding, in that any mistakes made by the falconer are often heavily paid for. It is impossible to overemphasise this fact. You may get away with the occasional lapse, but sooner or later you will make what seems a very small mistake and the results will be disastrous. You will find you have learnt your lesson the hard way, which may be good for you but often is not so good for your hawk. If this frightens you, so much the better – you will be more aware of the pitfalls that you may encounter. You will need patience and persistence, too, if you are to succeed. I do not believe there are 'born falconers', but I do think you need a 'feeling' for falconry. If you have this, and really want to train and fly a bird, then you can learn, so long as you are prepared to persevere.

Falconry suffers, both in' Europe and in North America, from what I call

'Robin Hood falconers' (or 'Drug-store falconers', as I once heard them called by a Canadian). Such people keep a bird just because it is unusual and draws attention to them. They dress up in various strange garbs, with large plumes in their hats, and so on. They rarely fly their birds except perhaps to a lure, yet their stories of their hawk's prowess grow, like those of armchair anglers, with each telling. They do falconry a lot of harm. Personally I have never found that a Robin Hood hat or a flying falcon design on my glove made any hawk put up a better performance.

4 Housing

When you first obtain a hawk, whether it is an eyass, a passager or a haggard, you will find it advisable to keep it indoors for at least a few days. This allows it to settle down and recover, in peace and quiet, from any stress put upon it by being caught. A bird imported from abroad will have undergone the additional fright and strain of travel (although now that quarantine has been imposed on imported birds they are in fact automatically subjected to a 35-day rest period). This rest period also allows for any veterinary checks to be carried out.

If the bird were to be put out of doors immediately after its arrival it would tend to bate (fly about) a great deal in an effort to get away, and would not only become even more frightened but would also very probably break some of its flight feathers. If, however, a newly-arrived bird is put into suitable indoor quarters, away from the bewildering sights and sounds that it would meet out of doors, it calms down quickly. Even when the bird is trained, indoor quarters are essential at times (for example, in very bad weather, or when it is ill). What sort of indoor set-up you have depends on what buildings are available, or what you can afford to build.

The more a bird can move around, the better, as this helps it to keep fit. The ideal indoor quarters would therefore be a room or shed in which the bird can fly around if it wishes to. The minimum width of this room must be more than the wingspan of the bird, otherwise it will break its wingtips. The longer the room, the better. There should be a perch at each end. For a small hawk the dimensions should be 6 ft by 4 ft at the very least; for a larger bird, such as a goshawk, at least 8 ft by 6 ft. There should be as much daylight as possible, and any windows must have vertical bamboo bars on the inside. There should also be a safety grid on the outside of the window, in case one of the bars breaks or becomes dislodged at any time. (A good alternative to bamboo is the black meshed Netlon used by gardeners as a windbreak.) Some form of ventilation is essential – either a glassless window, or the safety grid so arranged that the window can be opened or shut at will. Shutters are useful in very cold weather.

The room should be completely empty except for perches – with no old deck-chairs, bits of bicycle or lawn mowers lying around. Run a soft broom down the walls and you will feel it snag on any nails, screws or splinters left there by accident and likely to do the bird an injury. The floor can be covered with sand, peat or sawdust; I myself prefer sand. Perches can either run across from wall to wall or be fixed on brackets. It is a good plan to have a perch placed so that the bird can land on it as it flies towards the window; thus it will avoid crashing against the bars, will also get a view out and, if the perch can be so arranged, a bit of sun during the day.

If you are building a place especially for the purpose then you can have part, or all, of the roof transparent. If you do this then it will need to be insulated. This can be done by attaching transparent plastic sheeting under the roof, rather like double glazing.

The door should open outwards, so that one does not accidentally hit the hawk as one goes in. Outside this door there must be an outer room, or compartment, so that if the bird should go through the open door it cannot escape altogether. Sooner or later it will beat you to the door, and if you do not take this safety precaution you will have a lost hawk. Far worse can happen. One beginner I know ignored this advice and in his haste to prevent his lanner flying through the open door, shut it between the door edge and the jamb. It died a few days later from multiple injuries. There was no excuse for this. He knew the risks he was running, thought he would be clever enough to avoid them and failed. But it was bad luck on the lanner, to put it mildly.

Now since you are going to have an outer room you might just as well keep all your gear in it. It then becomes your weighing-room and general sanctum. How big it is, and how luxurious, is obviously a matter for you to decide. You can fill it with all mod. cons – an armchair, pictures on the wall, a refrigerator for the hawk's meat and so on – or you can make it strictly utilitarian.

As a safety precaution the windows in your outer room must have bamboo bars too. Thick bamboo is required, at least ½ in. in diameter, and since no staple will go over this size without crunching the bamboo and splitting it, it is best to drill the top end only, making the hole a little bigger than the shank of the nail that is being used; if it is a tight fit the bamboo will split. The nails should be galvanized and have big heads; roofing clouts are good for this job. Fix the top nail and then drill the hole for the bottom nail and fix that. If you try to drill both holes first you will find that the bamboo has turned slightly and one of your holes will be at the wrong angle. There should be no horizontal bars or supports for the bamboos, otherwise the hawk may grab these, put its tail through the bars and you will have some broken tail tips to repair. Using Netlon mesh prevents any feather damage.

Needless to say, the place must be dry and free from draughts. Either damp or draughts can cause illness in a bird, and both combined are killers of the first order.

A diagram of a typical housing plan is given (see page 54), and from this you should be able to design your own. Obviously this could be fairly expensive, particularly if you have to start from scratch. But there is a cheaper alternative which is simple to make and will cater for most hawks and falcons, provided it is adapted to their size.

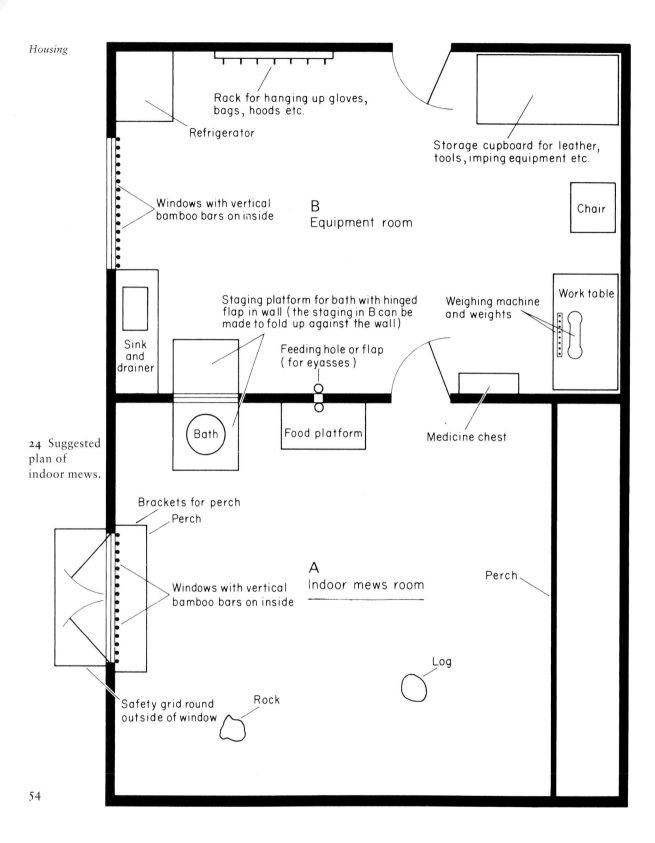

Rack for hanging up gloves,
bags, hoods etc.

Refrigerator

Storage cupboard for leather,
tools, imping equipment etc.

Windows with vertical
bamboo bars on inside

B
Equipment room

Chair

Sink
and
drainer

Staging platform for bath with hinged
flap in wall (the staging in B can be
made to fold up against the wall)

Feeding hole or flap
(for eyasses)

Weighing machine
and weights

Work table

Bath

Food platform

Medicine chest

24 Suggested
plan of
indoor mews.

Brackets for perch
Perch

Windows with vertical
bamboo bars on inside

A
Indoor mews room

Perch

Log

Safety grid round
outside of window

Rock

Take a tea-chest of the largest size, remove the top and turn the chest on its side. Make a 1 in. by 1 in. frame to fit the opening. Fix vertical bamboo bars on the back of this; the distance between them should be less than the width of the hawk's head. (Once again, Netlon could take the place of bamboos.) Fix this door to the box with hinges and add a catch. Now drill two holes in the sides of the box and screw a perch across at a height which will allow the hawk's head to clear the ceiling and its tail the floor. So the bird now has a compartment with a barred door and a perch to sit on (see fig. 25). You can cover the floor with newspaper, and if you care to add some sawdust on top of that, you can do so. The hawk goes in loose, with only its jesses on; if you hang the leash and swivel over the door catch then you will not forget the bird is inside.

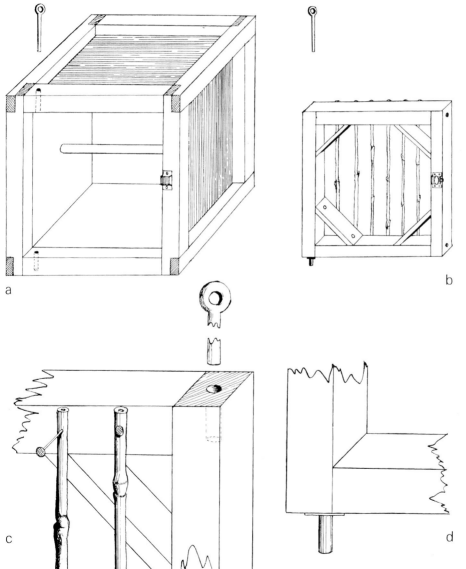

a

b

c

d

25 SIMPLE FORM OF NIGHT QUARTERS
a Night quarter without door, showing perch screwed into position and holes drilled for lift-off hinges. The wooden frame is lined with Formica.
b Completed door with corner struts, bamboo, bars, hinges and catch.
c Close-up view of back of door, showing roofing clouts passing through pre-drilled holes in the bamboo.
d Close-up of bottom of door, showing hinge.

55

This is one of the simplest forms of indoor accommodation that I know. You can use it in cold weather, for sick hawks and for travelling. You can improve on it in several ways. If you make a framework, line it with wood or ply, and stick a washable covering (such as Formica, Arborite, Ware-rite or Melamine) on the inside, you will find it much easier to keep the interior clean. If you use lift-off hinges the door will be simpler to scrub, and if you make the compartment the same size as your daily newspaper, fully spread, it will save you having to fold it to fit the floor. I use two sizes of compartment: 2 ft by 2 ft by 2ft for small hawks and falcons, and 3 ft by 3 ft by 3ft for larger ones. They take up far less room indoors than the now obsolete screen perch. Now and then you may have a bird which crashes around in one of these compartments at first, in which case you can drape a sack over it, or even fit a dark door as an extra. However, most hawks soon get used to these night quarters. Even if you have a shed, these small indoor quarters are still worth making, as they are ideal for travelling. You simply put the empty compartment in the boot of your car, and you have no housing problems when you reach the end of your journey.

Your hawk's room, or mews if you prefer the term (though strictly speaking a mews was simply the place where hawks were formerly put to be moulted) can also be used for housing an eyass bird until it has grown all its feathers full length and the quills have hardened properly. The small box-type night quarters would not be suitable for rearing eyasses.

Screen perches

Screen perches have long been the traditional indoor accommodation for hawks. A screen perch consists of a horizontal pole for the bird to perch on, mounted on a stand about 4 ft high. Beneath the pole there hangs a taut screen of cloth. The bird is tied up very short and can only move the length of its jesses on either side of the swivel. The screen stops it flying round the perch and tangling itself up, and helps it to climb back if it bates off.

Tradition is fine, but it should be tempered with common sense and altered if there is something better; and after long experience of screen perches I am now utterly opposed to their use. I do realise that many falconers will disagree with me, but I would ask them seriously to consider the following points.

Screen perches are very effective tail breakers, especially for short-winged hawks. The hawk bates along the perch, its tail goes either side, and in no time the centre feathers break and the others soon follow. Wingtips can also get broken, since if the bird does any wing-fanning exercises the tips hit the perch. All this can be avoided by keeping the bird in the dark, but no bird should be deprived of light if this can possibly be avoided.

Much worse, however, is the fact that screen perches can cause death to birds. Some hawks, especially sparrowhawks, take a long time to learn how to climb back up the screen on to the perch. They sometimes fail to do so, hang head down for too long and so die. Also, just like humans, hawks are sometimes taken ill during the night and, like humans, when they feel ill they want to lie down. A hawk on a screen perch cannot do this. She may try to fly down to the floor, and after one or more vain attempts will be too exhausted to scramble back, and will hang head down and die. When you find your bird dead in the morning you should have a post-mortem done. The results of this may show that your bird had frounce, coccidiosis or some other disease, and you will assume that this alone was the cause of death. But bear in mind that, had the bird been able to lie down, she might well have been alive in the morning, and you would have been able to treat her and might have had a good chance of curing her. The screen perch was the real killer, not the disease.

Screen perches do have a limited usefulness if you want to have your hawk indoors with you while you are manning her. But she should not be left alone on the perch for any length of time. I know there are dozens of falconers who have used screen perches for years without having any trouble of the kind I have mentioned; nevertheless it does occur far more often than is generally realised. Over the centuries that screen perches have been in use, they must have killed a great many hawks.

Outdoor housing

For your bird's outdoor quarters, again, you can spend a great deal of money. On the other hand you need spend nothing at all – apart from the cost of perches – simply putting your hawk out on the lawn when the weather is suitable, and bringing her in when it is not. But this is not a very satisfactory arrangement unless there is always someone at hand who is able to move the hawk under cover every time the weather turns bad. Even a well-trained wife who is willing to move the hawk before rescuing the washing from the line may well be out shopping when both hawk and washing get soaked in a thunderstorm. It is therefore advisable to provide some sort of shelter against the weather.

This needs a certain amount of consideration beforehand. The siting is important. The bird needs plenty of sun, but it also needs protection from the prevailing winds and shade in very hot weather. Although it should get used to seeing people around it, it is better not to put it in the front garden and have gaping crowds leaning over the fence and badgering you with questions.

While you are about it you may just as well make your shelter large enough to accommodate a big hawk, even if your bird is small, and so avoid having to make alterations later on. Small hawks can live in big shelters, but not vice versa.

A very simple form of roof can be made from corrugated plastic sheeting on a wooden frame. It can be supported against a screen fence or wall at the back; hedges, even evergreen ones, are not much use for this job as they soon go thin at the base and are by no means draughtproof. For the front roof supports see diagram 26. Side screens are another protection against wind; for these hedges will suffice, or you can use lap-board – there are many alternatives. It is best to make the roof fairly high – say 5 ft 6 in. at the front and 6 ft at the back – then the hawk will not be able to sit on the roof and you will not bang your head quite so often as you would if it were lower.

It is very pleasant to be able to go out knowing that your hawk will be getting the benefit of fresh air and sunshine and yet will be sheltered if need be. But you will still be left with other problems, such as stray dogs and cats, or even foxes, and inquisitive human beings. Also, swivels, leashes and other gear can break, and many hawks have been lost through this. You can avoid all these problems (barring the villain armed with a jemmy who is prepared to break in and steal your hawk) by making the whole area into an enclosure, with wire netting all round and over the top, and a padlocked gate. This enclosure (for it is not an aviary or a cage) will have to be made long enough and wide enough, so that unless the hawk breaks loose she cannot touch any part of the wire. This means you must make allowance for her wings when spread.

Do remember, if you make a wire enclosure, to use galvanized staples, and do not drive them right home. If you do so, you run the risk of cracking the galvanizing on the wire, which will make it prone to rust; also, should you ever wish to remove the staples you will find it very much easier if they have not been driven hard in. Remember also to make the gate of the enclosure wide enough to allow your lawn-mower and wheelbarrow inside.

The area under the roof should be sanded to a depth of at least 4 to 6 in. Every so often this will need raking, and, at longer intervals, will have to replaced

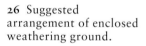

26 Suggested arrangement of enclosed weathering ground.

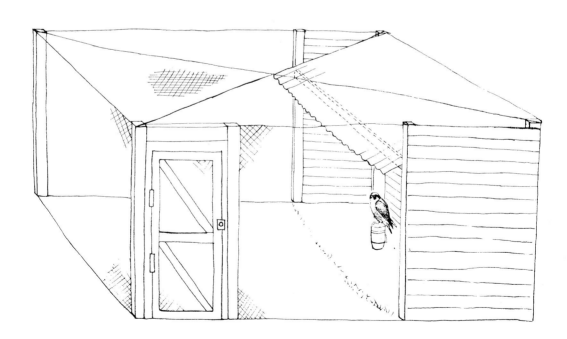

completely. If your hawk should contract a disease, then all the sand must be shovelled out and renewed. Outside the roof area, grass may be grown, but since not many hawks take kindly to the noise of a lawn-mower at close quarters, mowing should be done when the bird is not in the enclosure.

The illustration (fig. 26) will give you a fair idea of what an enclosure of this kind should be like. You can make various improvements of your own if you wish, such as putting up a gutter along the front edge of the roof to prevent drips from the roof being blown in by the wind. You can even put up a canvas roller blind, fixed so that if you pull it up to the back of the roof it will provide shade, and if you pull it down vertically in front it will give added protection against wind and rain. Incidentally, a small amount of rain will not do any harm to your bird; I find that many of my breeding birds in aviaries often sit out in the rain, even though they have plenty of shelter at hand. If you do put on a gutter, the down-pipe should lead into a soakaway, which can be dug outside the enclosure. Almost your only worry then will be in winter, when snow may build up on top of the roof and the wire netting which covers the enclosure; it is surprising how this can happen even on a large meshed netting. A good shake will usually clear it.

Blocks

There are many different designs for blocks. After years of trial and error I have found the most satisfactory to be the type illustrated here (fig. 27). Short-winged hawks dislike sitting on blocks, but falcons are perfectly happy on them, and as they are cheaper and easier to make than bow perches I therefore keep my falcons on blocks and reserve the bow perches for my hawks.

There has been a great deal of discussion as to what is the most suitable material for block tops. I myself use solid cork in preference to other materials, although I am at present experimenting with a synthetic turf (Astroturf) on the tops of some of my blocks; however, I am not entirely happy about this, and so cannot unreservedly recommend it. Stone and cement tops get far too hot in summer and cold in winter; padded tops take too long to dry out if they get wet (and no hawk in the wild sits on a padded perch). A block top should be slightly uneven, so that the surface does not always come into contact with exactly the same part of the bird's foot, and cork can easily be rasped into an asymmetrical shape. It is also easy to scrub and disinfect when necessary.

The best wood for blocks is either birch or alder, well-seasoned before being turned. The wooden part of the block should be varnished to protect it against the weather; boat varnish is far superior to the modern polyurethane varnishes, which tend to peel in the sun. The base of the block should be water-proofed as much as possible, as it is at this point that it is most susceptible to damp.

Make sure the ring is welded and not pinched, as pinched rings can open and let the leash slide out. Any non-ferrous metal will do for rings.

See figure 27A shows a block complete, and figure 27B shows the component parts. In figure 27A, a is the cork top, b is the top part of the block, and d is

A

B

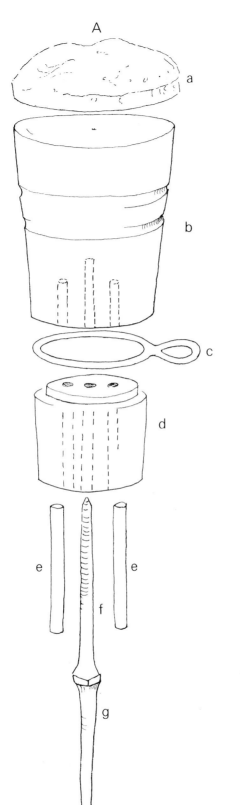

a

b

c

d

e   e

f

g

27 FALCON'S BLOCK
A Exploded view of
block.
a Cork top.
b Top part of block (the
holes are drilled before
sawing).
c Revolving ring of
welded iron.
d Lower part of block.
e Wooden dowel rods.
f Carriage screw, welded
to.
g Spike.
B The block after
assembly.

the lower part. These two are turned in one piece. The groove for the ring is turned a saw-cut's width wider than required, so that it is the right width when the block has been sawn in two. (The top grooves on the body of the block are purely ornamental.) This makes it easier to put the ring on, and is helpful in subsequent cleaning and greasing operations. But before sawing through the block, drill the three holes in the base. The central hole will take the carriage screw (not carriage bolt) which is previously welded to the spike; the outer two holes are simply alignment holes for the wooden dowel rods e1 and e2. If these are drilled before sawing they ensure that the grain of the wood lines up exactly when the block is reassembled. The central hole should be drilled to just beyond the groove with a small drill, so that the screw will bite, and then, after sawing, with a drill of a size which allows the shank of the screw to pass easily through the lower half of the block.

If you grease the dowel rods and the screw end of the spike, it will be easier to take the block to pieces, if at any time the ring jams because dirt has got into the groove or the wood has swelled. The ring itself should be painted before it is put on. A good contact adhesive will keep the cork top in place. See the following chart for dimensions of blocks.

Dimensions of blocks for falcons

	DIAMETER AT TOP (inches)	DIAMETER AT BASE (inches)	HEIGHT (inches)
Peregrine Gyr Saker Prairie falcon	5 (12 cm)	4 (10 cm)	11 (27 cm)
Tiercel Lanner Lugger Sakret Male prairie	4½ (11 cm)	3½ (8 cm)	9 (22 cm)
Merlin Kestrel	3½ (8 cm)	2½ (6 cm)	7 (17 cm)

Note: the ring groove should be about 2 in. (5 cm) from the base.
Spikes should be 9–11 in. (22–27 cm) long.

Bow perches

Besides being used for all the short-winged hawks, these are also used for buzzards and hawk-eagles. They are considerably more complicated to make than blocks, and unless you are an expert welder you will need to have the metal part made by a blacksmith. I have modified the traditional design of the bow perch, but the basic principle remains the same.

For the small hawks, such as sparrowhawks and shikras, it is fairly simple to find a piece of wood that can easily be bent to the required arc and which is of a diameter suitable to the bird's feet. For a sparrowhawk, 1 in. to 1¼ in. would be quite comfortable. It is best to leave the bark on the wood, although in the

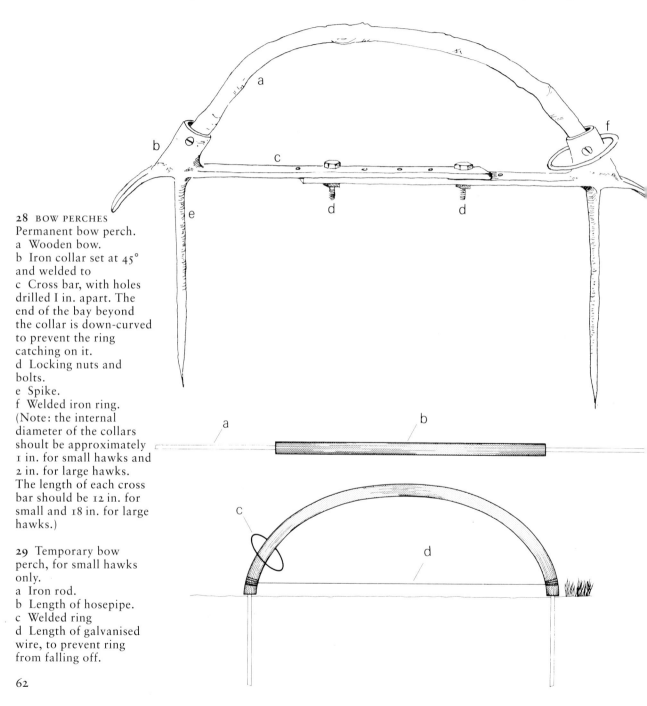

28 BOW PERCHES
Permanent bow perch.
a Wooden bow.
b Iron collar set at 45°
and welded to
c Cross bar, with holes
drilled 1 in. apart. The
end of the bay beyond
the collar is down-curved
to prevent the ring
catching on it.
d Locking nuts and
bolts.
e Spike.
f Welded iron ring.
(Note: the internal
diameter of the collars
shoult be approximately
1 in. for small hawks and
2 in. for large hawks.
The length of each cross
bar should be 12 in. for
small and 18 in. for large
hawks.)

29 Temporary bow
perch, for small hawks
only.
a Iron rod.
b Length of hosepipe.
c Welded ring
d Length of galvanised
wire, to prevent ring
from falling off.

case of bigger hawks this will soon get stripped off. When making bow perches for the larger hawks a problem arises in that the diameter of the wood required is such that it makes it very hard to bend – goshawks, for instance, need a perch of a good 2 in. diameter. I think you will do better to spend time, armed with a bow-saw, scouring the woods and hedgerows for a piece of wood which is already the right size and shape, rather than trying to bend a straight piece. People talk about steaming wood in order to bend it, but I think you would find this none too easy. According to the late Uffa Fox, steaming in any case tends to make the wood brittle, and he himself preferred to use boiling water when bending wood. Again, this would require rather specialized equipment. An alternative is to cut a series of V-shaped notches close together on the underside of the wood, which allow it to bend, and close up when it does so. Some woods bend much more easily than others – yew and hedge maple are good in this way. Cypress (not easy to procure as it is usually grown as an ornamental garden tree) grows naturally in curves that are often ideal for the purpose.

For the smaller perches one can use a bent metal rod with a covering of rubber or plastic hose slid over it. For larger perches, the canvas and rubber water pipes used in car cooling systems come in suitable lengths, curves and diameters, but one is still faced with the problem of what support to put inside them. The disadvantage of such artificial bows is that unlike wood they are symmetrical throughout their entire length, and also the texture of the surface will tend to stop the ring sliding easily along the perch. When fixing the wood it is better to use brass screws, countersunk into the metal cylinder that holds the bow, rather than a nut and bolt running straight through – otherwise the ring tends to get caught under the nut or the head of the bolt. Incidentally, the down-curving at the end of the metal base is to prevent the leash from getting caught underneath, and this protruding end is also very useful for putting one's foot on, when driving the perch into the ground.

A bow perch is best placed in the centre of the shelter, parallel with the sides. This prevents soiling of both back and side walls with mutes. A falcon on a block can only move in a circle, but the area covered by a hawk on a bow perch is elliptical. This should not be forgotten when siting the bow perch outside the shelter, otherwise the bird's wings may touch the wire of the enclosure.

Perches and blocks should be scrubbed and disinfected from time to time, and the paint on the metalwork kept in good condition. It is a good idea to have a spare perch in reserve for use while maintenance is being carried out.

Ring perches
Ring perches, an old Persian design which some modern falconers recommend, have two disadvantages. They have to be padded on the top, so if they are left out in the rain the padding gets soaked, takes a long time to dry, and this does not do your bird's feet any good. Also the leash can get caught up on the padding, and since the perch, being a complete circle, is higher than a bow perch, the leash tends to run through the bird's tail and break it. In the past I

have used ring perches, but have long since discarded them in favour of bow perches.

Baths

All birds of prey like to bathe at times, especially falcons. All that is required is a container for cold water, of sufficient size and depth. Since small hawks can bathe in big baths it is advisable to purchase a large one, and a diameter of 2 ft 6 in. is ample for all birds except eagles. I think that circular baths are best. The bottom six inches of a large cask makes a good bath, but it is very heavy and if you let it dry out it will leak and finally disintegrate. Fibreglass baths, preferably with the smooth side inside, are light and easy to clean; and those with inclined sides have the advantage of making the baths easy to stack. If the bird wants to bathe it will go in of its own accord, and if it does not there is nothing you can do to make it. You can either bring the bath to the hawk or vice versa.

Both perch and bath should be in the sun if there is any, for once your bird has had a bath she will go back to her perch and spread her wings and tail to dry. If the perch is not in the sun she may sit on the ground and get her tail tips muddy, and she will take longer to dry. You should place the bath in such a position that the hawk is able to reach as far as the middle and no further, so that she will not be able to get her leash tangled round it. If you do this then the bath will not be too close to her perch and become fouled with her mutes. If your bird is slightly wild then the bath should be on the side of the perch from which she is most likely to be approached by anyone. Then she will not bate into it as you go past or walk in to pick her up. If, on the other hand, she is already well manned, put the bath down so that when she bates towards you, keen for the day's flying, she does not go into the bath, get wet and so delay the start for you.

There are two other points concerning bathing – hawks do not often drink, but they ought to have water accessible, to give them the chance to do so if they wish. They do drink in hot weather and after long journeys, and when they are ill they may drink a great deal. Falcons, if they are not offered a bath before flying, especially in hot weather, may refuse to fly at quarry and go off, sometimes a very long way, looking for water. So you should allow up to an hour and a half for bathing, drying and preening before you take them out. At times falcons have been lost because their owners either did not know this fact, or ignored it.

Obviously baths should be kept clean and the water fresh. Do not think that cold weather will stop a falcon bathing. I have seen them bathe in icy cold weather with snow lying all around them.

By now you should have a good idea of what amount of space your bird will need and the various forms of housing. But do not leave your preparations until the last minute. It takes quite a time to get everything ready.

5 Tools and Equipment

It is not easy these days to buy good equipment ready-made, and most falconers find it advisable to make their own. This requires a certain amount of skill, and some of the tools needed would not normally be found in the average household. Assuming that you are going to make a large part of your own equipment, I have compiled the following list of tools and accessories that you will need.

leather punch
eyelet punches (varying sizes)
leather-cutting knives and blades (Stanley knives or surgical knives)
long-nosed pliers
parallel pliers
electricians' wire-cutters (preferably sprung)
saddler's awl and spare blades (small)
stitch marker
chisels, 7.5 mm (5/16 in.) and 9 mm (3/8 in.) (preferably wood-carver's chisels)
half-round file
scissors (American type leather scissors are very useful)
small blunt-ended marlin spike, or stag-horn winkle pin
needles (Sharps no. 3)
curved surgical or upholstery needles (size immaterial)
linen thread (Barbour's no. 18 – any colour)
beeswax
a packet of paraffin wax candles
a bottle of medicinal paraffin
two bulldog clips
contact adhesive (such as Evostick)
a packet of either Rapid Araldite or Super-Epoxy glue

In addition you will need the following gear. This chapter deals with the equipment which you must have before your bird arrives; the following chapter deals with equipment which needs the bird's presence in order to fit it properly.

The weighing machine
This is one of the most important items of a falconer's equipment, though

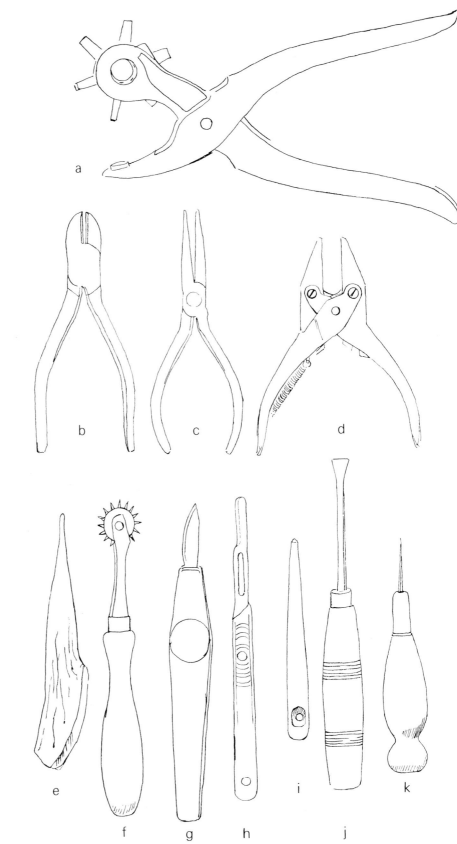

30 TOOLS
a Leather punch.
b Electrician's wire-
cutters.
c Long-nosed pliers.
d Parallel pliers
e Stag-horn 'winkle pin'.
f Stitch marker.
g Stanley Slimline knife.
h Surgical knife.
i Small blunt-ended
marlin spike.
j Wood-carvers chisel.
k Saddler's awl.

there are still a few people who do not use a weighing machine. It is of more value to the falconer than an exposure meter to a photographer, and you do not find professional photographers guessing exposures.

The kind of machine required is the old balance type with a pan at one end and weights at the other. The more modern spring balance will not do, since it tends to become inaccurate after a period of use. In place of the pan put a perch. There are several ways of doing this, depending on the construction of the pan-holder – very often two of the pan supports can be bent upwards to hold the perch, and the remaining two can be sawn off with a hacksaw, or may even unscrew. I make the perch out of metal tube, with a wooden bung at each end, and put a piece of carpet round it to stop the hawk slipping. Do not make the perch too high, or it will rock about and make the machine less accurate. Having added the perch you must now re-balance the machine. You can either replace the heavy platform with a lighter one, or you can add weight to the perch by filling its ends with the necessary amount of lead. Some machines can be finally balanced up by adding or taking away shot from the small box under the weighing platform.

The type of weights that the average ironmonger sells can be very inaccurate, and accuracy is of great importance. You should buy a set of government-tested weights. I use weights ranging from ¼ oz to about 2 lb – these will serve for any bird up to the size of a small eagle. A holder for the weights is useful, as it is all too easy to lose the smallest ones.

Hawking bag
This is a blind spot with many falconers. Either they are content with just any old haversack, or they go to the other extreme and have a leather-embossed, betasselled, embroidered, heavy, cumbersome 'Robin Hood' affair with a wide leather belt that looks like an heirloom from a pirate. The essentials of a good hawking bag are that it should be lightweight, washable and reasonably tear-proof, and should have several compartments so that the contents can be kept separate. There will be times when you will need something out of your bag in a hurry.

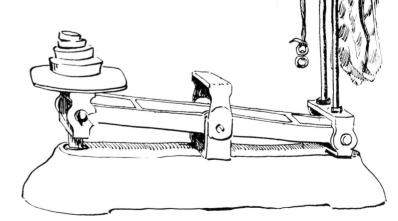

31 Hawk on modified weighing machine.

Basic contents will consist of a lure complete with lure stick and line, a pick-up piece (meat to pick the hawk up off the lure), a creance (a light line some 23 m (25 yds) long), a spare leash, a spare swivel and a knife. If you have only one compartment you may well pull out the lure to get your falcon back and the pick-up piece may drop out at the same time without your noticing it. The falcon will pick this up, carry it into a tree and eat it, and as a consequence may easily be lost.

I find canvas the ideal material for hawking bags, since it has all the properties I have mentioned. Patterns and instructions for making hawking bags are given in chapter 21.

Knives

I find a small, single-bladed lock knife the best. One should be able to open it with one hand, and it is useful to have a loop on the handle. The no. 8 Opinel knife, made in France but easily obtainable in England, is extremely good, but needs to be modified by cutting a semi-circular groove in the handle and by drilling the end and adding a loop. The enormous 'Falkners Heil' hunting knives, with hugely long blades and blood-gutters are, I think, more suited to tiger-hunters than to falconers, and merely add unnecessary weight to be carried around. Whatever knife you choose, remember to keep it sharp.

Creances

These are light lines on which you fly your hawk during training, before it can be trusted loose. They are best made of braided nylon (of a thickness suitable for the type of bird you are flying), since the wet does not affect this as it does cod line and most other alternatives. The ends of the creance should be sealed with heat to stop them fraying – this can be done by burning them with a match

32 CREANCE WINDING
a The creance is not tied to the stick. Hold the end in position with the thumb while starting to wind in a figure-of-eight.
b By turning the stick during winding, the creance is evenly distributed.
c How not to do it – this is the result if the stick is not turned.

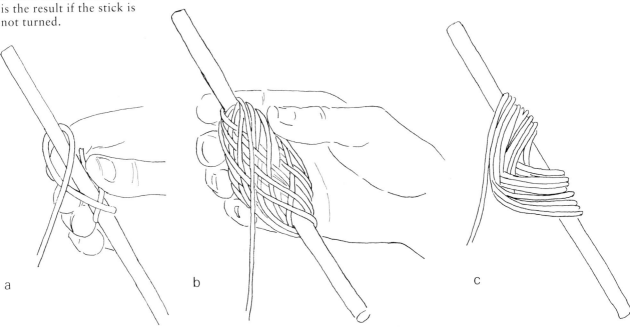

a   b   c

or lighter, and then squeezing them between a pair of pliers while they are still hot. (Do not do this with your fingers, or you will burn yourself.)

I find that 23 m (about 25 yds) is an ample length for a creance. When not in use the line is wound round a stick, but it is most unwise to attach it to this in any way. One winds a creance round the stick in the same way that one would cleat up a washing line, or a down-haul on a boat. It is done in a figure of eight fashion, but the creance stick is turned slightly at each wind so that the line does not build up on one side as it does on a cleat. This is not easy to explain, and it takes time to learn. You ought, after quite a bit of practice, to be able to do it one-handed with the hawk sitting quietly on your fist. Tension must be kept on the line whilst winding. This is best done by running it through the fingers of your left hand. Lure lines are wound in the same way. This way of winding is much quicker than others and it also allows one to unwind the creance very fast. There are times when speed makes all the difference to losing a bird or not.

A creance should always be carried in your hawking bag for there are times when it can be extremely useful in getting a bird back. Breaking strain of a creance for small hawks should be about 45 kg (100 lb), and for large hawks 110 kg (250 lb).

Lures

A lure is exactly what its name implies – something to tempt the bird back. The simplest form of lure is a dead animal or bird of a type that the hawk would normally be expected to take. This, however, is often inconvenient, since one does not always have to hand a dead grouse, say, for a grouse hawk, or a dead rook for a rook hawk. Most falconers therefore use artificial lures.

There are so many varieties of lure and so many opinions as to what is best that it can be bewildering for the beginner. There is the old padded horseshoe with dried wings attached – and maybe a bit of red tape into the bargain. There are plastic, fluttering, twisting lures – the range is endless. Some are certainly too hard and heavy, and are consequently dangerous to the hawk.

A lure should bear some resemblance to the type of quarry you propose to fly at, but I am quite sure that no hawk is ever fooled into believing the lure is the real thing. I find that the most convenient form of lure is a pair of dried wings with a piece of meat attached to them. Obviously the wings should be of the same type as the quarry that you are going to fly at, or at least similar in appearance and size. (Since, for reasons already gone into, you do not want your falcon to chase pigeons, do not use pigeons' wings for lures.) The wings should be cut off the dead bird as close to the body as possible, and hung up to dry. I put mine under the car bonnet, tied out of the way of any revolving machinery or very hot surfaces, and they dry there very quickly.

When made up, the lure is tied to a small swivel of a similar size to the swivels used for merlins. This in turn is attached to the lure line. For lure lines I prefer the braided cotton line used for ferrets and long-nets. Nylon is, of

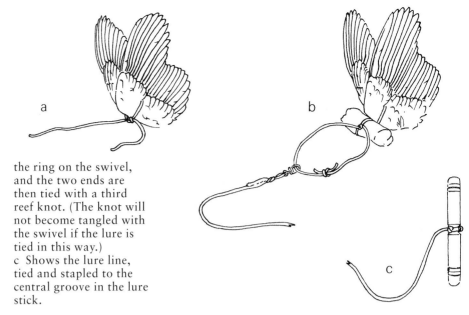

33 MAKING UP A LURE
a The dried wings are placed back to back and a piece of strong twine is passed between the primaries and secondaries of each and tied tightly with a reef knot as shown. (Note: one end of the string should be longer than the other.)
b The string is now tied tightly round the chosen piece of meat, with another reef knot; a small slit cut in each side of the meat helps the string to sink in and so hold it more securely. The longer end of string is now passed through the ring on the swivel, and the two ends are then tied with a third reef knot. (The knot will not become tangled with the swivel if the lure is tied in this way.)
c Shows the lure line, tied and stapled to the central groove in the lure stick.

course, stronger and more waterproof, but it tends to burn the fingers and raise blisters if used frequently. The length of the line is a matter of individual choice, but you will find it helpful to keep to the same length all the time, so that then you always know exactly how far your lure will reach. Personally I use 4 yds of line.

The other end of the line is attached to the lure stick, and should be tied and stapled round a groove in the centre of the stick. This stick will vary in size and weight according to the type of bird it is used for, and is best painted a bright colour such as yellow or blue. (Since birds are not colour-blind it is inadvisable to use red, and green or brown will not show up easily in grass.)

The string that ties the wings together and attaches them to the meat, and which in turn attaches the lure to the swivel, must be good strong twine. I once saw a falcon lost because the weak string used to tie the lure broke, the bird carried the lure away and was never seen again.

When training birds which are to hunt rabbits or hares, it is advisable to use a lure made up of a rabbit skin, sewn up and stuffed with some sort of material, and weighted to stop it bouncing up in the air when dragged along the ground at speed. At first, meat is attached to the lure at the head end, but once the bird has learned to associate the dummy with food, this practice ceases. This is purely a training device, and would be very inconvenient to carry around when out hunting, when a more normal type of lure will suffice. Rabbit and hare skins disintegrate very rapidly in the wear and tear of training. A piece of fox skin is tougher and will last longer.

Gloves

Most European falconers carry their birds on the left hand, and so only a left-hand glove is necessary. (If you happen to be left-handed you will of course need a right-hand glove.) For small hawks and falcons an ordinary leather glove is quite strong enough, but for the bigger birds you will certainly need a thicker glove, and for the very powerful ones this should be reinforced. If you do decide to train really big birds such as eagles, then a separate overlay on top of a reinforced glove will also be necessary.

Buckskin makes the best gloves, but is extremely hard to obtain. Do not confuse 'buckskin' with deerskin – although it comes from the same animal the tanning process is entirely different. Real buckskin is very dense, and it is extremely hard to push a needle through it; but deerskin, which is often sold as buckskin, does not have this property, and a big hawk, such as a female goshawk, will drive its talons straight through. If you want a really good glove, make your own, since ready-made gloves, for any of the big hawks, are certainly not sold in this country. You may see them advertized, but they are not well-made, nor is the leather real buckskin.

Gloves should be kept hung up – not stuffed into your hawking bag – out of the reach of dogs, who are particularly fond of chewing them. See chapter 22 for glove-making patterns and instructions.

Cadges

The old 'field cadge' is hardly ever used these days. It requires a minion to carry it, and the only time you would ever be likely to use it would be when out game-hawking. Falcons must never be left alone on a field cadge – however short they are tied up they may reach each other's wings when outstretched, and if left in the open country they are wide open to interference from stray dogs and strangers, and also from the falcon being flown at the time. Field cadges were ideal for the purpose for which they were intended, i.e. a means by which several birds could be carried at one time by one person.

Pole cadges are no better than field cadges, and are very easily overturned.

The box cadge is far more handy than a field cadge, and can be used when travelling by car or by train. It is simply a box without a lid, which has a perch running round all or some of the sides. It is far better than the pole contraptions one sees in station wagons and such vehicles, since it can be placed lower down, near the axle level. Thus the amount of movement is lessened, and the birds are therefore more comfortable. Two types of box cadge are shown in figure 34. The first is a very easily made cadge, for carrying only one bird at a time. It has a perch at each end – one for a small, the other for a larger, bird. The second shows a rather more complicated box cadge.

To make the simple version (fig. 34a) – find a wooden box, and carefully prise the top of the sides away from the ends. This will enable you to cut away the top three inches or so from each end. Now cut a piece of wood to fit in between the two sides. A piece of broomstick diameter will serve for kestrels,

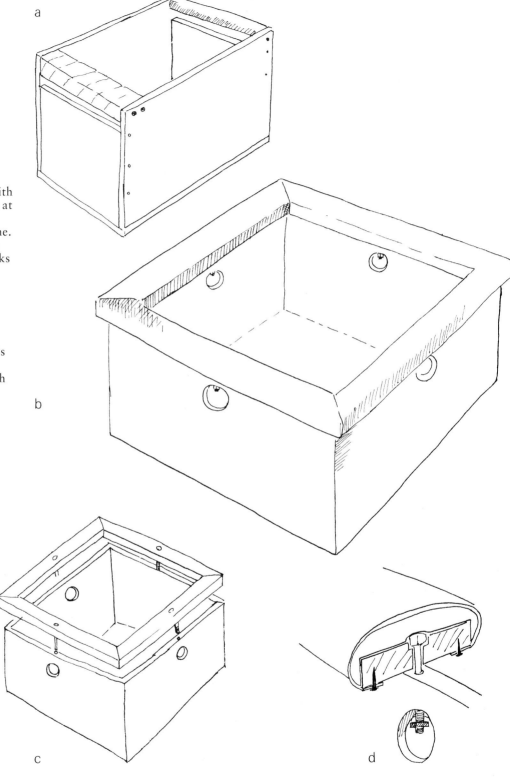

a

34 CADGES
a Simple box cadge with different sized perches at each end. Suitable for only one hawk at a time.
b More elaborate box cadge. Up to four hawks can be carried on this, provided that they are never left unattended.
c How the top is attached to the base.
d Cross-section in close-up. Note that it is easier to fix the perch cover on with the perch upside-down, before final assembly.

b

c

d

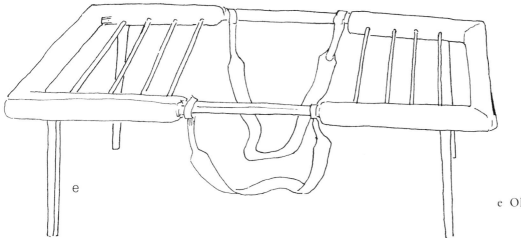

e

merlins, and sparrowhawks, and a piece of 5 cm by 2.5 cm (2 in. by 1 in.) with the edges rounded off will suffice for the larger birds. Screw these into position as shown, and pad them with material (such as old carpet) to help the hawk to grip. Paint the cadge, or varnish it, to help preserve it. When the cadge is in use in a car, a brick or heavy rock placed in the bottom will help to keep it steady.

To make the more sophisticated cadge (fig. 34b), you will again need a square or oblong wooden box. If starting from scratch, cut four pieces of wood, screw them together and add a base of ply, hardboard or any other suitable material. Drill four holes, one in each side. These can be as big as 3.8 cm (1½ in.) in diameter or more and will serve two purposes: firstly to tie the bird's leash to, and secondly to make bolting on the top frame of the cadge easier.

Figure 34c shows how the frame is attached to the main body of the cadge by means of coach bolts. Make the frame so that it overlaps the top of the box on either side. Place it on the main body of the cadge and mark the spot where the coach bolt holes are to be drilled. The holes should be slightly larger than the coach bolts so that they fit loosely into them. Drill the holes right through the top frame and down into the leash holes previously drilled. Insert the four coach bolts and knock them down tightly with a hammer. In this way they will countersink themselves and, since the shank of the bolt just below the head is squared, will be prevented from turning when the nuts are tightened.

Before putting on the padding and covering, check that the bolts line up properly and drop easily into the main frame. Next the padding can be glued on to the top frame, or roughly stapled with a staple gun. The cover must now be laid face down, and the top frame placed upside down on top of it (the coach bolts will now be sticking up). The cover can now be tacked on easily. All that is left to do is to put the top frame on to the main body and tighten up the four nuts. (When the cover gets worn out you can then simply undo the nuts, remove the top frame, strip off the old cover and renew it.) This may sound a rather elaborate way to make a box cadge, but if you have ever tried

73

tacking the cover to a non-removable frame, you will appreciate the reasons for this.

Obviously the sizes of box cadges vary according to the type of birds for which they are intended. The height should be such that there is plenty of clearance for the hawks' tails above the base. If you are carrying this type of cadge on a car seat, make sure you have no screws, nails or sharp corners protruding which might damage the seat cover. To help keep your car clean, the birds on the cadge should be facing outwards. To keep the inside of the cadge clean, line the bottom with newspaper.

The old type of cadge knot, similar to the screen perch knot (i.e. a half bow with the two ends pulled through, allowing the bird to move only the length of its jesses on each side of the swivel) is not what I would advise when tying a bird on a cadge. I tie my hawks up with a normal falconer's knot. This prevents broken tails should the birds bate off. No hawks should ever be left on a cadge unattended.

Car perch

Another way of carrying a bird in a car is on a perch fitted to the top of the front passenger seat. This is very easy to make using a clean sack and a piece of wood the width of the sack (or of the seat top – whichever is the smaller). Put the wood inside the sack about halfway down, so that it lies across its width, and tack or staple it into position. Screw a small ring bolt into the centre, countersinking the nut so that it does not protrude. Tie three or four tapes, evenly spaced, to the top and bottom edges of the sack. Drape the whole thing over the back of the seat, tie the tapes on the bottom edge to those on the top

35 PERCH ON BACK OF CAR SEAT
a Clean sack with tapes attached at top and bottom. The perch is inserted and then fixed centrally.
b The perch in position.

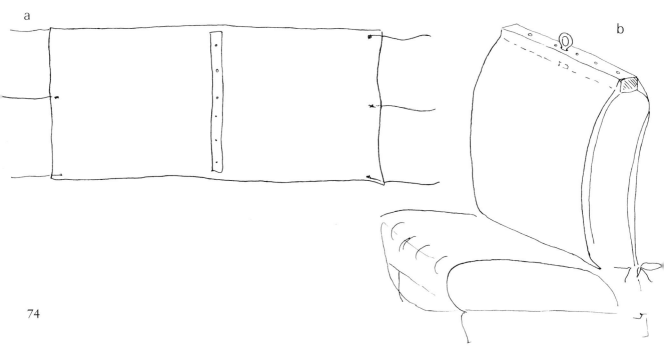

a

b

edge (see figure 30b) and you will now have a perch on the top of your passenger seat. Tie the hawk to the ring, and there you are. An unhooded hawk will soon learn to travel well like this, and since it can see what is going on it can compensate for the movement of the car, which it could not do if hooded. Travelling a bird unhooded means that it sees more of life in general, and this helps to man it more thoroughly. A hooded bird gains none of this experience.

Crates

Birds can, of course, travel in crates; indeed where air travel is concerned, they must. Good crates should be strong but as lightweight as possible. They must be dark inside, but must also have good ventilation. There should be something that the bird can grip on the floor of a crate – this should not, for obvious reasons, be completely flat, and I find that some crumpled sacking, with a piece of old carpet stapled down over it, is quite satisfactory.

Leashes

Until fairly recently leashes were nearly always made of leather, though braided cotton ones have long been used in the East. Now that nylon and Terylene are easily available, they are being used more often.

There is no doubt that man-made fibres are stronger and more reliable than leather. Also they show wear before breaking, instead of suddenly snapping without warning. But some birds will pick up braided leashes and peck at them until the whole thing looks like a forkful of spaghetti. For such birds leather must be used. The best is chrome tanned raw hide, ½ in. wide for large hawks, ⅜ in. for medium sized ones, and ¼ in. or slightly less for small birds. The thickness will vary slightly, but roughly speaking a leash should be about ⅛ in. thick.

To stop the leash running right through the swivel, one makes a button as in figure 36, using a leather punch (fig. 31b). Fold the thickest end of the leash; the number and length of the folds will depend on the size of the lower ring on your swivel. Obviously the button must be large enough to act as a stop, although if it is too big it will look clumsy, will weigh more and will tend to make the swivel swing when the hawk jumps onto its perch, so tangling the jesses. Now punch a hole right through the folds of leather. Do not hold the punch at right angles to the length of the leash, because on thick leashes with large buttons the punch will not travel through in a straight line (since it moves in an arc) and although the hole will start in the centre of the top fold, it will end up to one side in the bottom one. This will make a weak button. Having punched the holes, keeping the folds together you now thread the pointed end of the leash through them, and pull it right through until the button is completed, as in figure 36g.

The length of a leash is important. Many falconers tend to have their leashes far too long; 4 ft 6 in. is plenty for big hawks, 3 ft 6 in. for small ones. This will give your bird considerably more room in which to fly about than the average

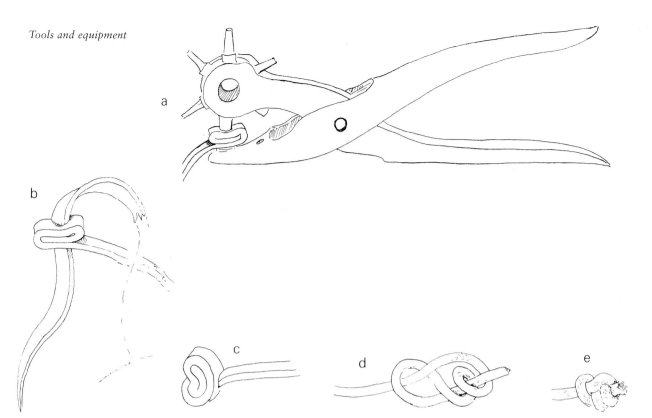

a

b

c

d

e

36 LEASH, HOOD BRACE AND AYLMERI BUTTONS
a, b, c Making a button on a leather leash. The buttons on hood braces and Aylmeri jesses are made in exactly the same way.
d, e The ends of Nylon and Terylene leashes must be knotted.

parrot or budgie cage allows its occupants. Too long a leash gives too much flying room and can result in a broken leg.

Nylon or Terylene leashes have a knot, as in figure 31c, instead of a button. The ends of leashes made of these two materials should be heat-sealed against fraying in the same way as creances. Often these leashes tend to be rather slippery and do not tie nicely, but if you run the leash through a lump of beeswax you will find this will help. The wax will wear off in time and then the process must be repeated. In the bigger sizes of leash a matt type of nylon or Terylene can be bought, and with this there is no slipping problem.

Obviously all leashes eventually wear out. The place where most wear occurs is just below the knot where the swivel comes. You can cut a leather leash button off when it begins to show signs of wear, and as the leash will have stretched a little by then, you can flatten out the end and make a new button. If in doubt always play safe and make up a new leash, rather than risk losing your hawk through a broken one.

Leather leashes should be greased at least once or twice a week to keep them supple. A recipe for jess grease is given in chapter 6.

Swivels
The object of a swivel is to prevent the leash from twisting and the jesses from winding round each other, but one swivel alone will not prevent the jesses

themselves from twisting. Good swivels are not easy to obtain, especially the larger ones (for of course they come in different sizes). When buying swivels you should look for the following points.

1   They should be either of stainless steel or some other strong, rust-free metal. Brass swivels are reasonably safe for small hawks, but on large hawks brass wears through much more quickly than one would imagine.

2   The top ring, or D, must be of sufficient size to allow you to get the jesses on reasonably easily; the bottom ring must be of the right size for your leash.

3   The joint of the bottom ring should never be just pinched together, but welded.

4   The shank to the bottom ring must be long enough for the whole of its length to be examined for signs of wear. (In some types of swivel, none of the shank is visible, and these should be avoided.)

5   The head of the shank should not only be threaded and screwed on, but also welded to ensure it cannot come off. The fairly large head stops the two rings coming apart, and it is at the junction of the head and the shank that trouble most often occurs.

Swivels for smaller hawks can be obtained from shops which sell sea-fishing tackle, but the larger ones are now no longer manufactured, as far as I know, and you may have to get an engineer to make one for you. Sometimes swivels are given a breaking strain, but this is not of much help to the falconer, since it is measured by gradually increasing the weight on the swivel until it breaks. Hawks when bating from a perch have no buffered action, as do fishing-rods, but are snatching at the swivel quite hard, so it is the snatch breaking strain that is important. For instance, a breaking strain of about 2 lb will not hold a 2 lb goshawk.

Should you experience difficulty in finding big swivels, try a ship's chandler and ask for Englefield clips, which are used for signal halyards. You will have to fill in the gap in the D with silver solder and also weld the head of the shank. Being usually made of brass, these wear very quickly. Swivels for big eagles, such as Bonelli's eagle, can sometimes be bought in harness shops – they are used on the end of lungeing-reins.

As I have mentioned before, the small swivels suitable for merlins also make good swivels for lure lines. When you are buying swivels it is as well to buy a few spares to keep in reserve.

Beating sticks

These are not necessary for falcons, but come in handy when flying short-wings. I like them to be about 4 ft to 4 ft 6 in. long, with a metal spike at the bottom end and a loop (as on a ski stick) about 6 in. below the top. Blackthorn or ash make good, solid, long-lasting sticks. Apart from using them for beating, you will find them useful if you are carrying heavy birds such as eagles – if you put the stick through your belt so that one end is underneath your gloved hand, and then press down with your free hand on the other end, you will give your gloved hand valuable support.

The spike on the bottom end of the stick allows you to leave it upright in the ground while you are calling your hawk back to the fist or the lure.

Whistles

The sound of a whistle will carry further than the human voice, and it is a good idea to get your hawk accustomed to coming when you whistle, like your dog. Some people find it difficult or even impossible to whistle, and have to use manufactured whistles. One of the best types is the kind used by shepherds. It is a circular disc of metal folded in half, with a gap of about ⅛ in. left between the two halves. A small hole is drilled in it. These whistles are easy to carry about, and have a very piercing note, but a certain amount of practice is required before you learn how to blow one.

Two points which may seem obvious – when whistling to your hawk, use a different series of notes from those you use for your dog, otherwise both will come at the same time. Also, if you can whistle without mechanical aid, this is better than using a manufactured whistle, since there is always a chance that the latter can be left behind when you go out hawking.

6 Equipment: Part II

This chapter deals with equipment that must be fitted to the bird itself, and the methods of fitting it. Jesses, bewits and, in some cases, tail bells, should be fitted directly the bird arrives. These operations can, and should, be practised in advance without the bird, so that when the time comes you are able to perform them quickly and with as little fuss as possible.

Leather

Since jesses, Aylmeri and bewits are all made of leather, it is as well to say a little about this subject first; although, since leather is extremely variable and is not always named after the animal from which it comes, the best course is to lay down a few guidelines to follow when buying it.

Good jess leather is hard to come by, as it must not only be strong, but also pliable and not too thick. Kangaroo hide, which can be bought in varying thicknesses, is extremely good for the purpose; goatskin, kip, elk and calf can also be suitable. But it is essential that you test all leather before buying it. First cut a strip the width of a jess, and test it by pulling sharply on both ends to see if it will break. If it does not, cut a small slit in it and see if this will rip easily. If it passes both these tests and has the qualities already mentioned, buy it. All leather has varying degrees of stretch, and it will also stretch more if you cut it down the length of the skin rather than across its width, so when cutting jesses to a pattern the stretch of the leather must be allowed for. Good jess leather is also suitable for Aylmeri and bewits, and for attaching tail bells.

Jesses

These are short straps, one round each leg (or, if you prefer to be anatomically correct, each tarsus, or foot) of the bird. Obviously their width, length and shape varies with the sizes of the birds for which they are intended – as a hawk's tarsus is longer than a falcon's, jesses for hawks can be cut wider and so give more support to the bird. It is very important not to have the jesses any longer than is absolutely necessary, otherwise the bird may straddle its block or perch, or, much worse, may when flying get caught up in a tree and die a slow, lingering death. All the jess patterns shown here are full size.

In figure 38 you will see the full details, stage by stage, of how to put the

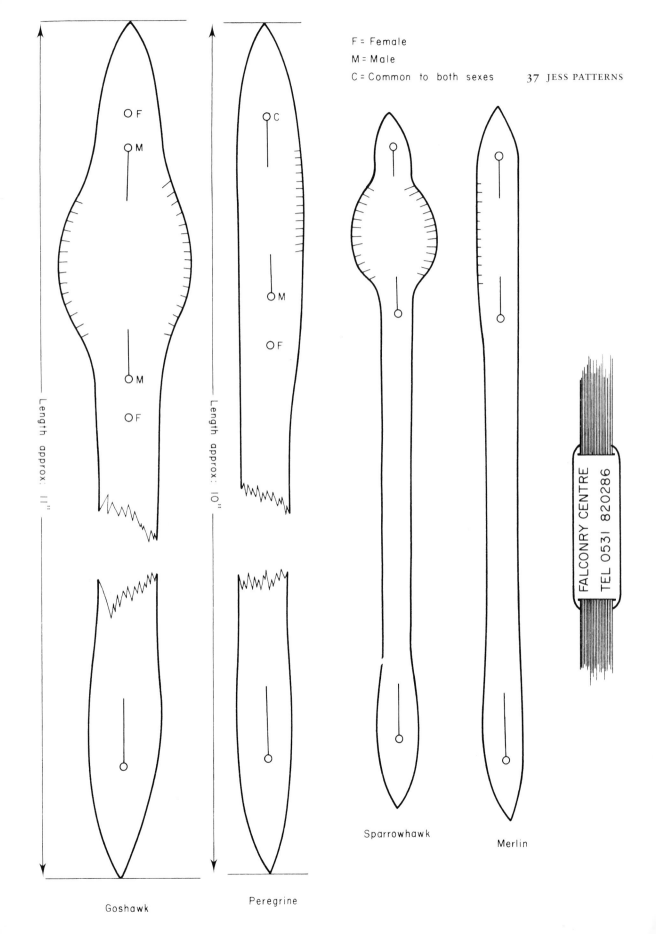

F = Female
M = Male
C = Common to both sexes   37 JESS PATTERNS

O F
O M

O C

O M
O F

Length approx: 11"

Length approx: 10"

FALCONRY CENTRE
TEL 0531 820286

Goshawk

Peregrine

Sparrowhawk

Merlin

jesses on. Although the snipe-nosed pliers are not essential, it makes the job considerably quicker and easier if you use them.

Put the jess round the leg, so that the leg lies between the two slits A and B. (Slit C is purely for the swivel and does not enter into this part of the proceedings at all.) You will find it easier if you keep slit A on the left of the leg as you look at it (see fig. 38b). Put the nose of the pliers, closed, through slit B. The jess should now be as in figure 38c. It should not be tight round the leg, but positioned so that A and B lie together.

Now take point X and the longer part of the jess in your left hand and put the pliers, closed again, through both slits A and B. Release the jess with your left hand and pick up the end somewhere around slit C. Open the pliers and grip point Y (fig. 38e). Pull the end through (fig. 38f). Now pull the jess through the two slits with your right hand. Use thumb and forefinger to ease it through at the last, and the jess will now be as illustrated in figure 38g. Repeat the procedure with the second jess on the other leg.

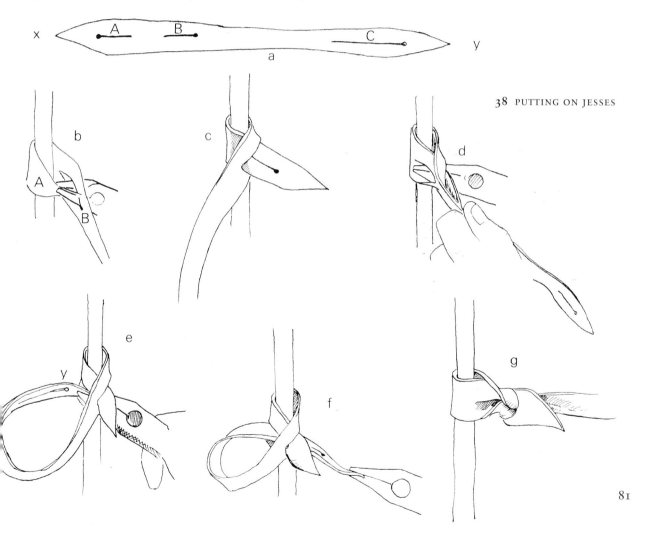

38 PUTTING ON JESSES

This is the correct way to put on jesses. I have seen another method used, but it is not so neat, and a bird which pulls at the jesses can manage to get them off, so I do not advise it and shall not describe it here.

Aylmeri

These are an invention of the late Guy Aylmer, and take the place of jesses. They consist of two leather anklets (fig. 39a), one on each leg, which are secured by a metal eyelet (fig. 39b). Through the eyelet is threaded a 'mews jess' of leather (fig. 39d) with a button at one end, to prevent it from pulling through the eyelet, and a swivel slit at the other. When in the field, 'hunting jesses' replace the mews jesses. These merely hold the hawk until the moment

39 AYLMERI

a Leather anklet.

b Metal eyelet.

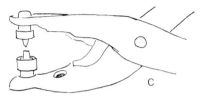

c Eyelet pliers (for attaching small eyelets).

d The anklet in place on the bird's leg. The mews jess is threaded through the eyelet.

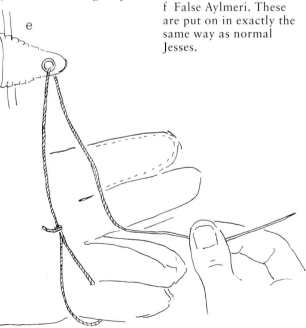

e Nylon or Terylene field jess with retaining loop.

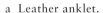

f False Aylmeri. These are put on in exactly the same way as normal Jesses.

g Attaching larger eyelets, which come in two sections:
1, 5 Eyelet punch and anvil.
2, 4 Top and bottom sections of eyelet.
3 Aylmeri.

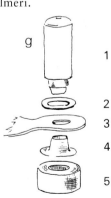

1

2

3

4

5

it starts to fly, when they pull out and remain in the falconer's hand (fig. 39e). In some cases the jesses are allowed to go with the hawk when it is flying, but should they get caught up in any obstruction such as thorns, twigs or barbed wire they pull out and so release the bird. I personally do not use this latter type of hunting jess.

Originally intended only for small hawks such as sparrowhawks, shikras and the like, Aylmeri are now rapidly coming into general use for all types of hawks and falcons, since most falconers now realize that even the larger birds can get hung up in the old type of jess. The sooner the old type disappears, the better, but there are some birds, particularly kestrels, who seem to take a delight in pulling the buttons off the ends of the mews jesses – for these, the old type of jess is the only answer.

In the case of small hawks the eyelets can be put on by means of eyelet pliers (fig. 39c) but where larger birds are concerned, larger eyelets are needed, and these must be put on with a hammer, a punch and an anvil.

When putting Aylmeri on a new bird it will be necessary to cast or hold the bird during the process, but later on, when new ones are required, they can, where eyelet pliers are used, be put on while the bird is on the fist.

There is an alternative form of Aylmeri made in the form of a small jess, onto which the eyelet is punched prior to the anklet being attached (fig. 39f). This form has one disadvantage in that it is sometimes possible for the bird's back talon to become hooked in the eyelet hole.

The procedure shown in figure 39e requires more explanation. The hunting jess of the type that I use has a loop at one end. This goes over your little finger on the gloved hand. The jesses go through the eyelet holes, down between the fingers and thumb, and are gripped between the second and third fingers. When the hawk is to be released you simply open your fingers and the ends of the hunting jesses pull through the eyelets as the hawk takes off. The jesses remain looped on the little finger. Braided nylon is very good for these jesses, as it slips easily through the eyelets. Different gauges can be bought from ships' chandlers. The ends of the jesses should be heat-sealed to stop them fraying, and to make them easier to thread through the eyelets.

Jess grease

Both jesses and Aylmeri should be kept greased, and the following recipe for for jess grease you can make up yourself.

Melt together 28 g (1 oz) beeswax and 70 g (2½ oz) paraffin wax (ordinary candles). Remove the candle wicks, and add 284 to 340 ml (10 to 15 fl. oz) of medicinal paraffin. Stir it well and pour it into a wide-mouthed, shallow jar or can, preferably with a lid to keep out the dirt. More liquid paraffin will be required in cold weather than in hot. Beeswax varies a great deal, and if the mixture is too stiff, melt it down again and add a little more liquid paraffin.

Rub this into the jesses at regular intervals; if the leather is allowed to become too hard it will be difficult to get it supple again.

Identity tags

A metal tag with your name, address and telephone number, and the word 'Reward' engraved on it, can be used on jesses as shown in figure 37. Light aluminium is the best metal to use. You can also have a similar message engraved on the bells, or round the brass eyelets on the larger Aylmeri.

Bells

Bells are attached either to the hawk's leg just above the jess (by means of a strap called a bewit), or, in some cases, to the bird's tail. They are of help in finding a lost hawk and in keeping track of it in cover. Bells come in different sizes. Small hawks can only be expected to carry one bell, but larger birds can carry two or even three. Obviously the louder the note, the better. There is a theory that bells from India are better than those from elsewhere, since the metal they are made of is not so pure and so gives a better note. This is not true – some of the bells made in America are very good indeed, and I myself have made bells that were better than Indian ones.

Good bells should not only be as loud, but as light, as possible. They can be made from brass, nickel, monel, silver and so on. The thinner the metal the better will be the sound, but the bell will have a shorter life. Bells bought from fishing tackle shops or pet shops are usually very poor, but better than no bells at all. Hawk bells do not have a hanging clapper inside them, but a loose dropper. This is best if made facetted rather than spherical, and can be of metal or glass. The old falconers used to say that, for the sound to carry really well, one of the hawk's bells should be a semi-tone higher than the other, but as far as I know no experiments have been made either to confirm or disprove this.

It is possible to make one's own bells, and instructions are given in chapter 21. (Those who do not feel equal to tackling bell-making themselves should enquire from the Falconry Centre at Newent for names and addresses of suppliers.)

Bewits

The metal loop on the top of the bell varies in size, and it is on the size of this loop that the width of the bewit will depend. The wider you can make your bewit, the stronger it will be, and so you should make it as wide as can be accommodated by the metal loop, or 'bewit strap'. The bewit must be long enough to go round your bird's leg and leave you some extra length to work with. (Figure 40a is long enough for a female goshawk.) Point each end of the bewit, and punch a hole approximately in its centre. Punch the second hole so that when the bell is on the bewit (see figs. 39b, c, and d) this second hole lies about halfway round the hawk's leg. Then just beyond the second hole, towards the right-hand end of the bewit (as in fig. 40a), cut two nicks, angled like an arrow-head. All this can be done before you start operations on the bird.

Now put the bewit round the bird's leg, just above the jess. Pass point A through hole 2, and pull it taut by hand. With your leather punch, punch hole 3 (fig. 40f). (You cannot make this hole until you get to this stage, as its position depends on the diameter of the individual bird's leg.) The hole should be made as close as possible to the point where the bewit passes through hole 2 – the anvil on the leather punch will not allow you to get it very close. Point B is now passed through hole 3, and the two nicks just by hole 2 should now open out, just beyond hole 3, and so prevent the bewit from coming off. To finish, cut off the spare ends A and B as shown in figure 40h. A pair of electrician's wire-cutters will do this job very well.

Watch for the next two or three days to see if the bewit gets slightly looser round the bird's leg. It should be able to rotate freely by then. If it is put on too tightly it will constrict the blood supply to the hawk's toes. If it stretches too much it will be too loose and will hang down too low. The bell will then

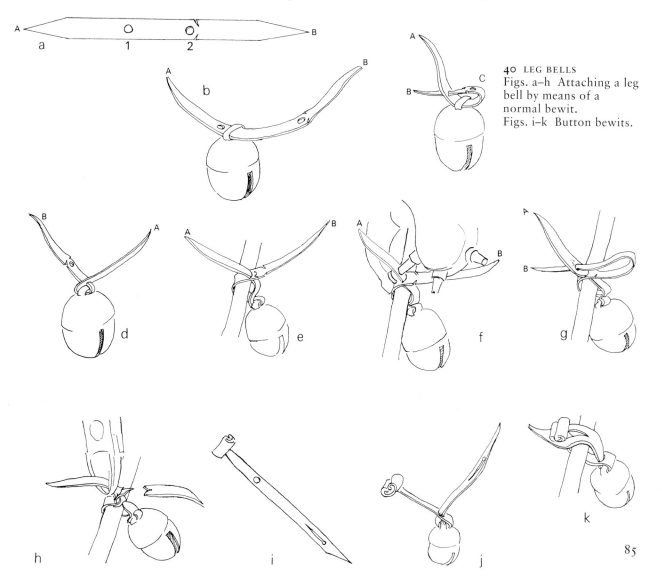

40 LEG BELLS
Figs. a–h Attaching a leg bell by means of a normal bewit.
Figs. i–k Button bewits.

get in the way of the hawk's foot and will also hit the perch and start to crack. In either case, cut the bewit off and put it on again properly.

There is another way of putting on leg bells with what are known as button bewits (see figure 40i, j and k). I do not advise this way, since the bell must always be too loose, but some falconers like it.

If you think it is a good idea to put bells on only when flying your bird, think again. Many hawks are lost from their perches through leashes, jesses or even swivels breaking unexpectedly. If this happens and there are no bells on your bird, your chances of recovering her are going to be very much reduced.

You can practise putting on leg bells and jesses before your bird arrives, and it is a good idea to do so. All you need is someone who will hold a pencil steady for you, while you perform the operation. Like jesses, bewits should be kept supple with jess grease.

Tail bells

Tail bells are generally used only on short-winged hawks, though there is no reason why they should not be used on falcons. Even on short-wings few people bother to use them. I think this is because they do not know how to put them on properly. Once you have used them you will never fly a short-wing again without one. This is because all short-winged hawks and buzzards have a curious habit of shaking their tails within a short time of flying or jumping onto a perch or a branch. If your hawk is carrying a tail bell, every time she moves you will have notice of the fact. A hawk on a kill also can be tracked down, since it balances with its tail every time it pulls at the meat and the tail bell rings. Leg bells give out very little sound when the hawk is on the ground.

Tail bells should not be very large. Figure 41a shows a nylon plectrum – these are used for plucking guitars, and can be bought at most music shops. A leather punch will make the two holes in it quite easily. Cut a small strip of leather and thread it through the bewit strap on the bell and then through these two holes (see figures 41b, c and d). Figure 41c shows perhaps a better way of attaching the bell, since it gives you an extra safety margin if, by any chance, one side of the strap gives way at any time. Figure 41d shows the strap threaded through the holes in the plectrum; the shaded area in the illustration indicates the portion of the *back* of the strap on which you should now spread a thin layer of contact adhesive.

Most birds of prey have 12 tail feathers. The two in the centre are called deck feathers (probably because they lie on top like the deck of a ship). Numbering from the outside, these feathers will be number six from the left and right. Lift these two feathers up and gently slide a piece of paper under them. Part the upper tail coverts and try to persuade them, too, under the paper. Now fold the paper round under the rest of the tail and clip it into position with two bulldog clips, to prevent it from slipping down (fig. 41e). You may find that the down at the top of the feather shafts gets in your way; damp this and smooth it up on either side of the shafts. Now, on the shafts just where the webbing starts put some more adhesive. Pick up the bell, plectrum and leather strip, and push the glued area on the back of the strip into contact with the glued area on the shafts, one strip to each shaft. This not only holds it in place while you are binding it on, but will also help to keep it there should your binding by any chance come off.

You now need a curved needle, of the type used by surgeons or upholsterers. The size is immaterial, so long as the thread will go through the eye. (To avoid pricking your fingers you can first blunt the point with a file.) Use a single strand of waxed linen thread; do not make a knot in the end. If you look at figure 41f you will see that although it is possible to perform this operation using a straight needle, a curved one makes things much easier. Bind the leather onto the shafts, with two bindings on each feather, by passing the thread twice round the shaft and then tying it off with a reef knot.

Now undo the clips and slide the paper out. Make sure you have not caught

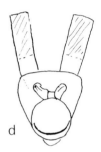

41 ATTACHING A TAIL BELL

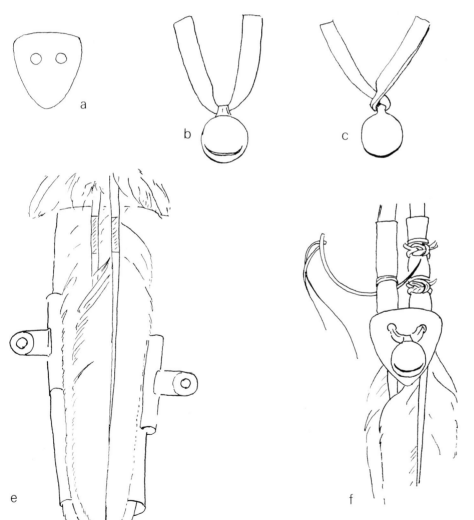

any little feathers while binding, by running the needle under each feather. Smooth the displaced feathers back into position. The bell should stay on and require no further attention until the bird moults. It will then come off when the deck feathers drop, or you can if you like cut it off at the start of the moult.

The purpose of the plectrum is to stop the bell dropping through the tail feathers and getting muffled by the undertail coverts. Tail bells attached in this way often last two or three seasons – much longer than the average leg bell– as they get very little wear. Given the choice I prefer tail bells to leg bells, but the more bells your bird can carry, the less likely you are to lose her.

The Japanese falconers sometimes bind the 'eye' of a peacock's tail feather onto their birds' tails, stripping the shaft of the peacock feather a short way below the eye so that it can be attached in the same way. The idea is that the sun, glinting on the irridescent peacock feather, helps them to see their birds in cover. I have never tried it myself, but you could if you wished do this by binding a peacock's feather in when you put on the tail bell.

Transmitters

As an addition, rather than an alternative to bells, one can now buy tiny, lightweight radio transmitters, which can be attached to the bird's tail and which give out a signal which is then picked up by a receiver. By using a direction-finding aerial, the whereabouts of your bird can then be placed. The complete equipment, at present available only in America, is very expensive, and is by no means foolproof. Although you may be able to pinpoint the direction in which your bird has gone, there is no way in which you can judge how far away it is. In mountainous areas the signal may get blocked by the hills, and in built-up areas you will probably run into radio interference. Nevertheless, as birds grow ever harder to obtain, and, consequently, more valuable, doubtless transmitters will be used more and more. (For information on where to obtain transmitters of this kind, see Appendix 1.)

Putting the swivel onto the jesses

Put the end of the first jess Y through the top ring of the swivel, and pull it through so that the whole of the swivel slit C is showing and you have enough of the jess to work with (see figure 42a). Open the slit C and push it over the bottom ring of the swivel (fig. 42b). Keep pushing it up to the top of the upper ring (fig. 42c), where it is pulled tight as in figure 42d. Now push the end of the second jess X through the upper ring, in the same direction as that in which the end of the first jess Y is now lying. Repeat the process as far as figure 42b. If at this point you thread the leash through the bottom ring of the swivel and hold it taut, you will find it easier to continue pushing the second jess into its final position, since the swivel will be kept steady.

A small point is worth mentioning here. I like whenever possible to bend leather in the same direction that it would bend on the animal, since it tends naturally to bend more easily like this and, I believe, will wear the better for it.

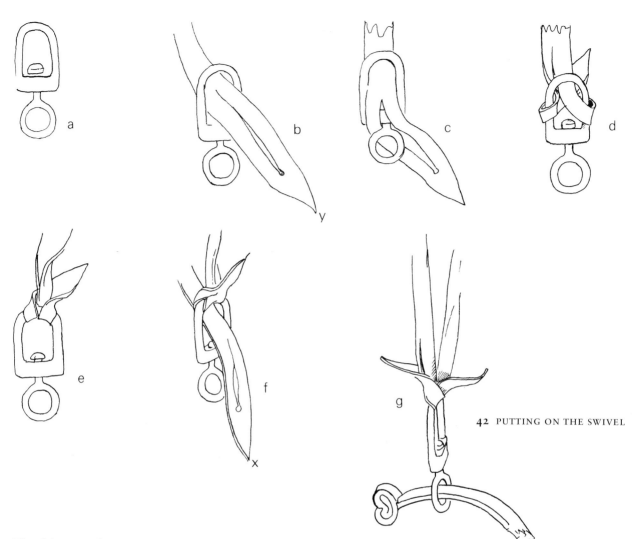

a

b

c

d

e

f

g

42 PUTTING ON THE SWIVEL

The falconer's knot

The falconer's knot has long been the traditional way of tying a hawk on an outside perch. I do not propose to go into the subject of cadge or screen perch knots, since for reasons already mentioned I am not in favour of them. In any case the falconer's knot is preferable when tying a bird on a cadge and, as I have already said, I cannot advise screen perches for anyone.

This is a knot which is tied with one hand while your bird is still on the other. Once it is learnt it can be tied and untied very quickly, if necessary in the dark. It is in fact a bow, one of whose loops goes through the perch ring, with the free end passed through the other loop – but it is not tied in the same way as a bow. With a little practice most people can become proficient in tying it in a few days.

See figure 43 and follow the different stages. They are illustrated as for a right-handed falconer; if you are left-handed you will have to reverse each procedure. This is not easy, but you will find it a help if you place a mirror opposite the illustration.

1 This is not part of the knot, but simply a safety measure, and an exceedingly wise one to get into the habit of employing. If you disregard it you may well end up with the too often heard cry of 'Oh – I've let it go!' (in which case turn hastily to the chapter on lost hawks). Normally when you are holding a hawk, the jesses will pass between the thumb and forefinger of your gloved hand, and lie across the breadth of your palm, with the swivel somewhere in the region of the base of your little finger and the leash looped round your fingers as in figure 38. However, when you are going to tie up or untie a bird, you should bring the swivel through to the back of your hand, with the jesses between the second and third fingers. Should your bird bate for any reason, the swivel will then be pulled tight against the back of your fingers, and act as a stop. If you do not employ this safety measure, it is quite possible that when the bird bates; the jesses and swivel will slip between your finger and thumb, and your hawk will fly off and be lost with the swivel still attached to the jesses. She will then very likely be caught up in a tree or a bush, and she may well die before you have a chance to find her again. So please, never neglect this simple procedure.

2 With, for the moment, an imaginary hawk on your glove and the leash full length, put the free end of the leash through the ring on the perch. Pull about two-thirds of the leash through and away to your left. Now pick up the part of the leash that has passed through the ring (this is called the 'working part'). It should lie over the ball of your forefinger, and the pressure of the second finger against the forefinger will hold it in position. Your thumb will be over the portion of the leash that has not passed through the ring (this is called the 'standing part'). Now move your gloved hand away from the perch until the leash is just taut. (When you are holding a bird, try to keep the perch out of her sight if you can – then she will not try to jump onto it until you are ready.)

3 Pass your thumb under the portion of leash between your forefinger and the ring. Try to do this within about I in. of the ring, so as not to use up more leash than is necessary. Otherwise you will not have enough spare leash on the working part to complete the knot.

4 In order to achieve the third stage, you will have curled your fingers up. Straighten them out now, but at the same time keep your thumb well up, so that the loop that is round it will not slip off.

5 This simply consists of turning your hand away from you, as if your thumb were the axis upon which it rotates. Keep the loop on your thumb. Instead of your palm, the back of your hand should now be uppermost.

6 Your thumb and your fingers now move in towards each other, like a crab's pincers closing.

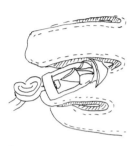

43 THE FALCONER'S KNOT

Stage 1

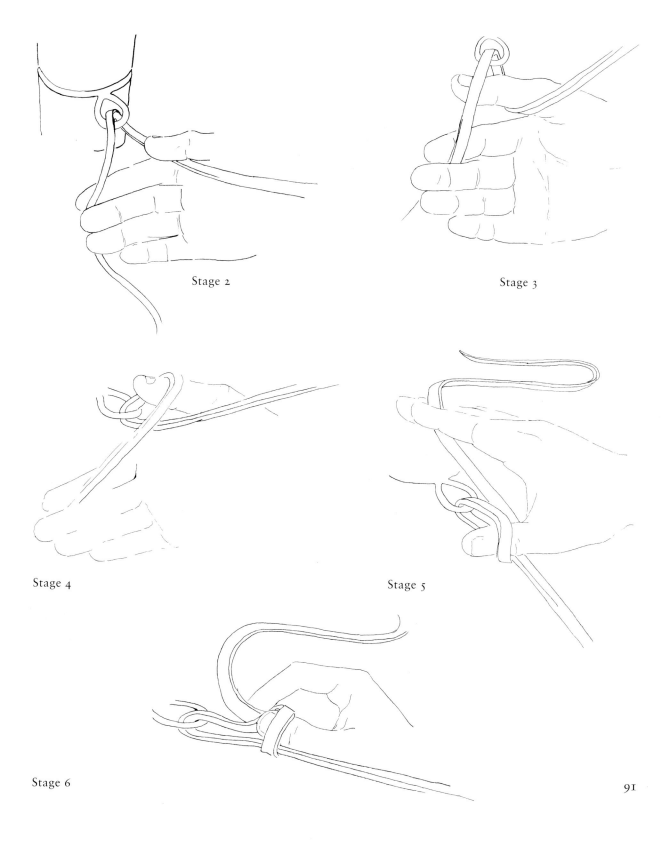

Stage 2

Stage 3

Stage 4

Stage 5

Stage 6

7 The part of the leash that is resting on the ball of your forefinger is now pushed through the loop on your thumb, and at the same time your thumb is pushed out of the way.

8 The working part is now pulled a short distance through the thumb loop, so that it itself forms a loop. If you now pull tight on the right-hand side of this second loop the thumb loop will tighten. (If you now look at stage 8 in the illustration, you will see why I described this knot as a bow – if the ring were not in the way, and you pulled both ends of the leash, the knot would now come undone in just the same way as a bow does when you pull both ends.)

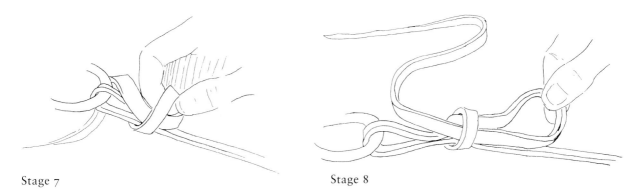

Stage 7   Stage 8

9 Having tightened the knot, you now put the free end of the leash through the newly-formed loop, and to complete the knot you tie a second one, exactly the same as the first, a little higher up the leash. (Some falconers do not put the free end of the leash through the second loop on this knot.)

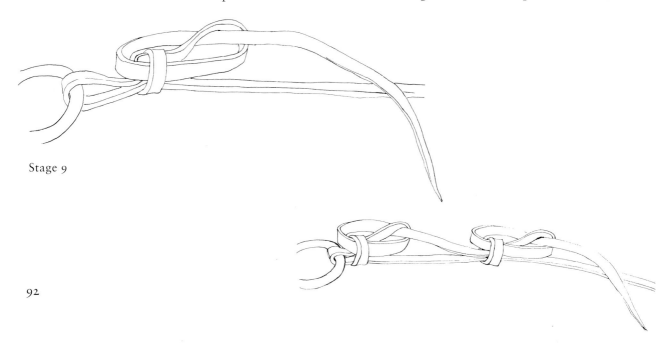

Stage 9

Once this process is completed you can allow the hawk to sit on the perch. The temptation to put her on the perch first and to use both hands to tie the knot must be avoided at all costs – it means you have no safety measure in operation, and if the bird bates off you may very easily lose her.

To untie the bird is a simple matter. Once she is on your fist and the swivel is in the safety position, you pull the free end of the leash clear of the second loop, pull hard on it and the second knot will corne undone. Repeat this once more, and the first knot will corne undone. You can now pull the leash out of the ring.

To begin with, when you are practising, you may have a few tying problems. If you run out of leash before completing the knot, this is because you either did not pull enough leash through the ring in the first place, or you started tying too far away from the ring. If the second knot you tie becomes a granny knot, you have again not allowed enough leash to work with and you have pulled the end right through the loop on your thumb. If when you undo the knot you find the whole thing is in a tangle, this will be because you did not tighten your knots enough in the first place.

Do not be put off by all these instructions and diagrams – the knot is not very difficult to master, and it is very useful once you have learnt how to tie it. It has many other uses – you can use it to tie up boats and cows, if you wish, as well as hawks. One great temptation is to use no knots at all, but to have a spring clip, as on a dog lead, at either end of the leash. Sooner or later this apparently easy method of fastening will come undone. It is not safe.

All the equipment mentioned in these two chapters may seem rather over-whelming at first sight, but if it is looked after well much of it will last for years and some of it for a lifetime. Depending on how good you are with your hands, you can save a certain amount of expense by making a fair proportion of it yourself. Do acquire the essentials, and practise what you can, before the hawk arrives.

7 Hoods and Hooding

I often receive enquiries from beginners who want a hood in a hurry and who appear to think that without one they will not be able to start training their bird. In fact, hooding will never help much towards manning a hawk, since manning is the process of getting the bird used to man, and therefore to all the strange things around him – dogs, cars, mowing machines and so forth. A new hawk will be alarmed by quite small things that we ourselves would not even notice – a rustling newspaper, a flapping curtain or a person sneezing – and certainly if it is hooded, and unable to see such things, it will not be upset by them. But unless it gradually becomes accustomed to strange sights and sounds, it will never get over its fear of them.

A friend of mine once bought himself a goshawk from a dealer in Lahore, who told him that on no account should he unhood the bird for three weeks. (Since it was hooded when he bought it, it could have been blind for all he knew.) Each day he fed the hawk through the hood and carried it around on his fist for several hours. Finally the great day came when the hood was removed. The bird was as wild as the day it was caught.

This is not to say that a hood does not have many uses. It is designed to blindfold the bird or, to use the original meaning of the word, to hoodwink, or fool, it into thinking that day is night. In complete darkness most animals will not move around, but will sit still. Since your hooded hawk is, to all intents and purposes, in the dark, and cannot see anything which would alarm her, she will not get upset and crash about breaking feathers and hurting herself; nor will she get jealous if another hawk is being flown. Even noises are to a certain extent muffled by the hood, although loud ones will still make the bird jump. The French word for a hood is *chaperon*, and in fact the hood does have rather the same effect as a chaperone. It gives the falconer some degree of control over his bird, and allows him to choose whom and what she may meet.

It is quite possible to train any raptor without hooding it at any time whatsoever. Indeed, the smaller falcons such as kestrels and merlins, which become tame very quickly, do not need a hood at all, and often the act of hooding upsets them far more than if they were carried around unhooded. Short-winged hawks will travel perfectly well without a hood, and although it can be useful if they are 'made to the hood' you may well come across some that will always dislike it. Buzzards become exceedingly tame and hooding them is almost a waste of time. The smaller hawk-eagles soon get used to car journeys, and my Changeable hawk-eagle often travels unhooded for several hundred miles without any fuss at all. Even peregrines can become so well manned that there is no need to hood them except when other falcons are being flown in their sight. But all large falcons should as a matter of course be 'made to the hood', and certainly this is also necessary with the larger eagles, since when travelling one cannot have such birds bating around a car.

On no account should hoods be used just for effect to impress people. Carrying a hooded kestrel about is more than likely to show other falconers that you do not know what you are about.

Types of hood

There are several different varieties of hood – Rufter hoods, Indian, Dutch and Arab hoods, and crosses between them.

Rufter hoods

These are rarely, if ever, used nowadays. They are really hawk trappers' hoods, and are not for falconry use at all. They are adjustable, and will fit only approximately a newly caught bird. Their purpose is simply to keep it quiet until a hood of a better fit can be put on.

Indian hoods

These are not much used in Britain now. They do not open and close at all, but fit on the hawk's head friction tight. Some birds soon learn how to remove them. In India, each bird has its own falconer, and as he is with it constantly he only has to pick up the hood and replace it each time the bird succeeds in removing it.

Arab hoods (sometimes called Bahreini hoods)

These are quite nice hoods as regards pattern, but generally they are made of very poor leather and so tend to lose their shape quickly. In my opinion the braces are invariably far too long, and they hang down over the bird's shoulders and irritate it. I would not advise the use of Arab hoods.

Dutch hoods

These are what are called block-built, or blocked hoods. That is to say that they are sewn lip inside out, soaked in water, turned the right way round and then dried on a wooden block to give them the correct shape, rather like felt hats. This makes them far more comfortable, since they conform to the shape of the bird's head. The old argument that this type of hood is too heavy can only be applied when they are used for small hawks – kestrels, merlins and so on – birds which in any case do not require hooding.

Some falconers dislike Dutch hoods because the beak opening is a different

44 DIFFERENT TYPES OF HOOD

Fakconry Centre pattern hoods

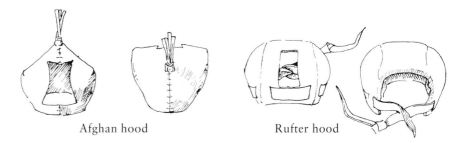

Afghan hood   Rufter hood

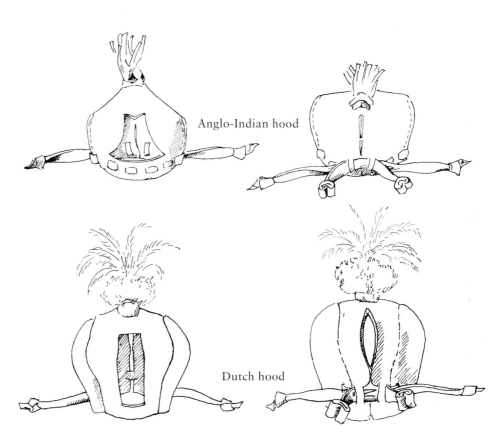

Anglo-Indian hood

Dutch hood

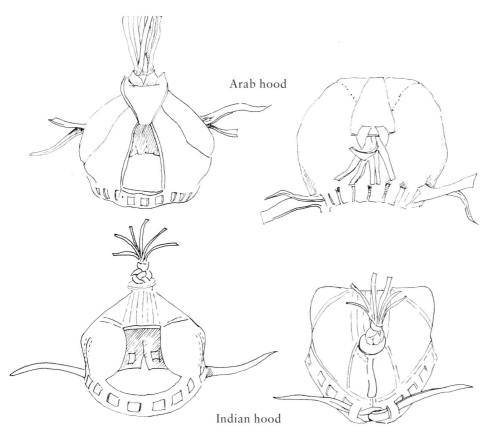

Arab hood

Indian hood

shape from those of the Indian and Anglo-Indian types. They argue that this makes it difficult for the bird either to feed or to cast through the hood. Personally I should like to blindfold any falconer who feeds his bird through the hood and then invite him to eat a plateful of spaghetti. He would soon find out how miserable it is. Quite apart from this, the hood soon gets filthy if the bird is fed through it. As far as casting through the hood is concerned, I can see no reason why any bird should need to be hooded at a time when it might be expected to cast. If the falconer manages his birds properly this problem should not arise at all. Hooded falcons fed on the fist will tear at the glove when keen – an expensive and irritating habit.

Dutch hoods are not particularly easy to make, but are worth the time and trouble involved.

Anglo-Indian hoods

These are basically Indian hoods, but the back is only sewn up for about three or four stitches at the top, and Dutch-type hood braces are added so that the hood can be opened and closed. Personally I do not use this type of hood, as I find it clumsy and ugly to look at. But it has the advantage of being relatively simple to make, and so is useful to the beginner who has not yet mastered the art of Dutch hood-making. Also it does not involve the use of a hood block, which is a difficult thing to obtain.

Falconry Centre hoods

After the Second World War the well-known family of Mollen, of Valkenswaard in Holland, ceased to make hoods. Dutch hoods became extremely difficult to obtain, and so I decided to try my own hand at making this type of hood, and managed to get some hood blocks for the purpose. Eventually I evolved a pattern of my own, now called the Falconry Centre type. This is a cross between the Dutch and Syrian types of hood, with some modifications. The main advantage is that I have eliminated the two weak seams on either side of the beak opening, which at the same time enables one to make the opening the same shape as that on an Indian hood, should one so wish it. It has also done away with the need for sewing a piece of soft leather round the base of the hood, which in a Dutch hood is necessary to prevent the material of the eye-pieces from fraying.

Patterns and instructions for making the Anglo-Indian and Falconry Centre types of hood are given in chapter 20 on hood-making.

Falconers in America have experimented with glued hoods, which require no stitching at all. So far I have not come across one where the glue held for any length of time when the hood was subjected to normal wear and tear. There have also been various other innovations, including spring-loaded hoods for easier opening, which to me seem extremely dangerous because of the wires inside the hood itself.

45–50 (opposite and following pages) Hooding a bird that is 'good to the hood'.

Hooding

The sooner you start hooding your hawk, the easier it will be, since a freshly caught bird will have most of her attention fixed on you rather than on the hood. If you wait until she is tame and well-manned, then she will dodge and duck and be extremely difficult to hood.

I dislike the phrase which is sometimes heard, 'to break a bird to the hood'. Like 'horse-breaking' and 'dog-breaking' it smacks too much of force. 'Making', rather than 'breaking', seems a more apt description of how the process should be carried out. The art of hooding can be summed up in one word deftness. There should be no need forcibly to cram the hood onto the bird's head, but neither should you be hesitant about it.

Success in hooding depends very much upon getting both yourself and the bird into the right position before you start. Bring the bird, from the normal carrying position, so that she is facing you at about eye-level. Hold the open hood by the plume, between the thumb and forefinger of your free hand. The hawk must be looking straight at you, and must be calm. If she shows any signs of bating, wait until she has settled again. Now very gently start to stroke the top of the bird's breast with the hood, which will be upside-down. Gradually work the hood a little higher, and finally, with one deft but unhurried movement, tip it over the hawk's head, so that her beak goes cleanly through the beak opening and the hood settles comfortably over her head.

45

46

47

48

49–50 Final stages of hooding.

51–54 (opposite page) In the case of a bird that is inclined to flick the hood off, the left-hand closing brace can immediately be tightened (the process is here seen from above).

A bird that is used to the hood will usually stay quite still and give you plenty of time to do up the braces. However, some birds give a quick shake of the head and send the hood flying off. In this case, the moment the hood is on the bird's head, grip the left-hand closing brace, which will be on your right, between the thumb and *second* finger (not the forefinger) of your free hand. Now press the tip of your forefinger against the side of the hood, immediately *below* the closing brace. If you now pull with your thumb and second finger, at the same time keeping your forefinger straight, you will tighten the brace without moving the hood at all. Then you can tighten the second brace with your teeth, still holding the brace which has already been closed so as to keep the hood steady. To do this easily and without fuss you will find it best to lower the hawk a little to your left, and at the same time to turn your head so that your left ear is almost touching your left shoulder. You are now in the best position to take the second brace in your teeth and tighten it.

Unhooding is not quite so easy as it sounds. Very often, as soon as the braces are undone, the hood comes off. This should not happen. Unhooding should be two separate movements – undoing the braces, and then removing the hood. This is because there will be times (as, for instance, when one is out rook hawking) when one wants to prevent one's falcon from seeing the quarry, and yet be able to unhood her and cast her off the moment it gets up. So one 'strikes' the braces and then one continues to stalk closer to the quarry with the falcon

51

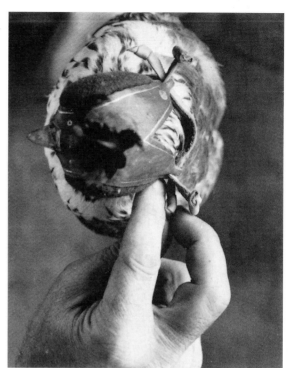

52

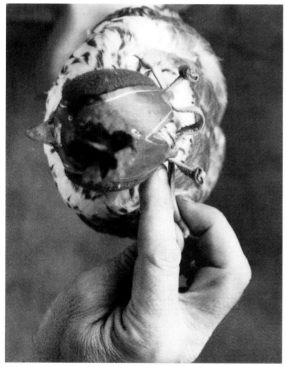

53

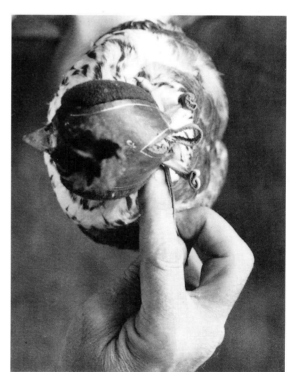

54

still hooded – if she were not, she might try to go too soon and therefore not get so close a 'slip' at the quarry.

It is just as important to get yourself and the bird into the correct position for unhooding as it is for hooding. Incline your head to the left and bring the bird round towards your mouth so that you can reach the right-hand brace with your teeth. At the same time, grip the left-hand brace with your right hand and pull both braces at once. The second you have the hood open, stop pulling. The hood is now undone, but still on the bird's head. Now, when you are ready, you can raise the bird to give her a bit of extra height, face her into the wind for a nice easy take-off and then, holding the plume only, gently remove the hood.

Good hoods deserve good treatment. Do not cram them into your pocket or your hawking bag, where they will quickly lose their shape and become messy. I use a roughly carved block of the right size, with a strip of leather screwed to its base, which slides onto the belt of my hawking bag. When the hawk is unhooded, as she leaves your fist, your hand should automatically put the hood onto the hood block, and both hands will then be free to tighten the braces to ensure that it stays there.

Once a bird has been made to the hood it will need hooding every so often to keep it 'good to the hood'. This does not mean it has to spend hours hooded each day. Some falconers leave their birds hooded all night, but I can see no particularly good reason for this. For the first few days after their arrival, large falcons will need to be hooded quite a lot of the time, as until they are fairly well-manned they will tend to bate a great deal and break their feathers.

It may seem an obvious thing to say, but a hood must comfortably fit the individual bird for which it is intended. You cannot just go out and buy 'a hood for a peregrine' – peregrines, just like people, vary in size. So you must fit the hood to the hawk, and not vice versa. See the chapter on hood-making.

Not many falconers are prepared to let you practise hooding on their hawks. It is only too easy to upset a bird, and once it dislikes the hood it will probably go on doing so, when it is said to be 'hood-shy'. It will bate and scream at the sight of a hood, and cannot then be hooded except by force, which is very undesirable as it will only upset the bird more. So do not feel hurt if a falconer refuses to let you try hooding his hawk. If you can get hold of a stuffed bird then you could practise the mechanics of hooding on that. Otherwise it will simply be a matter of having patience and perseverance when the time comes.

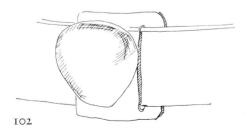

55 Belt hood block.

8 Handing the New Arrival

Before acquiring a bird you must find out what your country's laws are in relation to the taking or importing of birds of prey. In some countries you may even need a licence simply to keep such birds. The laws vary in different parts of the world, and it is most important that you abide by them.

Your hawk when it comes to you will be either an eyass (a young bird taken from the eyrie before it can fly), a passager (a bird that has left the nest but is still in its immature plumage), or a haggard (a bird in adult plumage, which will therefore have moulted at least once before it was caught). These names indicate the stage at which the bird was caught, and they do not change as the bird gets older. An eyass will remain an eyass for the rest of its life, although once it has moulted in captivity it will be known as an 'intermewed' eyass. The same applies to passage and haggard birds which have moulted in captivity.

In Britain, where the taking of passage and haggard birds from the wild is illegal, the bird is likely to be an eyass (unless it has been imported from abroad, or, possibly, comes from another falconer who no longer wishes to keep it). If this is so, then it must be put into the mews (not into a box-type night quarter as this will not give it enough room to exercise), to rest and become accustomed to its new surroundings, and to allow its feathers to develop fully and its quills to harden. If it is an imported bird, it will have had to remain in quarantine for 35 days, and this enforced period of rest will have helped it to get over the strain of its journey. But in my opinion any new bird that comes to you will be none the worse for a further rest period of from seven to ten days. This will give it a chance to get used to its new surroundings, and during this time you can collect samples of its mutes and send them to your nearest poultry laboratory for analysis. If the analysis shows that the bird has any internal parasites or pathological bacteria, these can then be treated. Although in the case of imported birds tests may already have been carried out, it is wise to double check on your own account.

Eyasses should not normally be taken until they are well-feathered and on the point of flying, but you may possibly get one which is much younger than this. Very small eyasses may even have to be hand-fed, and are of course far too young to have anything in the way of jesses or bells put on them. But, given that the bird is old enough to have such equipment put on it, in my opinion the sooner this is done, the better. Many falconers wait until training begins before putting jesses and bells on their birds. As the first stage of training is taming the bird, it has always seemed strange to me that one should start this by forcibly grabbing the bird in order to put on its equipment. I prefer to put it on at least some days beforehand so that the hawk has time to get over the upset and begins to get used to wearing equipment. The easiest time to do this is when the bird first arrives, provided that it is old enough.

Presumably the hawk will arrive in a box or hamper, and you must take certain important precautions before you open this. (It is to be hoped that you will not be so foolish as to open it out of doors, and so risk the bird immediately flying away.) Take the box into a room, close the windows and *draw the curtains.* A hawk does not understand glass, and if the window is uncovered it will fly straight at it. If it is a large bird it may go straight through the glass, leaving you with nothing but a broken window; it may equally well hit the glass with such force that it breaks its neck or is severely concussed; if you are very lucky it may only stun itself temporarily and recover in due course. But it is not worth risking any of these things happening.

Do not choose a room which is very large or very high – you may find yourself chasing the hawk round and round for a very long time, or she may perch somewhere out of reach. Do not go into a room where there are fragile ornaments which can be knocked down as the bird flies about. Your mews, if you have one, will be the ideal place for the operation.

CASTING A BIRD
56 About to take hold of the bird from the front . . .

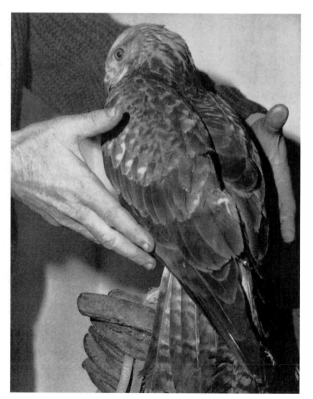
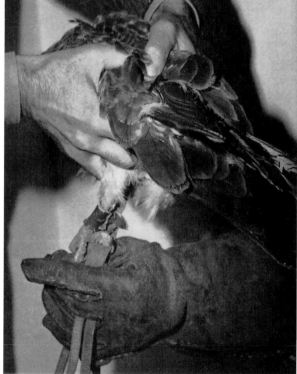

When you are in a suitable room, with the person who is going to help you (for you will need help when you put jesses and bells on the bird), lock the door, so that no one else can come in and let the bird fly out by mistake. Although not all birds will dash out of the box when it is opened and fly around, a great many do, and by taking these elementary precautions you can avoid accidents.

The bird can be discouraged from flying about if you open its box in a completely darkened room. After unfastening the box, but before actually opening it, switch off the light. When you remove the lid the hawk will sit quite quietly in the dark. Flash a torch so that you can see where and in what position she is. Then your helper can take hold of her by gently feeling his way in the dark. He should hold the bird with his thumbs over her back, while his palms keep her wings into her sides. He can either hold her legs back under her tail, or, if he prefers, between the second and third fingers of each hand, with his forefingers encircling her breast.

Before turning out the light you will have placed a rolled-up coat or a cushion in a convenient place – this is for the hawk to grip while her jesses are being put on. A frightened bird will clench its feet tightly, and if there is nothing for them to grip it may injure the undersides of them with its own talons. You now switch on the light, and your helper quickly puts the bird in such a position that its feet grip the cushion.

Falcons can and probably will peck; hawks are less inclined to do so. To

57, 58 . . . and lifting her from the glove.

59 The bird is placed so that her feet can grip the cushion.

60 Holding the bird from behind.

prevent this, put a scarf or handkerchief, or the open gauntlet of your hawking glove (or a hood, if you have one) over the bird's head. Now you can put the jesses on, as explained in chapter 6, and also the leg bell. If the bird is a short-winged hawk, and her feathers are 'hard down', now is the time to attach the tail bell as well. Obviously this cannot be done on a newly-caught eyass, as its feathers will still be 'in the blood', the quills will not have hardened, and the tail feathers will almost certainly be damaged in the course of the operation. Eyasses should be fitted with short jesses without swivel slits, rather than the normal type, to avoid any risk of their catching up. When training begins, these will be replaced by the ordinary type of jess or Aylmeri can be fitted.

While the bird is still being held down on the cushion, examine her flight feathers to see if they have become soiled with mutes during her journey. If so, they should be gently sponged with warm water and soap to clean them. If they are badly soiled they may even require the gentlest possible scrubbing with a nail-brush. Remember always to brush or rub down the webbing, not upwards. In the case of an eyass, once again the feathers must be handled with extreme care, as otherwise they will be very easily damaged.

Now spray the hawk with Johnson's Anti-mite*, to destroy any external parasites which she may be harbouring. Spray under the wings and tail as well as over the rest of the bird. Take care not to get it in her eyes.

* Not all other sprays are safe for raptors.

Now place the hawk on your gloved fist, holding the jesses in the safety position described in chapter 6 (brought through from your palm to the back of your hand, between the second and third fingers). She will almost certainly bate, and each time she does so you will have to help her back onto the glove. There are two ways of doing this – either you can put your free hand under her chest, fingers under her left wing and thumb under her right wing, and then lift her up and place her feet on the glove; or you can put your hand behind her, in the centre of her back, fingers under her right wing and thumb under her left wing, and lift her that way. If you use the second method she will be less likely to bite you, but neither way is completely bite-proof. A few bites are inevitably going to come your way in any case, and at this stage you must be brave and put up with it. The hawk is only biting you to try to stop you handling her, and if you do not attempt to take your hand away when this happens she will soon realize that she is not succeeding, and will cease to do it.

You may find that the bird refuses to grip the glove, or even to stand up at all – sparrowhawks in particular are liable to do this, until you wonder if their legs have become paralyzed – but try balancing her on the glove, removing your bare hand, and then rolling your gloved hand back and forth from the wrist. Finding herself unbalanced, she will very probably stand up properly and grip the glove.

Make sure that when the bird bates she cannot knock herself against the walls or perches (or, if you are in a room in your house, the furniture) as this will result in damaged or broken feathers.

She must now be weighed. This will be easier if the weighing-machine is placed so that the perch is to your left. If you have any idea of how much she is likely to weigh, it is a good idea to put the weights on the scales first, so that you will have to make as few unnecessary movements as possible while the hawk is on the perch. Try to get her sitting fairly calmly on the fist– then gently lower her onto the perch of the scales, so that she is facing the weights. Her tail should hang down over the back of the perch. She may step backwards onto the perch, but if she does not, continue to lower her until the perch is gently pressing against the backs of her legs. Feeling this, she will step up and back. Open your gloved hand and let the jesses go with the hawk. She is now loose. When you have weighed her and made a mental note of the weight, take the weights off the scales before picking her up again. This means that when you take her off the perch the scales will not suddenly tip with a crash in the opposite direction and frighten her. When you pick her up, you can either take hold of the jesses with your gloved hand, so that she must step forwards and up onto your fist, or you can take hold of them with your other hand, at the same time placing your gloved hand behind the bird, under her tail, and raising it gently until she must step backwards onto it.

Some birds can be very difficult to weigh on arrival, and in such cases it may have to be done in the dark – this is not so difficult as it sounds, since it is quite easy to tell by feel which weights you have on the scales, and whether the

LIFTING A BATING BIRD
ON TO THE FIST
61, 62, 63 From the
back . . .

61

62

63

64, 65, 66 . . . or from the front.

64

65

66

balance is level or not. When picking up the bird in the dark, you will have to get her to step backwards onto the glove, rather than forwards.

The bird should now be turned loose in the mews, wearing only her jesses (or Aylmeri) and bells, and left there for some days. If you are going to have a laboratory test done, put sheets of polythene on the floor under the perches, so that you can collect her mutes. During the time that she is in the mews, she should be given as much as she wants to eat, and there should be a bath of fresh water there for her. Both food and bath water should be changed daily, as unobtrusively as possible.

Food

Some people feel that a wild bird taken into captivity should whenever possible be fed on 'natural' food – i.e. the sort of food that it would be catching for itself in the wild. Apart from the obvious inconvenience and difficulty of keeping your bird supplied constantly with fresh, natural food, there seems to me to be another and much greater disadvantage in this type of feeding. In these days of toxic chemicals, in the form of dressings for seeds, and agricultural sprays, many of the animals and birds that a hawk would normally feed on are themselves contaminated by poisons in their own diet. Many hawks and other predators are killed in this way in the wild state, and it may very well be that in feeding 'natural' food to your hawk you will be endangering its life. So if you are going to feed natural food to your bird, take what precautions you can to avoid these poisons. Remove the crop, liver, guts and head from anything you are going to give her. This is not fool-proof, but it can help. Birds' crops in particular may contain dressed seed which could be fatal to your bird if she ate it. Of course, by doing this you will stop the food from being entirely natural, since the hawk would normally have eaten some of these organs.

Personally I feed my birds as little as possible on natural food. Instead I use beef, horse and a small amount of liver or heart – never pork or mutton. In addition I add a dietary supplement (called S.A.37) which provides the necessary vitamins, minerals and so on that are otherwise missing from this type of diet. For eyasses a certain amount of extra calcium must be added too, in the form of steamed bone flour. See chapter 23 on health and disease for further details of diet – here it is enough to say that very unpleasant things can happen to your bird as the result of an incorrect diet, and this should especially be remembered when dealing with eyasses, where a calcium deficiency can result in weak, deformed bones, which lead to broken legs and bowed wings.

There is also another form of food which is very free from toxins and is fairly easy to obtain in some places, namely, day-old cockerels from a hatchery. These are certainly good food for nearly all birds of prey of all ages, and provide not only some calcium in the bones, but also castings. However, I would still add a supplement when feeding them to hawks.

It is useful to have a deep-freeze to keep a stock of food for your hawk, and so save the trouble of having to buy fresh food every few days. But if you feed frozen meat to your bird, be sure that it has been properly thawed out in advance.

Castings

Although wild birds of prey will pluck a good deal of the fur or feathers from their quarry before eating it, they also swallow some of it, and bones as well. (Owls, for instance, will swallow mice whole.) The following day they will throw up the undigested material in the form of a pellet, known as a casting. (Fur, feathers and bones are called 'castings'.) Castings are presumed to do a hawk good. I have never noticed any ill effects in a bird that has not been given castings for some time; but certainly they do no harm, and the closer one can get to the bird's natural way of life then presumably so much the better. Pulling at bones and feathers also helps to keep the bird's beak in trim and prevents it from overgrowing.

The size of the pellet that your bird brings up will depend on the amount of casting swallowed. If a golden eagle and a kestrel both eat a mouse, their pellets will be approximately the same size, but as eagles usually require more than one mouse to keep them going, their pellets tend to be larger than those of kestrels.

Your new bird, be it eyass, passager or haggard, should certainly have some form of castings while it is in the mews. Natural food will automatically supply these. If you are feeding butcher's meat then you will have to provide the castings yourself, but this can be done quite easily by getting some fur or feathers and rubbing them over the meat. A certain amount will stick to it, and the bird will eat some. You could possibly get feathers from a poulterer, but beware of contamination by any disinfectant he may use. You could of course shoot a rabbit or a bird, and keep a supply of castings to hand in that way. Do not be afraid of giving too many castings to your hawk – for instance, a female goshawk will swallow all four pads and both ears of a rabbit.

Both eyasses and older birds must be weighed every day during the time that they are in the mews. This should be done more or less at the same time each day. Try to make it a time when the bird has 'put over' (that is, emptied) its crop and digested its food – this will make for more accurate measurements of weight loss or gain. Make a daily note of the bird's weight.

At this point the treatment of eyasses diverges from that of older birds. In the case of passagers and haggards, once the bird has settled down and the results of the laboratory tests have come through and prove to be satisfactory, you can begin to man your hawk and start its basic training. But an eyass must be left in the mews until its feathers are hard down – that is, until there is no longer any blood in the quills and the quills themselves have hardened off. (This is sometimes also called 'full-summed' or 'hard-penned'.) Just by looking at the bird you will be able to see when her feathers appear to be full length. But to make sure that they have not only stopped growing but have hard quills, you will have to examine the longest flight feathers at their roots. On a short-winged hawk these will be the two central feathers of her tail. On a falcon or a buzzard it will be the longest primary in either wing. As the quill hardens it changes colour, from blue (when it is still in the blood) to pink and then to off-white. Until the quills are off-white and hard the bird should not be handled unless it is absolutely necessary, because a very slight knock to a soft-quilled feather will mean that it will break off, and you will then have to wait some weeks while a new feather grows. If this does happen, the bird will bleed a little at the root of the feather, but this is rarely anything to worry about and it will heal by itself. The new feather will be of mature colour, and will be shorter than the first one, since, as I have mentioned elsewhere, mature flight feathers are shorter than immature ones. (In a peregrine this shortening of flight feathers continues for at least four years.)

Imprinting

There is another very good reason why you should not handle an eyass bird while it is in the mews (indeed it should see as little of you as possible during this time), and this is that you do not want it to develop into what is known as a 'screamer'. All young birds in the wild, when they see their parents coming to the nest with food, start to scream at them. When they grow up and leave the parent birds they naturally lose this habit, as there are no parents to scream at and they are hunting for themselves. If however your eyass sees you bringing food to it every day, you will be 'imprinted' on the bird's consciousness in place of its parent, and it will scream whenever it sees you coming, whether you are bringing food or not. This is most undesirable, particularly so in the case of falcons, who tend to have extremely penetrating voices and will some-times scream for hours on end without apparently getting the slightest bit hoarse. You will not only quickly find it very irritating yourself, but you will almost certainly receive complaints from your neighbours. A screaming eyass will become extremely tame, but this will hardly compensate for the annoyance.

There is no certain cure for screaming. The only times that I have known birds eventually to stop screaming were when they had a complete change of owner and locality. A friend of mine in Holland let me have a falcon, which he warned me was a screamer. I took the risk. From the day it arrived it never screamed once, and proved to be a good rook hawk. I myself had an eyass female goshawk which started screaming, but when I let her go to someone else she also stopped completely. This is however by no means an infallible cure. You could perhaps persuade another falconer to take on a screamer for a while, and if all goes well, to return it to you after three months or so. But he would have to fly the bird. Simply keeping it, without getting it into flying condition, might appear to do the trick, but once the bird was brought back to flying condition, it would tend to start screaming once more.

There are times when despite every precaution, a bird will suddenly start to scream long after handling has begun. There is no known reason for this. Again, the only cure that might work is the one I have already mentioned.

When bringing up two or more eyasses together it is possible to imprint them on each other as well as on human beings, and you are then less likely to have as much trouble with screaming as with the single eyass who has no contact with other birds. But even in this case it is not advisable to let the birds see who is bringing their food to them.

So be warned. Do not let your eyass see you bringing its food at any time, until it is old enough to be handled. Put the food into the mews through a flap in the door, and have a peephole here and there so that you can check from time to time that all is well, but *do not* go in and start fussing over the bird. You will only regret it later on. When you have to remove any old or stale food from the mews (this should be done every day, and the bath water should also be changed daily) do it at night, using a torch if necessary. It is the greatest temptation, especially to beginners, to go in and see their new birds, but it is a temptation that must be very firmly resisted.

However, there is one notable exception to this rule, and that is where eyass sparrowhawks are concerned. Here imprinting is actually desirable, in my opinion. Sparrowhawks are extremely temperamental, highly-strung birds, and are notoriously difficult to man (though not to train, as some books would have you believe). If you take an eyass sparrowhawk while it is still very young, and handle it constantly, it will become quite tame. This means that a lot of the temperamental difficulties you would otherwise come up against at the start of manning will never arise.

Manning is not the only trouble with sparrowhawks; they are delicate, and their very small size makes them hard to feed correctly. Many are killed by having their weight cut down too drastically during training. So it is a help to have ironed out at least one problem before you start. An eyass treated in this way will almost certainly be a screamer, but as sparrowhawks have tiny voices this is not a serious disadvantage, as it would be with other species. Later on, when you take your hawk out hunting, it may at times even be quite helpful to hear her kitten-like mew when she has disappeared from your sight in thick cover.

Do not, however, think that imprinting an eyass sparrowhawk will magically transform it into an easy bird for a beginner. I have said before, and repeat most emphatically, a sparrowhawk is the last bird that a beginner should attempt to man and train. You should not even consider one until you have had at least one successful season with a goshawk – and a gos is not a beginner's bird either.

Another bad habit that eyasses can get into is that of 'carrying' their food. A bird in the wild state will not normally eat at the spot where it has killed, but will carry its quarry off to some secluded spot where it can eat without danger of being disturbed. An eyass will naturally have this instinct, and will carry its food into a corner or onto a perch to eat it. If it is allowed to develop this habit it will continue to carry when out hunting or when flying to the lure, possibly with disastrous results. To nip this in the bud, you should tie or staple the food to a heavy plank of a suitable size to be pushed through the flap at the bottom of the door.

The length of time your new bird remains in the mews after her arrival will depend upon her age when she comes to you, her state of health and so on. But once the necessary rest period is over, you will be in a position to begin her training.

I regret to say that unscrupulous breeders often try to sell screaming imprints to unwitting falconers. So beware. You cannot be sure a bird is going to be a screamer until you have got it into condition for training. It may well not scream up to that point. So get some guarantee from the breeders that any imprinted screamer will be taken back and be replaced by either a decently behaved bird or your money returned.

9 Condition

Before you start actually training your bird, you must realise exactly what you are trying to do, why you are doing it, and how to set about it. It is therefore essential that you understand what is meant by 'condition'.

A bird whose owner can devote plenty of daylight hours, and, therefore, flying time, to her training will obviously be fitter than a hawk that can only be flown at irregular intervals. While it is possible to hunt at weekends with a goshawk that has been idle for most of the week, it would be unfair to expect her to perform to the same standard as a bird that has been flown every day. She will simply not be at the peak of her condition. Ideally, what you must aim for when training your hawk is to bring her, by careful manning, dieting and daily exercise, to the highest possible degree of fitness.

When a falconer uses the word 'condition' it is often to describe how fat or thin his bird is (a fat hawk is said to be in 'high' condition, while a thin one is said to be in 'low' condition). But falconers also talk about 'flying condition', and this term refers not only to the hawk's state of fatness but also to her state of fitness. The Turks have a word 'yarak', which describes the condition of a bird that is in perfect order to fly and hunt well. If you are to get the best from your bird she must be 'in yarak'; full of stamina, well-muscled, alert, neither too fat nor too thin – in fact, in splendid physical condition. Very few falconers today are in fact able to have their birds in the peak of condition, simply because they do not have the time to exercise them every day.

If you have not the time to exercise your bird every day do not, on any account, try to fly large falcons. Where daily exercise is desirable for other birds, for large falcons it is absolutely essential. Even if you can fulfil the other conditions required for flying them, it is useless to attempt it unless you have the necessary time.

When you pick up your bird to begin her training she will, as we have already seen, have spent a period of time in her mews (if she is an eyass) or in quarantine (if she is a passager or haggard). During this time she will have been relatively inactive and will have been eating all she wants. She will therefore be fat. (If she is not, then there is probably something wrong with her, and her training should not be started yet. Further veterinary checks should be carried out in such a case.) When you weigh her, her weight alone will not tell you whether she is 'high' or 'low', and you must judge this by feel.

In the past, before falconers realised the value of weighing-machines, this was how they judged their birds' condition and weight every day. I myself find that, even after many years of using a weighing-machine, I still like to feel my birds to check on whether they are fat or thin, and what the state of their muscles is. To carry out this check, feel your hawk's breast muscles on either side of the breastbone and under the wings. If her breast is plump and there is only a thin line of breastbone to be felt, then she is fat. If there is little flesh on her breast, and the breastbone sticks out sharply like the keel of a boat, she is too thin. A bird that has been inactive for some time will have rather flabby muscles, while one that has had plenty of regular exercise will have firm, resilient muscles. Feeling your bird is not a substitute for weighing her. The two methods must be used in conjunction with one another. Even a very experienced falconer will not be able to gauge by feel alone the small daily variations in his hawk's weight which show up so clearly on the scales.

Some falconers talk about the average weights of various species of birds of prey, but I find this tends to make for confusion, particularly where beginners are concerned. The beginner checks his bird's weight against the average weight, and is then alarmed because the two do not match up. What he does not realise is that birds, like human beings, come in different sizes, and that there can be considerable differences of size and weight between individuals of the same species and sex. Since a bird's actual weight is meaningless outside the context of its size and build, I strongly maintain that going by average weight charts is not only useless in many cases, but can also be dangerous.

The well-fed, under-exercised, fat hawk cannot possibly be fit, and before she can be expected to make any progress in actual training, she will have to lose some of her surplus weight. Once manning begins, you will only be offering her food while she is on your fist, and her fear of your presence, coupled with the fact that she is really not particularly hungry, will almost certainly inhibit her from feeding for some time. She will, however, be able to fast for quite a long period without doing herself harm, since she will be living off her internal fat reserves. (To begin with she may not even show a very marked decrease in weight.) There is no need to worry unduly about this fasting period, unless your scales indicate that the hawk is losing weight more rapidly than is good for her.

During her fast she will be getting more and more used to your presence, so that she will (except in very rare cases) have started to feed on the fist before any such danger point is reached. Wild birds do not feed at regular times, but only when they are hungry. If they have a large meal then they may not kill again for some days. This does them no harm, and although they are un-doubtedly fitter than your hawk, they do not have anything like her fat reserves to draw upon. The bigger the bird, the more it can eat at one sitting, and the longer the period may be between kills. So, the bigger your hawk, the longer she will most probably fast.

Having read the foregoing, do not on any account conceive the idea that you can train your bird simply by not feeding her, or by keeping her on very short commons indeed. This could kill her. Once your bird has used up her fat, she will start to lose weight more quickly. If a hawk loses weight too rapidly she is in danger of starvation. A rough guide to help you tell if your bird is nearing the danger point is that a bird weighing over 1 lb should not lose more than 1 oz in 24 hours; while a bird weighing under 1 lb should not lose more than ½ oz in the same period. I must emphasize that these figures are only approximate. Once your hawk starts to lose weight, she will need careful feeding to ensure that she does not get too low in condition. If you are in any doubt whatsoever, play safe and feed her more, rather than less – better a fat hawk than a dead one.

Falconers in the old days (and even some present-day ones) used to slow down the process of weight loss by feeding their birds 'washed meat' (i.e. meat soaked in water and then squeezed hard, so that all the nourishing juices are extracted and the bird is eating a pale, anaemic, almost completely valueless sort of food). I have tried this in the past, but never felt that I or the bird gained anything by it.

Another help in judging condition is simply to look at your bird, rather in the same way that you would look at your dog. A bird in good condition should have bright, full eyes, whereas a sick bird will have sunken, dull eyes, which tend to be half-closed. The bird's stance is also a guide to condition – healthy birds when tame and relaxed tend to fluff out their feathers and stand on one foot quite a lot of the time, but nevertheless take an interest in their surroundings. A sick bird will be even more fluffed out, may well sit on the ground, and will take little or no interest in what is going on around it. Experience can only be bought with time, and it will take the beginner a long time to recognize these symptoms. If you are in doubt about your bird's appearance, weigh her, feel her, and take any necessary action as indicated in chapter 23 on health and disease. A bird that is ill, or in low condition (and the two often go together) should not be fed large quantities at a time, but little and often, and no castings should be given.

Flying weight

In the same way as a boxer has a 'fighting weight', trained hawks have what is called a 'flying weight'. Many books would lead one to believe that once you have found the flying weight of your bird then most of your troubles are at an end, since so long as she is at this weight she is bound to fly well. This is far from true, since flying weight does not remain static.

There are several reasons for this. Initially, your bird will lack confidence, and will also still be in need of more manning (and therefore still rather frightened of you). This is usually the point at which she will be at her lowest weight. Once she starts to gain confidence, overcomes her fear and gets into the habit of returning to you, you will soon find that you can raise her flying weight. On no account, just because she comes a short distance at a certain weight, imagine that if you continue to lower her weight she will improve. Once she starts to respond, her weight should be levelled off and then, as she improves further, it can be raised.

All this is a matter of trial and error, and you may raise the bird's weight too much, find that she does not respond so well, and again have to lower it a little. Obviously the higher the weight at which you can fly your hawk, the better, but she must remain obedient. When you come to train your bird to fly at quarry, she will in due course make her first kill. If she is an eyass this will arouse instincts previously lying dormant; if she is a passager or haggard bird, it will doubtless bring back memories of the time when she hunted for herself in the wild. You may now find her keen to hunt, but not so obedient to fist or lure, and in order to restore discipline you will once again have to reduce her weight slightly.

As time goes on she will become accustomed to hunting and returning when you call her, and again her flying weight can be put up. By the end of her first season she may well be flying at a considerably heavier weight than at the beginning.

A bird can weigh the same in three different ways. This may sound nonsense, but it is true. Take a bird which usually flies well and is obedient at, say, 9 oz. If she weighs 9 oz today and weighed the same yesterday, she is at 9 oz level weight. If, however, she was over 9 oz yesterday, but is 9 oz today (because you gave her a smaller crop than usual in order to bring her weight down), then she is 9 oz 'coming down'. Similarly, if she was less than 9 oz yesterday, had a larger crop and is 9 oz today, she is 9 oz 'going up'. In all these circumstances she is at her correct flying weight today but, if you consider the matter carefully, it will be obvious that she is more likely to fly well if she is coming down (when she will be slightly keener) than if she is going up (when she will be less keen). This helps to explain why she may go well one day but not so well on another, even though her weight is the same on both occasions.

There can, of course, be other reasons for her not performing well, even though her weight is correct. Hawks are not machines, and they are just as subject to moods and temperaments as human beings. All of us have 'off' and 'on' days, without knowing why, and the same can be true of birds.

Apart from the actual amount of food which your bird eats each day, there are other factors which can affect her weight. Some of these may appear obvious, but" tend to be forgotten by beginners. Cold weather, particularly a sudden cold snap, will mean that your bird will need more food than normal to keep her flying weight level. In warm weather she will probably require less. The more exercise she takes, the more energy she will burn up, and once again she will need more food. If she is inactive, she will not need so much.

Different foods have different nutritive values. White meat, such as chicken or rabbit, is not so nourishing, weight for weight, as dark meat, such as pheasant or beef. Whilst training your bird this particular cause of weight variation can be entirely avoided by feeding her one type of food only, and this is a wise precaution for the beginner to take. Later on, as you gain experience, you will be able to assess the different values of different foods, and the effect these foods have on your individual bird, and you will thus be able to make the necessary allowances and adjustments in her diet.

A hawk that is given little or no food will lose weight, while one that eats a lot will gain weight; a moderate amount of food will keep her weight more or less level. However, a hawk that is in high condition will require far less food to keep her weight level than will a bird in low condition. Bearing this in mind, and the other factors I have just mentioned, you will see that a given weight of food will not always have the same effect on your hawk, unless all the circumstances are always the same.

Feeding

I have already discussed castings to a certain extent in the previous chapter. While you are training your bird it will be far easier for you not to feed her any castings at all. This will do her no harm, and will make it much simpler for you to ascertain how much food she is actually getting each day, since you will not have to allow for castings being included in the weight of food or the size of the bird's crop. Hawks should not be flown until they have cast; if a bird has not cast, she will probably not only refuse to respond to the lure, but will not even hunt. Also, hawks in training, until they are well-manned, may well cast at irregular times, and this again will complicate matters for the beginner.

Measuring the amount of food given can be done in several ways. With the exception of owls, all birds of prey have a crop into which their food goes after they have swallowed it. This can be felt by the falconer, and its size related to the size of some other object – a marble, a ping-pong ball and so on. In some ways this is rather haphazard, nevertheless it is a convenient method of judging a bird's food intake, and one which you should therefore get accustomed to using. In order to help measure the amount of food in this way, it is quite a good idea to have a series of different-sized objects which you can feel and compare with the size of the crop – perhaps a sort of falconer's crop-measuring necklace made of graded wooden beads. Also, by feeling the bird's crop in conjunction with weighing her, you will in time come to know roughly what size of crop corresponds with a given weight of food.

A more efficient and accurate method, and one which the beginner should certainly use, is to weigh the bird both before and after her meal. By subtracting the first weight from the second you will get the weight of food eaten. You can if you like weigh the food before feeding the bird, and weigh the remainder afterwards, but this is less efficient, since your bird may well feed from the lure as well as the 'pick-up piece', and so this will involve weighing both of them before you start. To make quite sure you are getting things right, it is best both to feel the hawk's crop and to weigh her.

Condition

67 Progress chart.

Date.	1	2	3	4	5	6	7	8	9	10	11	12	13	14	15	16	17	18
Weight	(graph: from 1.lb12ozs through 1.11, 1.10, 1.9, etc.)																	
Food	(graph: grade 5,4,3,2,1,0)																	
Behaviour.	F	F	G	G	F	G	P	G	G	F	P	G	G	G	VG	G	F	F
Time of weighing	7·30	8·0	7·30	6·0	5·30	4·0	4·30	3·0	3·30	2·0	2·0	4·0	2·0	3·15	2·0	3·0	10·0	11·0
Kills	–	–	–	–	–	–	–	–	–	–	–	–	–	–	–	–	–	–
Total	–	–	–	–	–	–	–	–	–	–	–	–	–	–	–	–	–	–

Remarks:

1. Newly caught in Sweden. Jessed up, put on tail bell etc. Tried him indoors. Did not feed
2. Carried indoors about 2 hours. Fairly quiet Refused to eat after 30 mins trying. Still too high
3. Carried him again in the evening. Fed on fist after 10 mins.
4. Carried again. Getting more used to people and dogs. Fed well. Jumped leash length.
5. Jumped indoors. Fed but would not jump outdoors.
6. Came 12ft on a creance. Getting better with dogs.
7. 12ft again No improvement. Too high.
8. 20ft on creance. Making sense now.
9. Out on the bow perch for the first time. Jumped from perch. 30ft on creance
10. Carried with dog. 20ft to fist.
11. As yesterday. Too high though. 15ft
12. Improved, Came 35ft. Better with dog
13. 30 yds, 2 people and dog
14. 50 yds. Not so distracted by distant traffic.
15. 70 yds. on a dragged creance.
16. Introduced to a lure, came 12ft then 20yds. 80yds to fist
17. 50 yds. lure and fist
18. Tried to fist from low tree. Slow but soon improved

Chart. Passage male gos.

Condition

	19	20	21	22	23	24	25	26	27	28	29	30	31	1	2	3	4	5	6
Condition	F	F	G	P	G	–	G	–	G	P	F	VG	P	VG	–	F			
Time	11·15	11·0	11·15	11·0	11·0	10·15	12·0	12·0	11·15	12·0	11·15	11·0	10·0	10·30	11·15	10·0			
Notes	Tree work again higher up. Not bad to fist came at once to lure.	Introduced to beating stick along hedge, disliked intensely at first 100 yds to fist.	More tree and hedge work. Tried at dummy rabbit dragged on line, went well.	A bit too much to eat yesterday. Took him in car. Bated a lot but settled later on	Very keen today. Needs a bit more manning yet. Flew a moorhen the dog pointed but the line caught up.	Rained all day. No flying. Fed early.	Tried for moorhens. Gos still on dragged creance. Flushed one from small pond & he took it well.	More rain, high wind. No flying.	Tried him on line with ferrets. Missed 2 rabbits caught 1. Good to fist.	Not quite keen enough. O.K. to lure though.	Had him loose for first time. Behaved very well. A bit uppish after chasing a pheasant.	Loose again. Caught 1 moorhen. Missed 2 more. Ended up getting a drake mallard	Wind and gos both a bit high. Flew a hen pheasant into a wood. Had to lure him down.	Very keen. Followed out of trees. Had a pheasant 2 rabbits and a stoat.	Did not fly.	Lost him for half an hour. Picked him up on a moorhen in a thick reed bed.			
	–	–	–	–	0	–	1	–	1	–	0	1	0	4	–	1			
	–	–	–	–	0	–	1	–	2	–	2	3	3	7	–	8			

121

Your hawk should be weighed every day at approximately the same time, or at least within an hour on either side of it. Weighing should be done just before the day's training session, and again immediately after feeding (which will take place at the end of the session). This means that you must decide, before you start to train the bird, what time of day is most convenient for you. (As I have said before, training must be done during the hours of daylight – do not confuse this with manning, which can be done at any time.)

The hawk's weight, the amount of food she has eaten, the time of weighing, and the bird's behaviour during training, should all be noted down each day. To do this efficiently, it is best to use a progress chart. The type of chart which I make out is in some respects similar to a hospital chart. From it one can tell at a glance how much weight the bird has gained or lost in one day, how much food she has eaten, and what her progress has been in manning and training.

On the sample chart illustrated, the top line is for the date, then comes a graph of the bird's weight (graph paper makes very good charts, for this reason); below this is the food graph. These two sections should be as large as possible so that small differences in weight can easily be shown. Next comes the time of weighing, then follow two sections showing progress in manning and training (here I use simple symbols – G for good, F for fair, P for poor and so on). Below these comes a section for short remarks on the bird's behaviour, and finally, two more rows – one for the number of kills per day, and the other for the total bag of the season to date. The larger the chart, the more information can be put on it. Clip it to a board and hang it near the weighing-machine for easy access; when it is completed it can be filed away and kept for future reference. It is not simply of passing interest to read back over old charts; there is often a great deal of useful information in them which you would otherwise almost certainly have forgotten.

In conjunction with your chart you can also keep a log book, if you wish. This can be very much more detailed, and can contain all the information shown on your chart as well. But it will not show you at a glance, as does your chart, how your bird is progressing.

Each day your chart should show some progress. In the early stages this will be very small, but once your bird is nearing her correct weight for that stage of training, and is also becoming tamer, you will find her improving by leaps and bounds. Of course there will be days (particularly if she is your first bird) when, probably because you have made an error in feeding, things seem to stand still or even regress. Do not let this worry you unduly – the important thing is that the chart, if correctly filled in, should show you where your error lies, and you will therefore know how to correct it. You must expect to make mistakes. However, so long as you err on the safe side, that is, by overfeeding rather than underfeeding, you have nothing to worry about. The bird will not suffer, and you will profit by learning from your mistakes. After all, if things went right all the time, half the fun would disappear.

10 Manning and Early Training

Your hawk's training must be done step by step, gradually building up to the desired result. You cannot miss out a step and you cannot move on until each stage has been properly learnt. This is where patience is required. Every movement you make must be slow and gentle, for in the early stages any sudden movements will startle the bird. However slowly she may seem to respond at times, you must never lose your temper with her. Punishing her by hitting or shouting at her will only terrify her. You can say 'naughty bird' as often as you like, but it will have no effect at all, except possibly to relieve your own feelings.

Now that she is hard down, or has finished her rest period, you can begin her training. Here you can take a very small short cut, by removing all food from her mews for at least a day before you actually pick her up for the first manning session. In the case of large birds, such as goshawks, this foodless period can be extended to two or even three days, providing the bird is alone in the mews. (If there is more than one bird in the mews this might well result in one killing the other.)

Carrying

Pick up your bird on the first day of training and weigh her ,as usual. If she is wearing short jesses without slits, you will either have to cut slits in them or replace them with normal jesses. Put the swivel onto the jesses as described in chapter 6, and then put on her leash. Since the leash is fairly long, it is best to halve its length by doubling it, and then to wind it first round the little finger of your gloved hand and then between the second and third fingers, as shown in figure 68. Should the hawk bate while you are carrying her, she will now run no risk of becoming entangled in the leash. The jesses should lie through the space between your thumb and forefinger and down across your palm. Depending on the length of the jesses, the swivel will lie either at the base of the little finger, or a little higher up the palm of your hand.

Carrying a bird is not quite so easy as it looks. Both the hawk's and your comfort are important. Your arm should be bent at the elbow so that your forearm is parallel with the ground. The back of your semi-clenched fist (relaxed, not tight) is to your left. If you are carrying a small hawk, her feet

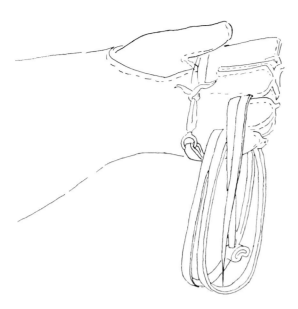
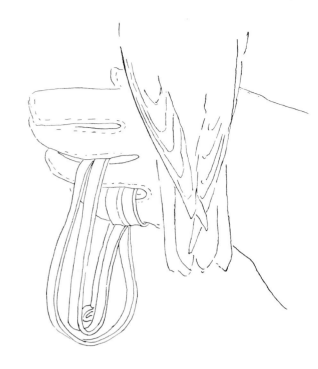

68 The correct way to
hold the leash.

will be on your thumb, or very nearly so. If she is a large bird, her left foot will
be on your thumb and her right foot on your wrist. She should be facing to
your right, with her tail over the back of your hand. (I find it more comfortable
to bring my forearm slightly inwards, towards my right, instead of keeping it
straight out towards the front; and to keep my elbow slightly back from the
line of my body.)

Do not tense up; try to be relaxed, or after a short time your arm will get
tired. Your whole arm should move easily up and down from the elbow, thus
acting as a shock-absorber, ironing out any jerky movements as you walk and
so giving the hawk a comfortable ride. There should be no need for her to grip
the glove tightly or to open her wings to balance herself. If you do this properly
(and it will take you time to learn) the bird will sit as comfortably on your fist
as on her perch, and eventually you will find that carrying her no longer tires
you at all.

At first it is quite common for hawks to persist in sitting the wrong way
round on your fist. To get your bird to face the right way, simply push or pull
her round very gently by applying pressure to the side of her tail. She may of
course bate off, but in a short time she will learn to turn the way you want.

Jesses will get twisted, even though you do have a swivel, and must be
untwisted when this happens. This will mean removing the swivel from time
to time, and whilst you are untwisting them, seize this opportunity to keep
them greased. One can untwist Aylmeri more easily.

Until your hawk begins to get tame it is not wise to put her on an outdoor
perch. If you do she will tend to bate a lot, and will break her feathers and

generally get upset. So she is best either in her mews or in her night quarters, when she is not with you.

One way of helping to avoid broken tail feathers is to bind her tail, when closed, with brown paper tape. Do this fairly high up the tail (see diagram 25) and on no account use any tape that cannot easily be removed by soaking in water. This is also a good thing to do when travelling a bird in a crate.

Manning

There is a general consensus of opinion among falconers that it is essential to carry a bird around a great deal in order to make her tame. This is not quite correct. If the hawk is wild and bates a lot then she is best *not* carried, except when she is being fed. Then, the food will hold most of her attention, and she will not be so easily frightened by strange things. The important thing is not to force the bird into doing things which she obviously hates. You do not want her to dread the sight and sound of your coming, which is what may easily happen if you start trying to man her too soon in crowded places.

Manning must begin slowly and quietly, and it only gradually builds up to the point where your bird has such confidence in you that she will put up with almost anything, from chain-saws and jet planes to fun-fairs. The process of manning never really stops, since your hawk will continually be meeting things she has never seen before. It is really worth your while to have your bird so well-manned that she will sit relaxed, fluffed-out and unworried on your fist, no matter where you take her. As Bert so rightly says (in his *Treatise of Hawkes and Hawking*, 1619) 'Worke out but your taske in this fashion, and you shall during your hawke's life finde none but playing-days'.

If you read some of the old books you will find accounts of the falconer taking his bird into a room dimly lit by a single candle, and sitting there for hours on end, waiting for the hawk to feed on his fist. This does work, but it is quite unnecessary. (If you have ever tried this method you will have found that the first time your hawk bates, the draught from her wings will blowout the candle.)

At this early stage the hawk will be distracted from feeding by anything that moves. So go into a quiet room on your own. If it is daylight then the hawk will see the outside world through the windows and will be inclined to bate towards them, so either draw the curtains or wait until it is dark. Just turn on the light, sit down in a comfortable chair, and try to persuade her to feed. Make yourself really comfortable, for you are going to be there for half an hour, and you want if possible to avoid moving around.

Make sure that if the hawk does bate, she cannot hit any hard or sharp projections, such as table edges, other chairs and so on, and so damage her feathers. Have a piece of tender meat, about the size of a rolled-up tobacco pouch, ready for her, and have a knife at hand in case you should need it. Settle down and wait – she will look around the room and perhaps bate off your

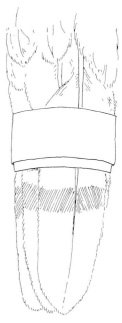

69 Taping a bird's tail.

fist. She may fly back again on her own, or she may hang head down, in which case you must gently lift her back.

Since any movement will attract her attention, you can use this to attract her to the meat. Simply squeeze it with your gloved hand, and with any luck she will look down and see it. Every time she looks away, do this again. After a while, she may take a tentative pull at it. This is why you want it to be tender – if she can tear a piece off easily she will probably swallow it, and having tasted it will continue to eat. But if the meat is tough she will be discouraged, and probably too frightened to pull hard enough to tear any off. Slashing the meat with a knife beforehand will help to make things easier for her.

If, however, she still ignores all your efforts, you can try another ploy. Quietly cut off a few pieces of meat, about peanut size, and gently offer them to her. If after half an hour she still has not fed at all, but has had a good chance of doing so, do not waste any more time. If you were to sit there for two hours she might feed, but there is little to be gained by this. She is not yet hungry enough for hunger to overcome fear.

If, on the other hand, she does feed, she will be likely to take only a small crop, since, once the edge has gone from her appetite, fear will once more overcome hunger. She may stop feeding after a little while, and appear not to want any more, but wait for a few minutes and give her a chance to reconsider. When it is obvious she will not take any more, remove the meat and then, if she is not bating too much, keep her on your fist and man her indoors for a while. But if she bates too much, put her back in her quarters.

Most small hawks will be feeding by the second day. Larger ones may not feed until the third or even the fourth day, sometimes longer still. This is where the beginner starts to get worried, and quite rightly so. But as I have said before, this is where the weighing-machine helps you. You will know how much overall weight the bird has lost over the period, and whether this is a steady, even loss or has started slowly and then gathered speed.

On very rare occasions you may get a bird that refuses to feed on your fist, no matter what you do or how long you sit with her. This is of course extremely worrying, especially if you consider she has reached the point where you feel it would be dangerous for her to drop in weight any further. I have found the following to work surprisingly well in such cases: pick up your problem bird and give her a chance to feed, as before. If she still refuses, put her back in the mews (or, if she is not too wild, tether her outside on her perch) and leave a piece of meat with her. Arrange matters so that you can watch her without her being aware of it. She is almost certain to feed now that you are not in sight. Let her take a very small amount and then, as quietly as possible, pick her up again and try her on the fist once more. She should start feeding again very quickly. Fortunately very few hawks are as stubborn as this, but should you encounter one, this is a method that I have never known to fail.

Once the hawk starts feeding on the fist you can make her mealtimes last longer, so that she can be carried about more while she is eating, and at the same time get used to things happening around her. To prolong her meal you can use tougher meat that takes her longer to eat, and you can also use 'tirings' (from the French *tirer*, to pull). These are simply foods at which she can pull and pluck – wings, legs etc. of birds and animals, which have very little meat on them, either because you have purposely removed it first, or because she has eaten most of it at a previous meal.

As she gets tamer and more friendly towards you, so you can carry her for longer periods and introduce her to more new things; for instance, if you are going to work her with a dog, she should be introduced to it early on. To begin with, when you feed her in the presence of other people, ask them to sit quietly and not to make sudden movements, rustle newspapers and so on. It will not take your bird long to get accustomed to them. I find it a good thing to bring hawks indoors in the evenings and let them share in the household activity. They bate far less once dusk has fallen, and this certainly helps to man them.

I once had a little gos from Japan. He was boarding with me and so, since I dislike flying other people's hawks, I did very little with him. His owner then gave him to me, and within ten days I had him flying loose. This was simply because, although all I had done was to feed him on the fist and then put him back on his perch, he looked forward to my visits, since they meant food. Once I started his training he was no trouble at all.

As your bird gradually becomes tamer and less inclined to bate at every strange sight and sound, she can be put out of doors on her block or bow perch in a quiet part of your garden, or in her weathering ground, for all or part of each day.

When putting a hawk down on an outdoor perch, you should go about it in the following way. Keep her facing towards you, not towards the perch, otherwise she will probably try to jump onto it; she must not be allowed to do this until she is tied up. If you put her on the perch first, you will have no safety measure in operation should she suddenly bate while you are tying her up, and may very well escape. Now unwind the leash from your fingers and pull it out full length so that the leash button is against the swivel. Bring the swivel through your fingers to the back of your hand, in the safety position. Now tie the free end of the leash to the ring on the block or bow perch with a falconer's knot.

You can now put the bird down on the perch. If she will not jump or step onto it of her own accord, place her so that her tail hangs down over the back of the perch and then lower her gently so that she must step up and back when it presses against the backs of her legs – just as if you were putting her on the weighing-machine, in fact. (This is the way that a hooded hawk must be put down on her perch, since she cannot see and will therefore not be able to step forward onto it.)

When you pick the bird up from her outdoor perch, the whole process goes into reverse. Get the hawk onto your fist (if she is hooded you will place your hand behind her, so that she can step backwards onto it) and pull the swivel into the safety position before you start to untie the knot. Then bring the swivel round into the palm of your hand, halve the leash and wind it round your fingers as previously explained.

If the hawk bates away from you as you go in to pick her up, run your gloved hand along the leash up to the swivel and lift her clear of the ground onto your fist. This will save her from exhausting herself through prolonged bating.

Flying to the fist

Now you can progress a little further. Next meal-time, offer her food on your fist, and after she has taken a few beakfuls remove the meat. Put her on the arm of a chair, or some other convenient perch, and offer the meat again, just far enough away from her so that she cannot reach it without stepping onto your glove. She is, of course, still on the leash. So that she can reach you, un-wind the leash, pulling it out to its full length so that the button is against the swivel, and either hold the free end or wind it a few times round the little finger of your gloved hand. The first time you try this it may take a long time before she steps up. She is like a child on the edge of a swimming-pool for the first time, hesitant and lacking in confidence. Persuasion and patience are needed. Once she has taken the plunge, and nothing terrible has happened to her, she will be willing to try again.

Your next step is to make her first jump and then fly to you for food. Each time you reward her, and each time you increase the distance she must come. With each reward the bird will be getting more food and so losing her keenness, so if you try to make her jump too often the moment will come when she refuses to do so and you will have to go closer to her. This is not progress – just the reverse. You must try to judge matters so that this does not happen. Three or four jumps (or flights) are enough at any training session, and this will apply all through her training. After her last trip, let her have her ration for the day, on your fist.

To begin with you may think it rather difficult to estimate the amount of food your hawk has eaten while she is on the fist. The last thing you want to do is to be continually taking the meat away from her and weighing her during the course of her meal to see how much she has eaten; this will only upset her and make her impatient. Weigh the meat, therefore, before the training session begins. (Do this out of sight of the bird or she will almost certainly try to grab it.) Having decided, when you have weighed your hawk, how much she will need to eat at her next meal, you can then judge by eye roughly how much of the meat she can be allowed.

It is not always easy to take meat away from a hawk. They often get their feet right round it and even one big inside talon of a goshawk will make it hard to get the meat away. If you take too long about it, the whole thing becomes an undignified tug-of-war, the hawk meanwhile gets more food than she ought, and your whole training session is set back. In the case of a big hawk which is holding the meat with one or two talons, you can roll your hand to and fro and the bird will probably shift her feet to keep her balance. You can then quickly pull the meat away. With small hawks this often does not work so well, and the best thing to do is to move each talon with your fingers, at the same time pulling the meat down into your gloved palm. Better still, as the bird flies or jumps towards you, pull the meat down a little with your free hand, into your gloved palm, so that when she lands on your fist her talons will be on the glove and not in the meat. If you see an expert taking the meat away it looks so easy that you hardly notice it being done. Nor does the hawk notice, which is exactly what the falconer wants. As she takes a beakful and raises her head to swallow, the meat is twitched away, and when she looks down again it has vanished.

It should only be a matter of a few days before your hawk is coming a leash length to your fist. By now when she bates she should have learnt how to get back to your fist without your having to assist her. She will most likely have learnt to jump onto the weighing machine perch and wait while you weigh her. Always offer her food when you go to pick her up and sooner or later you will find her jumping to you and being pleased to see you. After weighing, carry her a little to settle her down, and let her have a few beakfuls from the pick-up piece, just to remind her that you are her food supplier. Then carryon with the training session.

Once she is coming a leash length you must put the creance on so that she can come further. Put the swivel in the safety position and remove the leash, putting it somewhere safe (not in your hawking bag or your pocket, as it is all too easily lost in these places). Slip it onto your belt as in diagram 70. The creance is tied to the lower ring of the swivel with a falconer's knot. To help keep tension on the creance while tying it on, stand on it about 5 ft from the end.

A fairly open space is needed for your training sessions. For short distances a lawn the size of a tennis court will suffice, but later on, when the bird is coming further, you will need considerably more space, such as a field. Sports grounds make ideal training areas as the creance does not get caught up so easily when the grass is short. Keep away from trees, as hawks in training often swing off, away from your fist, and may well get the creance tangled if they fly into a tree and start to 'ladder' from branch to branch. You may then have to do some tree climbing, and by the time you have got your hawk back she will be upset and your training session will be spoilt.

Select a good place, away from anything that might disturb your bird, and put her onto a perch. A fence post or a field gate are the most likely convenient perches. The post is better as hawks on a gate will often walk up and down before plucking up courage to fly to you. She should be facing into the wind if there is any. Unroll a length of creance and either twist it round the little finger of your gloved hand or stand on it.

70 Leash and swivel
looped on to the belt.
Below, spring clip for
hawking bag.

The best way to unroll a creance is to hold both ends of the stick, one in each hand, and, treating the stick as an axle and allowing it to revolve, walk slowly backwards until the required amount of line has been unwound. Do not pull the hawk off the perch while you are doing this. If you pull the creance off one end of the stick, the line gets a twist in it at each turn. On your finger it will tend possibly to get in your way, but standing on it is not quite so safe as you may move and forget to keep your foot on it. (Some falconers tie the creance to the tassel on their glove. If you make your own gloves and are quite sure the tassel line is strong and safe then this is not a bad idea, but most bought gloves are poorly made and not to be trusted.)

Since your hawk came a leash length the previous day then start her off at this distance. Before you call her to the fist make sure the creance will not catch on anything, such as a crack in the post or a piece of barbed wire. Stand with your left side towards her and put your left arm straight out in front of you, holding the meat in your glove so that she can see it. Use a good-sized piece of meat (cut with the grain, about the size of a rolled up tobacco pouch) and one that looks tempting to the hawk, not a washed-out, anaemic, marble-sized lump of unattractive appearance.

If you stand like this your face is not directly behind the meat (which it will be if you stand facing her) and this means that she will be less likely to be distracted when you whistle or call to her. Also if she is a little nervous she may fly over the top of your fist (this is quite a commonplace happening with short-wings) and if this happens she will not come up into your face. Some hawks land quite gently on your fist while others come with a thump. You should 'ride the blow' as boxers say, letting the bird push your fist forwards and upwards. Once she comes to the first, reward her as usual and try her again, increasing the distance.

When your bird is coming readily on the creance some 3 or 4 m (12 ft) to the fist, you have now reached the point where the training of falcons differs from that of hawks and other birds of prey. In mediaeval times falcons were known as 'birds of the lure', while short-winged hawks were termed 'birds of the fist'. If your bird is a falcon she must now be 'entered' (introduced) to the lure; if she is a short-wing or a buzzard, you will for the time being simply continue to fly her to the fist, increasing the distance she must come each day.

The small falcons will, if you wish them to, come great distances to the fist (though there is little point in making them do this), but the bigger falcons, especially peregrines, have the instinct to fly very fast, chopping their quarry with their hind talons as they go past. If you try to make them come further than 6 to 12 ft to your fist they will chop at the meat in your fist and carryon. A falcon that does this is not, as some falconers think, being stupid. She is behaving as she should, and you should be delighted when she acts in this stylish way. When short-winged birds do this it is usually either from lack of confidence or, sometimes, from being just a little overweight.

Flying to the lure

The first time you introduce your falcon to the lure is a very important stage in her training. Rush it and you can build up a lot of trouble for yourself; take your time and you will save yourself not only endless hours later on, but also, possibly, the permanent loss of your falcon. It is important to have good weather. If it is raining or windy then delay matters until the weather is calm and dry.

I have already talked about lures and how to make them up in chapter 5. However, the lure you use for the first two or three times to introduce your falcon needs a few alterations, for the following reason. So far she has been accustomed to coming to you for just a piece of red meat. If you suddenly substitute a normal lure the meat will not be so obvious and may be partially or even entirely hidden by the wings on the lure. To avoid this I use a larger piece of meat than normal, and smaller wings. Young falcons especially may be puzzled if you do not do this, since they do not associate wings (or fur) with food. A passage or haggard bird understands all this already, but an eyass, unless the meat is obvious, will not realize the lure is edible.

Put your falcon on the post you are going to fly her from, and walk away, paying out more creance than hitherto. Today you are not interested in making the bird come any great distance, but since the lure line is about 12ft long you will want to stand a bit further back than you would if you were flying her to the fist.

Leave the lure itself in your bag for the time being. Make sure that it is not in the same compartment as your pick-up piece. Pull out the lure line to its full extent, holding the stick in your gloved hand with the line emerging between your second and third fingers. The stick will revolve in your hand while you do this, and so the line will not become twisted.

Take up a loop or two of slack line round the little finger of your gloved hand; each loop will take up about 2 ft of line. From there the line runs between the fingers and thumb, and then across, a matter of 3 to 4 ft, to your other hand. Then, as you whistle to your bird, take the lure out of the bag and swing it round vertically once or twice. The lure should just clear the ground at the bottom of each swing. Your right hand will be slightly higher than your elbow. The distance between the lure and your hand will depend on how tall you are and also (later on) whether you are standing on short grass or something taller, like clover or heather. Now throw the lure out to the full extent of the line, letting go of the line with both hands, but still holding the stick. The looped-up part should run off your fingers quite easily if you slightly open your gloved hand.

Throw the lure out to one side of you, never in front. Do make sure it lands where the hawk can see it – the grass around you should be quite short. The bird will watch it land, and once she sees the meat showing she should bob her head. This bobbing is a trait common to all falcons, but not to short-winged hawks, and is a sign of interest. Leave the lure lying on the ground for a slow count of seven. The falcon may well spread her wings as if to come, but then change her mind, fold them again and look away. If so, twitch the lure by pulling on the line, dragging it towards you about 6 in. or so. The movement will again attract her attention and again she will bob her head.

If she still does not come, pull the lure on to you, catch up the slack and swing it out once more. Even now she may not come – if not, go closer to her and throw out the lure. It is always better for a bird to come a short distance at once, rather than a long way after a period of waiting. Sooner or later, unless she is at the wrong weight or insufficiently manned, she will come. There is rarely much trouble over this part of the proceedings, as a rule, and she may even come to the lure a lot sooner than you ever expected.

Do not expect her to grab the lure the first time. More often than not a falcon, until she has learnt what it is all about, will more or less jump up into the air and then flutter down like a hesitant butterfly to within a short distance of the lure. Then, with that curious gait that a falcon has on the ground, rather like that of a drunken sailor, she will walk or even run up to it, and perhaps grab it with one foot. Stay quite still. Any movement on your part now may frighten her. Be patient, and let her consider the situation. She may try to pull the lure to her, and in this case you can allow her a few inches of play but no more.

Wait until she gets both feet on the lure, and once she is on it, pull in the creance so that it lies side by side with the lure line on the ground. Stand on them both; now, if you should alarm her and she should leave the lure and try to flyaway, you have her held fast. This should not happen, but it might, and so it is as well to be prepared. If by any misfortune it does, stay quite still and wait. The bird will settle down again if you give her time, and will grab the lure again.

While she is thinking about feeding, get out your pick-up piece of meat and your knife (you can do this before you start luring, if you like). Cut off four small pieces of meat about the size of peanuts (a little smaller for small falcons). Put knife and pick-up away, and put one of the little pieces of meat on your gloved forefinger. Keep the other three bits hidden in the palm of your hand by closing your glove over them.

By now she may have started to feed from the lure. If so, walk in towards her, step by step, stopping every time she stops feeding and going forward when she starts again. To begin with you will be about 12 ft from her, since this is the length of your lure line. Take your time – do not rush things. When you have covered half the distance to her, get down on one knee (however uncomfortable) and slowly, gently and quietly make in towards her. Hitherto she has for the most part seen only your top half, and now if you walk right up to her while she is on the ground you will look to her like a great giant towering above her, and she will be alarmed. So edge in little by little, and gently stretch out your gloved hand, offering her the piece of meat on your fingertip. After a while she will take it and swallow it. Withdraw your hand

71 Merlin flying to the fist on the leash. The end of the leash is tightly secured round the little finger.

72 Putting on the creance – the bird is an adult lanneret.

73 Winding up the creance while the merlin feeds on the fist. Tension is kept on the creance by running it through the gloved hand.

very slowly, and place another bit of meat on your finger. Again offer it to her, just as gently as before. If all goes as it should, by the time you offer her the last piece of meat she will be leaning forward to take it from you.

During all this time you should be kneeling on the creance and lure line, so that the hawk cannot pull the lure away as you make in to her. All wild hawks, when they have killed, tend to carry their quarry away to eat it. If you allow a trained hawk to follow her natural instinct and carry the lure, later on she will carry her kill when you take her hunting, and this could well result in your losing her. Once a hawk becomes a 'carrier' it is extremely hard to break her of the habit; and so it is better to prevent the habit from forming in the first place. It will not always be possible, but every attempt must be made to this end.

Once your bird has eaten the last of the small offerings, get out your pick-up piece (slowly of course). Holding it tightly in your glove, edge in a little closer, and place the pick-up over the meat on the lure, as low down as possible. A hawk feeds from her feet, and that is where the meat should be. When she next looks down she will see not the lure but the pick-up, and will start to pull from this. As she pulls, raise your hand. When it is level with her throat she will no longer be able to pull. Lower your hand again.

Continue to do this until she becomes annoyed with the meat because it will not stay still to be pulled, and puts one of her feet either onto your glove, or onto the meat to hold it down. Again she pulls – again you raise the meat. Soon she will put her other foot on it too. Now you have transferred her from lure to pick-up, just as you wanted. Let the bird take one or two bites of meat and then, raising your gloved hand, falcon and all, a few inches, gently remove the lure with your free hand and pop it into your hawking bag. Now put your free hand up under your gloved hand, take hold of the creance and follow it up to the swivel.

With as little disturbance as possible to the hawk, get the swivel and jesses into the reversed safety position. This is exactly what it says it is – the jesses hang down the back of your hand, and you simply pull them through between your second and third fingers so that the swivel lies on the inside of your hand instead of at the back. The reason for doing this is that it is not very easy to use the normal safety position when picking a bird up. You can now get slowly to your feet and let the falcon have a few more bites of meat. Then remove the meat and give her time to settle down.

Probably the bird's feet will still be gripping your glove. If you carry her towards her flying post she may try to fly back onto it, but will be unable to leave the glove because her feet are still gripping it. This quite commonly happens – 'sticky-footed' is the term often used to describe a bird that acts in this way. Roll your hand to make her shift her feet; you may have to do this several times, since some birds take quite a time to relax their grip.

Now she is back on her post again, you can try her once more to the lure, increasing the distance slightly. Do not rush things – some falcons, especially merlins, like to 'rouse' (shake their feathers) before flying again. The second

74 Getting the bird used to your approaching her from any angle while she is on the lure – here, an adult lanner.

75 Picking up a bird – the pick-up piece hides the meat on the lure.

time you call her to the lure you should find that she will come with very little delay, if any. Falcons get the idea very quickly, and from now on your training progress chart should show a considerable improvement.

As you increase the distance your bird comes to the lure each day, so there will come a point at which she is coming the full length of the creance, but at which you feel she is not yet ready to fly completely loose. You can now use a 'dragged creance'. This is a most useful way of increasing distance without having a longer creance (which would increase the weight the hawk has to pull). Take off the swivel and hang it on your leash, which you then loop over your belt. Tie the creance to only one of the jesses, through the swivel slit; this lessens the chances of the bird getting caught up. Instead of unrolling the creance out in front of the bird, lay it out behind her, so that when she starts to fly she will immediately have the full weight of the creance to pull, and it will run behind her and will be less likely to be caught up in the grass. The creance is not attached to the stick, of course.

Dragged creances work so well that with big birds like goshawks it is possible to start hunting while the hawk is still on a dragged creance. Of course it can catch up, but if you avoid going into really thick cover it is quite amazing how it snakes through long grass and branches. I was demonstrating this once with a male gos. He left my fist suddenly, and flew hard towards a nearby hedge, the creance dragging behind him. He went over the hedge and up into a tree, where he sat for a second or two on a branch about 20 ft up before crashing into some bushes below. I ran up and found him right in the middle of the bushes, on a grey squirrel. The far end of the creance was still over the tree branch. Yet when I lifted him up and walked away, the whole creance pulled through the branches without any snagging at all.

Small hawks and falcons do not have the strength to pull a creance through this sort of cover, but in the open it will work well. Of course, you must not expect a falcon to fly at quarry with a creance dragging behind her; the distance she flies is far too great. But with buzzards and goshawks it works well, and you can go hunting with a bird that is still a little nervous of strangers and that you dare not trust loose just yet, a few days earlier than would otherwise be the case.

However, there are two points to watch out for. First, if a hawk on a dragged creance goes into a tree, you must step in smartly, take hold of the end of the creance and keep it taut, in case the bird starts to 'ladder' from branch to branch. (This really gets the creance in a tangle and may well result in your having some tree climbing to do, so avoid using a dragged creance near very high trees.) Then set about getting your bird down to fist or lure.

Secondly, a bird does not fly at an even pace, but rows through the air rather like a boat, putting on speed at each downward stroke of its wings and slowing a little on the upward beats. The creance therefore alters speed too, and if it happens to go over a wire strand fence the last few inches will sometimes twirl round the wire and pull the hawk up short. The sooner you can dispense with the creance, the better.

To return to making in to the hawk and picking her up off the lure; each day you will only manage a couple of trips or so, as she will have had too much to need to go in fairly smartly, or she will be eating more from the lure than you intend her to. (So instead of being able to try her three or four times in a session you will only manage a couple of trips or so, as she will have had too much to eat.)

Later on, when hunting, you may temporarily lose your bird when she has killed in cover and has gone out of sight. If you are not sure exactly where she is, and are blundering about in, say, a reed-bed, thick heather, or long grass, you may well come upon her unexpectedly from behind and frighten her. You should therefore get her used to these surprises by making in to her from every possible angle. This is simple enough to do. Once she has got used to you making in and picking her up off the lure, alter the procedure on the last trip of the training session. Make in in the usual way, but after offering her a few bits of meat on your finger, instead of picking her up, take off the creance, put on her leash and swivel, and tie her up either to your hawking bag (which you have previously taken off) or to the ring spike. Wind up the creance as you walk away, leaving her feeding on the lure. Cut some small bits of meat from the pick-up, walk in to her again and offer her one. Walk away again and circle round her at a distance of a few yards, gradually spiralling in towards her, and approaching her this time from the side. Give her another piece and go away again. If you continue this, you will find you can walk in from any angle and she will be quite happy to see you. Once she has had about half the day's ration from the lure, pick her up and feed her the rest on the fist.

If you practise this every day, the hawk will become increasingly tame. Many hawks will jump to your fist as you go in, bringing the lure with them, once they are accustomed to you. Some will leave the lure on the ground and jump to you. I have had both hawks and falcons that would leave their kill and come to my fist.

As mentioned earlier, in mediaeval times short-winged hawks were called 'birds of the fist', and even today some falconers do not use a lure at all when flying short-wings. Personally I think this is a great mistake. Although it is very nice to have your hawk come to your fist and save you the trouble of getting out a lure, she should certainly be entered to one at some time during her training. You will find that short-wings will come more readily to the lure than to the fist, and this may prove to be a great help on days when your bird may be rather uppish, a little too high in weight, and slow to the fist. If you have no objections to using a lure, you will find that the training of hawks will not take so long as it would if no lure were used.

Entering a hawk to the lure is done in exactly the same way as for falcons. I would introduce her to it when she is coming some 50 yd to the fist. Of course, there is never any stooping to a swung lure where hawks are concerned, as they do not fly in the same way as falcons.

There is, however, a snag if your hawk comes only to the lure. You do not fly a falcon very many times during a day's hawking – perhaps four to six flights at most. But a hawk may have far more flights than this, some of which will be unsuccessful and will result in her having to return to the falconer. Then, if the grass is wet, or there is snow on the ground, each time she returns to the lure she will tend to get her wings and tail wet, and until they are dry again her flying will be impaired.

There is a happy medium, which combines both lure and fist, and which I find most useful. Instead of swinging out the lure full length, just unroll a few feet of line only, and then swing the lure. As the hawk comes towards you, swing the lure up onto your gloved fist, on which she will then land. This prevents her getting her flight feathers wet, and can also be useful at times for falcons, particularly merlins.

Not only during training, but later on as well, the falconer should take care not to let his bird get too one-track minded about certain things. For instance, there are some birds that after a time will only feed on the fist and refuse to eat either from the lure or from the ground. This can become a nuisance and should be avoided if possible. Also hawks can get used to one form of food, one locality, one form of dress and so on; this too must be avoided. Their usual food may not be available, and you may then find they will not come to you for a different sort. I have had Goshawks, Red-tails and Harris' hawks refuse to come a very short distance to beef, but on being offered a day-old chick, on which they had been fed during their moult, they would come a very long way. One man I know used a teddy bear as a lure when this happened, since it was chick-coloured.

You may train your hawk in warm weather, wearing a coloured shirt. Later on you may change to a white one, or wear a sweater or a jacket because the weather is colder. Your hawk, not being used to this, may fly badly or even refuse to fly at all. So change your clothing every so often.

If you always use the same field and the same post to fly the bird from each day, she may well be quite hopeless in another field or even off a different post in the same field. Ring the changes here too. All these little things can lead to trouble and often you may not realise why the hawk is acting badly. As her training progresses, the more people she sees, the better, otherwise she may end up working well for you only when you are alone.

On very rare occasions you may come across a bird that has a disliking for one particular person or thing. I have a Changeable hawk-eagle who loathes donkeys and will just sit up in a tree and refuse to come down if they are near, although he pays little attention to horses or cows. I have even had two birds that would refuse to fly if a lady was out with us – this may sound silly but it is true. (One was a merlin, which is the last bird one would expect to behave like this.) Short-winged hawks certainly dislike brightly coloured clothing if they are used to country colours. Plastic mackintoshes that rustle when you move can send some birds flying off into the next county. I flew a female goshawk once that simply could not stand tractors, but did not mind trains. These individual idiosyncrasies you find out by accident, although it is worth mentioning that no hawk becomes accustomed to a buzz-saw very easily.

Once your bird is trained, it is as well to get her used to car travel as soon as possible. To begin with, she will of course be travelling on your fist, so you will have to have a driver. Ensure that the car is facing in the right direction, with the engine running and the passenger door open, before you approach with the bird. She should be feeding on a tiring, to distract her attention. Get into the car as quietly and gently as possible, leaving the bird outside the door until you are seated. If she looks like bating, wait until she has settled before bringing her in. Once she is in, close the door as quietly as you can, and get your driver to move off at once, slowly and without jerking. Most birds take quite well to car travel but some, if travelling hooded, do tend to get car-sick on long journeys; so never travel a bird which has not put over its crop.

By now your hawk or falcon should be ready to fly loose. How long you have taken to arrive at this stage will depend on the amount of spare time which you have spent with her (it is very difficult to train a bird at times of the year when you are not able to have the training sessions in daylight except at weekends); and of course on the individual bird. A beginner will naturally take longer than an experienced falconer – this is only to be expected.

By the time you have reached the end of stage two of training, just prior to flying your bird free for the first time, you should have learnt at what weight she flies best, and approximately how much food she requires to keep her at that weight each day. By looking at your chart you should be able to estimate, to within a quarter of an ounce, what weight she will be, how she will behave when you fly her, and how much food she will need in order to give good results on the following day. If you can do all this reasonably accurately then you are well on the way to understanding condition and training, and you should have very little trouble from now on as far as getting your bird into yarak is concerned.

11 Flying Free and Getting Fit

The first time you fly your first hawk completely loose, off the creance, is not only a big moment for you, but also, naturally, a very anxious one. Because of this you may quite understandably be tempted to put it off from day to day, and the longer the delay, the more you will have to screw up your courage to take this step. (On the other hand, if you try to get her going loose too soon, you may well regret it; but this is not so likely, since nearly all beginners tend to start flying their birds loose too late rather than too early.) Each day's delay now means that later on your hawk will find hunting more difficult, since as the season progresses game will be getting stronger and hardier, and she will be less likely to get easy slips when first entered at quarry. And until your bird is going loose, you cannot move on to stage three of her training – getting her fit.

Falcons that are to be flown out of the hood at rooks, gulls and so forth are exercised daily by being stooped to the swung lure. Game hawks, on the other hand, must not be stooped to a lure, and it is therefore only constant flying at game which will muscle them up and get them fit. For this reason they take a great deal longer than rook hawks to reach their peak of fitness. One could compare a game hawk's daily exercise with that of someone playing a gentle game of croquet, with an occasional dash to answer the telephone; whereas the exercise taken by 'a rook hawk each day is more like several strenuous games of squash. The old-fashioned idea that game hawks require to be flown in far higher condition than rook hawks is really too ridiculous when you examine it carefully. Any bird should always be as fit as possible, and in the highest possible condition, provided that it remains obedient; and, moreover, a rook hawk frequently has far longer and more energetic flights than does the average game hawk.

In the case of short-winged hawks and buzzards you should make quite sure, before having them loose, that they will come out of trees. Quite a number of hawks will come 50 to 150 yd from a post to your fist, yet once you put them 15ft up in a tree they may well refuse to have anything to do with you. Eventually they change their minds and come down, but it certainly would be foolish to fly a hawk completely loose before you know what effect trees have on her behaviour. You can check on this while she is still on the dragged creance.

Pull her jesses really taut between your second and third fingers, as it were in the safety position, and make sure she is not sticky-footed on the glove. Face in the direction in which you wish the bird to go. Now bring your carrying arm back, so that it is in line with your shoulder but only slightly higher than your waist, at the same time swinging your body in the same direction from the hips. This is done quite gently. Now reverse the movement (this time bringing your arm forwards and upwards) accelerating as much as possible, until you are facing forwards. Now stop your swing as sharply as you can, and at the same time open your hand to release the jesses. This sudden stop will give the bird forward impetus, in much the same way that a passenger in a car is thrown forwards if the brakes are suddenly applied. This method of throwing a hawk off is applicable whether she is on the dragged creance or not, but she should never be thrown off at quarry in this fashion.

Where falcons are concerned you must ensure that if they overshoot the lure they will turn and come back to you, since every now and again you will come across one that flies straight on without a backward glance. One of my tiercels once did this – luckily I was in open country when it happened. He flew for well over a mile before stopping. Falcons can be tested for this, also, while still on the dragged creance.

Most falconers drop their hawks' weight a fraction for the first free flight. This is reasonable enough, since it ensures that extra bit of keenness, and will not harm the bird so long as it is not overdone.

Flying free

Let us assume that your hawk is well-manned, obedient and at the right weight; that she has had a bath or the chance of one, and that the weather is fine but not windy. Away you go. There is no need to alter your normal routine in any way. You can if you like take a pair of binoculars with you as an added safety precaution, but otherwise there is not much you can do that will be of any extra help. However, if you know a friendly falconer, you could ask him to come and stand on the sidelines. If you are flying a falcon and he happens also to have a similar bird in flying condition, ask him to bring it with him. For if your falcon should by any mischance get lost, flying another falcon will be the quickest way to attract her back, so long as she has not killed in the meantime. (This will not work with short-winged hawks; but for more of this see chapter 17 on lost hawks.)

When you fly your bird free for the first time, do not be surprised if she suddenly seems to be much faster. Now that the drag of the creance has gone she will have more speed and may well fly higher above the ground than hitherto.

If you are all set but the weather is not right then you would be wiser to delay matters. In a high wind a young falcon free of the creance for the first time feels the lift under her wings and may well go quite high without even meaning to. Not having flown much before, she will not be in full control as far as manoeuvring is concerned, and she may find it difficult to come back in to your lure. On a gusty day the wind may suddenly blow a bit harder just at the wrong moment, and she will be carried away. So remember the old falconers' saying: 'If the wind be high, do not fly.'

However, given that all the conditions are right, you should not run into any trouble the first time you fly your bird loose – although doubtless you will heave a sigh of relief when her jesses are safely in your hand once more and you have put on her leash and swivel. (You should also have a great feeling of satisfaction.) You are far more likely to lose her a few days later, when things have been going along spinningly and you feel just a little over-confident and fly her in too high a wind or at too high a weight; or, because you are so pleased at seeing her fly, you overdo things and have just one more go, when it would have been wiser to have stopped.

Stage two of your bird's training is now almost over, although there is really no point at which either training or manning can be said to be completed. Like people, hawks go on learning all their lives.

How you get your bird fit depends on what quarry you intend to fly her at. As I have already said, if you are going to fly at game you should never stoop your falcon to a swung lure. There are some falconers who do this, but I have found it to be a very great mistake. This is because the falcon, instead of climbing up to a good height when out hunting, will tend to go up only a short way and then circle round, waiting for the lure to be thrown out. But if you are going to fly a large falcon at rooks, crows or gulls (or a merlin at larks) then the swung lure is the ideal way to get her fit.

Swinging the lure

A lure has three uses. It lures or tempts the bird back to you. Properly swung, it exercises her. It also teaches her that her quarry is not just going to flyaway in a straight line and be caught easily, but is going to try to avoid her stoop in many different ways. Lure-swinging requires much practice and work on your part if you are to become really proficient at it. One could compare it with the way in which a matador swings his cloak. The closer he allows the bull to come to him, and the more fluently and smoothly he performs the different passes, the better he is.

Good lure-swinging is a delight to watch. It combines fluency of movement of arms and hands, feet and body, with perfect timing. There should be no jerkiness about it. The falcon should feel that if she flew just a little harder she would catch the lure, yet when she does so she still finds it eluding her by a fraction – so she tries harder still. She should enjoy it and should not become discouraged in any way, which means that you must watch her closely. If you see that she is beginning to tire then you must let her have her reward.

To learn how to swing a lure is extremely difficult. Breaking the different passes up into separate movements can make things easier. If you have played

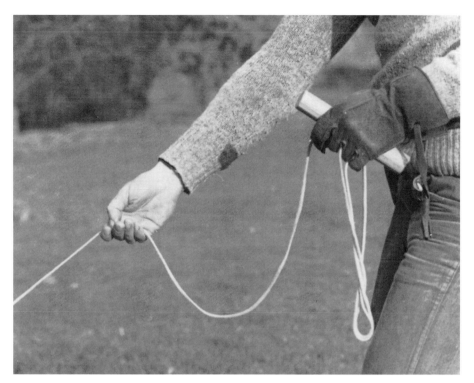

LURE SWINGING
76 The lure is just starting to swing towards the falcon. It is fully unwound; the stick is in the gloved hand. The line passed between the second and thrid fingers, is looped on the little finger and then once again between the finger and thumb. From there it runs across to the finger and thumb of the right hand and thence to the lure itself.

77 As the falcon approaches, the line is allowed to slide through the right hand until both hands come together. Just before the falcon reaches the lure the line is shortened by pulling with the left hand.

143

78–81 The lure is swung vertically, in a clockwise direction, so that it just clears the ground by your right foot.

tennis or squash then you will find that the way in which a lure is swung may remind you of some of the strokes. You will need to practise a great deal, first without the falcon, of course, and later with it. The mechanical side of lure-swinging should become automatic, so that you can concentrate entirely on the bird. It will take you some time before you become even reasonably proficient at lure-swinging, but obviously the more you practise the better you will get.

You already know how you should hold the lure. Now practise some simple lure-swinging movements. The lure should be swung clockwise in a vertical plane, completing a full circle just above the ground by your right foot. Swing it slowly, just fast enough to keep it turning. If you go any faster it will make no difference to the bird, but it will very soon give you a blister on your right forefinger. In fact it is advisable in any case when practising to protect the middle joint of this finger with sticking plaster.

Now imagine that your falcon is in a tree and that there is only a small patch of open ground where she could come down to the lure with ease. Practise throwing the lure out on to a predetermined spot on the ground. As you throw it out, the loops of spare line should peel off your little finger, and the lure line will be at its full length. (See figure 76.) If you throw the lure out too hard it will jerk as it reaches the full extent of the line, and will bounce back towards you. If you do not throw it hard enough, obviously it will not reach your chosen spot.

If your falcon refuses to come to the lure, then you must haul in the line, again gathering two loops of slack round the little finger of your gloved hand. Once more you are back in the position you first started in, as in figure 71.

Once your falcon is going loose to a lure just thrown out on the ground for her, you can begin to exercise her fully by stooping her to the swung lure (except in the case of a game hawk, as already discussed). Here again you must practise all the passes, first of all without the falcon. The more varied and difficult you can make your passes, the more the falcon's skill will increase, and this will be of the greatest help to her once she starts flying at quarry. For although no lure swinging ever reproduces all the tricks that her quarry will think up, it goes a long way to teaching your falcon at least to expect difficulties and to be prepared to try to do something about them. A falcon that has not had some sort of preparation for what lies ahead will not only disappoint you but will herself soon get discouraged and lack confidence in her powers of flight. This may result in your having difficulty in entering her at quarry at all.

The passes are varied, and some are easier than others. Probably the most difficult one to learn is the overhead pass – it is certainly the hardest to teach. The pass to the left is easier than the one to the right, but practice will soon get you into the way of doing either without any trouble. The simplest pass of all is the straightforward ground pass, where you throw the lure out full length on the ground and then, just before the falcon reaches it, jerk it towards you. This requires little practice, but you must not be content to leave it at this. In

82–89 PASS TO THE LEFT

82, 83 The falcon approaches. Take a step forward so that your weight is on your right foot. At the same time your left hand moves forward towards your right hand. The slack line previously between the two hands is pulled out through your right hand by the weight of the lure.

84 The falcon is almost on the lure. Your left hand, acting as an accelerator, pulls the line back through your right hand, so that the lure moves away in front of the bird.

85, 86 As the bird follows the lure through, turn towards her (i.e. to your left), pivoting on both feet.

87 The falcon flies on, and the swing continues.

88, 89 You have now turned through 180° and are still facing the bird. The vertical swing is resumed as before.

no time at all she will learn that the lure is suddenly going to move towards you, and she will then start to aim for the spot where she thinks you will jerk it to. You will then find her catching it every time, and you will then have to bluff her by pretending to jerk it away but not doing so. However, you will then have to lower the lure line, so that she does not hit it as she cuts in towards you. Pretty soon she will learn this trick (since lowering the line is a different movement from jerking it), will work out what is going to be the result of your movements, and will beat you again.

Study the series of photographs which illustrate the various other passes. These, with the accompanying captions, clearly explain the various movements which go to make up each pass.

Practice is the only thing that will make you perfect, and you will find you need to put in a good deal of time swinging a dummy lure, without a falcon, before the movements become automatic. A good dummy lure can be made by putting some sand in a small canvas bag (to give it the necessary weight) and attaching this to your lure line. Get one pass perfect before moving on to the next. Having mastered the second, go back to the first again. Try to alternate the two. You will probably find you get very muddled at first, but keep working at them and eventually you will find you are able to do all the passes whenever you want to.

Now imagine your falcon is in the sky, circling round you. Swing your dummy lure round slowly, always turning with your imaginary bird. Imagine

90, 91
(see over for caption)

that she has now decided to stoop – which side will you take her? It is always your decision, remember. Decide, and then carry it out. Now she is up again and is circling, and you are turning with her. Once again she is coming in; this time, pass her on the opposite side. Now try and speed up the whole process. Try, when you are practising on your own, not to let yourself get into any set rhythm, such as three swings and a pass, three swings and a pass and so on. You will soon realise when you swing the lure for your bird that timing is the essence of the whole thing. A falcon will not stoop at regular intervals – she may put in two stoops very quickly and then circle round for some time before stooping again. Once she starts to stoop you must be able to make up your mind very quickly indeed, and you may well have to increase the speed of your swing as she comes in, so as to get the lure in the right position at exactly the right split second.

It is worth remembering that even a comparatively unfit falcon may be stooping at between 40 and 50 mph, and that if she is stooping downwind she will have added speed, and will be coming in much more quickly than if she is stooping into the wind, which will slow her up. As she gets fitter and better muscled, too, her speed will increase. If she is stooping out of the sun, you will find it more difficult to judge at what moment to pull the lure away. All these are things which you will have to take into consideration.

You may well find yourself getting into bad habits which you will have to correct. Some of these are fairly common. I have already mentioned that if you

90–96 PASS TO THE RIGHT

The falcon has turned and is approaching again. This time your left foot moves forward, hands go forward and together, and the line is again pulled out in front of you. As your left hand pulls in the line and the falcon follows through, pivot on both feet, turning towards her (i.e. to your right). Once again you will have turned through 180, and you continue to swing the lure vertically as before.

97 The lure is swung up as if the falcon were about to take it in mid-air. If the right hand released the line now, the bird would catch the lure.

98 But at the critical moment the lure is pulled down sharply, and the falcon swings up overhead.

swing too fast (what I call propeller-type lure-swinging) you will soon get a blister on your forefinger. If you swing with too long a line, the lure will hit the ground. Shorten it, but not too much, or you will tend to swing with too short a line. To help to correct this, find the place where you should be holding the line (this will depend on your height and arm length) and with a needle thread a bit of coloured wool through the line at this point. After you have executed a pass, see if you are still holding the line in the same place.

Stooping to a swung lure

Your falcon will also need to practise, and you will both improve together. Kestrels will seldom stoop well, but tend to run a shuttle service from post to post, with a pass or two at the lure as they go by. One rarely sees a trained kestrel hovering, although as I have already said, they are superb at this in the wild. One way to induce a kestrel to hover is to take her, once she is flying free to the lure, to a hillside on a day when there is a breeze blowing up the slope. Put the bird down on a suitable perch at the top, walk away downhill and swing the lure. As she comes towards you, hide the lure. The breeze will give her height as she throws up above you, and she will start to hover while waiting for the lure to reappear. Later on she will learn to hover on windless days and over flat ground.

Lanners and luggers perform very well, but are slower than peregrines.

99 Throwing up the lure for the falcon to catch requires a certain amount of practice and timing on the falconer's part. If you let go of the stick, as illustrated, make sure that you are well away from trees or fences, as the bird will sometimes carry the lure some distance before landing on the ground.

Merlins are probably the most difficult birds to stoop to the swung lure, as they are so quick on the turn. It is of course much easier for a beginner to learn to swing a lure with a young, inexperienced bird that is itself learning, rather than with an older bird which will already be up to most of the tricks of the trade.

With a newly trained falcon it is most important not to keep her too long on the wing at any time, or she will get tired and go and sit in a tree or on some other convenient perch until she gets her breath back. This will quickly develop into a habit, and it is one that should be avoided at all costs. If her beak is open, if her pace slows up or she flies lower, these are sure signs that she is tiring. So you must judge for yourself when she has had enough, and let her have the lure at the next stoop. This you can do by throwing it out on the ground and letting her bind to it. She may cut over it, turn and cut again, and then bind to it, or she may grab it the first time. Whichever she does is not important. I like to see a falcon cut at the lure once or twice first, as this usually means she has style and is not losing speed but is making her cut fast and with good effect. (Sometimes a falcon will cut so hard that the lure lifts and then falls back again.)

When she binds to the lure, if she is going any speed at all, she will carry it with her at least some distance. This is why you need a heavier lure stick for larger falcons, as the weight slows them up and prevents them from going on too far. I have seen comparatively light lures, with no lure sticks at all, being carried for a very considerable distance indeed. There is no need for you to pull up the bird with a jerk when she takes the lure; the lure stick will be a satisfactory brake on its own, so let it go with her. Do not confuse her action in carrying the lure on with the bad habit of 'carrying' – it is only her own impetus which takes her on, and not any particular desire to carry off the quarry.

The alternative to throwing the lure out on the ground is to let the falcon catch it in the air. This is frowned upon by some falconers, and I have seen it stated that a falcon should never have the lure thrown up to her, since it is 'unnatural and unrealistic (no quarry being stooped at would or could perform such a manoeuvre)'. One can only assume that the writer of this had never seen a cunning old grouse leap up from the ground and go right over the falcon as she stooped at him. A crafty magpie will do much the same, and a rook will twist right round at the bottom of the stoop and throw up some considerable way into the air.

I personally think that you should teach your falcon to catch the lure in mid-air, since I have seen a falcon lost for good simply because her owner had failed to teach her this. He was standing in long heather at the time, and every time he threw the lure out on the ground it fell out of sight. The falcon was young and newly-trained, and perhaps not as keen as she should have been. By the time he had run to a bare patch of ground where she could see the lure, she had already become bored and had flown out of sight. The same thing can happen in long grass and particularly in clover. Whether or not you consider it unnatural to throw the lure up to the falcon, it still requires dexterity on her part to take it, and this, surely, is what you are trying to teach her. Again, see figure 99 for the correct method of throwing up the lure.

Each day you should increase the number of stoops that your falcon must put in before you allow her to take the lure. When she is capable of about 50 consecutive stoops without getting short of breath, then she is fit enough to have a reasonable chance at quarry.

Where short-wings and buzzards are concerned, lures can be exactly the same as for falcons, but they should be used as sparingly as possible. As I have already explained, it is preferable to have your short-wing coming to the fist.

Getting short-wings fit

To get a short-wing fit one cannot stoop her to a lure. Most falconers simply call their birds to the fist a few times each day. This is not really sufficient exercise to get a hawk properly fit, however, and such birds are likely to disappoint their owners when it comes to pheasant or partridge hawking.

One frequently reads such statements as 'A hawk should know no perch but her master's fist' or 'Never let your bird take stand in a tree' (though how to prevent her doing so is not explained) and 'On no account should goshawks be flown from trees at quarry'. This may be all very well if one has an unlimited supply of game at which to fly, but most austringers today are lucky to achieve half a dozen flights in a day. These flights will rarely be more than 100 yd of hard flying, and by the end of the day the hawk will only have flown 600 yd or so. This cannot be sufficient to keep a hawk fit, let alone bring it into top flying condition from an unfit state, and it is the main reason (combined with the small amount of flying time that most birds receive) why most short-wings often do not succeed at partridges or pheasants unless the slip is very close.

Flying a hawk for more than three or four trips in each training session can lead to disaster, as I have already said. And so you must do something better than this in order to get your bird fit to attempt the more exciting flights. Admittedly most flights with short-wings do tend to be fairly short, but all the same a fit bird will go an amazing distance, once she has confidence in her powers of flight. A really fit goshawk will take on partridges that rise about 100 yd or more distant, and will gradually overhaul them and put them into cover. Provided you have a good dog you can still emulate Bert, who in the early seventeenth century took over 80 partridges in about a month with a single goshawk.

I make my short-wings fit by putting them up into a tree, after giving them a few pecks at the pick-up piece to remind them who provides the food. Then I persuade them to follow me, rather like dogs out for a walk, from tree to tree along the hedges, always keeping an eye on them to make sure they are never very far away. By doing this I can walk two miles and my hawk can fly two miles, and we both keep fit.

100

It is not very difficult to get a hawk to do this. Put her up in a tree and walk away from her. When you think it is time she caught up with you, call her to fist or lure, but as soon as she gets close to you hide the food. She will swing past and up into the next available tree. Every so often leave the food there and reward her, so that she does not get bored with the proceedings. You can also use the dummy rabbit (see chapter 5 on tools and equipment) more at this stage, and you can make this more and more difficult for her to catch, once she gets used to chasing it, by pulling the dummy away sharply just before she reaches it, so that she must put on extra speed.

It is helpful at times to have an assistant for this, who can pull the dummy at an awkward angle to try to surprise the hawk. If you have a helper, you can also get him to hide behind a tree, a hedge, or even in a ditch and by pre-arrangement get him to throw out a dead bird, so that your hawk will become more vigilant, and quicker off the mark, as you progress. After a week or so of this kind of work your short-wing will be ready to be entered at quarry. She

101

will have a far greater chance of success than a bird which has been carried on the fist and called off a mere 150 yd or so four times a day.

Harris' hawks, Red-tails, Cooper's hawks and hawk-eagles can all be treated in the same way, although the big hawk-eagles will take a long time to learn and, consequently, to get fit. Indeed, I think that the main reason why most falconers have not had a great deal of success with hawk-eagles is that they are difficult to get fit. In the wild I think these birds 'still hunt' more than goshawks, just waiting for something to come unsuspectingly along. Certainly my old Changeable hawk-eagle takes quite a time to get fit again after moulting and is very slow off the mark at the beginning of the season. Yet I have caught 44 rabbits and a rather easy pheasant with this bird, in only eight evenings' flying. The bird visibly improved evening by evening and at the end was a really efficient, and at times spectacular flier, taking on slips at rabbits that broke cover a long way off down the hill, and pursuing them across the glen and up the other side.

Where sparrowhawks are concerned I do not think it is necessary to exercise them in this fashion, though it does no harm. They are such efficient birds that it is hard to tell if they are unfit; and as most flights with sparrowhawks are very close indeed, they probably do not need in any case to be as fit as the larger short-wings. If you do exercise them in the way I have described, they will soon come to realize what it is all about and will follow you from tree to tree.

Of course it often happens that while you are exercising a short-wing in this way you unintentionally put up suitable quarry; so you may well have a successful flight sooner than you expected. But do make sure that if you fly hawks in this manner, you still maintain discipline. There are some falconers whose enthusiasm for hunting makes them forget to keep their birds good to the fist or lure. They end up by only being able to get their birds back off a kill, or, if by luck the hawk takes stand very low down, by occasionally managing to entice it a short distance back to the fist. Such hawks are a nuisance, and usually get lost in the end.

Training to fly at game

As I have mentioned previously, there are very few people lucky enough to be able to fly large falcons at game in the proper manner, and if you are a beginner, it is unlikely that your first bird will be a large falcon. I repeat once again that if you have not the time and money necessary for successful game hawking, then you will be well advised to leave it strictly alone.

The main problem in the training of game hawks is teaching them to climb up high and then wait-on overhead while the game is flushed. This really is the only way to take game, since very few falcons can overhaul an old grouse or partridge from a standing start off your fist. When the falcon is released, before the game is flushed, there is no quarry in sight, and so she will have no incentive to climb up. This is what you must teach her to do, by some means or other.

There are many methods used to teach game hawks to wait-on; I have tried most of them and have had little success with any. Several of the methods used, although they do produce results, can encourage some very bad habits in falcons, which will lead to their being very easily lost. For instance, the old idea of allowing falcons to chase pigeons is, in my opinion, utterly and completely wrong. It leads to lost hawks only too easily and can wreck hawking wherever wild pigeons are common. The old falconers, when intending to fly eyasses at game, used to hack them first. Hacking, in my opinion, is not necessary at all and today one cannot afford to hack falcons in Britain – it would be far too risky. But, since it has other uses, I have dealt with it separately in chapter 18.

Let us assume that you have two young eyass falcons, both well-manned and good to the hood, which have been flying off the creance for a couple of days. They are coming to a lure thrown out on the ground, but they have not been stooped to a swung lure. (This is most important – as I have already said, it is much more difficult to persuade a game hawk to circle round, gain height and, eventually, wait-on, if she has been stooped to the lure. The swung lure discourages falcons from going up and indeed even stops them doing so.) By the time you have reached this stage in your eyasses' training it will be the end of July or the beginning of August. Now is the time to move to the grouse moor. If you have to travel far, give your falcons a day or two to recover after their journey. When they have done so, and are in the right condition, you can proceed with their training.

Normal daily procedure is as follows. First thing in the morning make sure they have cast and give them the chance to bathe, dry and preen. Get ready your pick-up pieces (one for each falcon), lure, and other equipment. Hood and weigh the birds and put them on the cadge. If you have anyone who can help you and will carry one of the birds on his fist, so much the better. Take the falcons, with your dog, onto the moor. Move as far as possible from any trees, fence posts, rocks or other places where a tired falcon might be tempted to have a rest. Now take whichever bird you think is the keenest and remove her leash and swivel. Keep your dog close in, since you do not want a point at this stage. Unhood the falcon, face her into the wind and let her go when she wants to. Do not throw her off – let her take off in her own time.

As soon as she has left your fist, take out your lure stick and unwind the lure line, but leave the lure itself in your bag, since it is most important that she should not see it at this point. She will probably circle round you, but if she starts to go off on her own you must whistle to her and try to make her turn back without showing her the lure. Only use the lure if she refuses to turn, and once she is on her way back hide it immediately.

She is certainly not likely to get up very high, and flying around will soon tire her, since at this stage she is not very fit. But if she does get up to any height at all, even only 30 ft, then shout to her (do not whistle) and throw the lure out on the ground where she can see it easily. Once she is on the lure (and she may well, if she has any style at all, cut over the top of it a few times before binding to it) make in to her slowly. Pick her up on the fist and give her a small reward; then take away the meat and hood her. If she does not gain any height while flying, but shows signs of tiring, shout and throw out the lure. At all costs try to prevent her perching anywhere, since, as I have said earlier, this will quickly become a habit with her if you do not. At no point at all during the proceedings must you stoop her to the swung lure. Simply allow her to take it on the ground.

Now change birds, giving the first one a rest while you go through exactly the same procedure with the second. You can give each falcon three to four sessions, with rests in between. After the last session, feed the birds up, first on the lure on the ground and finally on the fist. Then take them back home.

All this will take you some time, and you will soon realise that if you had more than three falcons to deal with you would not have enough hours in the day to manage them all properly.

Continue in the same way every day that the weather allows you to fly. Keep the falcons longer on the wing at each training session, so that day by day they become fitter. If at any time one of them gets up high, cut short the session, shout and let her have the lure. Do not expect too much at first – you may be lucky and have a bird that does get up high right from the start, but the odds are against it. You can sometimes help by getting your assistant to cast the bird off from some high ground, while you remain lower down in the valley; then, as the falcon flies over you, shout and throw out the lure. In this way she will gradually learn that height is desirable.

During all these training sessions you will of course have your dog with you. If it is not fully trained, you must be careful never to let it run in on the falcon while she is on the lure. But it should be brought close to her while she feeds from the lure so that they get accustomed to one another.

By the start of the grouse season your falcons should be keeping on the wing, circling round you, for five to ten minutes or so without getting tired. How high they go will vary with each bird. Even if they are only 30 to 40 ft up you are well on the way to success. If they start to rake away, then a whistle from you should bring them back without your having to show the lure. Birds tend to rake away more on windy days – be careful not to let them get too far off, because the grouse will be watching the falcon and will seize any opportunity that occurs to get up and fly in the opposite direction.

Assuming that your game hawk is now waiting-on, your rook hawk is putting in a good number of consecutive stoops to the swung lure, or your short-wing is flying a fair distance each day without tiring, you are now ready to move on to the final stage of training, and the object of the whole exercise so far – hunting.

previous page Hogson's Hawk Eagle. Used widely by Japanese falconers.

right Harris's Hawks in aviary (photograph by T. Cullen).

below Captive bred Kestrels on top of nest box.

opposite page Greenland phase of Gyr.

Goshawk on a pine tree by G.E. Lodge. Interestingly, Lodge painted this in Japan and signed it in Japanese.

right Icelandic phase of Gyr, looking for a ptarmigan which has put into cover, by G.E. Lodge *(copyright reserved)*.

above Redtail Buzzard (Redtail Hawk in USA) returning to the fist.

left Immature Peregrine on a Hoodie Crow.

opposite page Adult Peregrine on a cliff, by G.E. Lodge *(copyright reserved)*.

following page Sparrow Hawk on fist.

12 Flying Falcons Out of the Hood

If you intend to fly any of the large falcons out of the hood then you have the choice of several different types of quarry – rooks, crows, gulls, magpies and, at times, duck. You will not succeed in catching game with a falcon flown in this manner, for game birds fly too fast and she will not be able to overtake them. Quite apart from this the main object of flying falcons is to see good flights with stoops, and not just a stern chase.

In rook hawking the stoops are generally shorter than in game hawking, and tend to take place further away; but they are far more frequent, and so the flight is still just as exciting, though in a different way. In all cases open country is of course essential.

Before the Second World War the best rook hawking ground in Britain was Salisbury Plain, which was at that time mainly sheep pasture and by no means as flat as its name suggests. Apart from the Army ranges, the Plain is now vastly altered. After the war, cattle began to take the place of sheep and, since the Plain is very windswept in winter, shelter belts of trees were planted. Also the use of artificial fertilizers greatly increased the growing of corn crops there, and these had to be enclosed with wire fences. Wire fences are, to a rook, a crow or a magpie, a safe refuge from a falcon's stoop; they also mean that one can now no longer keep up with one's falcon on horseback, as was possible formerly (a falcon flies very much faster than a pack of foxhounds can run).

The increase in corn on the Plain has meant an increase in the number of partridges, and this in turn has made it very difficult for the falconer to obtain permission to fly his birds. (It is hard to convince a shooting man that a rook hawk will not take partridges, nor will it drive the game away.) The shelter belts of trees also provide cover for pheasants, so the austringer who hopes for permission to fly at rabbits will also have great difficulty in obtaining it. So, the last really good area of rook hawking country in England has been spoilt. There are, of course, other open areas in Britain, such as Dartmoor, Exmoor and Bodmin, and parts of northern England, Scotland and Wales; but in none of these places does one find rooks in sufficient numbers out in the open. Parts of Ireland are probably the only places left in the British Isles which are still really suitable for this sort of flight.

Rooks, crows and magpies will seldom take to the air and try to beat the falcon in fair flight if cover is near. Certainly you can still fly falcons out of the hood on Salisbury Plain, but the percentage of high, ringing flights you will get will be very small.

Rook hawking cannot start until August, since your falcons, if old, will not be through the moult, and if young, will not be fully trained until then. But it is at its best in the spring, when the rooks are stronger on the wing and the weather tends to be more windy. This tests the falcon's powers of flight to the full and makes the whole thing more exciting. But autumn rook hawking is not to be despised, for although some of the old rooks are moulting, and therefore easy to catch, you will find the young rooks evenly matched with your falcon, and, on occasions, quite capable of beating her. Some falconers fly the same falcons at rooks in the spring that they flew at game in the autumn. Personally I think this is a great mistake, for it is only too easy to spoil a good game hawk by doing this.

Once your falcon is stooping hard at a rook lure and does not run out of breath after, say, 50 consecutive stoops, you can consider her ready to go at a wild rook; 50 stoops sounds a large number, but it will take a remarkably short time. She will do far more than that if you want her to, but there is little point in it. It is just a simple way of measuring whether she is fit enough to have a fair chance at the average rook. If you fly her before she is properly fit, she will be most unlikely to catch anything. This will discourage her, she will have no confidence, and she may end up by refusing to fly at quarry at all.

As in all branches of falconry, the first few flights at quarry should be carefully selected so as to give your bird the greatest possible chance of success. Some years ago I discovered, by accident, a means of helping a new falcon at the start of her career. On one piece of ground where I could fly at rooks there was a small hawthorn bush which had spoilt a number of flights in previous years by providing cover for rooks, which would have gone up had it not been there. If you can, find a flock of rooks, or, better still, a single rook, near a small piece of cover like this, approach as near as you can; loosen the hood braces, but leave the hood on. The moment the rooks start to rise, off comes the hood and you raise your falcon into the air and cast her off. Then make for the cover yourself immediately. The rook that the falcon singles out will almost certainly go into it. The falcon should circle round, and if you are close at hand you will be able to chivvy the rook out for her.

Although the flight may not be anything spectacular at least she will have a good chance and, with skill and luck, may be successful. If she is, do not rush in to her; make in gently, help her by plucking some of the feathers out of her way, using your knife so that she can get at the rook more easily. Put her leash and swivel on while she is still on the ground, and then lift her on to your fist, with the rook, and feed her her normal rations. Bear in mind that freshly killed rook meat will put more weight on her than cold beef.

Do not be tempted to fly her again this day; it is better for a falcon at this stage to end her day's flying on a kill. Some falconers give their hawks a gorge (i.e. as much as they can eat) on their first kill. If you do this she will not be fit to fly the following day, and so she will have longer to forget how clever she was and how good fresh rook tasted. It has been said that falcons do not like eating fresh rook, and letting them do so will eventually put them off taking rooks, but I have never found this to be the case. The sooner you can fly again, the better, for now she has confidence she will try all the harder, having already been successful.

There is however a danger that your falcon can become so keen on hunting that you lose control, and eventually, of course, you will lose the falcon if you allow this to continue. A judicious degree of luring, particularly from long distances, combined with hunting, will produce a good rook hawk.

There is one thing that I think it is very important to mention here, and that is the use of bagged quarry. Most of the old books talk of using bagged quarry to get a bird started. I am told that abroad there are even falconry competitions in which bagged quarry is used. I feel very strongly indeed about this. Any falconer who uses bagged quarry at any time is doing something *utterly inexcusable*. It is simply an admission that he does not know how to train a falcon properly. In an official enquiry into field sports some years ago, it was agreed that falconry was the least 'cruel' of them all. But using bagged quarry is the quickest way to get the sport banned. The falconer who does so is risking the future of falconry, and the sooner this kind of thing is stopped everywhere, so much the better.

From close, easy slips you can progress to more distant ones, and then, instead of merely casting your bird off just as the rooks are getting up, try her at one on passage. If the rook is high up, it is best to let it get away a little, so that the angle of climb is less steep. An experienced falcon will take on a rook 150 ft up, a quarter of a mile away, and think nothing of it.

You can stalk rooks either in a car or on foot. If you slip your falcon from a car (a sunshine roof is a great help here) make sure you are going very slowly, otherwise she will have to battle against the wind made by the vehicle's movement. (If you are constantly rook hawking in the same area, it will only take about a week for the rooks to recognize your car as it approaches.) If you are stalking on foot, it is best to walk in quite boldly at a slight angle to the rooks, as if you were going to pass them on one side. Carry your falcon carefully, so that she need not flap her wings to keep balance, as this will immediately give the game away.

Falcons which have been fed through the hood are often a nuisance on such occasions; being keen they tend to hunt for food on your fist and tear at the glove. This unbalances them, and your stalk is then spoilt. Also such birds are often so impatient that it is very difficult to strike (undo) the hood braces, and when one succeeds in doing so they frequently flick the hood off in an ill-mannered way.

Always slip your falcon at rooks upwind. The higher the wind, the more the advantage seems to lie with the rook, but also the better the flight as a rule. It is often stated that falcons should not be flown once the wind reaches a certain speed (though as far as I know few falconers understand the Beaufort Scale or carry anemometers). I find this rather odd. Do such statements refer to wind speed at ground level, and do they take into account the fact that higher up the wind may be far stronger, and that individual falcons vary a great deal in their response to wind? Some birds enjoy flying in strong winds; others, particularly most sakers, are hopeless. You must try to find out what your particular falcons like, and then ask yourself just how far you are prepared to risk losing them. Also take into account the lie of the land, how many helpers you have, the chances of the weather worsening, and so on.

Never try to fly in mist or fog or falling snow, all of which are almost certain to lose you your hawk. She will disappear very quickly and even if she does kill, you will not see the flight. So you will gain nothing and stand to lose everything. However, once snow has fallen (providing it is reasonably easy to get about and there are no signs of another imminent fall) there is no reason why you should not fly; in fact, the flight is usually easier to follow. Snow will clog up a falcon's leg bells once she is on the ground, and if you are likely to be flying her much in these conditions it is a good idea to bell her tail. I used to fly a great deal at rooks and hoodie crows during the winter in the north of Scotland, and had some very enjoyable flying.

Carrion crows are more difficult than rooks, and Hoodie crows more difficult still. In Scotland one often finds the normal hoodie crow together with a bird that looks like a carrion crow (i.e. black all over) but that is obviously paired off with a hoodie, and this, if flown at, will act just like a hoodie. Ornithologists are of the opinion that the hoodie and carrion crows cross-breed, and in some books there are pictures of hybrids between the two species, showing a mixture of plumage.

Where crows are concerned you must be careful; occasionally so with rooks. They will sometimes gang up on a falcon which has caught one of their number, and can damage her if the falconer does not get in quickly. On two or three occasions I have had falcons fly ravens. They never succeeded in catching one, but the flights were high up and very exciting to watch. However, a friend of mine did catch one once, in Ireland. Ravens are protected throughout Great Britain. Jackdaws are often found in the company of rooks, and may occasionally be caught, but they are very agile birds and unless they are right out in the open they are rarely taken. Wild peregrines seldom seem to take any of the crow family, though I have found the remains of *Corvidae* in some eyries. Probably the wild peregrine soon learns the danger involved in tackling these birds, and leaves them alone.

At the start of a flight rooks will usually fly upwind, if no cover is available; but once the falcon gets above them they will nearly always make for the nearest cover downwind. One should be prepared for this; in the days of the Old Hawking Club a number of lookouts used to be positioned in a line across country down-wind of the flying area in order to mark a kill and so prevent falcons being lost. Obviously it is unlikely that you will be able to afford the luxury of lookouts. It is often wiser to stay where you are, rather than to go up-wind, and should the flight then turn down-wind it is probably better to stand still and to use binoculars than to try to follow. You are more likely to lose sight of your falcon while you are running.

All the crow family are exceedingly cunning. I once flew a falcon at a hoodie crow, a good mile from the nearest trees. At no time could my falcon get in a stoop at him, for he flew quite slowly down a road, dodging in and out of the telephone wires the whole way to cover. One crow I flew at in Scotland took refuge in the gentlemen's lavatory at the local railway station and the falcon, being a lady, was unable to follow him. But rooks and crows also vary a great deal in flying ability. Some will take to the air and give a high, ringing flight even when there is cover close at hand; others, seemingly spellbound at the appearance of a falcon, are easily caught. One such was a rook I once came across who, as soon as the falcon was cast off, fell off his fence-post onto the ground, like a Victorian lady in a swoon.

It is important to get a falcon entered to rooks, or any other quarry, as soon as she is fit; otherwise the quarry is, in many cases, older and wiser, and also the falcon can easily have too much luring and become 'lure-bound'. A typical example of this was a falcon that I should have entered in early August but, because I was using her for filming, did not get a chance until September. Day after day I flew her at rooks – single rooks, rooks in pairs, flocks of rooks; rooks close by, rooks in the middle distance, rooks sitting and flying. She ignored them all, simply circling round me waiting for the lure.

However I persisted, and after some eight to ten days of frustration I found a small flock of rooks close to a road where it ran through a cutting. I cast her off over the top of the bank and immediately ducked down so that I was out of her sight. I waited, expecting her to come circling back overhead looking for the lure. When she did not appear I looked over the top, to see her sitting on one of the rooks a short distance off. Presumably because she could not see me she had decided that a rook was the next best thing to my lure. After this she never looked back, since success had given her the confidence she needed, and over the next seven weeks she took 88 rooks and crows.

A number of the flights were poor, since there were far too many wire fences about, under which most of the rooks took refuge; but we had a few high ringing flights from rooks who thought they could beat the falcon in the air. All 88 birds were taken before 8.30 in the morning, since I had to be at work by 9 o'clock. (It is quite simple to condition a hawk so that she will fly at any time convenient to you.) Then, as the winter drew in and the early mists stopped morning flying, I tried her a few week-ends at rooks, the only time I could spare. But she soon became unfit, and I had to go goshawking instead.

When flying peregrines at gulls one must realise that cover, to a gull, is not trees and bushes, but water. However, you still need open country to be able to follow the flight. The bigger gulls are nowhere near as manoeuvrable as the smaller ones, and this in fact turns out well for British falconers, since common and black-headed gulls are both protected species, while the herring gull and the two black-backs are not. I have only once caught a great black-backed gull with a peregrine, but herring gulls are comparatively easy quarry and it is not uncommon to catch a lesser black-backed gull.

The late Gilbert Blaine used to fly a cast of tiercels at common gulls (before they were protected) with success. But I think that tiercels flown at the bigger gulls would not be able to handle this quarry on the ground where a large gull can do a lot of damage with its beak. Most hawking of this sort was done with passager peregrine falcons caught in Holland, but trapping there ceased in 1928.

I had a very badly battered passager peregrine from India once, and I had to do a considerable amount of imping before she was even presentable. She was quite small compared with the Scottish eyasses I had at the time, but she certainly knew all the answers. I flew her at rooks, hoodies and gulls, and she went equally well at all of them – rather surprisingly, since one would not imagine that her quarry in India would have resembled them in the least. But she never hesitated, even in her first attempts as a trained bird. She would appear to pay little or no attention to the quarry; indeed, on her first flight I thought she was not interested, and from the way the quarry behaved it obviously thought the same. I think she flew in this way deliberately to make it appear uncertain as to whether she was hunting or just having an afternoon outing. (Most birds, and indeed most falconers, can tell at once whether a hawk is out to hunt or simply fooling around, since she will fly in a completely different way.) But once she had gained height she soon showed that she meant business, and the rest of the flock scattered to safety, shouting the odds, as she singled out her choice.

However, her real merit did not show until the bottom of the first stoop. Usually crows and gulls, if they have any height, will drop down in order to avoid a falcon's stoop, and when the falcon is closing fast they start to dodge. Most falcons will try to follow their twists and turns. Sometimes they are successful, but more often than not the quarry's evasive action pays off, and also makes the falcon lose speed as she tries to follow. This particular falcon never lost speed trying to follow the quarry when it used these tactics at the bottom of the stoop; she just went on flying, so that when the quarry threw up she did so too, and having more speed was able to rise further. At the point where the quarry was losing flying speed and had to get on an even keel to avoid stalling, she was able to grab it from below at the precise moment when, due to lack of speed, it was unable to take any more evading action.

She was a very lethal falcon, and I lost her far too soon for my liking. One day, when she caught a herring gull out of my sight, a farm labourer threw stones at her and chased her off, and I never got her back. I wonder what he would have said if someone had chased him off his dinner.

When I trained the falcons and falconers for the Royal Naval Air Station, HMS Fulmar, at Lossiemouth in the north of Scotland, we flew far more at gulls than at rooks or crows. Of course this was not proper falconry in the generally accepted sense of the word; that is, we were not out to see good flights or to catch something to eat. The object was to keep the duty runway clear of all birds, in order to avoid 'bird strikes' (i.e. planes running into flocks of birds, which can cause immense damage, and even loss of life to crew and passengers). We used peregrines, for they are the only birds, except, possibly, for prairie falcons, capable of doing this work. Lanners, luggers and sakers have been tried by others, and have proved useless under the conditions imposed by the job. We soon found that even tiercel peregrines were not good enough, since if left on the wing too long they tended to draw in gulls, and were mobbed by them. But the falcons were extremely efficient, and during the first few months the better of our two accounted for 47 head, mainly gulls. The local gull populace soon learned to clear off in haste when they sighted our hawking wagon.

When the experiment was first tried out we somewhat naturally met with a certain amount of opposition from some of the officers, who did not believe it would work and did not fancy having a bunch of crazy falconers let loose on their airfield. This opposition had to be overcome. Luckily there was a disused airfield close by, where we could practise, and when I considered that our team was ready we laid on a demonstration to which we invited our doubting friends and the Press.

Usually this sort of thing backfires, everything goes wrong and one is left looking quite foolish. However, for once everything went according to plan. The onlookers assembled, we gave them a briefing as to what we were trying to do and invited them to look at a large flock of gulls that were conveniently sitting on the runway in what would have been the worst possible place had a plane been about to take off. I suggested to the pressmen that a few photo graphs of the gulls would be a good idea, as they could then follow them up with a shot after we had dispersed them. One of the naval falconers I had trained then cast off the best falcon and in a matter of seconds the gulls had gone, apart from one large herring gull which the falcon (cheered on, to my delight, by the officer whom I considered to be the leader of the opposition) caught in mid-air after a brief but exciting chase. The whole thing took under five minutes, and was really most impressive.

In southern England gulls so often occur in mixed flocks with rooks that it might well be difficult to persuade a falcon to stick to gulls alone; but in Scotland they are frequently found on their own, and so this problem does not arise. Very often the great black-backed gull can be found right out in the middle of moorland.

I found my falcons all ate gull meat quite happily, although the small downy feathers tended to make it hard for them to break into the flesh. This can usually be overcome with a little help from the falconer.

Magpie hawking is quite a different affair. Here the onlookers must be pressed into service, to help keep the magpie away from cover or to drive him out if he does get in. Whatever cover there is must be small; the magpie will be impossible to shift out of anything sizeable.

It is a very clever falcon that manages to take a magpie single-handed, for although magpies are slow fliers they are extremely crafty and difficult to catch. So often I meet with falconers who tell me that their bird nearly caught a magpie – 'missed it by inches', they say, not realizing that this is exactly what the magpie intended. When hard-pressed, magpies will drop onto the ground; they are past masters at playing last-across, and it is only by a split-second jump at the critical moment that they avoid the falcon's stoop. By repeating this manoeuvre again and again they gradually work their way to cover. Just as the falconer thinks his falcon is going to catch a magpie single-handed, the quarry disappears into cover, and once there, is extremely hard to dislodge.

Magpie hawks start off being flown out of the hood, but they must also do a fair amount of waiting-on if they are to be successful. This is because they must be on the wing, waiting for the field to drive the magpie out of cover once he has reached it. Almost any cover serves as a refuge for magpies; they will even go into a flock of sheep and, when you move the flock, will cling to a sheep and travel with it.

Ireland or Spain are good places for magpie hawking. Although there are plenty of magpies in England they are generally found in unsuitable country for flying falcons; they can be taken with short-wings, but this is an entirely different type of flight. A cast of lannerets would be ideal at magpies. Male luggers, too, should do quite well at this flight. I think they are more manoeuvrable than peregrines, because of their smaller size, and this makes up for their lack of speed; given a chance, luggers might very well prove better than expected in this field.

The point of flying a cast of falcons at a magpie is that as the quarry jumps away from one pursuer, he runs into the other. A cast that flies well together is most impressive, each falcon taking it in turn to stoop while the other is getting into position again, like two men driving in a post with a sledgehammer. The timing must be perfect or things are apt to go very much awry. When flying a cast of falcons two falconers are essential. The birds should be used to flying together, otherwise they may well 'crab' (that is, one may catch the other). This can lead to disaster in more than one way, since the falconers are then likely to fall out with one another. I think eyasses are more prone to crab, since they tend to be more inclined to jealousy than passage hawks, but this has been known to happen in the case of passage hawks as well. Another problem that can arise is that one falcon may be flying the intended quarry well, but will give up because the owner of the second bird is having to use his lure to avoid losing her. And certainly both falconers should make in quickly to avoid any bickering between the cast when on the kill.

Flights at herons and kites, once considered by far the most spectacular of all, are now quite out of the question in Britain. Both species are protected, and the kite is extremely rare. Also the country needs to be even more open, since such flights might sometimes go for very considerable distances.

Twice I have had a falcon tackle a buzzard, when she was already in the air

and there was nothing I could do to stop her. However, we did not infringe the
Bird Protection Act, as on both occasions the buzzards escaped. The falcon
beat them in the air after an exciting chase, and bound to them, but after
tumbling earthwards (on one occasion for quite a long way) decided to break
off the engagement and released her hold.

My uncle, the late Captain C.W.R. Knight, had a tiercel that was intended
for rooks but ignored all our efforts at this quarry. (Few tiercels seem to like
rook hawking, though some take well to it.) He would have made an excellent
partridge hawk, for he mounted well without any encouragement from us.
High up he would at times attract the attention of kestrels, who seem to be
over-curious at times, and I regret to say that he took several of these before we
finally lost him. There are several past records of peregrines flying merlins and
sparrowhawks; but it is to be hoped that few falconers these days would wish
to fly at such quarry.

Duck hawking can be done in two different ways. You can fly your falcon
out of the hood as the duck get up, so that a stern chase then develops and can
go on for a very long distance, depending upon how far away the next stretch
of water is. If it is a very long way off the duck may decide it is too far, and
double back to the place they came from. It is very hard to flush duck once they
are in the water. Even mallard, which do not normally dive, will do so time and
time again. When hard pressed by a falcon, duck will drop into water from a
considerable height, the falcon stooping after them and very often getting wet
from the column of water that shoots up as the duck dives in. A lot of falcons
dislike stooping over water, but some do not seem to mind.

You can, alternatively, use a falcon trained to wait-on, and try to flush the
duck under her. If they are on a large sheet of water you will find it virtually
impossible, even with a large number of helpers and dogs. On the other hand,
from small ponds in open country you can get some very exciting flights; but
this sort of situation is by no means common.

Wild peregrines take a lot of duck, and peregrines that winter round an
estuary feed mainly on wildfowl and waders, such as curlew, whimbrel, sand-
pipers and so on. But to fly a trained falcon near such a place would be asking
for trouble, since she might very easily go across the water and leave you
stranded.

Very few peregrines will touch fur, although they are sometimes flown at
desert hares in North Africa and Saudi Arabia. Why they dislike taking
mammals I do not know; gyrs, sakers, prairie falcons and luggers certainly
take them, even seeming to prefer them. Some lanners take small mammals
and even lizards, depending on what is available in their own locality.

Obviously I have not been able to cover in this chapter all the eventualities.
No book can do this. You must build up experience as you go along, and you
must not be surprised if you come across falcons that do not conform to the
normal pattern. As I have said earlier, all living things are individuals, and if
some did not occasionally break what natural historians call the 'behaviour
pattern' then we would not have evolution.

13 Flying Short-Wings

If you can fly your short-wing for half an hour or more each day, she should be reasonably muscled up after a week or two; so that stage three of her training will be over quite quickly. As Mr Jorrocks said after the first heavy frost: 'Good, the dahlias are dead. Now we can go 'unting.' Harris' hawks, red-tails and others of the Buteo genus will perhaps need a little more flying, especially at the dummy, to get into the swing of things. It will depend very much on your individual bird and on how much time you can spend on her.

The hawk should have been accustomed to your dog during training. If she is not used to a dog, on no account take one out with you when you first start hunting, for this could well lead to disaster. Take one or two friends with you, if you like, but not too many. They should be people who understand that this will only be a trial trip; if they are falconers then so much the better. Try to plan your flying in advance for this occasion. Time spent in reconnaissance is seldom wasted, and you will give your hawk a better chance of success if you know the places where you are most likely to find quarry, and the places that you should avoid (large woods, fields that are being worked by tractors, and so on). You and your helpers can be armed with beating sticks, but the hawk must be used to them and the beaters should not be over-enthusiastic – a gentle tapping is all that is needed, not a mad thrashing of bushes.

By now you will have decided whether to hunt your hawk from the fist or out of a tree; you can, of course, do a little of both. When flying her from the fist, remember that the hawk is much quicker than you at seeing things. I think a lot of falconers tend to hold on to their birds until they themselves have seen what it is that the hawk is bating at, simply because they are afraid that if she goes into a tree it may take them some time to get her down. (If this is the case, they should not even be flying her loose yet.) If you are not going to let your hawk go until you have seen the quarry yourself then most probably you will be too late and the hawk will have bated off your fist and be hanging upside down. This is why I like to let my hawks fly at any time they feel like it, once we are on the field of operations. If I break this rule I often find that I regret it. Very often your bird will go off and it will take some time before you yourself actually see what she is flying at. There are times when she may disappear into a hedge or long grass and catch something that you never even saw at all. In time you will come to recognize at a glance the difference between a hawk that is flying for fun and one which is hunting.

I remember the first time that I ever took out a passage gas. She was still on a dragged creance. Suddenly she took off, although neither I nor my companion could see anything. She went low and fast across the field, swung up into a tree in the hedge, touched a branch for a fleeting second and then dropped down into the hedge. Still we had seen nothing; but she had caught a stoat.

A few days later we went out again with her to a different place. This time she was loose. It was fairly open country, and as we came into the first field a covey of partridges rose and went off over the far hedge. The gas bated, but I kept hold of her. 'You can't catch them at that distance,' I told her. (She looked rather annoyed.) We went on and found nothing, and it began to get late. On the way back, another covey got up in front of us, but these were even further away; later we calculated their distance at about 135 m (150 yd). I let her go and she went immediately, disappearing over the top of a rise in front of us. 'She hasn't a hope at that distance,' I said. We ran to the top of the rise and looked around. I expected to see her close by in a tree, but there was no sign. I looked further afield and there she was, having gone down the hill and half-way up the side of the next rise, sitting on a fence post. I walked over to her, and was about to hold out my fist, when up flew a partridge at my feet, and at once the rest of the covey rose all round me. The hawk had marked them down and settled right beside them, but could not actually spot any of them. As they rose she was off the fence post and grabbed the one nearest to her.

This was my first introduction to a passage gas. All my previous goshawks had been eyasses, and although I had caught the odd partridge and pheasant with them, they would rarely try any long slips. If they did, they soon gave up and sat in a tree. But this particular passage bird had obviously lived, and successfully hunted, in game country. Hares she refused to try at all, even though one day I had her up in a tree with a hare standing up on its hind legs directly below her. Still she was utterly uninterested. I think that like most wild goshawks she had come into contact with hares before she was trapped. Probably she had been buck-jumped off a few and had wisely given them up for good.

Hare hawking seems to have a great attraction for beginners, possibly because a hare is a big thing to show people, to impress them with your hawk's prowess. But personally I would rather take a pheasant or a partridge than several hares. If you must fly at them then I feel that a Bonelli's eagle or one of the hawk-eagles is better than a gas, which is not really strong enough to hold a hare. Some of the big red-tailed buzzards have done well at hares, too. I myself feel that hare hawking is a boring affair, only worth considering if there is nothing else to fly at.

My passage gas would go any distance at all after game, and would stick to quarry like glue. She was not fast enough to overtake and catch game unless it rose up very close to her, but she would tag along behind it until it put into cover, and then she would wait there. At that time I had no dog, and so we caught comparatively little, but we had flight after flight, sometimes over amazingly long distances. (I found later on, with subsequent passage goshawks, that she was nothing out of the ordinary.) Once I had a pointer again we really began to catch a good deal of game with comparative ease. Without a dog you will have a lot of difficulty finding game, once the hawk has flown it into cover; you have very nearly to step on it, in many cases, before it will get up.

So – if your hawk wants to go, let her. If she kills, you will be pleased, and if she misses and goes into a tree, then it will be good practice for you, and for her, to bring her down to the fist. The more flying she gets like this (whether she kills or not), the more she is being exercised and the more she is getting into the habit of returning to you. All this is important. It does not matter if she is still on a dragged creance – she may miss some quarry because the creance gets caught up, but at least she is practising and getting exercise, and you are having fun and learning too. And all the while your bird is still being manned, and is enjoying it.

Goshawks flown at game birds vary enormously. Wild hawks very often tend to the same quarry most of the time; or they may have previously lived in an area where there was no quarry of the sort at which you want to fly. So it is quite possible to have two passage goshawks, one of which is very keen on ground game but ignores pheasants, while the other is the exact opposite. Some are exceptionally keen to fly at what may seem to you to be quite the wrong kind of game. The call of a jay will make some passage goshawks sit up and take notice at once, but others will completely ignore it.

Short-wings are often described in books as being sprinters, and not long distance fliers at all. If you have an eyass goshawk and can only fly at weekends then this tends to be true, but if you can fly her more often she will soon become as good as a passage bird. A passager that has already caught pheasants in the wild will have learnt that although she may not be able to overtake the pheasant, if she persists she may very likely catch it as it puts into cover. Pheasants often land outside cover and then run into it, and this is where a gos frequently captures them. Once she learns she can keep up with partridge or pheasant she will fly for very long distances indeed; a quarter of a mile or more is not unusual, and as long as you are able to keep your gos in sight and go and help her with the pointer, you will find yourself having flights that will surprise you.

From all this it will be obvious that fitness is just as important to a short-wing as it is to a falcon, if you want to get the best from your bird. But whereas short-wings will still perform reasonably well when not absolutely fit, falcons when laid up for only a few days become completely out of condition, will refuse to fly any but the easiest quarry, and are very disappointing indeed.

There are many falconers who are very scathing about flying goshawks at moorhens – 'Far too easy', they say. Moorhens can be easy, it is true, but they can also be quite tricky on occasions. However, generally a gos has a good chance of catching them, and as you do not want a very difficult flight for your hawk on her first outing, moorhens are quite a suitable quarry at which to enter her.

I had a female gos once that had been in a zoo for a long time before she came to me. She was very sulky at first and it took me a long time to train her; and when I finally got her flying loose she seemed to have lost all idea of hunting. I gave her an easy chance at a number of moorhens running into a small brook under some trees, but she refused to look at them. However, as the last one disappeared from sight she left my fist and flew towards the trees, where she pitched on a branch. I left her there, hoping she might drop down onto one of the moorhens, and after a short time she suddenly dived out of the tree. When she did not reappear I and my companion walked over to see if perhaps she had caught one. At first we could not find her, but then we suddenly saw her, wings outstretched, floating in the water. I scooped her out to find that she was still tightly gripping a teal she had caught!

Incidentally, moorhens are very good to eat, both for hawks and humans, but they should be skinned first. For some unknown reason, hawks that eat moorhen skin seem to be thrown out of condition; and where human beings are concerned, the skin is distasteful when cooked. To keep moorhens from getting dry during cooking, it is best to wrap them in bacon and baste them frequently. Buttered cooking foil would probably be a good substitute for the bacon, and you would not then need to baste so often. My father once took my uncle and myself to lunch at a well-known London club. Golden plover were on the menu, but when they appeared my uncle pointed out that they were very curious plover, as they had moorhens' feet – however, other less observant club members were happily eating them, quite unaware of the deception!

Some falconers believe that if you start a gos or sparrowhawk off at small, easy quarry, such as moorhens or sparrows, the hawk will not take larger quarry later on. In my opinion this is quite incorrect. Once a hawk starts killing it gives her an immense amount of confidence and she will generally go on from strength to strength. Some hawks become so keen on hunting that their discipline suffers and they become bad at returning to their owners. This must not be permitted, and their weight should be brought down a little until they behave themselves, for a disobedient bird should not be tolerated on any account. Later, when they have learnt both to hunt and to return, their weight can be put up once more.

Many passage and haggard goshawks (and sparrowhawks too), regardless of how well-manned they may be, will often freeze as you approach them on a kill. That is to say, they remain utterly motionless, neither plucking nor eating. When they do this, their bells are silent, and if they are in very thick cover it can be extremely hard to find them, even though they may be only a short distance away from you. I and two companions were out one day with a gos, and we found a dead rook, which had been freshly shot. To encourage the hawk, who was fairly new, one of us threw the rook high in the air. The hawk went straight off, bound to it and carried it into a tall wide, overhanging hedge. We knew almost exactly where she had gone with it, but her camouflage was so good, and she froze so completely, that it took the three of us over ten

102, 103 Changeable hawk eagle watching a moorhen from a willow. The moorhen escapes by diving and the eagle lands in the water ....

104 . . . but rows herself to the shore.

minutes to find her. I am sure this freezing habit is instinctive, and protects a wild bird from being spotted on a kill. Probably many a gamekeeper has walked straight past the scene of a kill without ever seeing the hawk at all.

When rabbits are not lying out, you can go ferreting with your hawk. If you have white ferrets, and not the polecat variety, and get the hawk used to them in advance by having their hutch and run in her view, she will not try to catch them when out hunting. I bolted a white rabbit one day and my gos refused to fly it because of its colour, since she associated it with the ferrets. At the start of the season it is too early in the year to begin ferreting, and it is best left until the leaves are off the trees and the vegetation has died down, so that one can see the rabbit holes more easily. When hawking with ferrets you should go quietly and not stamp about on top of the burrows, so that the rabbits will not be alert to danger and will therefore be more likely to bolt well. But very large warrens are difficult to work with a hawk, since more often than not the rabbits will not leave the warren, but come up out of one hole and then pop straight down the next.

Ferrets must be really tame and easy to pick up and handle. You should be able to curl your ferret into a ball and toss her over the hedge for your assistant to catch. If you cannot do this sort of thing then you have not trained her well. Gills (females) are more often used than hobs (males) since they are smaller and can therefore go down smaller holes. I like to feed my ferrets half their daily ration in the morning before taking them out hunting, since they are not then so likely to lie up. Incidentally, I have often wondered why so many ferret owners feed their animals entirely on bread and milk. Although ferrets will eat bread and milk, this is not their natural diet – they are meat-eaters, and were it not so they would not chase rabbits and rats for you – and they do not do particularly well on it.

I suppose that people have been arguing over the respective merits of male and female goshawks ever since man first started to train them. All one can say is that if you take two birds of prey of the same species, the bigger one (usually the female) will most probably be the faster over long distances. But speed alone is not the only desirable quality in a hawk, and in the end one's prefer-ences can only be governed by one's experience of individual hawks.

One can safely say that female goshawks have a better chance of holding big quarry (such as brown hares) by virtue of their greater weight and larger feet. But a tiercel gos is quite capable of taking mountain hares and rabbits. He will be at a slight disadvantage where taking cock pheasants is concerned, but his success at them will also depend upon whether he has learnt to hold their front, rather than their tail, end. (Pheasants have a very thick layer of upper tail coverts, and many a gos has helped a pheasant towards an untimely moult.) Much as I admire Bert's *Treatise of Hawkes and Hawking*, I cannot agree with him that female goshawks are always to be preferred to the males.

No matter how carefully you condition your bird, there will be times when you may have difficulty with her, either because she is a little overweight or is just being temperamental. A goshawk that refuses steadfastly to come down out of a high tree (particularly on a cold winter's day) is a nuisance; and if there are any onlookers she soon becomes an embarrassment as well. You can resort to various tricks to get her down – for instance, tying your lure to the creance instead of the lure line, hiding it in long grass, brambles or the like, and then suddenly jerking it out beneath her when you are the full length of your creance some 25 yd away. This may well bring her down with surprising alacrity. You can also try throwing the lure out towards her, leaving it on the ground, and then walking off and watching from a distance. Also, a gos that has been trained to follow you from tree to tree will probably do so, from force of habit, if you simply walk away from her, and by and by she will probably perch lower down in another tree, from which it will be easier to get her down. Make sure that anyone who is with you keeps well out of the way at such a time; it may simply be the presence of a stranger that is making the hawk uneasy. If she still refuses to come down, you may have to resort to one or other of the devices mentioned in chapter 17 on lost hawks.

If you are flying along a river bank, make sure you know where the nearest bridge is, or you may find yourself having to swim, or at best to wade, in order to retrieve your hawk. This is certainly not to be recommended as a winter pastime.

Buzzards and hawk-eagles are generally flown in exactly the same way as goshawks. Although they can never be as efficient in performance, they are certainly not to be despised, as is shown by the increasingly large numbers of falconers who fly them. Some people even prefer the larger species, such as red-tails and ferruginous buzzards, to goshawks, since they are so much less temperamental.

Certainly the first Red-tail I had was a great success. Although she was a bit on the lazy side she gave us a lot of fun on her favourable days. One thing she really enjoyed was snakes. Whether Red-tails take a lot of snakes in the wild I do not know, but this one certainly knew how to go about it. She would puff herself out all over when catching a snake, presumably as an automatic safety precaution against being bitten, since the snake would strike at the feathers, and not reach the bird at all. (Honey buzzards also do this, when digging out the nests of bees and wasps.) This Redtail also became very clever at taking moorhens over water, and occasionally we caught pheasant and the odd mallard with her. Another Red-tail of mine will wait-on for short periods – about ten minutes at the most – and falconers in America report the same of Ferruginous buzzards; and this certainly cannot but increase their potential as good falconry birds.

Buzzards and hawk-eagles have the advantage over most *Accipiters* of re-maining tame for quite a long time, even when they are not being handled. A goshawk can become really wild if she is not handled for a period of about ten days, but you will not have this problem with a buzzard. Although strictly speaking it is not absolutely necessary to make them to the hood (their phlegmatic temperament makes them far less jumpy than most short-wings), it is not a bad idea to do so. One of my red-tails was so good to the hood that she would even go to sleep with it on, sitting on my fist with her head tucked under her wing, and only the plume showing in the middle of her back. She looked rather like the headless lady in the 'Silent Woman' public house sign.

As I have said earlier, another advantage that buzzards have over short-wings is that they are far less likely to get lost. Whereas a gos will spot something three fields away and set off after it, a buzzard is far less inclined to do this, and the danger of her getting out of your sight is smaller.

One thing to watch out for when training buzzards, but perhaps especially the eyass common buzzard (passage and haggards of this species are virtually useless for falconry): get them entered at quarry at the earliest possible opportunity, otherwise they very easily become lure-bound.

As I have already said, sparrowhawks are definitely not birds for beginners, but the rules for flying them apply to all small short-wings, and to deal with each species separately would simply be repetitive. If you are intending to progress to a sparrowhawk after having already successfully flown a gos, you will find that hunting with her is in many ways superior to hunting with a larger short-wing.

If you are interested in the quality of your flights, rather than the amount of game you bring home for the larder, then a sparrowhawk will be a most rewarding bird for you to fly. To be sure, trained sparrowhawks will take fairly sizeable birds on occasions – I have caught teal, partridges, pheasants and magpies with mine – but they really excel in flights at smaller things, such as starlings and blackbirds, which are far more difficult quarry and which test their speed and agility to the full. Sparrows on the whole are too easy a quarry for female sparrowhawks, but you will get good flights at them with shikras and with muskets – although in my opinion muskets are best left alone, even by experienced falconers.

Moorhens are a possible quarry, but I would avoid flying at them, as a sparrow hawk is not strong enough to carry a moorhen for any distance, and may well be pulled down and drowned if she binds to it over water. You may wonder why she does not let go when she finds herself being dragged into the water, but sparrowhawks are very sticky-footed, and seem to have great difficulty in releasing their hold quickly. In fact, when you have called your sparrowhawk back to the fist, rewarded her and removed the meat, do not attempt to fly her again until her grip has completely relaxed, otherwise you may find her bating at the quarry and trying to take you with her. (It is worth noting that ospreys are sometimes picked up drowned with their feet still firmly fixed in fish too big for them to carry, so this sticky-footedness is not confined to sparrowhawks alone.)

A quarry that female sparrowhawks seem to be fond of taking is the Little owl. Although little owls are protected, there is not much you can do to stop your hawk once she has taken off after one, but it is frequently quite easy to remove the owl from her grip unharmed, and to release it when she is not looking.

The main difference between flying a sparrowhawk and a gos is that it is very much easier to find flights for the former, since few land-owners will refuse you permission to fly at starlings and sparrows.

One rarely gets very long flights with sparrowhawks. They are essentially sprinters, and in the wild they kill mainly by surprising their quarry, either by nipping over a hedge or coming fast round the edge of a wood, and catching it before it has time to reach cover. I once happened to see a wild sparrowhawk come over a hedge into a mixed flock of sparrows and starlings; she caught a starling on the ground, bent down and dislocated its neck with one twist of her beak, and was up and away over the hedge with it before I had time even to draw my companion's attention to what was happening.

Birds seem to recognise very quickly whether a sparrow hawk is hunting or not. Starlings will mob a hawk that has a full crop, following her in flight and making rude noises as they go; but when they know she means business, they do not wait around.

You will not often take the larger types of quarry I have mentioned with a sparrow hawk; for one thing, you need very close slips, since a teal or a partridge, once it gets up speed, will leave the hawk standing. Also, the few sparrowhawks that will take this type of quarry are nearly always eyasses or young passage hawks, which have not learnt in the wild that if they tackled such birds on their own, they would have very little chance of success. Rather like eyass goshawks at hares, their inexperience tends to make them foolhardy. One of my hawks took a number of magpies, but had she not had me at hand to help her, she would soon have learnt that magpies, like crows, will often come to the rescue of a friend in trouble.

Sparrowhawks are extremely agile. One of mine once flew at a sparrow in a farmyard. The sparrow saw her and dodged into a very small pony stable, through the slightly open top of the half-door. My hawk had to turn at least 135 degrees to get into the stable, but not only did she do so with the greatest ease, but also she reappeared almost immediately with the sparrow in her feet. So she must have caught it in mid-air, swung round a full circle inside the stable and come out again, all without stopping. Sparrowhawks will sometimes stoop like falcons – I have once seen a wild hawk do this from well over 30 m (100 ft) up, although the stoop was unsuccessful on that particular occasion.

Hedgerows are good hunting-grounds for small short-wings, but it is best to wait until the leaves are more or less off the trees before working your hawk in this fashion. Cut and laid hedges are the best; very tall or thick hedges should be avoided, as the quarry can get away in them. Sparrowhawks will unhesitatingly dive into the thickest of cover in pursuit of quarry, and can at times run themselves on thorns and so become injured. You should be careful always to examine your bird to see that she has no thorns in her, if she has plunged into cover in this way.

All the small short-wings can be flown out of trees or off the fist. If you are doing the former, choose a suitable tree in a hedgerow, put your hawk in it and leave her. Then start beating the hedge at a distance, gradually working up towards the tree, so that any quarry will tend to break in the direction of your hawk.

An alternative method to flying a small hawk from the fist in the normal way is to throw her from the palm of your free hand in the Eastern manner. (This is of particular help to shikras, which are not such fast or agile performers as Cooper's hawks or sparrowhawks.) This gives her a slight added impetus on take-off, but more important still, means that she cannot fly until you want her to. If you are beating a hedge with your hawk on your fist in the normal manner, and quarry emerges, she will immediately take off after it and nine times out of ten the quarry will turn straight back into cover. But if you hold your bird as shown in figure 105, you can let the quarry get well clear of cover before throwing her off, and so give her a better chance of catching it. Do not throw her too hard – if you do, her head will snap back at the end of the throw, and she will lose, rather than gain, impetus.

There is a fourth method of slipping short-wings at quarry, which can be applied to large and small hawks, and which also originated in the East. The falconer carries the bird in the normal way on his fist, but round her neck is placed a loop of soft leather or woven cotton, whose free end hangs down the hawk's front. When he wishes to slip his bird at quarry, the falconer takes the

179

free end of the loop between finger and thumb and pulls it taut, so that the hawk's head is pulled down and she is in a crouching position. He then throws her off, releasing the end of the loop at just the right moment. This device (known in the East as a *jangaoli*, and called *Halsband* by the Germans) gives the bird extra impetus, and prevents her head from being snapped back by the thrust. I personally can see no real advantage in using it on birds such as goshawks. In any case, it requires a great deal of skill and experience on the falconer's part to use it correctly. If the jangaoli is not released at exactly the right moment, the hawk can very easily be injured. In my opinion this method of slipping a hawk is best left well alone.

Sooner or later, unless you are very lucky indeed, your sparrowhawk will start to carry. Sparrowhawks so often take their prey in mid-air that they are more inclined to swing up into a tree with it than to land on the ground. Here I feel that Cooper's hawks have a slight advantage; the fact that they are slightly larger means that if they do carry a small bird into a tree and eat it, they will generally still be keen enough to return to you afterwards. A male Cooper's hawk that I flew for some seasons would carry a sparrow into a tree, where it would take him about twenty minutes to eat it. He invariably dropped the last few remains onto the ground, as they were too difficult for him to hold on the branch, and would then fly down after them. I could then quite easily pick him up, and occasionally, if I was quick enough to beat him to it, he would come to the fist. But once this had happened, all hunting was over for the day. Had he repeated the performance after another flight, he would have had a full crop, and then no amount of persuasion would have brought him down.

Most sparrowhawks will learn to carry eventually; haggards, which have already lived at least a year in the wild, are always confirmed carriers, and are usually very quickly lost because of it.

Despite all the difficulties inherent in manning and training a sparrowhawk, it is a most rewarding bird, and I think this is well illustrated by the following. A friend of mine had a female gos while he was at Oxford, and he flew her there as much as possible; but he found it hard to get permission to fly, and in the places where he was able to do so there was very little quarry. I suggested that he try a sparrowhawk instead. A few months later we met again, and his remark summed up the whole situation. 'Don't ever talk about goshawks to me again,' he said. 'I've had more fun with my spar in one week than with my gos in a month.' So, if you have had a successful season or so with a gos, and are not too set on being a 'big game falconer' and having yourself photographed carrying an eagle, with a row of dead hares laid out at your feet – try a sparrowhawk. Fly nothing else at the same time, but really concentrate on her and work hard with her, and you will find it well worth your while.

The austringer who can regularly fly a sparrowhawk, consistently catch quarry with her, moult her out and then repeat the performance the following season, can consider himself to have reached the height of achievement as far as short-wings are concerned.

Just because you happen to live in open country does not mean you cannot fly short-wings. They can be flown anywhere except in towns and woods, and as a rule they are by far the most suitable birds for present-day falconers. Unfortunately many falconers have the only too often encountered idea that short-wings are dull and uninteresting compared with falcons. One frequently hears the phrase 'I'm a long-wing man myself' (which usually means that the speaker has neither the patience nor the competence to train and fly short-wings). That they are more difficult to train, particularly in the early stages, there can be no doubt. But once you have flown one properly you will admit that falcons are not for you, unless you have the time and money to fly them to a really high standard.

I would say that the good austringer is far better at training birds, and a far more careful man, than the good falconer – simply because he has to be. For the falconer who really does not have a great deal of time to spare for hawking, a member of the buzzard family is probably even better suited to his needs than a short-wing, since once he has trained it, it will not require so much attention to keep it in flying order.

But if you are still convinced that you are a 'long-wing man', why not try a compromise? Fly a merlin for three or four weeks during your summer holiday, and then hack it back to the wild and fly a short-wing for the rest of the season. This way, you will get the best of both worlds.

14 Merlins

Before it became so hard to obtain a licence for a merlin, very few falconers even considered wintering these birds. Merlins were summer holiday falcons and ideal for that purpose. In those days most people flew them from the beginning of August until about mid-September, and then hacked them back to the wild, often on the moor where they were bred. This not only kept the number of merlins on that moor at normal level; it did if anything increase it, since if gamekeepers knew they could get a few pounds each year for young merlins, they left the old birds alone. On some moors this hacking back swelled the number of breeding pairs quite considerably over a few years, since the young birds had been removed at the start of the shooting season (the most dangerous time for them) and put back later on. In the future, the answer to the problem of obtaining merlins for falconry must lie in captive breeding.

Jack merlins are seldom such good performers as females, though of course there are always exceptions that go to disprove this statement.

Like all small falcons, merlins grow very quickly, so that the time they must spend in the mews until they are old enough to be trained is relatively short – a week or two at the outside. Once you have decided that your merlin is ready to be picked up, you can save yourself a day of training by removing all food from the mews on the morning of the day before you intend training to begin. Thus your bird will be getting keen, and will very likely feed on your fist the next evening. Merlins can be trained in an amazingly short time; a week is plenty for the average bird, and I have had a female which took only four days from the time I picked her up to the time I flew her loose and killed with her. This may sound extraordinarily quick, but it is in fact not unduly so; merlins are easier to train than kestrels, which, I regret to say, sometimes seem rather stupid.

Since merlins are so small their feeding must be very carefully watched, and your weighing machine must be accurate to within at least ¼ oz. A matter of an hour or two will make all the difference to a merlin's weight and behaviour; at three o'clock in the afternoon she may sit on a fence post and utterly refuse to come to the lure, but at half-past four she may well come 100 yd without the least hesitation. As a very rough guide, most female merlins will keep in good condition on two sparrows a day during the summer months; the average jack will need slightly less. But beware – your merlin may not be average; she may need slightly more, or maybe even a fraction less. Some falconers always feed their merlins twice a day; I have found this to be a bit tricky when gauging the amount of food they should have at each meal, and prefer to give only one feed a day. If you do feed your bird twice, avoid giving her castings at the morning feed.

If you have the time, you can give your merlin two training sessions a day – one in the morning (with a very small crop as a reward), and the second in the afternoon, after which she will of course eat her ration for the day. Offer her a bath every day without fail. Some merlins will bathe twice or even three times a day in hot weather. Never fly her (or any falcon) without first giving her a chance to bathe.

Once your bird is flying loose, start stooping her to the swung lure. Being so small, she will be very quick on the turn and her stoops will not be very high, so your lure-swinging will need to be first-class. When you have got her stooping hard to the swung lure, and she is beginning to get muscled up, you will find it useful to teach her to come to a lure swung on a very short line and then caught on your fist, so that she comes onto the fist direct. When you start hunting with her, there will be times when you want her on your fist in a hurry, after she has put a bird into cover.

Most merlins will go at the first bird you flush for them, although jacks can sometimes be a little reluctant. I knew one whose owner carted him around for days before he would hunt; possibly this was due to the fact that he had not been entered soon enough and had become lure-bound. However, in the end he decided to go, and after that turned into a good flier. I had a female once who was also a slow starter and would ignore birds put up right under her. But one day she suddenly went for a lark that another merlin had chased up to 100 ft or so and had then abandoned; from there on, she never looked back.

Young merlins at the start of their careers will try to fly almost any small bird, including swallows and martins. Of course, they cannot catch these, and after a few unsuccessful flights they soon stop trying. They are extremely quick to learn what they can and cannot catch.

I have said earlier that the best quarry for merlins is larks. Just in case you feel that by flying merlins at larks you are endangering one of our song-birds, think again. The trained merlin will most probably catch far fewer larks whilst being handled by a falconer than she would do if left in the wild. The number of larks you take are not only limited by your permit; if you go for high quality flights over down land (as you certainly should do) then you will perhaps have three or four flights in an afternoon and be lucky if more than one ends in a meal for your merlin. Of course, you do not have to fly at larks; you can try starlings if you prefer, but no starling is going to give you a ringing flight, and I personally feel that this is rather a waste of a merlin.

Larks found on down land seem to be very much stronger on the wing than their stubble-dwelling relatives in the valley below. So if you want good high flights (and I have seen merlins go straight up overhead out of sight of binoculars), go onto downland. You will probably have to do this anyway these days, as modern farmers tend to cut corn much later, and the stubble often stands only a matter of days before ploughing begins; moreover, nowadays the straw is often not used, but burnt on the ground.

Moorland is not very good hawking country for merlins. Certainly larks are not very common on some of the southern moors, and although one finds a fair number of them on some Scottish moorland, the heather makes flights difficult, since it provides so much cover. A good dog can help you to find larks when they are scarce – almost any kind of dog will suffice, as it puts the larks up simply by ranging about.

I was once flying a merlin on a disused airfield in Scotland, and had taken my old German pointer, Trudy, along with me just for exercise. I kept her in to heel at first, but when we had difficulty in finding any larks I let her range and we soon had a flight. The merlin put the lark into cover, so I used the dog in an endeavour to find the lark. Trudy soon caught the idea, but to my horror she started pointing larks as the day went on, and I began to worry that she would point them the next day when we were grouse-hawking with the peregrines. There is nothing worse than one's dog pointing small birds when one is after grouse, and I rather expected I should regret having taken Trudy out with the merlin.

However, she made no mistakes the next day, and after that, on days when the wind was too strong to take the falcons to the hill, we would take the merlin on to the low ground and Trudy would point larks for us. This was something she taught herself, and I would certainly not care to risk it with any other dog. But then Trudy was a rather special dog anyway. When she grew too old to go to the hill I taught her to retrieve when we went shooting. She never liked picking birds up, but would do so if I persuaded her gently.

A merlin putting a lark down into heather will be far more easily found if you can get a cross bearing from two onlookers who are a good distance apart. Once you have agreed with them where the merlin was last seen, put a marker, such as a handkerchief, on the spot. Then you can use this as the centre of the search. But watch out, if there are cattle around, or you may find your marker disappearing down a cow. Until you have tried, you can have no idea of how hard it can be to find a merlin in heather. Two of us once spent three hours looking for one, and finally had to give up the search. Yet when we went out the next day and swung a lure, the merlin jumped out of the heather only a short distance away from our marker.

One might think that snipe would be an excellent quarry for merlins, but in fact this has not been borne out by the experience of people who have attempted this flight. In the few cases where merlins have taken snipe, the flights were very disappointing; the snipe put in after only flying a very short way, and were taken on the ground. In cases where the snipe decided to take to the air, they left the merlin standing, and she soon gave up.

It is rarely much use throwing a merlin off the fist as quarry gets up. This may on occasion work with peregrines at rooks and crows, and with some of the buzzard family; but where merlins and short-wings are concerned, it usually seems to put them off their stroke. Another thing worth remembering when flying merlins is, that very often, after a flight at quarry or the lure, they will refuse to go again until they have roused. They can frequently disappoint you if they have not done so before being slipped a second time at quarry.

Merlins seem to vary considerably, some being very persistent indeed, and ringing up to great heights, while others give up the contest only too easily. (But this may well be the fault of the falconer rather than his bird.) It is quite possible to fly them in a cast, and this can produce some very exciting flights, as each bird takes it in turn to stoop at the quarry, rather like a cast of peregrines at a gull. There is one thing to look out for when training a merlin: take care that when you make in to her after first entering her at the lure, you do not make her carry. A merlin that carries is all too soon a lost merlin, and you will find this most frustrating, to say the least. Merlins need never be hooded, as they become tame so quickly; and properly managed, they are the most charming and delightful of small falcons.

15 Game Hawking

Doubtless most shooting men would like, ideally, to own a pair of Purdeys and a grouse moor. But only the fortunate few can afford to do so; the vast majority realise that they can never fulfil this dream, and settle for other less grand, but none the less enjoyable, forms of shooting. Similarly there are a great number of falconers who would like to fly large falcons at game; but for some curious reason many of these simply refuse to recognise their limitations in a sensible way.

Game hawking, like rook, crow and gull hawking, is extremely demanding of time, and if you cannot give up several months in the year to it, you are really best advised to leave it firmly alone. It is no good pretending to yourself that you are going to get top-quality flights at game when you can only have three weeks or so of uninterrupted holiday; or when you are only able to fly at week-ends. As explained in chapter 11, a game hawk takes far longer than a rook hawk to get really fit, since she cannot be stooped to the swung lure. To make her ready for the start of the season you will have to be on the grouse moor, or whatever, right from the time she begins to fly loose.

No falcons will produce really good flights until late September (at grouse) or early October (at partridge). Young falcons are, obviously, inexperienced; while for older birds there will be little worth flying at before this time, as for the most part the game will still be young and weak on the wing. It will be more a case of 'cradle snatching' than proper game hawking. The good falconer should really regard the first month of the game hawking season as a rehearsal period, during which he and his team of falcons and dog are learning their parts, as it were. Only when they are all working smoothly together can the curtain go up on the real performance.

If you do not actually own land yourself, you are likely to find it difficult to obtain permission to fly over someone else's estate, particularly if it is well enough stocked with game to give you regular daily flights. (A point every 20 or 30 minutes is admirable, but this does pre-suppose plenty of game.) Most land of this type will in any case be shot over, so that the game will soon be too wild to lie to your dog.

Falcons are ideal for grouse because of their greater weight; tiercels are more suited to partridge hawking because they are smaller and can turn more quickly, which is of help in the more enclosed country where partridges are found. (Tiercels can be flown at grouse, but should really have a season or two at partridges first.) Do not attempt to fly more than two birds during your first season. Three should be considered the maximum for any falconer j more than this means that he cannot give enough flights to each bird, so that he either ends up with one or two star performers and several very poor ones, or a completely mediocre team. The old records show that quite often more than three birds were used, but if you examine them carefully you will find that as a general rule more than one falconer was employed, and that where quite a number of falcons were used the season often ended with a very poor score.

For game hawking you must have a trained pointer or setter – hawk trained, not a gun dog.

Last, but by no means least, you must fly every day that the weather permits. If your falcons are grounded for three days in a row because of bad weather, you will at once notice how their performance has deteriorated when next you fly them.

You should by now be convinced that game hawking is not a sport for week-end or holiday falconers. Properly done it is very expensive. If you cannot meet all the necessary conditions then your results will be sub-standard, and you ought to be disappointed. I say 'ought' because, sadly, there are all too many falconers nowadays who seem perfectly happy to accept low standards as the norm. Make no mistake about it, although you may take quite a number of young grouse early in the season, you will have to be a good falconer, with a good falcon and a good dog, if you are to do well right through into November and December, when grouse hawking is at its best.

Grouse hawking

Let us assume that it is 12 August, the first day of the grouse season. (If the 'Glorious Twelfth' falls on a Sunday, you must wait until 13 August.) You are out on the hill with your falcons j and your dog, after ranging in front of you (into the wind, of course) has come on a point. If you have any helpers or onlookers with you, position them where they can see, not to their best advantage, but to yours. As early in the season as this, you are not out for their enjoyment – at present spectators must take pot-luck. Their turn will come in another four to six weeks when rehearsals are over. Right now, you want them placed so that if the grouse fly into dead ground (ground out of vision) they will be able to see and advise you.

Do not on any account rush matters. For her first flight at grouse you will obviously want to give each falcon the best chance you can; for only by succeeding will she gain confidence and improve and become a good game hawk. So for the moment the falcon you have chosen to fly first remains hooded on your fist.

Now flush the grouse. A really well-trained pointer for hawking will flush on command (pointers for shooting are not trained to do this). But you may well have a dog which is not yet up to this standard, in which case you must go in yourself. (It is most unwise to teach a young dog to flush in its first season; if you do, it will tend to creep in towards the game instead of remaining steady on the point.) So, steady your dog if necessary, and leaving it behind you, still on point, move in. Some falconers use a second dog, such as a spaniel, to flush the game. This seems to me to complicate matters unduly, involving as it does an extra dog to handle; I can see no advantage in it at all.

As the grouse rise you will be able to see if there are any young birds among them. If there is simply a single old bird, or a barren pair, forget about them. At this stage they are not suitable quarry for your young and inexperienced falcon. But if there are any young birds, try to mark the covey down. A covey of young grouse will not usually fly far. The old birds with them realise that the young quickly tire, and so they put into cover quite soon. If other members of your field can also mark the grouse down you will have cross-bearings, and therefore a better chance of finding them again. Beware of one thing here – grouse flying over the top of a rise often look as though they are pitching (landing), but more often than not they have gone further than you think.

Once again, do not rush things. It is so easy to get excited and dash off madly, and this is just the wrong thing to do. Let the grouse settle down. They will move around a bit and may well end up not exactly where you marked them down, but if you move in too soon you will only make things more difficult. They will soon forget about you if you all stay put quietly. This waiting period will also give time for the wind to carry the scent of the birds towards you, so that the dog can point them again. If you move in too soon the scent will not have had time to travel, the birds may well jump up before the dog can point them, and you will have spoilt the whole thing and have to start again from scratch. Ten to fifteen minutes is a reasonable time to wait.

Now move in gently towards the spot where you marked the grouse down, and try to get another point. If you succeed, the chances are that they are the same birds, and so you already know there are young, inexperienced grouse there for your equally young, inexperienced falcon to have a crack at. Again, quietly position your field. Unhood the falcon (her jesses and swivel will of course have been removed long ago) and let her fly off your fist as soon as she is ready. Do not cast her off hurriedly. You have plenty of time and she might like to look around her first, possibly even to rouse before she flies off. She now circles round as she has been doing for the past week or more; perhaps with luck she gains some height.

Now comes the difficult part. You want her overhead almost immediately behind the grouse, so that when they rise up they will be almost underneath her and all she will have to do is turn over and stoop. This is where many things can go wrong. The less wind there is, the better. From the previous point you will have gained some idea of how far scent is travelling and, therefore, roughly how far in front of you the birds are. Using this knowledge you must decide when to flush the birds. When you think the falcon is well placed and is heading towards them, run in and flush them. The moment they rise, shout to your falcon just as you would if you were throwing out the lure. This will attract her attention and as the birds get up she should, if she is in the right position, stoop. If you are very lucky she will have picked out a young bird; if you are luckier still, she may even knock it down in the first stoop.

In spite of the oft-repeated statement that falcons tend to kill weak and sickly birds, I think you will find, where game hawking is concerned, that they go for the first bird that moves. It is frequently the old bird in the covey that makes the first move, and the young ones then follow; though this does of course depend to a certain extent on how the covey is lying. (If, for instance, there is a young bird nearer to you than the old bird then that may very well be the first to be flushed.)

If the falcon does stoop at the old bird then naturally she is most unlikely to take it. In this case you will probably have to bring her back to the lure and start all over again. You might be able to mark the birds down once more, but if not, go right back to the beginning and act as before. However, if a young bird rises under her she has a greater chance of success. She may knock it down, throw up, circle round and land on her kill. But more likely she will miss it and the young bird will dive into cover. A falcon will sometimes go into cover after a bird, and if yours does this, she may with the greatest of luck catch the grouse on the ground.

Very probably however she will not find it. In this case, stand still. If you move now you may well flush the grouse, and the falcon may try to follow it. As she is considerably slower at getting up from the ground, a stern chase may well result. This is something you want to avoid if you possibly can, because she might conceivably overtake the grouse and this will lead her into bad habits. If she once finds she can catch a grouse in this way she will continue trying to do so instead of going up, and later on in the season she will be unable to catch anything at all.

If she does not kill, whistle to her, throw out your lure and, as soon as she comes back, hood her. Now move in gently with your dog, who will almost certainly find it easy to point the grouse in hiding. Once the dog is on the point, put the falcon up in the air again, and when she is in the right position flush the grouse once more. This time, with any luck, she will be successful in catching it. However, if it gets into cover again and the falcon, instead of following it, circles round overhead, go in quickly with the dog and flush it again as soon as she is in the right position. If you work on these lines you are bound to have success sooner or later. Very few falcons will refuse to fly game in these circum-stances, and if they are placed right and the game is flushed at the correct moment the odds are in their favour.

Grouse have many natural enemies. When they are still in the egg, hoodies, gulls, crows, foxes and ravens are pleased to eat them; once hatched, they are threatened by stoats, wild cats, faxes, eagles, harriers and so on, not to mention man. So do not assume that they have never seen a falcon before; there are still a reasonable number of wild peregrines in Scotland, and the grouse may well have met one already. Evasive tactics are instinctive in them, and they can be remarkably clever. They will dive into thick heather and hide in peat hags; they will even pitch on a loch an, bobbing up and down on the water. Grouse cannot swim, but they can float, and seem to know that very few falcons like picking them off water. In due course they are blown back to the shore, where they creep into the heather again. Small islands in lochans are a great attraction to a hard-pressed grouse. Fortunately these islands provide good cover, since they cannot be grazed by deer or sheep, and once the grouse is there your falcon will be foiled. (I say 'fortunately' because otherwise you might find yourself having to swim in extremely cold water to retrieve her.)

Of course many things can, and often do, go wrong in these early stages of game hawking. It is surprising how often a falcon may seem to be heading just where you want her yet, between the time you decide to put the birds up and the time they actually rise, will turn away and spoil her chances. A strong wind is your worst enemy on your first few days out. A young falcon finds it very easy to turn down-wind, but hard work to keep flying against it. Your falcon will frequently go for an old bird, rather than a young one, and so make things difficult for herself. The grouse may not be so easy to flush as you could hope, for they are not fools. You can run right through a covey and fail to put them up at all if they can see your falcon directly overhead. Of course, a dog that will flush on command is worth untold gold to you. Its nose will tell it exactly where the birds are, and it will put them up far more efficiently than you can on your own.

Some people think that the game should be flushed down-wind, towards the dog. They leave their pointer on the point and, taking their spaniel with them, they work round in a large half circle till they are up-wind of the grouse. This is not quite as simple as it sounds, since one can never know the exact where-abouts of the grouse and it is only too easy to put them up by mistake at quite the wrong moment. The falcon must be persuaded to get well up-wind of the pointer and the falconer. The spaniel is then sent in to flush the game. So one is asking the spaniel to find the game when in fact the scent, on which the dog relies to do its job, is blowing away from it. (Frequently what happens is that the spaniel goes past a grouse and then, catching the scent, turns and flushes the grouse *up-wind*. This gives the falcon the most difficult shot of all – a stoop head-on; and if she misses she is then going in quite the wrong direction.)

Any man who can train a pointer (and some take on two pointers or even more), a spaniel and two or three falcons to do all this, seems to me to be taking on a completely unnecessary number of tasks, and to be making life consider-ably more difficult for himself. Some of his difficulties can be resolved if he employs a dog handler, but this obviously adds to the expense and can also lead to arguments between falconer and dog handler, each blaming the other when things go wrong.

I have never seen any logical reason in flushing down-wind, though I have tried it on occasions. Very few falcons like to stoop down-wind, which is what they must do if you flush the game in this direction. The reason for this is quite simple – although they may go somewhat faster, it is far more difficult for them to steer accurately. (Any sailing man will tell you that it is far easier to steer against, rather than with a current.) Quite apart from this, if the wind is such that it will make any appreciable difference, game will not fly down-wind unless you force them; and when the wind is really strong they will, if forced to start down-wind, turn and go up-wind at the first opportunity. Their short wings enable them to fly lower than the longer-winged falcon, and since higher up the wind is stronger, they are immediately at an advantage. They can also steer better, and so avoid the falcon more easily.

I once tried to flush a covey of grouse down-wind and downhill. By having a line of people close together advancing towards the pointer I succeeded in getting them up, but they turned at once and flew over our heads and between us, and went off uphill and up-wind, since they knew this was their safest way out of a tricky situation. If there is little or no wind then it makes no great difference to you, the falcon or the game, which way you flush them, but it is easier to do it by approaching from the pointer. In nearly all circumstances this is the best method; the only time you might prefer to do otherwise is when the best cover (or something like a wire fence that could be a danger to your falcon) lies up-wind, close to the line of flight.

Once your falcon has caught a grouse, do not on any account rush in to her. This is a moment when she deserves her reward, and she might carry if you make in too quickly. Falcons do not hurry their meals; they like to pluck a good deal before starting to eat. A falcon of mine once took a grouse. It was just over two hours before I found her; all she had eaten was the head, but the bird was completely plucked. So make in slowly, and put on her swivel and leash while she is plucking and eating her kill on the ground. (I like to lie down in front of her and with my knife cut pieces off the kill and give them to her.) When she has had nearly all her ration for the day, lift her up, kill and all, and finish feeding her on the fist. Then hood her up. She should go well the next day.

Do not be tempted to overfly falcons during the first fortnight or so; three flights a day are plenty, unless some happen to be very easy. Gradually your falcons will go higher and learn the ways of grouse and what the dog is about. And all the time they will be getting more experienced and more confident.

By the middle or end of September the whole affair becomes amazingly easy. The whole team now knows its job, and the falconer can begin to relax and enjoy things. At the beginning of the season a young falcon is doing well to take one in every four grouse put up for her; but by October the grouse are strong on the wing and will fly far greater distances, and the flights are really worth watching. The falcon is at her peak of fitness, wastes very little effort in getting up to her pitch (the height at which she waits-on), and once there uses virtually no energy at all, simply cruising around on outstretched wings. The dog, too, should be steady by now. The rehearsal period is over.

How high will a falcon wait-on? One reads in books of falcons waiting-on at 300 m (1000 ft), and I have even seen one magazine report of a falcon at 450 m (1500 ft). I am afraid that I simply do not believe it. Judging heights is extremely difficult; if you ask six people to judge the height of a tall tree you will find their answers vary enormously, and it is much harder to tell how high a falcon is in the sky. I feel that falconers often tend to exaggerate. One day out on the hill a falcon of mine went up far higher than her normal pitch. I had three companions, and asked them all to estimate very carefully her height above us. We kept her waiting there, and the general consensus of opinion was that she was certainly no higher than 750 ft, but more likely around 600 ft. She looked tiny, and when we flushed the grouse it took her so long to come down that they were in cover before she could get on terms with them. In fact, she was too high up.

This applies even more in the case of partridge hawking, where the birds are usually closer to the cover of a hedge or fence. Between 200 and 300 ft is a suitable height for a game hawk to wait-on. Once she has learnt how efficient she is at this height she will invariably go up to it with no trouble at all.

Old falcons can become very lethal indeed. One of mine once took 43 grouse without a miss, and went on to kill over 100 that season. But this is certainly no record. I flew this particular falcon at partridges one day when the wind was too strong to go to the hill. We found a large covey in very open ground, and she took five of them in about 30 minutes. Had we had a good dog out with us I expect she would have taken even more. But this is by no means the normal pattern of things; and of course, the number of birds you kill has little or nothing to do with the quality of the flying. You can have a very exciting day and yet come home empty-handed. If you went out shooting and came home with nothing, the guns would consider it very poor indeed. But although he can only judge his skill at shooting by whether he hits or misses, a discriminating shot will prefer the difficult birds, just as a discriminating falconer would rather have a hard, testing flight, even if there is no kill.

Getting to know each individual falcon's ways (and your dog's, too) is very important. They all vary, and you can make use of a particular falcon's style of flying. I had a falcon that I trained very badly in her first season so that she very rarely waited-on at any height. But she would fly very fast in tight circles round the dog, and if one timed things correctly she would knock down a grouse before it had gone any distance at all. She relied entirely on speed, and took a great many grouse over the six seasons that I flew her. She would hunt them out on the ground rather like a spaniel, poking around where she thought they might be hiding. Very funny she looked, trotting around like an inebriated sailor in feathered plus-fours. As soon as a grouse ran she would jump up into the air and make short dashes at him like a sparrowhawk. She became very good at it indeed.

I once saw one of the late Kim Muir's falcons take three partridges out of one covey in one flight. The first she hit fell into thick clover and disappeared from her view. She turned over and hit another, which went the same way. She repeated the process with a third, which fell onto stubble where she could see it, and she immediately took possession of it. One of my own falcons once hit a grouse at the bottom of her stoop and, as she threw up, delivered a smart undercut to another bird that was in her direct line of fire, hitting it under one wing and tipping it out of control. However, taking more than one bird in a single flight is a very rare occurrence.

Occasionally when grouse hawking you may be lucky enough to get a flight at black game. These are heavier and quite a bit faster than red grouse, but a good falcon can take them. Ptarmigan seldom come down below 1500 ft above sea-level; I have never myself flown at them, but there is no reason why trained falcons should not catch them, particularly as they frequently do so in the wild.

Partridge hawking

The partridge season starts nearly three weeks later than the grouse season, and this can have both advantages and disadvantages to the falconer. It gives you more time to train your birds, but if you are not very careful they can become lure-bound, and there is a point where, once they are fit, they should be entered at game straight away. But a skilled falconer may well have his birds ready several weeks before the law allows him to fly at partridges. The easiest way to overcome this problem is to start training your partridge hawk a week or so later than you would a grouse hawk.

Partridges are certainly slower on the wing than grouse, and are therefore easier to catch. But whereas on a grouse moor there is seldom anything that might tempt your falcon to give chase when you do not wish it, in areas where you find partridges there are other birds, in particular wood-pigeons, which can lead her astray.

As in grouse hawking, a good pointer is essential. You can catch the occasional bird just by driving over the stubbles in a car and putting your falcon on the wing as soon as you see any partridges rise up, but if the falcon misses and the game goes into cover you will find it almost impossible to flush it again without a dog. I think many people, particularly those who shoot, do not realise how a game bird's attitude to man alters when a falcon is waiting-on overhead. If there were no falcon then the game would rise without hesitation, and you would not have to search for them; but in the presence of a falcon they will sit so tightly that at times you can even pick them up by hand.

You can fly grouse hawks at partridges and partridge hawks at grouse, but it is a great mistake to use either for anything but game. Obviously if you un-hood your falcon at one minute, expecting her to climb up and wait-on, and half an hour later expect her to chase a crow, she will be thoroughly bewildered and will fly well at neither.

I am quite convinced that training game hawks is nowhere near as difficult as it is generally made out to be, although there are problems inherent in game hawking which do not make it more difficult than other branches of falconry. Nor do I believe that only a few peregrines make good game hawks – in fact, I think the reverse. As I see it, any peregrine, properly trained, will make a good game hawk. (I fully realize many falconers will disagree with this statement; but I think this is because not only are their methods different from mine, but also they often have too many falcons at one time, so that the slow starters never really get a chance to prove themselves.)

I myself have mainly flown unhacked eyasses at game. (I have seen hacked eyasses flown, and they were no better and no worse than my unhacked birds.) My few passage and haggard peregrines never turned out so well as the eyasses, since they would often be led off by the sight of a crow or a pigeon and so were very easily lost. They were certainly never as steady and reliable as the experienced eyasses, and none was any better.

There is one particular trait that eyass peregrines seem to have to a much greater degree than other falcons. Most of them, once they have been flown for a month or so, will, if they fail to kill, come back and look for you, even if the flight ended out of sight a mile or more away.

As regards flying at pheasants with game hawks, this is not easy to do in this country, since pheasants are primarily a woodland bird. I have caught the odd one at times, but have never tried to do so on purpose. A pheasant, when put into cover by a falcon will act entirely differently from the way it would if a goshawk or Harris' hawk were after it. When pursued by hawks, pheasants appear extremely cunning; but when trying to avoid a falcon they seem quite stupid.

Cock pheasants are rather heavy for a falcon, and personally I prefer to fly a goshawk at pheasants, but I would not be dogmatic about this. To fly falcons successfully at pheasants obviously depends to a certain extent on the sort of country you are in. I believe that in parts of America, where pheasants can be found in very open country, one can get extremely good flights at them with falcons; and I have been told that no gos would have a chance at them there because the country is so open. (This I doubt. So many goshawks never show their capabilities to the full, simply because they are not really fit.) I feel that gyrs might be better than peregrines at pheasants in the open.

When woodcock are flown with a falcon they act very like snipe, mounting high and fast and giving a most exciting chase. On some moors woodcock come in during late autumn, in quite large numbers. They like bracken, and this, from a falconer's viewpoint, is one of the worst things to have on a moor; although small patches are not too bad, any large areas of bracken will spoil flight after flight.

To go out game hawking when your whole team is working to perfection and the season is in full swing is a splendid experience. To have trained both falcons and dog yourself makes it doubly satisfying; if they are home-bred, it is still better. But to reach this ideal you will have to endure many set-backs and moments of despair. So many falconry books tend to dwell on how marvellously well the author's game hawks flew, and one gets the impression that nothing ever went wrong. If it is of any encouragement I can assure you that things do in fact go wrong far more often than they go right (particularly when one is trying to demonstrate to others how the thing should be done properly). Do not become despondent if everything does not seem to fall into place immediately. My first season at game hawking was one that I should not care to go through again; I made a great many mistakes and had very few successes. In the end, as you and your falcons gain more and more experience and confidence, it will gradually sort itself out, and you will feel well rewarded for the trouble you have taken.

16 Moulting, Imping and Coping

Moulting

A bird's flying power depends mainly on three sets of feathers – primaries and secondaries (in the wings) and tail feathers. Most birds of prey have ten primaries in each wing (the number of secondaries varies between species) and 12 tail feathers. The primaries are numbered one to ten from the outer edge inwards (i.e. number one primary is the one furthest from the hawk's body when the wing is spread); while the tail feathers are numbered one to six on each side, again from the outer edge inwards. (The two central feathers, which lie above the others, are known as the deck feathers.) These, with the false wings, are the most important of the bird's flight feathers, giving her lift and speed, brakes and steering.

When a bird moults, naturally it does not drop its feathers all at once. If it did, it would not only catch cold, but would also be unable to fly; and therefore it could not catch its food or avoid its enemies. (A partial exception to this occurs in the case of ducks and geese, which drop all their flight feathers almost simultaneously, and replace them in six to eight weeks. During this time they are flightless, but as they can still swim and dive they are able to avoid predators, and can continue to find food in the normal way, either grazing on land or dabbling in the water.)

A bird of prey must be able to fly efficiently at all times, or she would starve. Her moult is therefore spread over some five or six months; she normally drops only one pair of primaries and one pair of tail feathers at a time, and not until the new feathers are half-grown does she drop another pair. So in effect she is seldom short of more than one and a half feathers in each wing and one and a half feathers in each side of her tail, at anyone time. This does not seriously impair her flying power.

Many falconers tend to think of moulting as something almost akin to a disease, which requires special treatment and must be got over as quickly as possible. Some even resort to drugs in an effort to speed up the rate at which their birds drop their feathers. They seem to forget moulting is a perfectly normal and natural process, common to all birds and very many animals, including man himself. The falconer may look ruefully at his hairbrush and wonder if he is going bald; meanwhile his wife is busily sweeping up the dog's hairs off the carpets. In fact, both dog and falconer are moulting, and neither of them is the least incapacitated by it. Nor are hawks. But even so, a great many people still believe that a hawk cannot be flown while she is moulting, and that she should be shut away and handled as little as possible, if at all.

If you think about this, you will see that of course it *is* possible to fly a moulting hawk; after all, wild hawks have to fly in the moult in order to survive. It will not harm your bird's health if you fly her during this period (although it can slow down her moult, or delay the start of it until such time as she is put down for a rest). There is however a practical reason for not flying at this time. Most British raptors start to moult between April and June (though birds from abroad may begin at an entirely different time, before becoming acclimatised). From this time on, for the next few months, the trees are covered with leaves, crops and hay are standing, and it is far easier to lose your hawk than at other times of the year. (If you do lose her, and have to go ploughing through fields of standing corn in search of her, you will certainly not be very popular with the farmers.)

If you have game hawks, they will naturally be taking an enforced rest in any case, since this is the close season. It never hurts a bird to have a rest from hawking, and so the moulting period is the logical time to rest your hawks. But they can quite well be flown then, if need be. Indeed, very few grouse hawks will have completely finished moulting before the time comes to pick them up and get them going for the start of the season.

Many old books recommend that once a hawk starts to drop her feathers she should be shut up in a loft, or some other unfrequented place, and her food should be thrown to her, so that she has very little contact with human beings at all. This seems to me quite ridiculous. To begin with, lofts are among the worst places for keeping birds – they are usually very hot in summer and cold at night and in winter, and they seldom get enough fresh air and sunlight. (Cellars, obviously, are equally hopeless.) By shutting your bird away like this, you are depriving her of air and light and human companionship at a stroke. Your hawk should be your friend, just as much as your dog is. (If she is not, then you should never have had her in the first place.) And this is no way to treat a friend; even a nice tame hawk will become quite wild in such conditions, and once she is hard down you will have to start manning her all over again. This seems quite pointless.

Keep your hawk in her usual weathering-ground, so that she continues to see you every day and stays accustomed to your presence; feed her on the fist from time to time, and generally treat her just as you would normally. It will not affect her moult, and it will save you trouble when you pick her up again at the start of the season.

In the past it was believed that a hawk, during her moult, built up a reserve of surplus fat in her stomach and intestines, and that she must be purged of her 'grease' before she could be brought into flying condition again. The old falconers used various methods to bring this about, and the process was known as 'enseaming'. The bird was fed well-washed meat, and given purgatives such as sugar candy crushed and mixed with fresh butter. She was also given 'rangle' (small smooth pebbles, which when she cast them were supposed to emerge coated with 'glut or evill humor' – Latham). Enseaming, which is recommended as early as 1610 (in Latham's *The Faulcon's Lure and Cure*) has survived in practice until recent times; but whether it does in fact make a great deal of difference to a hawk I cannot say.

Obviously, when you pick up a well-fed, well-rested hawk from the mews after her moult, she will be in very high condition, and will need to be lowered before re-training begins. There may be a case for the use of washed meat here (a good alternative is rabbit, which being a white meat has little nutritional value); but unless you know exactly what you are doing I would not specially recommend it. I have never used rangle on my birds; forcibly to fill a hawk's stomach with stones seems to me an extreme method of purging her – rather like using steel wool on a saucepan when a cloth would do just as well. Some falconers leave a small pile of stones close to the hawk's perch so that she can swallow them if she wishes. I have never known any of my hawks voluntarily to swallow stones. .

However, in 1974 Mr Nicholas Fox's observations of wild New Zealand falcons (*Falco novaeseelandiae*) showed that in some cases these birds do take rangle, females taking stones approximately ⅜ in. in diameter, males taking stones about ⅕ in. in diameter. Rangle was found in two castings out of some 600 examined. This is certainly interesting, and could be used to argue a case for leaving rangle by a hawk's perch at all times. But I still do not think that rangle should be forcibly given.

When my hawks have finished moulting I simply cut down their food (gradually, not drastically); and as soon as they respond enough to be exercised, I give them as much exercise as they can take. This will do as much, and more, for a hawk as any amount of patent purges and pills.

Be careful, if your hawk is in very high condition when taken up after moulting (or indeed, after any period of rest in her mews) that she does not bate a great deal. Excessive bating, especially on very hot days, is always to be avoided, and its effect on an unfit hawk can be disastrous. Here again is a reason for keeping your hawk well-manned during her moult.

One thing that always amazes me is that peregrines (particularly game hawks) will be fit and flying hard within a week of being taken up. I have an old falcon at the moment that I can leave on her block for weeks on end; but give me three days' notice and I will have her flying loose. Although she will get short of breath after a few stoops, her flight is extraordinarily strong and powerful, quite contrary to what one would expect, and after another four days of exercise she will be fit.

Some people like to think that hawks moult to a kind of pattern. This is not always the case. Do not think that birds always drop their feathers in the same order at every moult.

Moulting can on occasions be delayed by certain factors. If you fly a hawk constantly during the time when she would normally be moulting, this may slow down the process, and she will take longer to drop her feathers than she would do if she were resting. A hawk that is flown throughout the year may, on rare occasions, not moult at all. But once she is put down for a rest she will usually catch up pretty quickly; some trained hawks whose moult is delayed by flying may, once they are put down, drop more than the normal number of flight feathers simultaneously, to make up for lost time, as it were.

Another thing that can affect a bird's moult is an abrupt change of location. A hawk that goes to a new owner or a new home while she is dropping her feathers may stop altogether for a time; but once the strangeness has worn off and she has settled down, she will usually resume her interrupted moult. These delays and interruptions do not seem to affect a hawk's general health in any way, but if she is badly frightened or shocked during a change of location there may be 'fret marks' on her new feathers when they grow down, and these bring their own problems.

The 'hunger streak', or 'hunger trace', as it is sometimes called, is a curious mark sometimes seen on new feathers, making them look as if someone had drawn a razor blade across the webbing at a sharp angle. The feather shaft, too, may be marked by a bump, and this may be a slightly different colour from the rest of the shaft. People used to believe this was caused by the bird not getting enough to eat while her new feathers were growing; and because of this you will find a number of old-fashioned books advising you not to fly your hawks at all during the moult, but to rest them and feed them as much as they can eat. But these so-called 'hunger' marks can be found not only on the feathers of poultry, domestic pigeons and wild birds, but also on trained hawks which have been eating plenty of food. Personally I believe that they are not caused by malnutrition at all, but by stress or a sudden severe shock to the hawk, and for this reason I prefer to call them 'fret marks'.

Many things can frighten a bird enough to produce feather deformities – a car back-firing close at hand, a strange dog running in suddenly; and, in the case of eyasses, the experience of being taken from the nest and transported to completely foreign surroundings. The hormonal imbalance produced by shock or nervous strain affects the growing points of the feathers, and although the damage may simply be confined to the webbing, in severe cases the feathers can 'pinch out' (that is to say, they drop out, and if you examine them you will see that the shafts come to a point and look as though someone had nipped them with a pair of pincers). A parallel can be found in the case of human beings who have undergone extreme shock or prolonged nervous strain, and who thereafter find that their hair changes colour or even drops out, and that there are colour or growth irregularities in their fingernails. You will not see any fret marks on your bird until the feathers are clear of the blood sheath and have grown down beyond the coverts; this will be quite some time after the bird suffered the shock which caused the marks.

Where a feather has pinched out, a new one will eventually grow in its place. In the case of a young bird, this feather will be different from the others, both in colour and length, since it will be mature, not immature plumage. (The flight feathers of birds of prey tend to shorten after each moult, though over how many years this shortening continues is not definitely known.)

A feather which has a fret mark on it will be weaker than a perfect one, and is therefore far more liable to break. Once a flight feather breaks, the ones on either side of it are likely to follow suit in time; even if they are not fret-marked themselves, they will have an extra strain put on them, and will be weakened if the broken feather is not repaired. A gap will appear, and it will be only a matter of time before more break. Young eyasses, whose immature flight feathers all grow down at much the same time, can have the entire tailor wing fret-marked, and when this occurs you are likely to have a good deal of repairing to do before long.

A flight feather that 'breaks' while still in the blood does not actually snap off, since the shaft is still soft. What happens is that the whole thing pulls out, leaving a wound which will bleed. This should not cause any problems (though it will probably make the surrounding plumage messy) provided that you dust it with sulphanilamide to prevent any infection from developing. It is, however, most advisable not to handle the bird until a new feather has grown (although this does take time and is very frustrating for the falconer). Eyasses, and older birds trapped during the moult, can sometimes arrive with a number of feathers broken in the blood, due to being roughly handled during transport; and there is nothing you can do except wait for the new feathers to grow down.

Occasionally a bird may have been wing-clipped by the trapper; in this case, if the stumps of feather shafts are no shorter than 3.8 cm (1½ in.), they can be repaired. Repairing, or 'imping' (from the Latin verb *imponere* – to place in) is not difficult, but it does require time and a good deal of patience. Manning a hawk that has many broken feathers (particularly if they are the primaries on her right wing) can be quite painful, as the broken ends will scratch your face every time she bates. But she should be fairly well-manned before you consider imping her.

One of your main difficulties, particularly if this is your first bird, will be to find new feathers to replace her broken ones. Once she has moulted, you will be able to keep any flight feathers that are in good condition, and these will come in useful in the future. But to begin with it is unlikely that you will have a set of suitable flight feathers for the bird you want to imp, and you will have to find someone who can let you have some. Obviously the best feathers are going to be those from a bird of the same species and sex, but you can use others. For instance, it is quite possible to put a jackdaw's tail onto a sparrowhawk. It will look slightly odd and will certainly confuse ornithologists, but so long as the feathers are about the same size and are strong, they can perfectly well be used.

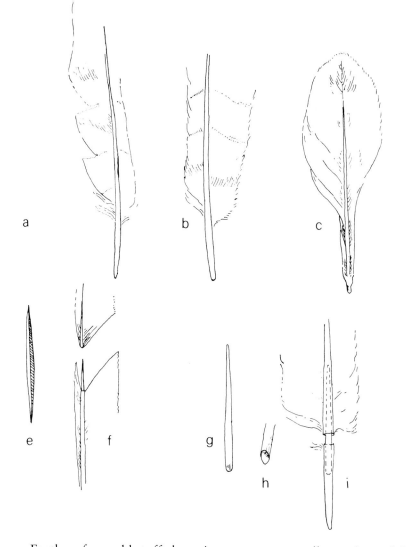

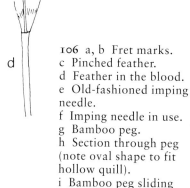

106 a, b Fret marks.
c Pinched feather.
d Feather in the blood.
e Old-fashioned imping
needle.
f Imping needle in use.
g Bamboo peg.
h Section through peg
(note oval shape to fit
hollow quill).
i Bamboo peg sliding
into position.

Feathers from old stuffed specimens are not usually much good for imping, as they grow very brittle with age. If you collect moulted feathers from your own birds, they too will need to be carefully kept, free from moths and other feather eaters. Each set of feathers should be kept separately, since individual birds vary in size, and once you start mixing one bird's feathers with those of another they will not necessarily make up a matching set.

Imping

The process of imping is comparatively simple, but it does require a fair amount of manual dexterity and common sense. All that one is doing is repairing a broken feather by cutting it where it is hollow and joining a new, similar feather to it by means of a bamboo peg, carefully cut to fit, and glued into position. The difficult part is getting the new piece of feather at exactly the right length and angle in relation to those next to it. Whittling the bamboo pegs is a long, tedious job that needs to be done carefully, in order not to split either the shaft of the new feather or the stump of the old one, and yet to be a good friction-tight fit. If you should split a shaft it must be bound round with thin waxed thread after the imping peg has been inserted.

The new feathers can be prepared, and the thinner end of the pegs already glued into them, without the bird having to be present. But first you must examine her, to see which feathers need imping. (You may well have to cast her for this.) If by good fortune you do happen to have another bird of the same species, you can carefully examine her to see the varying distances between feathers corresponding to those which need imping on your bird; this will be a considerable help to you. But if you have to estimate, then it is better to have the new feathers shorter than normal, rather than too long.

Once you have made a note of the feathers which need imping, put your bird away and begin your preparations. You will need the following tools: a very sharp knife, a pair of electrician's wire-cutters, a tube of glue (Super Epoxy or Araldite are good for the purpose), a fair-sized needle, some thin waxed thread, and a supply of bamboo cane. I know of nothing that equals bamboo, although I have tried many different substitutes – metal and plastic knitting needles, piano wire, orange sticks and so forth. Ordinary garden bamboos are fine for making pegs for small or medium hawks; for very big birds you will have to find bigger bamboo. (Try carpet shops for this; carpets are sometimes rolled round large bamboos.)

Now sort out your replacement feathers. Once you have decided which ones you are going to use, it is a very good idea to punch small holes in an old box lid and stick the feathers in these holes in the correct order – then you will not mix them up, and when you bring the bird in to be imped, she will not send them flying with one flap of her wings.

Pick up a feather and take a good look at the quill end. A short way from the end you will see a mark right round the shaft. This is the flesh line; originally all the part between this line and the end of the quill was sticking in the bird. (Your imping peg should reach no further than the flesh line.) A little further down the shaft the fluffy feathering begins, and then comes the webbing proper. It is about here that you must cut the feather, though this does depend on its size. (The bigger the bird, the more room you have; the smaller the bird, the trickier it is.) Tail feathers are always easier to imp than primaries, since the coverts are easier to push aside out of the way.

Cut straight across the quill with the wire-cutters, ignoring any webbing; all these joins will be out of sight when the job is completed. Keep both pieces of feather, as you will need them. Now cut a section of bamboo, about 3 in. long (this gives you something to hold on to while you are whittling) and split it into pegs. (At this point of the proceedings they will be too big to fit into the hollow quill. Their finished size and length will obviously vary according to feather size.) Your pegs will have to be oval in section, to match the shape of the feather shafts.

I find when whittling a peg that it is easier to shape the thin end (which will, obviously, fit into the replacement feather) first. Once the peg is roughly the right size, it is better to stop cutting, and to scrape along it with the edge of the knife blade; this stops you getting bumps and hollows on it. Try fitting the peg into the replacement feather every so often, to check on the size, but do not force it into the shaft too hard, as this will split the quill. Once you have shaped the sharp end so that it fits into the feather shaft, make sure it cannot rotate. (If it does, it is too loose and you will have to cut another peg.) Then you can shape the other end, which will be thicker and blunter, since the lower part of the shaft has a greater diameter. Check this against the quill which you cut off (this is why it is necessary to keep both pieces of the replacement feather after cutting). When both ends of the peg fit, you will see what a neat join it makes– nothing will show except the actual cut. Pull the peg out of the feather, glue the pointed end, and then push it back into the new feather again and wipe off any surplus glue. (The quill end can now be discarded.)

The feather is now ready for use, so you can replace it in its hole in the box lid and continue with the next one. When all the feathers have been prepared, the bird can be brought in again, and the operation can begin. It is best to imp your hawk just before you feed her, so that the minute the job is done she will be occupied with her food and will not try to preen her new feathers. This will give the glue time to set properly.

The hawk can be hooded or not. Although it is not essential to hood her, I personally think it is better to do so. I have already described how to hold a hawk; if there is a great deal of imping to do, make sure that you, and the person who is going to hold her for you, are as comfortable as possible. Some people advise putting a silk handkerchief over the bird's back if she is to be held for any length of time. This is supposed to prevent her plumage from becoming disarranged; but I find that it makes matters worse, since silk is so slippery. You will need a good strong light in which to work – preferably one of those desk lights that can be put at any angle. A cup of cold water is useful for damping down the fluffy under-feathers which would otherwise get in the way while working.

It is best to operate on the tail first, because the wings are probably short if they need imping, and so there is less to get in your way. If you only have one feather to imp, the job will be fairly simple, because you will have the feathers on either side of it to help you gauge the length correctly. But if you have many to do, then it is best to start on the inner side, closest to the hawk's body, and work outwards. This is where it is so helpful to be able to compare your bird's feathers with the wing or tail of another bird. As I have already said, it is better, if you have nothing you can use as a yardstick, to have the new feathers too short rather than too long.

Imagine, then, that your assistant is holding your hawk with her tail towards you. Her feet are gripping an old cushion placed on the table. Both you and your helper are comfortable, and have everything necessary to hand. Take the first feather that needs imping and pick out its replacement from your box. Push the coverts aside, damp down any fluff that is in your way, and lay the new feather alongside the broken one. Match it for length, and where the new feather ends, make a mark with a felt-tipped pen on the shaft of the broken feather. Put the new feather down, and cut the broken feather cleanly, straight across where you made the mark.

Now try the blunt end of the peg (which is sticking out of the new feather) and see if it will slide tightly into the old feather. If it fits snugly, and the length is correct, and the feather lies at the right angle to those on either side, pull it out, glue it and replace it. (Never try using a contact adhesive, for obvious reasons.) If the feather is too long, this can be corrected by cutting a piece off the stump. If it is too short, you can cut a tiny piece off the quill end of the broken feather you removed, and slide it over the peg in order to lengthen the new feather. If the peg is too tight, whittle it down until it fits; if by any chance it is too loose, then you will have to pull it out of the replacement feather and make an entirely new peg.

There are times, especially with small hawks, when you may find, after cutting the broken feather across at the mark, that the hollow shaft is clogged up. A little careful manipulation with a needle should remove the obstruction, and imping can then go ahead as normal.

When you have finished repairing all the broken feathers, take the bird on your fist and feed her. While she is eating, have a careful look at your handiwork and, should you notice a feather lying at slightly the wrong angle, you may be able gently but firmly to twist it back into the correct position before the glue sets hard. If a hawk is not really well-manned, it is advisable to tape her tail after imping. Before setting her back on her perch, check that none of the coverts (either upper or lower) have by accident got stuck to the imped feathers. If they have, run the blunt end of your needle between the coverts and the newly-imped quill.

The only other advice I can give is to take your time over imping. It is not a job that should ever be rushed. When it has been well done, it is almost impossible for anyone to see that the bird has imped feathers. Do not be frightened of imping; it takes patience, time and care, but it is not really difficult. If you are really worried about it, have a trial run with a tailor wing from something like a wood-pigeon or a crow.

If a bird bends a flight feather, but does not actually break it, you can straighten it out in very hot water (but take care not to scald the bird). This really works extraordinarily well. One of my golden eagles will frequently pick up one of her moulted primary or tail feathers and chew it along the shaft until it looks a complete wreck. Provided she has not broken the webbing, the whole feather can be rescued by pouring boiling water over it. This hot water trick is very useful, but should only be done when absolutely necessary; too many applications will weaken a feather. And very often a hawk will preen out a bend in a flight feather herself.

There are times when a bird comes to one in a terrible mess – really filthy, with dirt so ingrained in her feathers that it is obvious that no amount of bathing on her part will clean her up. For instance, a lost merlin of mine was picked up by someone and put in a coal-shed. When she was returned she was really dirty, and it was clear that she would have to be washed if her plumage was to become properly clean again. If you are faced with such a problem, the best thing to do is to melt some soap-flakes (*not* detergent) in a small quantity of hot water, and then add cold water until it is lukewarm. Immerse the bird completely in this, except for her head, and after a brief soaking lift her out and gently but thoroughly stroke the lather all over her. Stroke in the direction in which the feathers lie, not against them. You will see the dirt coming out in the lather. Then give her a couple of rinses and put her on your fist. If the weather is warm and the sun is shining, she can sit out of doors on her perch to dry. If it is cold or wet, she can soon be dried with the aid of a hair-drier or an electric fan-heater, but do not have it at too hot a setting. Once she is dry, let her preen.

Washing like this does unfortunately take away a lot of the bird's natural weather-proofing, and it will be at least two or three months before her feathers will be reasonably shower-proof again. (Her plumage will never really return to normal until after her next moult.) Another thing which will remove a hawk's water-proofing is constant stroking, particularly on her back. The less you stroke your bird, the more resistant her plumage will be to rain. The Japanese falconers use wisteria sticks, teased out at the ends, to stroke their hawks, so as to avoid touching them with the hand.

A young bird that has recently grown all her feathers, or an old one who has just finished moulting, will have a kind of bloom on her plumage rather like the bloom on a grape. I am inclined to think that this bloom may be the breaking up of the blood sheaths into a fine powder, which helps to protect the feathers.

In time you will learn to look at a hawk's plumage with a critical eye; and it will not be long before you literally wince if you see a bird in such a position that it would be possible for her to break feathers. You will have realised, like any good falconer, that to fly really well a hawk needs to have her feathers in the best possible condition; and although of course accidents do sometimes happen, you will try to foresee them and to avoid them as far as you possibly can.

Coping

There are times when talons and beaks overgrow and need cutting back. The process of cutting and trimming is known as coping. Although overgrown talons are rare, some falconers are of the opinion that they should be coped every so often. This is not because they are overgrown, but because they are 'too sharp'. I find this an extraordinary attitude – one might just as well give

soldiers blunted bayonets or take the guns off a battleship. Overgrown beaks occur more frequently, and I have on one occasion seen a beak so badly over-grown that the bird died, simply because it could not open its beak to eat. (This, I hasten to add, was not a falconer's bird; but there are nevertheless some raptor owners – one would not call them falconers, whatever they may call themselves – who seem unable to recognise a beak that is overgrown.) Figure 102 shows the extent to which beaks can overgrow, though these are of course extreme examples.

Talons and claws (technically speaking, a falcon has talons, while a hawk has claws) can, if badly overgrown, be clipped back with a strong pair of electrical wire-clippers. These are far better for the purpose than ordinary nail-clippers, although these can be used quite successfully on small hawks and falcons. If the bird is being flown at quarry, the talons should be re-sharpened after clipping with a file; if not, they will reshape themselves naturally after a few weeks.

Beaks can also be clipped back in the same way; at least, as far as the tip of the upper mandible is concerned. I do not advise the use of clippers on any other part of the beak, as clipping may well split it and make matters worse. Some people advocate the use of a sharp knife to pare an overgrown beak; I would consider this a most difficult tool for the purpose, and extremely danger-ous into the bargain. A coarse file, to remove the worst of the growth, followed by a finer file to finish off, is far less risky. Beaks often start to split, and if this

109, 110 Kestrel, before
and after coping.

happens then the sooner they are filed back beyond the split, the better. If the split is allowed to go too far, it will not be possible to file back far enough, without filing into the tender part of the beak (which, obviously, one must not do).

Falcons' upper mandibles have a small, sharp 'tooth' at each side. Hawks, buzzards and eagles have a 'festoon', which is simply a curved portion in the same place. So when coping, this should be borne in mind.

Most overgrown beaks are caused by a lack of tirings and bones, which help to keep the beak down. Overgrown talons are caused mainly by soft perches (some people pad their perches, in spite of the fact that no wild hawk would sit on a padded perch) or by perches of insufficient diameter (so that the talons go right round the perch and never rest hard down on it). Where birds are in aviaries, the perches should be of varying sizes; rocks and large stones also help to keep talons in good order. (Where birds on blocks are concerned, do not use stone blocks. They may sound very good, but they get unbearably hot in summer and cold in winter.)

If you can avoid coping then do so. Once a bird has had to be coped, you will find that you will have to continue to cope it every so often. Correct diet and proper perches should make it largely unnecessary.

17 Lost Hawks

As I have said earlier, falconry is a very demanding sport, since no falconer can really afford to make a mistake at any time. All too often the smallest error can lead to disaster in some shape or form, and all too often that disaster could have been avoided.

Sooner or later all falconers lose a hawk; most often this is the result of using faulty equipment, or just plain carelessness on the falconer's part. Of course, unforeseeable accidents can and do happen, and the falconer who loses his hawk in fair flight has no reason to blame himself, provided that he has taken all possible precautions beforehand to avoid such an occurrence. But much more frequently hawks are lost because some item of their equipment breaks (I cannot over-emphasise the importance of daily checks on equipment); and in the early stages of training the beginner's despairing cry of 'Oh, I've let it go!' is all too often heard.

It is often very tempting to fly when your bird is not quite in yarak, or when weather conditions are against you; it does require a certain amount of self-control to keep oneself from flying in such cases – especially when perhaps one has asked a few friends to come out and see the hawk fly.

But whatever the reason for losing your hawk, when it happens the important thing is to know what to do, and to have a rescue procedure worked out in advance, which can be put into operation without delay. You will need a certain amount of gear, and this should always be kept in readiness, so that when disaster strikes you will not have to waste valuable time hunting around for it.

All kinds of things can be of help in retrieving a lost bird. The following list is fairly comprehensive; some of the things you may consider unnecessary or too expensive, or you may have devices of your own which you think will serve you better.

binoculars
telescope
landing net
climbing irons
long pole with hook or noose at the end
ladders

light nylon net about 6 m by 1.8 m (20 ft by 6 ft)
torches
torch pole
long pole (or old fishing rod) with noose and light
traps
maps
small roll of adhesive tape
pen and paper (or visiting cards)
whistles
spare gloves, bags with lures, pick-ups, creances etc.

Binoculars   The best binoculars for hawking will be those with a magnification power of not less than × 8 and not more than × 12. The greater the magnification, the more difficult it is to keep the glasses steady enough to get a clear image, particularly when the bird is in flight; and binoculars with a big magnification are correspondingly larger and heavier than those with lesser magnification. (This is worth remembering when buying them; weight, or the lack of it, can make a great deal of difference when you have a long way to walk.)

Telescope   Although telescopes are not much good for following a bird in flight, they can be very useful for identifying a motionless bird at a distance, since their magnification power is greater than that of binoculars (× 20 or more).

Landing net   This should be of the light, folding type, with large mesh and as long a handle as possible. It is of use when the bird is in a tree, in such a position that her jesses cannot be hooked up from below, and cannot be reached by hand; or when she is in long grass and there is too much vegetation around her for you to 'wind her up' (see below).

Climbing irons   These metal spikes, which are strapped to one's ankles, can be of great help in ascending trees which would otherwise be unclimbable (although if a tree is too big to get your arms around, climbing irons on their own will not solve the problem). You should practise using climbing irons beforehand, rather than waiting until you actually lose your hawk and have to scale a difficult tree to retrieve her.

Climbing ropes   If you can throw a light line over a strong branch then you can pull up a heavier, stronger climbing rope. However, these are probably not worth buying as a general rule; you might need to use one only once in a lifetime.

Long pole with hook or noose at the end   This is best made of the large type of bamboo described in the previous chapter, as this does not weigh much, but is strong. The hook at the top end can be made of wire, and is best fixed by drilling a couple of holes through the bamboo, threading the wire through them and then binding it into position. This hook can be passed through one of the jess slits (though it takes a steady hand to do it), and is also very useful if, as can happen, the bird has escaped with her swivel still attached to the jesses, owing to her leash breaking. Swimming pool manufacturers now make very useful light, metal poles (in two sections) which are used for pool cleaning. As this type of pole is hollow, you can fix a noose at the top and run the line down inside the shaft. A pull on the line will tighten the noose round a jess and hold it securely. (To transport any of these long pole devices you will probably need to have a roof-rack on your car.)

Ladders   I am not suggesting that you carry these around the countryside with you when out hawking. But often, if one marks down a lost hawk to her roosting place at night, a ladder is much easier to use than ropes or climbing irons. Ladders can often be borrowed from a nearby farm.

Net   A light nylon net about 6 m by 1.8 m (20 ft by 6 ft) is quite good for most purposes. Two people are needed to use the net, one at each end, holding a corner in each hand. This is a convenient catching device, which can be raised or lowered depending on circumstances. Carry it in a small bag, otherwise it will snag and tangle on every projection you come across.

Torches   The bigger and brighter they are, the better. Here I should say that it is a good scheme to have accustomed your bird to having a torch shone on her at night and to being picked lip by torchlight. This will make your task easier should you ever have to retrieve her at night.

Torch pole   This is a long pole (again, best made from bamboo) with a torch reflector, bulb-holder and bulb at the top end. The wires from these run down the pole to a battery which you can carry in your pocket. (This keeps the top of the pole as light-weight as possible.) The reflector should throw the light downwards from the top of the pole. A short way below it a noose of nylon spinning-line is securely fixed. (Adhesive tape will help to keep this noose in place, and can also be used to keep the wires close to the pole.) This device is also for night use, and is simple, though rather frightening, to operate. Once you have located your hawk in a tree, you move in, first using your big torch and then, as you get nearer, your pole light. (You can of course use it in conjunction with a ladder, if necessary.) With the aid of the light you can see enough to get the noose over the hawk's head; then, with a short, sharp movement, pull her down off her perch. Immediately run in and release her, or she will strangle. In the past, this was a method used for trapping wild hawks.

Traps   There are very many types of trap, and I have illustrated and described two of these (see figures 111–112). They are of little or no use for falcons.

Maps   You may know the district very well, but a large scale Ordnance Survey Map is still a very useful thing to have. It will tell you and your helpers where everything is – bridges over rivers that you may encounter, telephone boxes,

TRAPS

111 German trap for short-wings, with passage gowhawk. Note the food and water containers for the decoy homing pigeon. As the trap is sprung, the door to the decoy compartment automatically opens and releases the pigeon. The twin bows are activated by a double-coiled spring at each end.

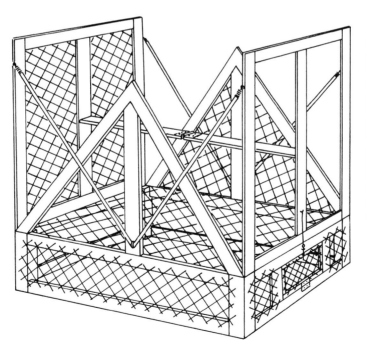

112 Swedish trap. This works on a similar principle to the German trap, but is activated by strong elastic luggage straps, and the hinged trigger bar is a separate piece held in place by tension. This is a very efficient form of trap and is simple to make. Decoy birds must be properly cared for, and must never be left out in bad weather.

public houses and so on. (Public houses can be very useful in as much as you can advertise among the clientele the fact that you are looking for a lost hawk.) In any case, you should certainly study a map of the area before going out on an organised search for a lost hawk. There may well be good vantage points (such as a hill or an old castle) near the spot where your hawk disappeared, and it may well pay you to go there first of all and reconnoitre the area.

Adhesive tape   This is very handy for silencing the bells on other hawks that may be out with you, and which can cause confusion.

Pen and paper   Carry these, so that you can give your name, .address, and telephone number to anyone you meet who might possibly see the hawk later on. Visiting cards are even better, as they save time. As an added inducement to people to keep a look-out for the bird, you can offer a reasonable reward, too.

Whistles   These are very useful, as you and your helpers can signal to each other from a distance, using a pre-arranged code. Do not make this too complicated, though. For example, one blast on the whistle means that you have sighted a hawk, but are not sure if it is the lost one. (You can point in the right direction, and flap your arms up and down if you want to indicate that the bird is flying.) Two blasts mean that you have definitely identified it as the lost bird, from seeing the jesses or hearing the bells. Three blasts mean you have captured the bird, her jesses are actually in your hand, and the search party can either join you or make their way back to their own transport. (Do be careful, though, that everyone knows the search has been called off before you go on your way rejoicing. If you leave anyone stranded you will be most unpopular. I and two other people once walked, quite unnecessarily, for five hours, not knowing that the hawk had been found. When we got home after dark, tired, cold, wet and hungry, and found everyone else had changed, had hot baths and fed hours earlier, our feelings were less than cordial, to say the least!)

Spare bags, lures, etc.   It is only worth handing these out to people who know how to use them, otherwise they can do more harm than good. Usually the people who know how to swing a lure will have all their own equipment to hand, and will bring it with them if you ask them. But they may use a different type of lure from yours, and they will not know all your bird's little idiosyncrasies, so brief them first.

The more people you can enlist to help you search, the better your chances will be of finding your hawk. Plan your search in advance, and work across country with your helpers, rather like a line of beaters. The distance between you will of course vary; in close country, when looking for a lost goshawk, you will be much closer to each other than when out on an open moor, looking for a lost falcon. In close country no piece of cover should be overlooked, and so your helpers will not always be travelling in a straight line – they will have to deviate at times in order to make a proper search. Do make them understand this before you set off; otherwise some may take the line of least resistance, so to speak, and will skirt round the places that are difficult to walk through. And it is in just such thick cover that your hawk may well be concealed.

All kinds of things can help you in your search for the hawk. Of course, her bells will lead you to her in many cases; indeed, a bird without bells is extremely difficult to find. Radio direction-finders, used in conjunction with a tiny transmitter attached to the bird, are obviously very expensive but can be a useful aid. However, they are not infallible by any manner of means, and should never be used as a substitute for bells, but in conjunction with them. You should practise using them beforehand; you do not need to have the transmitter on the bird for this. Just send one person out carrying a transmitter, and see at what distance you can pick up the signal and how best to find him. Try this in different weather conditions, in different types of country and so on. The range of the signal is often far less than one is led to believe, except in the best of conditions, when the bird is high up and there is no interference caused by other radio waves or hilly terrain. The transmitters made in America are illegal in Britain, and must be altered to a wave-length acceptable to the Post Office Authorities before they can be licensed.

A direction-finder that is easy to carry and would pick up a signal and lead you to where your hawk had killed in cover, say only half a mile away, would be extremely helpful. Being unable to find a lost hawk that has killed before she has eaten a large crop (and will therefore ignore the lure) is one of the main reasons why hawks are lost while being flown.

Some form of labelling on the jesses and bells is not a bad idea, and is one that has been current for many years. (I have a bell in the Falconry Centre museum engraved 'Captain Hawkins Fisher, Stroud'; Hawkins Fisher lived in the late nineteenth century.) But labels on bells, or on Aylmeri, are often over-looked, since a person who finds a hawk is often too frightened to go close enough to read them.

Not only bells and direction-finders, but also the behaviour of other birds (and, sometimes, animals) can help you to locate your bird. Any of the crow family (rooks, jays, magpies and so on) will mob a lost hawk, though not for long. Carrion crows, in particular, have an easily identifiable alarm call which carries a long distance. Magpies will chatter and keep flying in and out of trees where a hawk is sitting. Rooks and jackdaws will fly round overhead, stooping and calling. Domestic poultry will create a commotion at times, if your bird is near. If the hawk is on a fence, or on the ground in a field after a kill, cattle, especially young stock, will sometimes gather round to gaze at her. This last applies particularly to falcons, which kill in the open a long way off more often than hawks. So keep a sharp look-out for any of these signs.

Lost hawks do not as a general rule fly very far, but falcons usually set off down-wind, and can go for considerable distances on the breeze. In hot weather they will sometimes go on the soar, looking for cooler air currents, and will then drift away too fast for you to have any hope of following them. They can on occasion be chased by wild falcons – lance lost a merlin in this way, because I was unwittingly flying her too close to a wild hobby's eyrie, and the old hobby chased her away out of sight. Wild peregrines will sometimes join in with your trained bird and stoop at the same covey of grouse, and I have had trained peregrines led away by a wild falcon; whether because of jealousy, or in play, it was hard to tell.

As I have already said, one of the easy ways to lose your hawk is to fly her in too high condition. Then she refuses to come back to you and you will have to chase after her to find her. If you are out flying and anticipate having this kind of trouble, get your field to move into strategic positions, so that they can at any rate cover as much ground as possible and see where the hawk goes. She is halfway to being recovered if you can keep her in sight; but once she is out of sight there is little you can do until you find her again. If the hawk is spotted flying into a wood (or a large tree) station your field around it, so that she cannot make her exit unseen.

If it is a falcon that you have lost, flying another falcon will generally bring her back quite quickly, provided she has not already killed. This can be a little difficult. It is best to have two lures. Bring the lost bird down first, then immediately throw your second lure out to your decoy bird, as some falcons will crab. I have never known this to work with hawks.

Where peregrines are concerned, it is always wise to keep an eye on the area where you lost your bird. Very often she may come back, looking for you.

If your bird does not return to you of her own accord, then you will have to start searching for her in the direction in which you saw her go. While you are looking for her, ask anyone you meet if they have seen her. (They will probably think you are quite mad, especially if you are swinging a lure, but this is something you will have to endure.) Tell them the size and colour of your bird, and describe the bells and jesses (since few people will know what you mean) so it is better to say 'short leather straps on its legs that hang down when it's flying'. Give them your name, address and telephone number, and ask them to contact you immediately if they see anything which looks like your bird.

Incidentally, do not forget to keep your telephone manned at home if you have been handing out your name and number around the countryside. If you are going to be out all day, make sure you telephone home every so often. There is nothing more infuriating than to return home after a fruitless search, only to find that someone had rung ten minutes after you left, and had you known you might have recovered the hawk quite easily, instead of searching for hours in the wrong direction.

You will also probably receive many false alarms. So often the informant at the other end of the telephone has been watching a wild kestrel or a buzzard. You will need to do some gentle interrogation. Always ask the person when the bird was sighted; I have had people telephone me to tell me about a hawk they saw three weeks before and 300 miles away. Always ask whether the bird seen was hovering, if it had jesses, and if your informant heard the bell.

If, by the time night falls, you have still had no luck, either call in at local public houses, police stations, the RSPCA and so on, or telephone them as soon as you get home.

However, you may find your hawk. She may well have killed and eaten a large crop, and very likely she will not let you pick her up. You have a choice of action. You can wait until dark and watch to see where she goes to roost; then you can try to retrieve her at night by using some of the devices already mentioned. Or you can leave her until first light and then go out after her. If she has taken a really big crop late the previous day then she will not be keen early, and will be disinclined to move much until she has cast and begins to feel hungry again. This may not happen for a considerable time. Once, when I had lost a falcon, I was out early the next morning looking for her, and at about 7.30 a.m. I saw her flying across a field towards me. She completely ignored my lure and pitched in a willow near by. It was not until 3 o'clock in the afternoon that she was keen enough to come down to my lure.

Sometimes your bird will come down to the lure, but will not allow you to pick her up. She may leave the lure and fly off a short distance. This is where a simple procedure known as 'winding-up' may be used to advantage. Take your creance and your knife, and tie the line to the loop on the knife-handle. (Alternatively, cut a strong wooden peg and tie the creance to that.) Then throw your lure out into the most open place there is, and walk away. Let her come to the lure. Now walk towards her until you are as close as you think you can get without disturbing her. Stick your knife (or peg) into the ground, unwind the creance, and walk round her three and a half times, holding the free end of the creance. As you go round, the creance will wind round her legs. When you stop (on the far side of the circle from your knife) and walk in to her, keeping the creance taut, she will be unable to fly off.

When winding a bird up the grass should be as short as possible, so that the creance does not catch up. When you pass behind the hawk you may have to twitch the line under her tail, or wait until she lifts her tail as she balances herself to eat. It is almost impossible to wind a hawk up in long heather, but I

113 Winding up a hawk on the lure.

have done it by cutting some turfs, putting them upside down in a pile, and pegging the lure down on top. It is quite easy to do, and in this way the creance does not get caught up as it would otherwise.

'How long should I go on looking for a lost hawk?' is a difficult question to answer. Goshawks soon become wild, and then your only hope of recovery is by re-trapping. A peregrine will be tricky to pick up after ten days or so, though if you are lucky enough to find her on a fresh kill you can probably wind her up quite easily. I had a sparrowhawk back after a week, and within two days she was back in flying order. One of my merlins was recovered after 163 days. But of course, as each day goes by one's hopes (and one's chances of success) certainly diminish. Retrieving a lost bird means persistence on your part, as well as luck.

If you enlist the help of others when searching for your bird, then do not be surprised if they expect you to help them in similar circumstances, and be ready to do so. This is so obvious that it should not require saying at all, but I regret to say that people are not always prepared to repay one kindness with another.

One final word about broken equipment. A hawk lost due to a broken leash is in dire trouble, and every effort should be made to find her as soon as possible. The swivel will be bound to get caught up on a branch sooner or later, and then the bird is doomed unless someone is there to help her. But now that Terylene leashes have almost entirely superseded leather ones, a broken leash is a rare occurrence. Proper care will ensure that any sign of wear is spotted straight away. Leather leashes will sometimes break without any warning, and should not be used unless it is impossible to avoid doing so. (My Changeable hawk-eagle will chew braided leashes, and there is nothing I can do that will stop him.) Bad, cheap swivels will break very easily, particularly at the joint. Penny-pinching on equipment, and carelessness, will only lose you your hawk; and if you value her, not just financially but as a friend, then she is quite irreplaceable.

18 Hack and Hacking Back

Hack is a period of a few weeks during which young eyasses are allowed to fly free, the idea being that they learn how to use air currents, how to take off and land efficiently, and generally get themselves fit and ready for a normal life of hunting. There are various advantages and disadvantages to hack, and these have long been a matter for discussion and argument among falconers.

In my own opinion, hack is unnecessary and (which is more important) largely impracticable at the present day. In the past none of the old falconers would have dreamed of not hacking their eyass falcons, since it was generally believed that unhacked birds were no good at all. However, this has now been completely disproved; indeed, there are some cases where it is actually desirable to have an unhacked, rather than a hacked eyass, particularly if she is to be flown at game; but more of this later.

Conditions have changed a great deal in the last 50 years or so. Whereas before it was possible for the professional falconer to hack his hawks on his employer's estate, nowadays nearly all falconers are amateurs, and few of them have much land of their own. To hack falcons successfully one requires control over a considerable area, since birds at hack can travel quite long distances (I have seen peregrines at hack as much as 15 miles away from their hack place). Once they pass beyond the limits of their owner's jurisdiction, they are at great risk from any trigger-happy gentleman with a shotgun (and there are, unfortunately, a great many of these around).

Another difficulty that arises is that for the more usual method of hack (there are two methods which can be employed) at least two, and preferably three or four young birds are required. In these days, when the licensing laws allow only one licence per person per year, it would mean that several falconers would have to band together in order to get enough licences to be able to hack their birds together.

This in its turn would present problems, since it is quite usual to lose a bird at hack; one can easily imagine heated arguments arising as to whose bird had actually been lost. The old falconers knew full well that they were likely to lose some of their hack birds, and actually took more eyasses than they needed to cover themselves against this contingency. In any case, it did not matter so much in those days, since birds were far easier to obtain in the first place. As I see it, the risk of losing birds at hack is so great that it far outweighs any advantage that might be gained by hacking them.

The main use of hack nowadays is to return birds to the wild. In the field of captive breeding, too, it is very probable that hack would have a definite value, if used to prevent imprinting in hand-reared eyasses. But the risks I have already mentioned still remain.

There are two methods of hack. The one generally adopted is to put two or more young eyasses out onto an artificial nest with some sort of shelter from rain, wind and sun. They are provided with very short jesses (without swivel slits), which are usually of different colours to make it easy to identify them. Some falconers also put heavy bells on them, but I feel these are not so advantageous as they were thought to be in the past. The idea was that a heavy bell makes it more difficult for a young hawk to kill for herself. Unfortunately it also draws attention to the bird, and this can easily lead to her being shot.

Some falconers use a loft, or even a flat roof, from which to hack their hawks; others prefer a nest in a tree, an old farm cart or a barn. What you choose is really a matter of what is most convenient. The birds should be protected as far as possible against predators such as cats, foxes, and stray dogs, by a temporary fence of wire netting around the hack place. They must be fed twice a day, at regular hours, and the food must be tied or stapled down to a board or block, so that they cannot carry it. Before you put them out in the hack place, you must arrange things so that you can watch them when they come back to feed, and trap them when the time comes. Once they can leave the nest, a bath should be provided.

During the early stages of hack the young birds will remain on the nest. As they grow, however, they will start moving around more. If the hack place is situated so that they can jump or scramble into a tree, this will be of help to them. (A shallow-angled ramp with footholds, leading from the nest to a branch is a good idea.) Should an eyass miss her footing and fall, then the anti-vermin fence will stop her wandering away too far.

Very soon the eyasses will be on the wing. At first they will only be taking short flights, but gradually they will be learning and improving their powers of flight, and the distance they go will increase each day. They will play with each other, like all young creatures, and even with other birds too. I have seen hack hawks stooping at jackdaws, and once on the Black Sea coast I watched three wild eyass peregrines, which had only recently left the eyrie, trying to catch a hoodie crow. At first I thought they were hunting in earnest, but I soon realised that although the hoodie used the trees by the shore to take cover at times, he kept coming back for more, and was obviously enjoying what appeared to me to be a dangerous game of 'last-across'. Hack hawks at play are certainly a great delight to watch.

The important thing about this method of hack is that the young birds must be put out in the hack place when they are well-feathered, but before they are able to fly. In this way they establish it as a base, and become used to returning to it for food at regular intervals. The fact that there are several birds together means that, should one go a little too far away, the others act rather like a magnet, drawing it back. Thus they develop a homing instinct, rather like young pigeons. One bird hacked on its own in this way would almost certainly be lost very quickly, as she would not have such a strong focal point to return to. Similarly, if you put your birds out too late, after they are able to fly, they will not be conditioned to return in this way, and will soon be lost and will probably die because they have not yet learnt how to hunt for themselves.

As the eyasses grow stronger on the wing and go further afield, you should watch them carefully. Check at each meal-time, after pegging out the food on the hack board, that the full complement of birds returns to feed. (Do this, of course, by watching from a distance; you can build yourself a hide of some sort, so that the birds do not realise that you are there.) Some falconers whistle or call to their birds when the food is put out, in the same way that they will whistle to them later on, when luring.

If one of your eyasses does not return for food, you must assume that she has killed for herself. At the next meal-time she may arrive early – in which case it was a small kill and she is already hungry again – or she may be late, which implies a larger kill which has taken her longer to digest. When this happens, this is the time to take them all up. You can do this using either a trap, a noose or a bow-net. They can either be trapped singly, or all at once when they are feeding. If you decide to take them one by one, you must trap each bird at a time when none of the others is present; otherwise they will be scared off by seeing one of their companions taken. (In the case of the larger falcons, it is generally the tiercels that start killing first, because they are usually more advanced than their sisters.)

The second method of hack is little used nowadays, though there is much to recommend it. This is 'hacking to the lure'. The birds are trained before hack begins, and are then called to the lure each day for food, and picked up and fed on the fist. In this way they retain much of their training and stay relatively tame. After feeding they are released to choose their own roosting places. So they are free to fly around and play with each other until the next feeding time, when they are once more called down to the lure, fed on the fist and released. The advantages of hacking to the lure, are, firstly, that trapping, once hack is over, is not necessary; secondly, that a single bird can quite well be hacked in this way; and thirdly, that training can proceed without any period of in-activity on the bird's part, since manning problems were overcome before hack ever began. The moment your bird starts coming loose to a lure is the time to begin hacking her in this way.

Although, as I have said, I think the risks involved in hacking eyasses nowa-days are too great, I fully agree with those who say that hack is the best possible way of getting the birds muscled up and turning them into efficient flyers. However, I do not at all agree with the many people who have said that un-hacked birds are no good. I have successfully flown unhacked peregrines both at game and out of the hood at rooks, crows and gulls; and indeed, where game hawks are concerned, I would never hack one on any account whatsoever. I realize this is a sweeping statement to make, but I will explain my reasons for doing so.

When training falcons for grouse and partridge hawking, there are two problems which constantly crop up and which are not very easy to overcome. Firstly, game hawks will chase birds other than the type you want them to catch; and secondly, when they begin to get tired they will sit down in trees or on fence posts. To take the first problem: over most of England it is difficult to find any area that is not full of wood-pigeons, stock doves, turtle doves and collared doves. And as I have said before, these are the last birds you want your game hawk to learn to chase. Now although trained hawks are unlikely to catch pigeons, hack hawks, who have no falconer with them to advertise their presence, can quite often succeed in taking them by surprise, and will acquire the bad habit of pigeon-chasing only too easily. But the unhacked eyass, who has never actually caught a pigeon, although she may chase them once or twice, will soon give up when she finds she has little hope of success.

When it comes to sitting down on the nearest convenient tree or post, hacked hawks are very much more inclined to do this than unhacked ones, since they have learnt, during their few weeks of freedom, that such spots make good resting-places, and have been accustomed to sit down after every flight they make. Where the birds are to be used for rook and gull hawking this does not matter so much, but a game hawk that sits down instead of waiting-on at a good height is not going to be much use.

Unhacked eyasses have never learnt to sit down when tired (if they have, it is a sign that your training sessions have been over-long and that you have kept them up in the air when they were beginning to tire) and so this problem does not arise. In my opinion they are preferable to hacked birds at game, and are just as good at rooks and gulls. (Of course, for the best flights at rooks and gulls you should have a passage peregrine – though this is impossible nowadays, unfortunately.)

There are times when hack is extremely useful in returning birds to the wild. For instance, a clutch of young kestrels or hobbies may suddenly find their tree felled, or some young owls may have to be moved so that a farmer can have access to his hay. All you have to do is use the first method I have described. Of course, you do not put jesses on the young birds; you can, if you like, close-ring them, or contact the British Trust for Ornithology, who will send one of their members to do it for you.

Then hack them in the normal way, but instead of trapping them when they start to kill, go on feeding them until they are all hunting well for themselves. In the case of kestrels this may take as long as eight to ten weeks; and you should continue to put food out for them for a few days after they have stopped coming back to feed. A day of bad weather may make things difficult for them at first, and they will be glad of your supply.

In such cases, young birds should be hacked back in an area which not only provides them with good hunting, but is also suitable for them to nest in; for they will be homed to this area just as young house-martins are homed to your house, or salmon to the river down which they first swam to the sea. Young peregrines, for instance, should be hacked back from a cliff ledge, with an overhang to protect them from bad weather (their food can be dropped onto the ledge through a length of drainpipe).

I believe it would be possible to establish tree-nesting peregrines (of which there are still examples in Europe), or even peregrines that would be inclined to nest on buildings, as they have done on a few occasions in the past. Twice during this century peregrines have nested on Salisbury Cathedral. In the early 1900s two eyasses were taken from there by the Old Hawking Club (which in itself refutes the statement that the birds were in fact kestrels, since the Old Hawking Club would certainly not have bothered with this species). In the 1950s, when I myself was living in Salisbury, a pair took up residence once again – a pity that the Old Hawking Club probably spoilt the first attempt by taking the young – but the old tiercel was shot and was brought to me, still alive, in a paper bag. He was desperately thin, and had a single shot-gun pellet in his brain, and he died only a few hours later. Peregrines have nested on factory buildings, both here and in North America. Perhaps we could persuade architects to provide suitable nesting-sites on such buildings in the future.

Old birds that have been brought in sick or injured, and which have recovered enough to fend for themselves, can simply be turned loose (preferably in the neighbourhood of the place where they were picked up). It is not a bad plan to put a pair of old jesses and a long creance on such birds, and tryout their flying ability before actually releasing them. If they have been in captivity for a long time, they may have forgotten how to hunt for themselves; in this case, they should be hacked back to the lure.

Birds which a falconer no longer wants (such as a kestrel or a buzzard that has been used to teach a beginner) can also be hacked back to the lure. But do not try to hack such birds back in winter. They must go at a time when food is abundant and the weather is reasonably good.

Owls that are too young to hunt, but can already fly, are more of a problem. If it is possible, they are best put in an aviary for some weeks, after which time the top should be opened up so that they can come and go as they please. It may take some considerable time before they are away for good.

Although you are not likely to be faced with the problem of hacking back eagles, here is a word of warning in case you are. Not a great deal is known about young eagles and how long it takes before they become independent of their parents, but it certainly is a very considerable period (Crowned hawk-eagles are said to nest only every second year, since the previous year's young need to be looked after for such a long time). It must be remembered that all young birds in the wild have the advantage of seeing how their parents hunt and learning from them, and they will therefore become self-sufficient more slowly if they have to teach themselves.

Hack is already being used in America to put captive-bred peregrines and prairie falcons back in the wild. Unfortunately we do not as yet have any such plans in Britain (apart from some rather strange, isolated attempts at re-introducing the White-tailed Sea eagle and the Great bustard). Perhaps, now that we have learnt a great deal more about breeding and rearing young raptors, advantage will be taken in future of the falconer's knowledge and methods of hack to increase the wild population of the rarer species.

19 Dogs for Hawking

Let me say straightaway that I have never been a professional dog-trainer. But I have trained quite a few dogs to work with falcons at game, and with goshawks, sparrowhawks and even merlins. (No dog is needed for rook, crow and magpie hawking; indeed it would very likely be in the way.) I have also seen all sorts of dogs used for hawking – poodles, spaniels, labradors, dalmatians, terriers and the various types of setter and pointer. Without wishing to be disparaging about the other breeds, I must say that I am quite convinced that a well-trained German pointer is the best dog you can have for hawking. A good pointer is worth its weight in gold to the falconer, and although other breeds besides setters and pointers will point, this is rare.

You cannot buy a trained hawking dog as you can a trained gun-dog; although you can use a gun-dog with hawks, you must not expect it to understand what is required of it beyond a certain point. It cannot suddenly switch from one type of work to another.

It must be fairly obvious that you are more likely to get a good dog if you choose a puppy bred from working parents. Avoid show dogs; however beautiful they may be, they will have had a great many of their working characteristics bred out of them. I would also avoid Field Trial dogs (though not necessarily their offspring) as although they point marvellously they are seldom bred for stamina, and this is quite important. Do not be misled into thinking that a gun-shy dog will necessarily be good for hawking – it will not. A gun-shy dog is a very nervous, temperamental animal, and will prove difficult to train, so avoid it.

The earlier you get your puppy, the easier it will be to train. But no pup should be taken from its mother before it is at least eight weeks old. In these first weeks of a dog's life, and for the next few months, good feeding is all-important. If it does not receive the right treatment to start with, nothing can compensate for it later on.

Pointer puppies will not point when they are very young indeed, and the age at which they begin to do so can vary. Some will start to point at three months, others will take longer. Pointing is a characteristic which is bred into the dog, not something you can teach it; if your dog does not point, there is nothing you can do to make it.

I intensely dislike kennel-housed dogs. A pup kept penned up for most of the day runs riot for the first 20 minutes or so after it is let out, and until it has worked off its surplus energy it is a waste of time to try to concentrate on training. All my pointers have been very great house pets, but once they go out to work all this is forgotten. Once your dog is old enough, let it roam around the house and garden during the day (preferably in your company) ; then, when you begin a training session, it will be more biddable.

I do not think you need to teach pointers a great many things; m fact, the fewer basic things they have to be taught, the more quickly they learn. You must teach them obedience. They must learn to come at once when called, to sit when told, to walk to heel on your right-hand side (not on the left for a hawking dog) and, most important of all, to stay still when told. In their second season of working they can learn to flush game on command.

At first you reward your puppy with food and make much of it when it does what you tell it. Later on, food will not be necessary; the dog will be happy to come to you when called, or to sit when told, just because you show you are pleased when it does. The tone of voice you use to your dog is very important. Words do not matter at all, provided the dog knows from the tone of your voice whether you are pleased or angry.

Making a puppy 'stay' when told is quite easy if you start early enough. At feeding time it is only a step from making it 'sit' to making it 'stay' while you walk away with the food bowl and put it down where the dog can see it. You can use hand signals in conjunction with your commands, too; the pup will soon connect your hand signal with a particular command, and in due course will work to either. (But do not rely entirely on hand signals; if you do, there will come a time when the dog cannot see you, and you will run into trouble.)

Another important thing that all puppies must be taught from a very early age is that they must on no account chase sheep, deer, or similar animals. This is not always so easy to insure against, especially where deer are concerned (unless you have a deer park nearby where you can accustom the dog to seeing them) but it is something you must try to do. A dog that chases livestock is a menace. Of course, your dog must not chase hawks either, but this is a much easier problem to get over. Once the puppy will sit and stay on command, you can have her around while you are training your hawk. Gradually you let her come closer while the bird is feeding on the ground, and so they will become used to each other in no time.

Of course, one of the things you do not teach a hawking dog is how to retrieve. It is most embarrassing to have your dog come back triumphantly carrying the hawk, while the pheasant runs away.

Being over-dogged is like being over-hawked – if you have too many, none shows at its best and you end up in trouble. Personally I prefer to have one dog only. Then it receives your concentrated attention and is much the better for it. Certainly it is most ill-advised to have two puppies at once; like ammunition, they are far too prone to sympathetic detonation.

Once your dog begins to point, then it is simply a question of encouraging it to do so at the right quarry. Quite often dogs start off by pointing at pigeons or house-sparrows, and this worries their owners. Do not let it bother you. Pointers enjoy pointing. The first time my dog ever pointed was at a cow on the other side of the hedge! During the off season she would spend hours in the garden, day after day, embarrassing a blackbird on its nest. What a dog is doing when it points is exactly what faxes or cats do when they are hunting. The scent of their quarry drifts down-wind to them, and at once they stop. They then begin a slow stalk, moving forward very gently until their prey is within range, and finally gathering themselves up and springing forward to catch it. Your pointer is acting in a similar way. What you want it to do is to stop, as soon as it has caught the scent, and to *stay still*. Teach your puppy to stay when you tell it, first for food, then on command; then, when it begins to point, you will have no difficulty in persuading it to stay still, and you will have no need of check cords or other awkward equipment.

A good pointer for hawking should stay on a point for as long as you need it to – an average of ten minutes at least. It is no more difficult for it to hold a point for ten minutes than for ten seconds. Once, when filming, I kept my dog on a point for 35 minutes, with the single grouse in full view of her the whole time. Any dog that will point should be able to do this – there is nothing outstandingly clever about it. Shooting requirements, however, are different.

Scent can be divided into two categories: ground scent, which is where the birds have come into contact with the ground and the surrounding herbage;

114 German pointer on point.

225

and air scent, which drifts or blows on the air with the breeze. Pointers must therefore be worked into the wind, either directly or across it. They range to and fro (or 'quarter'), trying to pick up the scent. Some people are very strict as to how far on either side of them their dog should range, and if it does not turn within a certain distance and begin working out to the other flank, whistles are blown, hands are waved and sometimes much bad language floats across the moor. To be told 'My dog ranges like clockwork – never goes more than 60 yds to either flank' impresses me not at all. If you want a machine, you are welcome.

However, let us examine ranging for a moment, and see what exactly it is that you want your dog to do. At the beginning of the day, you consider which is the best way to take things, where the grouse are likely to be found in view of the weather conditions, and so on. When you start out, encourage your dog to range out to the flanks and work the ground in front of you. When you think she has gone far enough, whistle to her. She will turn and work back to you, and with a hand wave you can then send her out on the other flank. But, before you whistle her, do watch her carefully. She may have just caught a trace of scent and be working up to a point. Once you have seen a pointer working you will get the idea. When it has caught a whiff of scent it slows up and goes slightly stiff-legged, and if you leave it to work things out it may very soon come on a point. On the other hand, it may decide the scent is a 'has-been', that there is no game there any longer, and its speed will pick up again. This is the time to turn the dog.

While your dog is still being trained you should not have a crowd of people out with you. When you do start taking out a field with you, they are better kept in a group while the dog is ranging, so that their voices need not be raised any more than is necessary. (This is exactly the opposite of shooting. You do *not* want your field to walk in a line, spaced out, as the birds may then be put up before the dog points them.)

A good dog will soon learn the sort of place that it is likely to find grouse, and will go and work a promising area without being told. As far as distance of ranging is concerned, if you have confidence in your dog and it does go further than usual, why worry? If it finds a point, it will wait for you to come up. Of course, if you are afraid that it will creep or run in on the game, then you will have to keep it ranging closer to you – it takes the best part of a season at game for a young dog to gain experience, and you must give it time to learn the ropes.

I like my pointers to flush the birds on command, but this is something that I feel one should not attempt to teach them in their first season, or they may start to run in and flush the grouse before they are told to do so. This is why some people like to use a spaniel for flushing. Many shooting people teach their dogs to drop as soon as the birds get up (or when a gun is fired). I am very much against this for hawking. I like the dog to stand and watch. If the birds put in again close by, I then get the dog over there with me, try to get a fresh point and serve the falcon as quickly as possible. In time, the dog learns to do this of its own accord, since it can see the spot where the grouse put in (which it could not do if it were lying on the ground), and can be sent in on its own to flush the birds once more.

If your falcon kills, bring the dog close in to her while she is on the kill, and it will soon learn that it is grouse or partridge that you are interested in, and should start to point them more consistently. With German pointers you can often tell the difference between a point at game birds and a point at hares or rabbits. At game, the dog will remain quite still, except for its mouth slowly opening and closing (for dogs use their mouths as well as their noses to scent game). But if it is pointing a rabbit, its tail will quiver, or even wag. At larks and pipits the tail will wave even more (soon most dogs learn not to point small birds at all). I think snipe must smell very strongly; dogs will point them very steadily as a rule. Possibly this is because snipe are usually found in damp places, and the humidity helps the scent.

How far off will a dog point game? This depends on the weather conditions, how many birds are there, and for how long they have been in one spot. In dry weather scent is usually rather poor. In damp weather it tends to be good. A gentle breeze will carry scent a long way without dispersing it; a strong wind disperses it more quickly and dries up the ground too. Some types of ground hold scent better than others. Heather is good, short grass less good, and I have seen dogs unable to point grouse until they were only about 2m (6 ft) away from them; but on good days they can point them as far off as 225 m (250 yd).

There has in recent years been a peculiar tendency among some breeders to make pointers faster than they used to be. Why this is supposed to be desirable I do not know; indeed, some of these greyhound-type pointers go so fast that on a poor scenting day they run right into the game and flush it, simply because the breeders have been unable to endow them with brakes to match their increased speed. Since man is slower, if anything, than he used to be, there seems little reason for making dogs faster, and plenty of reasons against it. But I am talking here of hawking dogs only; shooting gentlemen doubtless have other ideas on what constitutes a good dog. One of my reasons for preferring German pointers to other dogs of similar type is that they are not too fast. (They are also better in cover than English pointers, and they have not yet been spoilt by show breeding.)

20 Hood-Making

There are very few people making really good hoods for sale today, so it is well worth taking the time and trouble to learn how to make your own. Not only is hood-making satisfying; it also saves you money, and, once you have mastered the technique, you will find that your own hoods will fit your birds far better than anything bought 'off the peg'. Bought hoods are seldom entirely satisfactory, and you may well have to actually take your bird to a hood-maker before you find something that is an exact fit. If you do buy a hood, and then find that it does not fit, a reputable maker will usually exchange it, or make alterations where possible. But do not start trying to make your own alterations and then expect him to change it.

The tools you need for hood-making are few, and have already been described in chapter 5:

sharp knife
leather punch
small saddler's awl
two sharp chisels 6 mm (¼ in.) and 9 mm (⅜ in.)
stitch marker
pair of parallel grips
Sharps no. 3 sewing needles (or a smaller size, if making very small hoods of very thin leather)
blunt-ended marlin spike or stag-horn 'winkle-pin'
strong linen thread (gauge 18 for large hoods; gauge 40 for smaller ones)
beeswax for waxing the thread

In addition to these, a heavy metal 'straight edge' is useful when cutting hood braces (or throat lashes for Indian hoods). You will also need a hardboard or plywood cutting board; 12 in. by 6 in. is an adequate size; it is not worth having anything more substantial, as the surface of the board soon becomes pitted, and you will then have to replace it.

If you are making a blocked hood you will need knitting wool and feathers to make the plume; also some thin brass wire, a pair of wire-cutters and a piece of file card (a kind of stiff bristled wire brush on a canvas backing, normally used for cleaning files and rasps, but here used for teasing out the wool of the plume). And as blocked hoods have cloth-covered eyepieces, you will need some kind of very closely woven cloth. (I use good quality billiard-table cloth for green eyepieces; hunting pink serves well for red ones.)

The best leather for the main body of your hood is cowhide (sometimes known as 'skirt' or 'belly') as this is stiff, and keeps its shape well. It varies in thickness; thicker leather of about ⅛ in. can be used for large hoods, while the thinner type of about 1/16 in. is kept for smaller ones. Anything thicker than ⅛ in. tends to be too heavy.

For hood braces one requires a leather that is both stiff and pliable; this sounds like a contradiction in terms, but in fact it is possible to find such leather in the shape of kangaroo hide, which is excellent for the purpose. Good braces must be stiff enough to stand out from the hood; if they droop down like a mandarin's moustaches you will find them difficult to do up and strike when the hawk is on your fist.

For the throat lash (the strip that runs round the base of Indian and Anglo-Indian hoods) and for the leather plumes on Indian hoods, any fairly thin leather, such as skiver, will do. As it does not need to be particularly strong, you can if you like make the hood gayer by using a bright, contrasting colour (dyed leathers often tend to be brittle, and so are best not used when there is any strain going to be put upon them). Some falconers put feathered plumes on Indian hoods, but being a traditionalist myself I prefer to use leather for these, and to keep feathered plumes for block-built hoods.

Anglo-Indian hood

The easiest of all the different kinds of hood which you can make yourself is undoubtedly the Anglo-Indian type. This is simply an Indian hood with Dutch hood braces. The back seam is sewn down a shorter distance than it would be on an Indian hood. Although it is an ugly type of hood, and can never be as comfortable as a block-built hood (since it does not conform to the shape of the bird's head), it certainly has its uses. Once you are reasonably proficient at hood-making you should be able to run one up in a couple of hours, and this can be most useful at times when you may need a hood in a hurry and have not the time to make a blocked one.

Whether you have a selection of patterns available, or are having to start from scratch, the first thing you must do is measure the bird's head. Only one measurement is necessary – the width of the head just behind the eyes, where the skull is widest. (Unless the bird is very well-manned indeed, you will probably have to ask someone to hold her while you measure her.) It is most important that you measure her accurately; accuracy in constructing a pattern is also essential, otherwise errors multiply themselves and the pattern will not be symmetrical when finished.

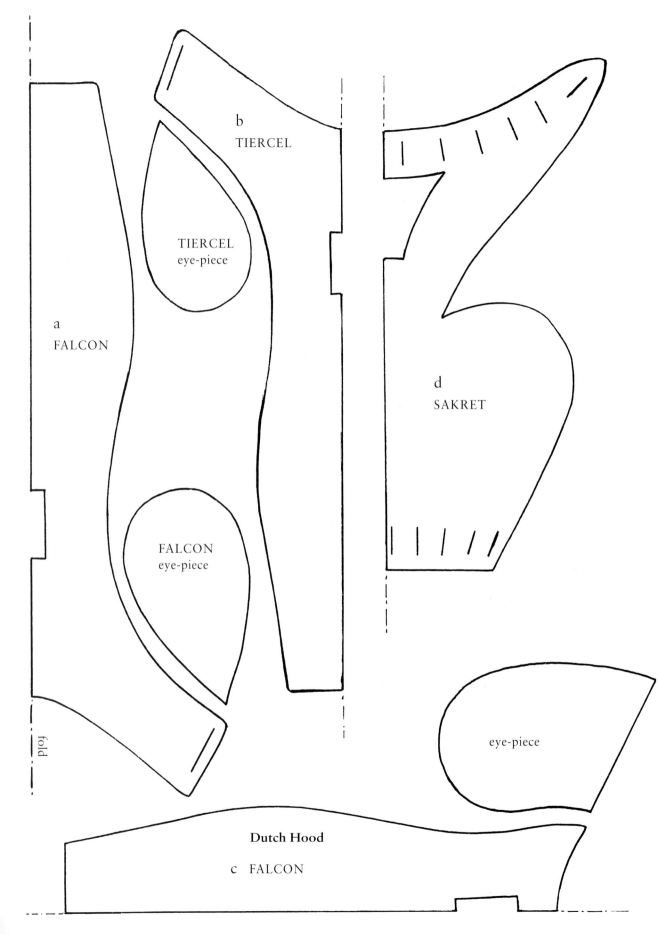

a
FALCON

fold

b
TIERCEL

TIERCEL
eye-piece

FALCON
eye-piece

d
SAKRET

eye-piece

Dutch Hood

c FALCON

116   Select a hood pattern of the correct size. The distance A–B is double the measurement across your hawk's head.

117   Place the leather, suede side up, on a flat surface, lay the pattern on it and draw round it.

118   Remove the pattern and cut out the hood. Keep the knife at right angles to the leather and try to cut right through in one stroke. Always cut *away* from corners, not into them, or you will have nicks in the leather of the hood. Cut on the inside of the outer lines, and on the outside of the lines round the beak opening.

119   Turn the leather right side up. Place the pattern on it and with a sharp point (a needle or bradawl) mark each end of the hood and brace slits. Mark the centre of the holes showing the position of the throat lash slits.

120   Mark the stitches with a stitch marker (from C–A, C–E, D–B and D–F) about 3 mm (⅛ in.) in from the cut edge of the leather. There should be an equal number of stitches between each of these points. Mark four to five stitches from Z towards X and Y (either side of the back opening). Stitch holes begin slightly below the corners C, D and Z, not directly on them. The last stitches of Z–X and Z–Y can be a little more than 3 mm (i in.) from the edge, to make them stronger. Do *not* try to drive the points of the marker right through the leather.

121   Cut the plume and brace slits with a 9 mm (⅜ in.) chisel. Cut the throat lash slits with a 6 mm (¼ in.) chisel. (You can punch holes for the throat lash if you wish, but although this is easier it does not give such a good finish.)

122   With a saddler's awl make the stitch holes at the points you have marked. Angle them, so that the point of the awl emerges halfway down the cut edge of the leather.

123   Thread your needle with strong linen thread, previously waxed. Pass the needle through the first stitch hole below D and pull half the thread through, leaving a long end. (No knot is required in the thread at this point.) Now pass the needle through the first hole above D, entering the leather through the cut edge.

124   From the top side of the leather, pass the needle through the second hole above D, and through the opposite hole in the cut edge below D. Continue like this until you have reached the last hole, making sure meanwhile that you hold the two edges butted together and pull the stitches tight. (The top few stitches will tend to slacken, until you start sewing down the remaining end of thread.)

125   Re-thread the needle at the top, with the spare end of thread. Sew down the seam again, filling in the gaps between your first stitches.

opposite page
115 VARIOUS HOOD PATTERNS
a Falconry Centre Pattern (Falcon)
b Falconry Centre Pattern (Tiercal)
c Dutch pattern (Falcon)
d Arab pattern (Sakret)
(See page 308 for patterns for New Zealand Falcons)
(Patterns shapes are shown halved, but all are full-size)

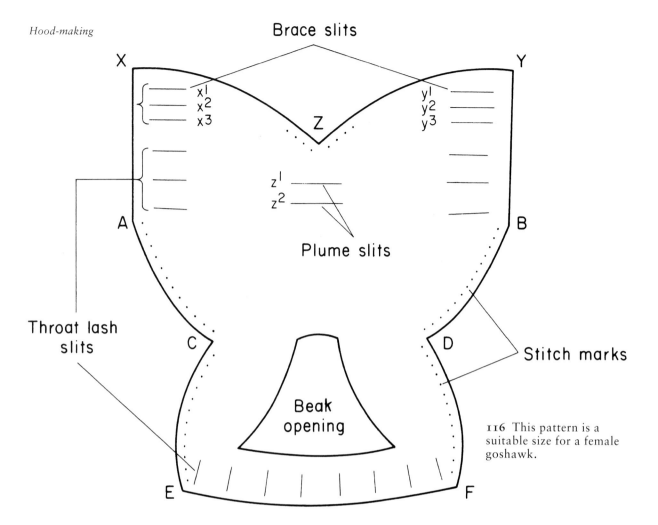

Brace slits

X   Y

x^1
x^2
x^3

y^1
y^2
y^3

Z

z^1
z^2

A   B

Plume slits

Throat lash
slits

C   D

Stitch marks

Beak
opening

116 This pattern is a
suitable size for a female
goshawk.

E   F

If it is hard to push the needle through, pull it with the parallel grips as shown. Grip the needle along its length (not across it, as this will bend or even break it.) Unthread the needle.

126   When you reach the last hole, unthread the needle and tie off the two ends of thread with a reef knot on the outside. (Later on, this will be hidden by the throat lash.)

127 and 128   Damp the seam. Place a suitable piece of wood (such as the handle of the stitch marker) under the seam on the inside. Hold the hood firmly, and hit all the way down the seam with another piece of wood, thus driving the stitches home, closing the seam, and shaping both the top corner and the seam into a curve, rather than a sharp angle. (If this is done properly, the noise should sound just as though you were hitting two pieces of wood together, without any leather in between.) Sew the other side seam in exactly the same way.

117

118

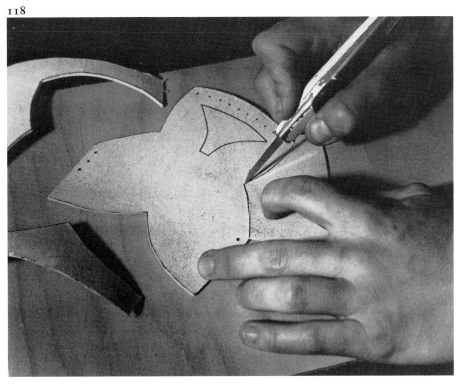

119–121

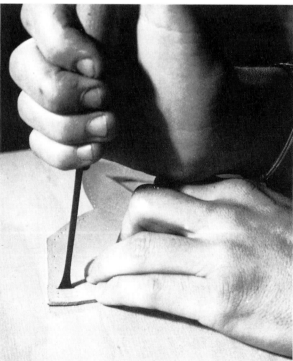

122

123

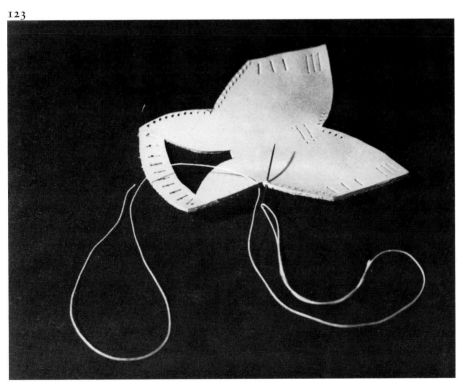

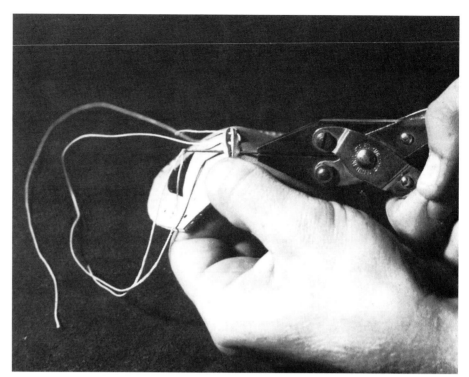

124
125

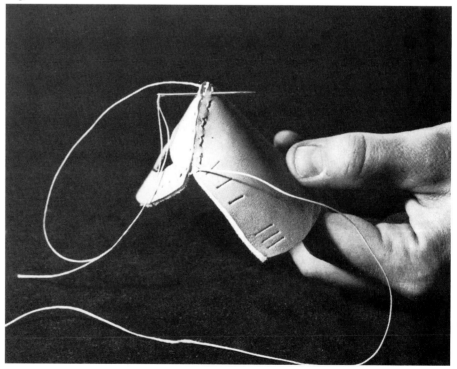

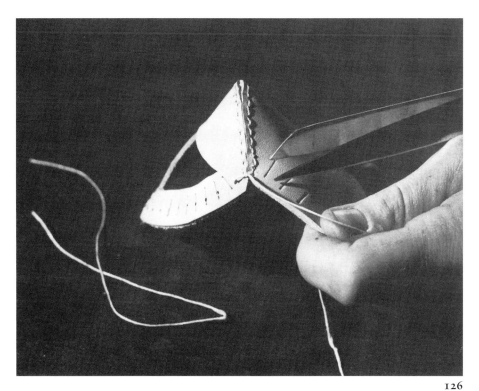

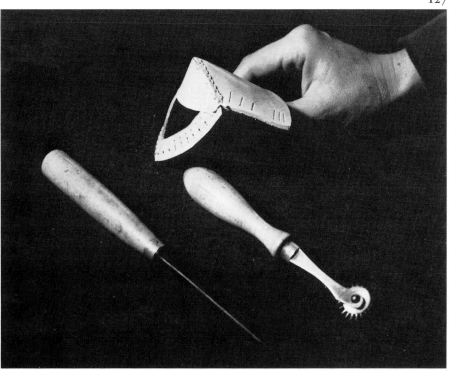

126
127

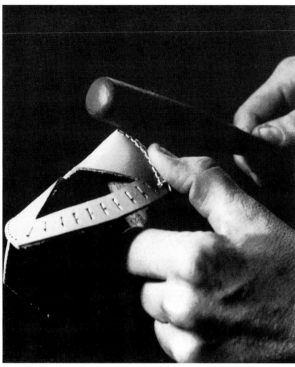

128

129 The back is sewn likewise, but when you reach the last stitch you must drive the bradawl *straight down* through the last stitch hole on the opposite side, and pass the needle through (crossing over the seam) so that the end of the thread is now on the inside of the hood. Repeat this with the second thread, and tie the two ends off in a reef knot inside the hood. Again damp the seam and the corner, and hit them as before. The throat lash can be entirely omitted in this type of hood if you wish. However, there are three advantages in having a throat lash, though the last is rarely made use of:

a) it helps to stiffen and strengthen the throat strap

b) it improves the look of the hood, and hides the two knots at the bottom of the side seams (though you can tie these on the inside if you prefer)

c) if you sew the two side seams only to within about 6 mm (¼ in.) of the bottom (this will depend to some extent on the size of the hood) then you can alter the circumference of the bottom of the hood, by pulling the throat lash tighter, so that the bottoms of the seams close

130 Cut the throat lash (a strip of leather slightly longer than the circumference of the hood base) and point it at one end to make it easier to thread through the slits.

131 With a small blunt-ended marlin spike or stag-horn 'winkle-pin' gently open up each throat lash slit. Begin on the inside of the hood at the back, and

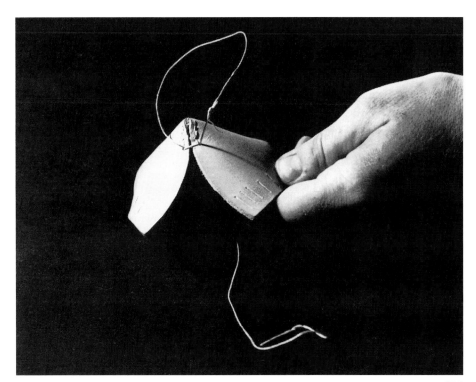

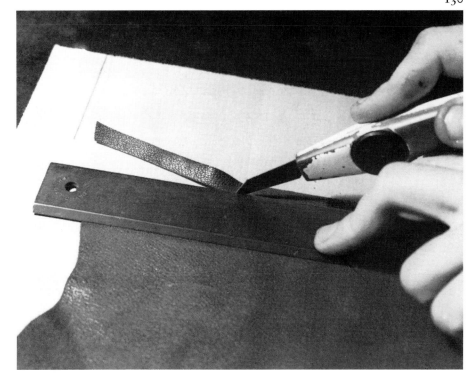

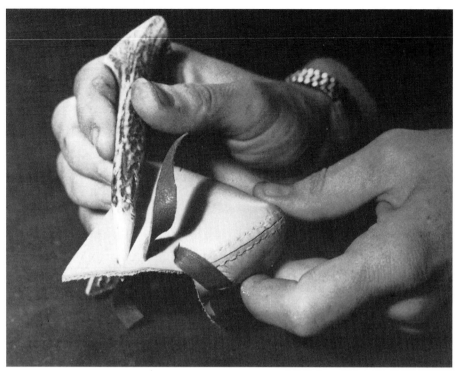

131

thread the lash in and out of the slits. If the number of slits at the sides of the hood is odd, and the number on the throat strap is even, the lash will hide the knots at the bottom of the seams, and will end up inside the hood.

132   Cut the ends of the throat lash straight across, so that when they are stuck down they just clear the brace slits x3 and y3. When gluing them down, you can at the same time put a dab of glue on the reef knot inside the back seam – this will stick the ends of the thread down.

133   With a very sharp small blade (I use a no. 15 surgical blade) chamfer the inside edges all round the beak opening, to make the hood fit more comfortably. A lighted match, very carefully applied, will burn off any surplus rough bits of leather on the chamfered surface.

   Cut the braces the same width as the brace slits on your hood, and about 23 cm (9 in.) long. Make a button at the end of each one (see the diagram of a leash button on page 72) and point the other end. About 12 mm–19 mm (½ in. – ¾ in.) away from the button punch a small hole in the centre of each brace. Note that one of the commonest faults made by both amateur and professional hood-makers is placing this hole too far from the button. This lengthens not only the button end of the brace but the other end as well, and because they are too long the braces then droop down. This makes them difficult to get hold of; in some cases they even touch the hawk's shoulders and

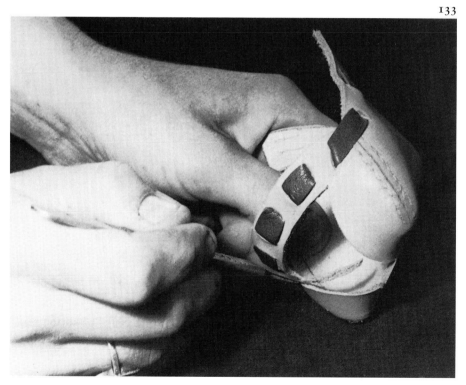

irritate her. From the hole, cut a slit in the direction of the pointed end; the length of these slits will vary according to the size of the hood, but one should in any case be slightly longer than the other.

To put the braces onto the hood see the diagrams on figure 134. These show how to put braces onto a blocked hood, but in fact the procedure is exactly the same in either case. Note that in the captions, the word 'down' implies direction from the outside to the inside of the hood; while 'up' implies direction from the inside to the outside.

a   The back of the hood, showing the brace slits numbered 1, 2 and 3 from the back opening.

b   Using a winkle-pin, as for the throat lash, and keeping the brace suede side uppermost, pass it down 2 and up 3.

c   Pass the end through the slit in the brace, down through 2 and up 1.

d   Pull the brace tight, leaving the punched hole just showing by brace slit 2. Repeat the procedure on the other side. The skin side of both braces will now be uppermost.

e   The pointed end of each brace is now leading towards the opposite side. The brace with the shorter slit now passes up through the slit in the other brace. (It is not important on which side you have the longer slit.) Should no slits be showing, cut a slit in one of the braces, taking care not to cut the hood while doing so. Note that this is the only process which is not duplicated.

f   Take one of the braces, and push the pointed end down slit 1, up slit 2 and out at the back of the button end of the opposite brace. Now pull both pointed ends, and the hood will close. Gently pull both button ends of the braces, and the hood will open (though it may be rather stiff at this juncture). Do this several times until the hood opens and closes easily. Now put the other brace through the opposite side in exactly the same way, and again open and close the hood several times. Should it still be very stiff, apply a tiny amount of jess grease on the parts of the braces that lie between the V at the back when the hood is open.

g   Open the hood fully, by pulling on the two buttons, and grasp one of the closing braces (i.e. the pointed ends) at point 4 – just beyond the point parallel with the button on the opening brace.

h   Now close the hood, and at point 4 tie an ordinary over-hand (granny) knot, keeping it as flat as possible. Before pulling it tight, make sure that when the hood is open this closing brace is slightly longer than the opening brace which lies above it. Cut off the surplus pointed end. Now repeat the procedure on the other side.

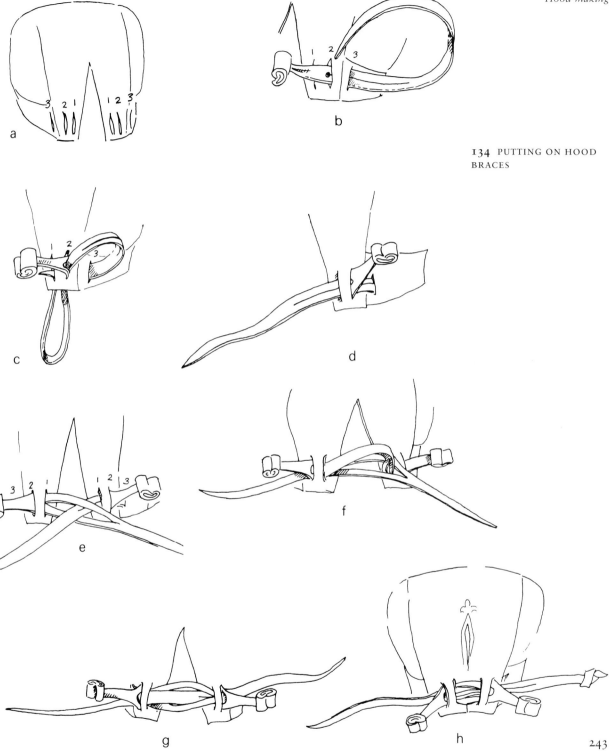

134 PUTTING ON HOOD
BRACES

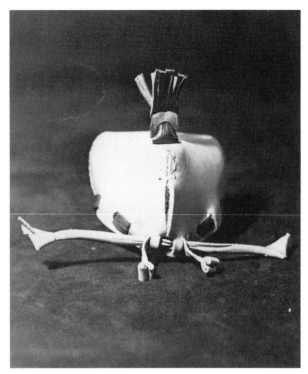

135

136

137

138

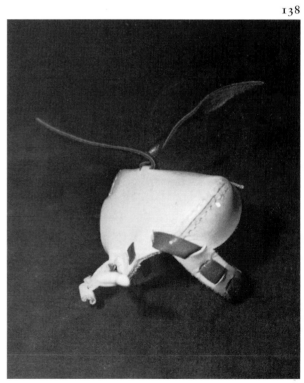

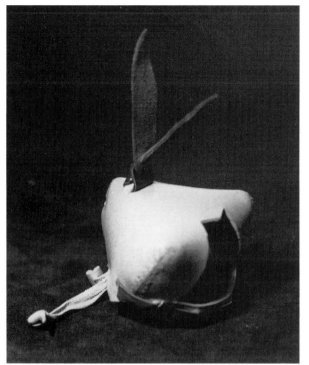

135 and 136   An Anglo-Indian hood in the closed and open positions.

137   Putting on a simple leather plume. Cut a strip of leather about the same width as the hood plume slits and point it at both ends. With the aid of a winkle-pin, thread it through the hood plume slits for approximately half its length. Punch a hole in it, close to where it emerges from the front slit.

138   Put the point of the back half of the strip through the hole in the front half, and pull it through. It now becomes the front half.

139 and 140   Punch another hole in what is now the front half, and thread the back half through this hole. You can now either leave it like this, or cut it straight across and fringe the ends with a knife.

Falconry Centre hood

Once you have made a few Anglo-Indian hoods, you can move on to the block built type with a considerable degree of confidence, as the actual sewing is much the same and all the leather is identical.

To make what I call a Falconry Centre hood (this is a Syrian/Dutch cross with some modifications of my own) you will need the tools I have already listed, plus cloth to cover the eyepieces; wool, feathers and wire for the plume; a pair of wire-cutters; a file card and some impact adhesive. You will also need a hood block of the right shape and size. This is where you will almost certainly start to encounter difficulties, since hood blocks are extremely difficult to obtain (although it is hoped that they may be on the market in the near future). If you cannot get hold of a set of ready-made hood blocks, you will either have to make your own by a process of trial and error, or copy blocks belonging to another falconer who makes his own hoods. If you have an old blocked hood which fits your bird well, you could take an impression of this (in the open position) by putting a balloon inside it and then running some kind of liquid cement into the balloon. When it sets, you can slide the balloon out of the hood, and use this as a guide for making a block.

Hood blocks are not exactly the same shape as a hawk's head, and so measuring your bird's head is not going to be a great deal of help to you. The block bulges out over the eyes, so that when the hood is on the bird, the eyepieces will not touch her eyes and irritate them. It is also much wider than normal at the back of the head, since a hood must be blocked in the open, not the closed position. Blocks can be made of any durable, hard substance; it must be something which will stand up to knife blades, as part of the cutting of the hood is done while it is on the block. Wood is obviously the best material, as it does not blunt knives as badly as most hard surfaces. But if you are making wood blocks then you will have to have some skill in carpentry.

Once you have got a suitable block, or blocks, you will have to adjust the given pattern to fit them. This, again, is a matter of trial and error; it can be a long and tedious business, or you can be lucky at the first or second attempt. Do not think that you can make a hood pattern simply by pulling an old blocked hood to pieces and then drawing round it. In the process of hood-making, the leather is stretched during the soaking and blocking, and then shrinks slightly as it dries, so it will not make a satisfactory pattern for new leather.

However, for present purposes let us assume that you have a hood block and that your pattern fits it. As you did with your Anglo-Indian hood, place the leather suede side up on a flat surface, lay the pattern on top and draw round it. When drawing round the eyepieces, make sure that the grain of the leather runs the same way in each one, so that they will both have the same amount of stretch. The beak opening and the V at the back of the hood are not accurately drawn at this stage (indeed, the back of the central piece of the hood is purposely left too long, to allow for any slight variations caused by individual styles of sewing). They will be trimmed to the correct size later on, when the hood is on the block. In any case, it is always better to cut the beak opening too small, rather than too large, since it can then be adjusted exactly to fit the individual bird for which the hood is intended. The base of the hood will also be trimmed later on. (This is an advantage of this design over the traditional Dutch hood, where the measurement of the base must be completely accurate right from the start.)

Probably the hardest part of the hood to cut out is the curve of the eyepieces.

Try if you can to make the whole curve in one single cut, going right through the leather; otherwise it will be untidy and will not fit well into the central part of the hood when you come to sew it up. Remember when cutting always to keep your knife at right angles to the leather.

You now have the two eyepieces and the central part of the hood cut out. Coat the suede side of the eyepieces with a thin film of adhesive, and stick them to your cloth. (The cloth, as I have said, should be a good-quality, closely woven material. Felt, which some people seem to think will suffice for eye-pieces, is not nearly strong enough; the hawk has only to scratch it with a talon and it will rip.) Once the cloth is firmly stuck to the leather, cut it round the eyepieces, leaving an overlap of at least ⅜ in.

With your ⅜ in. chisel, cut the two no. 3 brace slits on the central part of the hood, as shown on the pattern; these you will previously have marked with your awl. (They are, of course, cut on the skin side of the leather.)

Now take your awl and carefully make stitch holes all round the eyepieces, about 4.5 mm (³⁄₁₆ in.) from the edge on the skin side, just as you did on your Anglo-Indian hood. A stitch marker will not be of much use to you here, as the distance between the stitches along the straight edges will be greater than the distance between them on the curved edges. (This is because on the curve the stitches will be radiating outwards, and by making them closer together you will in fact ensure that they emerge from the edge about the right distance apart.) Do not at this stage make any stitch holes on the central piece of the hood; you will have to do this as you sew on the eyepieces, to ensure that you align them with the holes on the eyepieces, so you will not be able to make more than one or two at a time.

Wax a piece of strong linen thread, tie a figure-of-eight knot in the end and thread your needle. With your awl make three stitch holes in the central piece of the hood, the first of which will emerge in the top end of the brace slit (see fig. 141c). Now you can start sewing. As blocked hoods are sewn up inside out, the skin side of the central piece and the cloth of the eyepieces will both be on the inside.

Pass your needle through the first stitch hole on the lower edge of the eye piece by the pointed end (on the pattern, point A or point X), and through the cloth overlap. Pull the thread through so that the knot lies close against the leather. (You can, if you like, gently squeeze the leather at this point with a pair of pliers, to make the knot sink in, but in fact it will in any case countersink itself later on, when you soak the hood.) Now pass the needle through the stitch hole leading into the top of the no. 3 brace slit (on the central part of the hood). Look at your pattern again – point A (X) on the eyepiece should line up exactly with point B (Y) on the central piece, so that ABC (XYZ) appear as an unbroken line.

Now stitch the eyepiece to the central piece, sewing the leather edge to edge as in figures 141c, d, e and f. The overlap of cloth will in fact be lying between the two edges of the leather (this is trimmed off later). Make sure, while sewing,

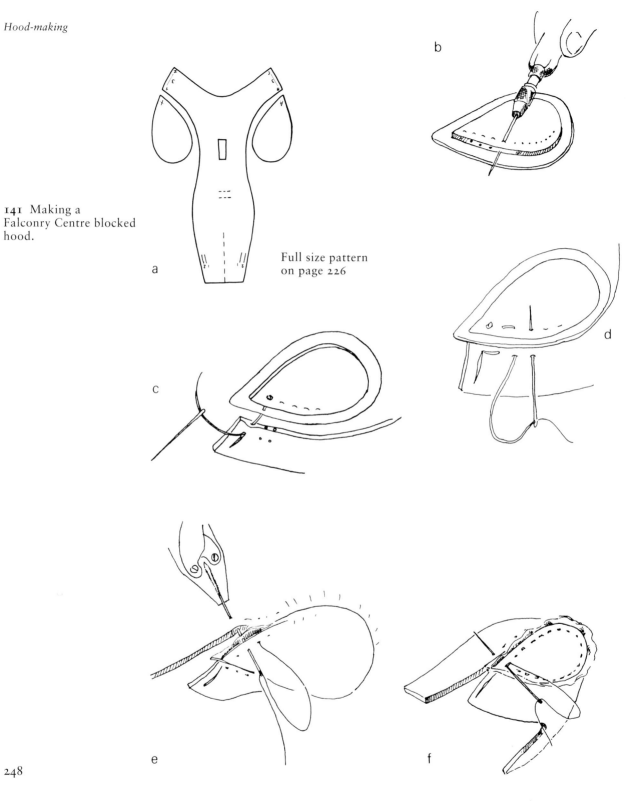

141 Making a
Falconry Centre blocked
hood.

Full size pattern
on page 226

a

b

c

d

e

f

that you hold the two pieces of the hood together all the time, so that they curve together at the seam and do not stand at right angles to one another. Use the parallel grips to help you pull the needle through if things get difficult.

When you come round to the final stitch of the eyepiece (fig. 141f), hold the back of the central piece so that it butts against the edge BC (YZ), next to the brace slit, where you first started sewing (i.e. in the position it will occupy when the hood is finished). Carefully aligning it with the no. 3 brace slit already cut, mark your no. 2 brace slit (shown on the pattern by a dotted line) with a pencil. Then cut it out with the chisel on your cutting board, keeping the chisel at an angle of 90° to the leather.

Now with your awl make stitch holes from the inside of no. 1 brace slit into the centre of the edge BC (YZ) and from the inside of no. 2 brace slit into the edge opposite BC (YZ). The final stitch holes will be 3 mm (⅛ in.) below the brace slits. Sew the two edges together as shown in figures 141 h and i, and finish off with a couple of half stitches, as in figure 141j.

Now sew on the second eyepiece in exactly the same way. But keep checking, as you sew, that it is going to finish symmetrical with the first eyepiece. There may be a slight variation in your sewing, or the leather may have slightly more or less stretch, and if you just sew gaily round without checking, you may find at the end that your hood is lop-sided when seen from the back. If it looks to you as though it is going to come out unevenly, you will have to adjust your stitching to correct it, making the stitches longer on one side and shorter on the other. A very slight unevenness can be rectified immediately after the hood is blocked (see below).

Now you can neatly and carefully trim off the surplus margin of cloth round the seams, using scissors. Then, with your sharp knife, cut the slit up the centre of the back (this appears as a dotted line on the pattern). The length of this slit will vary according to the pattern and the size of the hood, but it is better to cut it too short than too long. If it is too short, your hood will probably not go over the block, and you will have to lengthen it a little; but if you make it too long then your hood will be spoilt and you will have wasted a lot of sewing time.

During all the cutting and sewing process, keep your hands as clean as possible; otherwise the leather will get dirty and your hood will look scruffy.

The hood must now be soaked; simply drop it into clean, lukewarm water and gently rub along both sides of the seams with your fingers. Once it is well soaked (when it will be very flabby) you can turn it. At this point a lot of strain will be put on your stitching, and to minimize this you should turn the hood as shown in figure 141m, pressing both thumbs in on the curved ends of the eyepieces.

Next, slide the hood onto the block. If the back slit is the right length it should go on quite easily. Make sure that it is on straight, and then dry it on the outside with a clean towel, gently squeezing the water out of the cloth of the eyepieces. With your fingers, press down on the leather surrounding the

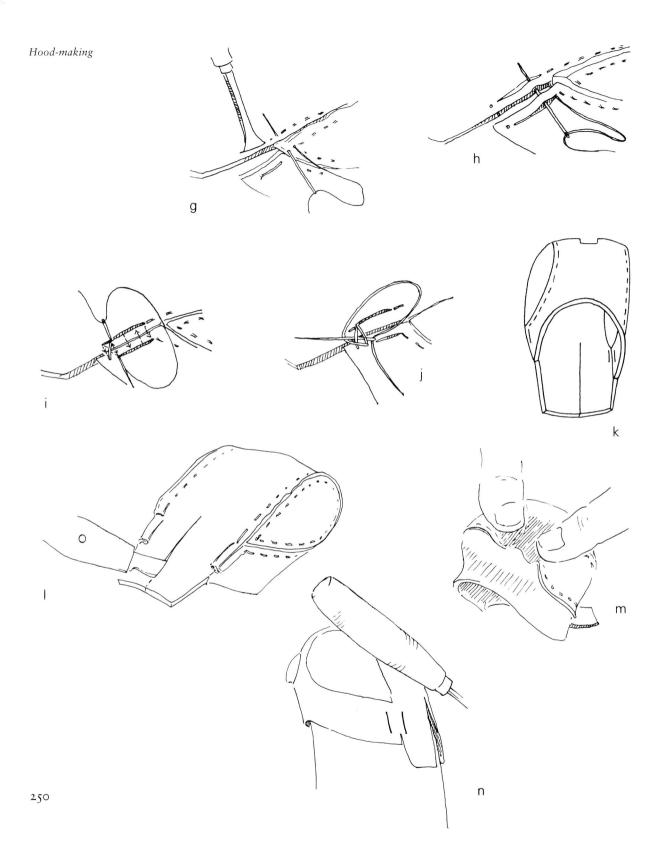

g

h

i

j

k

l

m

n

eyepieces, and check that you have a nice clean-cut edge lying all round. Sometimes uneven stitching, or awl holes slightly too near the surface, may cause irregularities round the eyepieces, which of course spoil the look of the hood. With the wooden handle of a chisel, lightly tap all round the seams, paying particular attention to the area between the brace slits, which will tend to stand proud because of the half hitches underneath. The back slit will have opened out slightly to become a narrow V.

Having made sure that the hood is centred properly on the block, look at the back, and if one side of the V is obviously higher than the other, take hold of the surplus part sticking out beyond the base of the hood with your parallel grips, pull it down hard and try to stretch it until both sides are level. Now let the hood dry out on the block; you can either leave it until it dries of its own accord, or you can hasten the procedure by placing it in front of a fan-heater. In my opinion forced drying, which takes some of the natural grease out of the leather, usually produces a better hood. But be careful, if you do use some form of heat, that you do not singe the hood. Beware also of leaving any tool marks or finger-prints on the hood while it is wet, as once it dries these will show up even more.

When the hood is really dry, gently ease it off the block (it should come off fairly easily). It may well still feel damp on the inside, in which case you should leave it off the block so that the air can get to it and dry it out. Once both the inside and outside of the hood are completely dry, replace it on the block and lightly mark with a pencil the surplus leather to be cut off from round the base.

Mark the V to be cut out at the back, again in pencil, and then cut it out as shown in figure 141p. (Remember to leave space for the no. 1 brace slits on

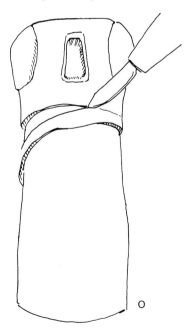
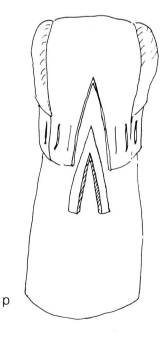

o   p

s

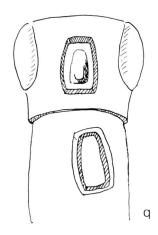

q

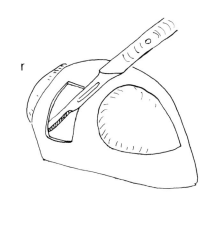

r

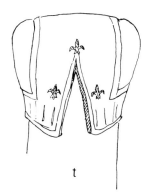

t

either side.) The finished size and shape of the hood will depend largely upon the way you cut the V – if you cut it too high you will notice when the hood is closed that it sticks up at the back and looks out of proportion; if you cut it too wide at the bottom, the hood may be too small round the base, since the base circumference of the finished hood will depend on how much you have cut away. (A hood that is too big round the base, but otherwise seems to fit perfectly, can be made smaller simply by cutting the V slightly bigger.) This is a matter of trial and error.

Now cut the no. 1 brace slits with your ⅜ in. chisel, carefully aligning them so that they are parallel with the no. 2 slits.

Next, mark out the beak opening in pencil. Cut it out, and take the hood off the block so that you can chamfer the inside edges. Both the width and the actual shape of the beak opening will make a difference to the way a hood fits a particular bird. Gauging this correctly is something you can only assess and adjust by experiment to begin with. Later on, your previous experience will make it easier for you.

I decorate my hoods with gold leaf, but this is a complicated business and something of a luxury, and I do not propose to go into it here. However, if you want to decorate your hoods, you can do so with simple patterns made with a thin-edged creasing iron.

The hood braces are put on in exactly the same way as has already been described in the instructions for making an Anglo-Indian hood.

To cut the plume slits, hold the hood in the closed position and mark them on the outside, about ⅛ in. apart. The gap between the slits should be exactly central between the top of the V and the top of the beak opening. The slits themselves should be ⅜ in. to ½ in. long. Put the hood back on the block, and cut them with your chisel.

To make the plume: cut a small strip of leather, the same width as the plume slits and about 75 mm (3 in.) long, and pass it through the slits as in figure 142a. Pull the two ends of the leather up and cut straight across them, so that you

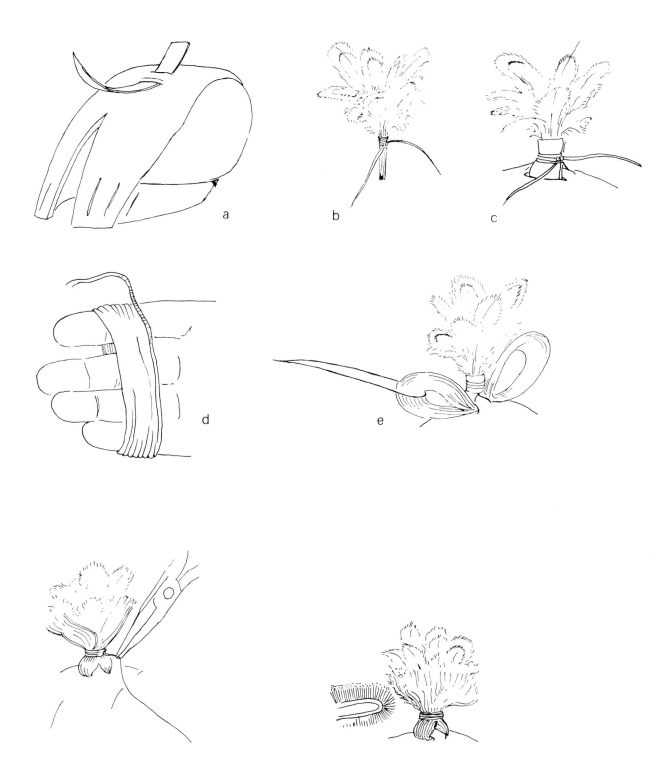

a

b

c

d

e

f

g

253

have about 19 mm (¾ in.) on either side. Make a small plume of suitable feathers, neatly arranged (fig. 142b) and bind them together with waxed thread just above the ends. Place the plume between the two leather strips. If it stands too high, cut off the quill ends until it is the right length. Bind the two strips of leather round the plume base with waxed thread (fig. 142c) and tie the thread off securely. Cut off any spare ends. Loop a length of ordinary knitting wool round your fingers of one hand (I use red wool for hoods with green eyepieces and vice versa) keeping your fingers slightly apart, so that it will slide off easily. The number of loops required will depend on the size of your hood.

Cut a length of thin copper or brass wire about 25 mm (1 in.) and slide this through the looped wool. Bend it in half and twist the ends together tightly with a pair of pliers for about 12 mm (½ in.). Snip off the extreme ends to make a good point. With your winkle-pin, open the plume slits under the leather strip securing the plume, and thread the wire through. Pull the wool about halfway through the slits (fig. 142e), snip off the twisted ends of the wire and smooth it back into a straight length. Snip through the wool loops with scissors. Leaving a short end of wire sticking out, wind it neatly several times round the wool (fig. 142f), cut off the spare end, leaving a short end which can then be twisted tightly together with the first end to a distance of about 6 mm (¼ in.). Bend the twisted ends down and towards the centre of the plume, tucking them neatly away under the wool at the side (fig. 142g). Take your file card, and tease out the wool that lies above the wire; a certain amount of wool will be pulled out during this process. (The file card will do no harm to the feathers on the plume.)

Finally trim all round the wool at the top with a pair of scissors, so that it looks neat and tidy.

Hackles from cockerels are the longest lasting feathers for making plumes, but almost any small feathers will serve – breast feathers from mallard, flank feathers from French partridge, neck feathers from pheasant and so on. (Guinea fowl feathers look particularly smart.) If you can find a small pin-feather, you can place this in the centre of your plume for a touch of extra *chic*. But keep the feathers quite small and short – a plume that is too long looks top-heavy and ungainly. Feathered plumes do not as a general rule keep smart for very long if the hood is receiving a lot of use, but as they are easily replaced, this does not matter.

Once you have made a few blocked hoods, you can try your hand at some of the other types – Dutch, Bahreini and so on. Although hood-making certainly does require care and patience, it is really not so difficult as many people would have you believe.

21 Making Bells and Hawking Bags

Making bells

I do not propose to go very deeply into the subject of bell-making. It is by no means easy to make bells, and it takes quite a long time before one is competent enough to produce any that are worth while. Also it is an extremely noisy affair, and you need quite a lot of rather specialized equipment (some of which is expensive and not easy to obtain). Unless you are a confirmed 'do-it-yourself craftsman, you are probably better off buying bells.

Bells can be made of brass, monel, silver and other metals. They are usually made in two hemispheres; a loose dropper is then put inside the lower one and the two halves are silver soldered together. A bewit strap is soldered to the top of the bell, and finally a slot is cut in the bottom to allow the sound to come out. Basic equipment for bell-making must include the following:

doming block (see figure 143)
doming punch with a thin shank
blow-lamp (gas blow-lamps are best)
hammer
supply of suitable sheet metal

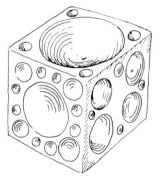

143 Doming block

First cut two discs of metal, heat one of them in the flame of a blow-lamp and then plunge it into cold water while hot. (This softens the metal.) Drop the disc into the largest and shallowest depression in the doming block, and shape it with the aid of a hammer and a doming punch. As it gradually takes on the shape of the depression, move it to a smaller, deeper depression, and continue to do this until you have hammered it into a hemisphere. When this point is reached you will have to turn the hemisphere almost at right angles, so as to be able to hammer round the top edges (this is why it is essential to have a thin shank on the punch; if you do not, it is impossible to get at the edge properly). The hammering stretches the metal; like a drum skin, the more it is stretched, the higher the note of the bell. Treat the second disc in the same way, and then clean off and level the edges with a file or on a grindstone.

Next the edges must be fluxed, and a thin line of silver solder run round them with the blow-lamp (this requires a very small but intense flame). Allow both halves to cool naturally; do not try to cool them in water. Check that their circumference is exactly the same by placing one half on top of the other. Make a dropper (a small piece of an old square section flooring nail will do; or a section from a hexagonal glass rod, cut off with the blow-lamp and then squeezed into a rough ball with long-nosed pliers) and put this into the lower half of the bell. This is best placed in a small depression made in an old block (not the doming block) to keep it steady. Line up the top half all round, and then join the two halves by gently running the blow-lamp round until the silver solder on the two edges melts and holds the two halves together.

Next, cut a narrow strip of metal and shape it to fit the top of the bell. This is the bewit strap. It is then soldered into place. Finally, when the bell is completely cool again, you can make the slot in the lower half of the bell, by cutting the metal with a hacksaw. Some people drill a hole at each end of the slot to help prevent the metal splitting.

'Acorn' type bells (where one half overlaps the other) are liked by some, but my own opinion is that they are no better and no worse than the normal type.

The lighter and louder the bell, the better; but this also means that it will be made of thinner metal (as this will have been stretched more by hammering) and so it will have a shorter life.

When choosing a bell from among several, get someone to take a bell in each hand and stand a little distance away from you. Ask him to shake each one in turn, with as little variation in shake as possible. Discard the one you like least and replace it with another. Repeat this procedure until you have exhausted the whole batch of bells; the last bell you prefer is the best one for you. But it will not necessarily be the best for someone else; human hearing varies a great deal, and what may sound good to you may sound bad to another person.

Making a hawking bag

To make your hawking bag you will need the following equipment:

1.14 m–1.37 m (1¼–1½ yd) of canvas, 91 cm (3 ft) wide if possible
a strip of 1.9 cm (¾ in.) Velcro about 30 cm (1 ft) in length
a gloving needle (or a sewing-machine with heavy duty needle)
strong linen thread
a piece of bamboo about 25 cm (10 in.) long
a 3.75 cm (1½ in.) split-pin (or cotter pin), preferably made of brass
a swivel (the size you would use for a peregrine)
impact adhesive
scissors or sharp knife for cutting out canvas

The diagram of the bag pattern given is to scale, except for the gusset, which is 91 cm (3 ft) long and 11 cm (4½ in.) wide. Having made your pattern on thick card and cut it out, lay the pieces out on your canvas. As far as possible you want to avoid unnecessary sewing, so you should use the selvage edge of the

144 (opposite page) Pattern for a hawking bag. (The entire pattern is to scale – one square = 2 cm (¾ in.) – with the exception of the gusset.

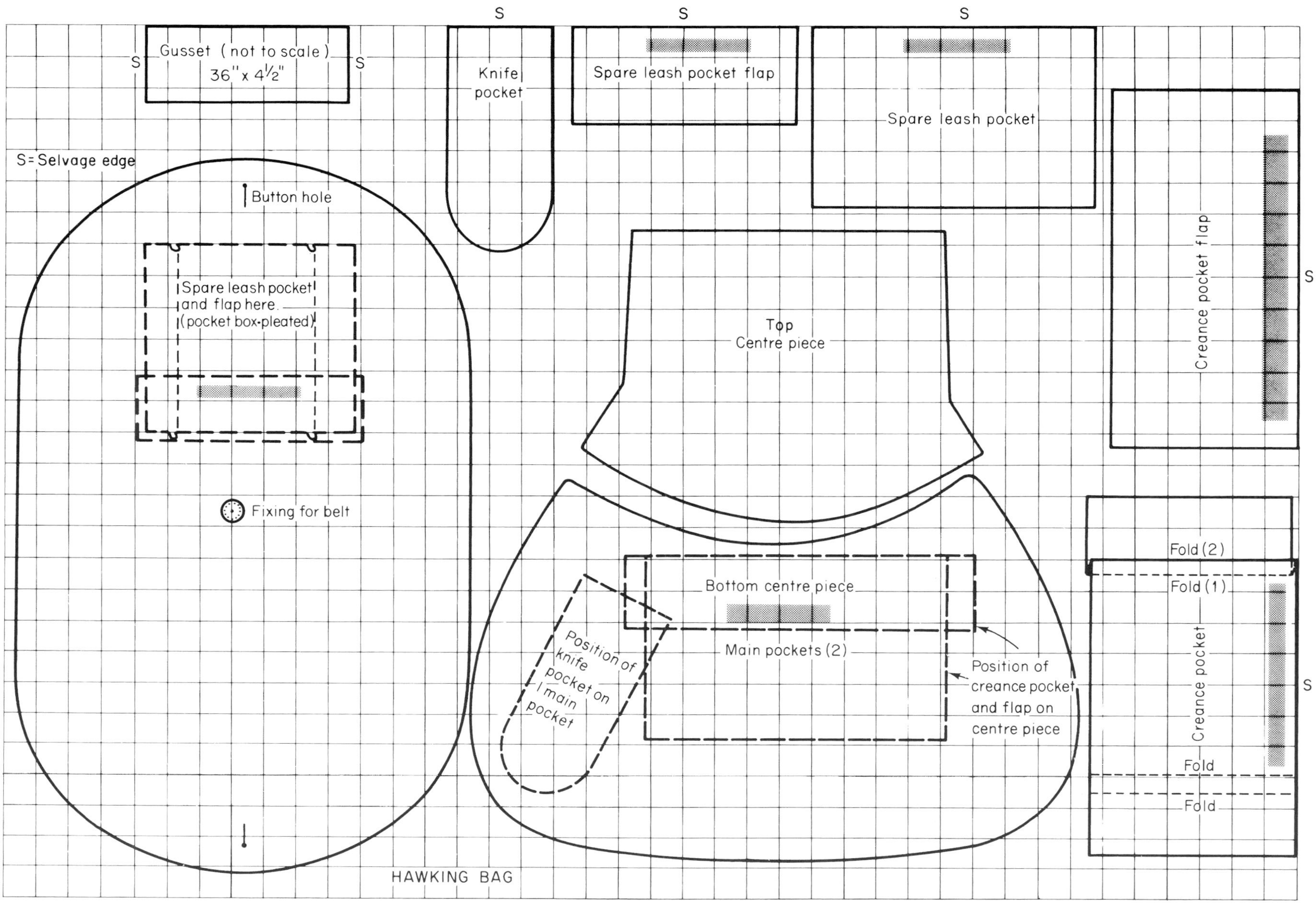

Creance pocket flap

S

Fold (2)
Fold (1)
Creance pocket
Fold
Fold

S

Spare leash pocket

S

Spare leash pocket flap

S

Knife pocket

S

Top Centre piece

Position of creance pocket and flap on centre piece

Bottom centre piece

Main pockets (2)

Position of knife pocket on main pocket

Gusset (not to scale) 36" x 4½"

S
S

S
S

Button hole

Spare leash pocket and flap here (pocket box-pleated)

Fixing for belt

S = Selvage edge

HAWKING BAG

canvas as much as you can. Lay the pieces out so that the following edges are on the selvage:

top edge of knife pocket
top edge of creance pocket
top edge of spare leash pocket
bottom edge of spare leash pocket flap
bottom edge of creance pocket flap

If your canvas is 91 cm (3 ft) wide, by laying your gusset pattern across the width of the material you will get selvages at each end. If the canvas is wider, you will have to make the gusset a little longer in order to give yourself a turning at each end. The pattern for the main pockets must be cut out twice (since there are two pockets); when pushed up to fit into the top centrepiece, it also does duty as the lower centrepiece (cut top and lower centrepieces together in one piece). Draw round all the pieces of your pattern, and cut them out. On the following pieces, all the edges that are not on the selvage will have to have 6 mm (¼ in.) turnings made on them, which are glued down:

knife pocket
spare leash pocket
main flap
the two ends of the spare leash pocket flap
creance pocket
the two ends of the creance pocket flap
the top edges of the two main pockets

Before assembly the following glued turnings must also be stitched:

main flap
the two ends of the spare leash pocket flap
the two ends of the creance pocket flap
the top edges of the two main pockets

On the reverse side of the gusset, draw a line down its full length, 5 cm (2 in.) from one side; it will be 6.25 cm (2½ in.) from the other side. Also make a halfway mark on the reverse side of the gusset. Now fold the main flap in half, and mark the centre of the fold. Fold the two main pockets in half and mark the halfway point on the bottom edge of each (on the reverse side).

Take the spare leash pocket and make a fairly wide box pleat in it. In the middle of the box pleat, about 6 mm (¼ in.) below the top (selvage) edge, sew on a strip of Velcro. As your box pleat will be about 7.5 cm–8 cm (3 in.–3¼ in.) wide, the strip of Velcro should be about 6.25 cm (2½ in.) long. Now sew a corresponding strip of Velcro to the reverse side of the selvage edge on the spare leash pocket flap, also about 6 mm (¼ in.) from the edge. Stick the two strips of Velcro together, and fold the flap over the top of your pocket. Glue round the turned edges on the reverse side of the pocket, and glue the part of the flap now folded over behind the top of the pocket. Stick them centrally on the main flap, about 5 cm (2 in.) below the fold. Now stitch from the top corner of the pocket down one side, across the bottom (here, if you are using a machine, you will have to miss out the bottom of the pleats, as they will be too thick, and sew them by hand later on) and up the other side. Pull down the front of the pocket out of your way and stitch across the back of the pocket flap to the point where you started. Run down over your first line of stitching for about 2.5 cm (1 in.) to give it extra strength. Now both the spare leash pocket and the spare leash pocket flap are secured, and for the time being you have nothing further to do on the main flap.

You now attach the creance pocket and creance pocket flap to the centre-piece in exactly the same way. Box pleat the pocket, sew the Velcro on both pocket and flap, fold the flap over the top of the pocket, and glue and stitch both pieces on to the centrepiece as shown in figure 144.

Now take the gusset, and on the reverse side, along the whole length of the off-centre line, run a bead of glue about 6 mm (¼ in.) wide. The glue should be on the side of the line where the canvas is widest.

Take the centrepiece and make a mark at the edge on either side, 10 cm (4 in.) below the two top corners. Starting at one of these marks, run a bead of glue right round the lower edge of the centrepiece, until you reach the second mark. Now align the centre mark at the base of the centrepiece with the halfway mark on the glued side of the gusset, so that the two are stuck together at this point. Stick down the gusset right round the edge of the centrepiece – the selvage edges of the gusset should now reach the two marks where you started and ended the gluing on the centrepiece.

Next, glue the turned edges (i.e. the reverse side) of the knife pocket, taking care not to glue the selvage edge. Take one of the main pockets and stick the knife pocket to it on the outside, off-centre and slightly at an angle (see figure 144). Stitch round the knife pocket, double-stitching for about 2.5 cm (1 in.) below the two top corners. Note that the size of the knife pocket can be adjusted to fit whatever knife you normally use. For those who prefer sheath knives, the knife pocket can be omitted altogether.

The main pockets must now be stuck to the gusset, and this is the point at which many people tend to make mistakes. All round the unturned and unsewn edge of the pockets, run a narrow bead of glue – on the *outside* edge. Also run a bead of glue along the *outside* edge of the gusset, starting and ending 5 cm (2 in.) below the selvage ends. Take one pocket, and stick it to the gusset in the *inside out* position, starting from the centre point at the base. You will find it more convenient to have your knife pocket on the same side as the creance pocket when the bag is made up; to attach the main pocket which has the knife pocket on its outside, lay the centrepiece, creance pocket side down, on the table, and pull the lower half of the gusset up towards you.

Stick the glued outside bottom edge of the main pocket to the glued outside edge of the gusset. You will be left with approximately 5 cm (2 in.) of unsewn, unturned and unglued gusset above the top corner of the pocket on either side. Fold this down in a triangular shape, so that it aligns with the top corner of the pocket (you can glue it down if you wish, but this is unnecessary). From this corner will protrude the unturned, unglued top part of the centrepiece. Turn these two side edges over and glue them.

Now sew from the top corner of the centrepiece down this turned and glued edge, down the turned edge of the gusset, and right round the lower edge of the pocket where it is stuck to the gusset. Continue up the other side until you have reached the top corner on the other side of the centrepiece. At this juncture the bag will be inside out. Turn it to the right way round, and then proceed to glue and sew the other main pocket on to the gusset in exactly the same way, inside out. (As you have already sewn the turnings on the top part of the centrepiece, this will not need to be done again.) Now turn it the right side out again, and you will have a pocket on each side of the centrepiece, one with creance pocket inside and knife pocket outside.

Now make a 6 mm (¼in.) turning on the top edge of the centrepiece (there is no need to glue this) and then fold the top part over to a depth of about 5 cm (1 in.). Sew along the turned edge in the folded-down position. This makes a tunnel into which you will put your piece of bamboo. Take a small piece of leather, not too thick, and cut out a circle about 2.3 cm (⅞ in.) in diameter (the size of a 5p. piece). Punch a hole in the centre of this, glue the back of it, and stick it so that the central hole coincides with the mark showing the centre of the main flap. (The size of the punched hole in the leather must be sufficient to allow your split-pin to pass through.) Now punch a tiny hole in the canvas where the mark is.

If you wish to have buttons on your two main pockets, you can now mark the position of the buttonholes on the main flap, and cut out and stick on two small pieces of leather as strengtheners. Sew them round the edges, and then cut the buttonholes straight through the leather and the canvas.

Next, take your piece of bamboo, whose length should be slightly less than the width of the top of the main flap. Roughly round off the ends with a rasp or a file. Now drill a hole through the centre of the bamboo, at the halfway point, which must be large enough to accommodate your split-pin. Push the piece of bamboo through the tunnel at the top of the centrepiece, lining the hole up with the mark which you previously made. (This is best done by sticking a needle or the point of an awl through the mark on the canvas, and then rotating the bamboo back and forth until you find the hole with the point. Then slightly bend the tunnel up towards you, and push the needle through the bamboo so that its point emerges through the canvas at the bottom of the tunnel.)

Now hold the canvas and bamboo very firmly and withdraw the needle. With the sharp point of your knife make small cross cuts through the canvas at the points where the needle entered and emerged. Open your split-pin enough to allow you to slide the swivel into the ring at the top. Then close it again, and push the pin through the hole in the centre of the leather on the main flap, through the canvas at the top of the tunnel, through the hole in the bamboo and out through the canvas at the bottom of the tunnel. Open up the protruding ends of the split-pin, bending them at right angles so that they lie to right and left along the stitching at the bottom of the tunnel. The main flap is now secured to the body of the bag. Hold the swivel and, if necessary, turn the main flap so that the spare leash pocket lies on the same side of the bag as the knife pocket. Sew the main flap to the centrepiece just below the bamboo, about 2.5 cm (1 in.) inwards from the edge on either side, parallel with the bamboo.

If you are having buttons on your bag, you can now line up the buttonholes on the main flap with the main pockets, mark the spot where the buttons are to be placed, and sew them on firmly. If you wish, you can replace the Velcro on the spare leash pocket with a button. Staghorn buttons look very smart.

All you now need is a 2.5 cm (1 in.) shoulder strap with a buckle at one end and holes punched in the other (to make it adjustable). Onto this you slide a spring clip with a belt fixing (see figure 144) which is clipped to the swivel on the top of the bag. You will also require a belt, to stop the bag swinging out-wards when you are on the move; you can slide a roughly carved hood block onto the belt where you can put the hood when flying.

This type of bag is very lightweight, quite easily washable, and will stand up to a good deal of wear and tear. Some falconers make spongeable linings for the two main pockets in their bags; these are difficult to put in and make the bag heavier. In any case, your bag should not need scrubbing out all that often, provided you remember never to leave your pick-up piece or lure in it when you hang it up after use.

22 Glove-Making

Gloves for small hawks and falcons can easily be bought, at a price. Leather driving gloves are as comfortable and as good as any; pigskin is probably the best, though doeskin, if thick enough, is also very good. For slightly larger birds, such as lanners, luggers and Cooper's hawks, you need something a bit thicker. Motor cycling gauntlets, sometimes to be found in army surplus shops, will serve, though most of these gloves are made with the skin side outermost, and this quickly gets picked by the bird's talons. The chrome-tanned industrial or gardening types of gloves are usually extremely hard and uncomfortable. (In the case of industrial gloves one should make sure that they have not been impregnated with chemicals, as is sometimes the case.)

At the time of writing there is nowhere in Britain where really good gloves for the more powerful birds can be bought. The large falcons, Red-tailed and Ferruginous buzzards, Harris' hawks, goshawks and hawk-eagles all have a very strong grip, and it is only too easy for their talons to drive right through what appears to be quite thick leather. In fact, good glove leather is not judged by its thickness – it is its density which is more important, as this is what stops talons from penetrating it. Also one does want a certain degree of flexibility and comfort in a glove, and thick leather will provide neither. These qualities do not only depend on the type of skin used, but also on the way in which it is tanned.

Bucksin, which I have found to be the only leather which combines strength, flexibility (even after getting damp), long life and comfort, is made from the skins of many species of deer. But unless it is tanned correctly it is not buckskin, but deerskin, which is not at all the same thing as far as gloves are concerned. Real buckskin is very hard to obtain, and although one may well be offered a 'buckskin' glove, one all too often finds, after paying a lot of money for it, that one has been deceived. Many so-called buckskin gloves are also cut and sewn incorrectly (particularly if they are the reinforced type).

Another disadvantage of bought gloves is that although they are, of course, sold in varying sizes, the lengths of the fingers are always the same. Most normal gloves have a large degree of stretch in the leather, but the same is not true of large falconry gloves. The only way to get a really comfortable glove is to make it yourself, and cut it to fit your hand.

As buckskin is so very difficult to obtain nowadays, if you are lucky enough to find any, you cannot afford to be fussy about the colour. Brown is probably the most serviceable, but one does find buckskin of other colours too. A possible source of supply would be an old pair of buckskin breeches, such as the House-hold Cavalry wear (or used to wear). I have a glove that has now been in daily use for 20 years, and before that the leather had seen several years' service as breeches; this should give you some idea of buckskin's lasting qualities. (Here may I say that the idea put forward by some veterinary surgeons that gloves should be thrown away as soon as they become cracked or greasy, is in my opinion quite impractical. One simply cannot afford to discard gloves of this type.)

Since it is unlikely that you will be able to find any real buckskin, you will obviously have to settle for a good 'second-best' alternative. Some of the old blacksmiths' leather aprons (usually grey in colour, denoting chrome-tanning) are quite good, if you can get hold of them. Elk hide from Scandinavia is also a reasonably good alternative, too; but both these tend to be on the stiff side. When choosing glove leather, the points to look for are that it should be difficult to push a needle through it, that it should be pliable, if possible suede on both sides, and should be free from holes caused by warble-flies or bad flensing. If you do come across the right kind of leather, buy plenty of it, so that you have some to use later. If you are making a reinforced glove with an overlay, you should have enough leather for a spare overlay in the future.

For the gauntlet lining you can use any soft leather, such as sheep or chamois, preferably as thick as possible.

Gloves are not difficult to make, providing you cut them carefully and take time and trouble sewing them up. For your first glove it is not a bad idea to do a trial run on a piece of inferior leather. It is also a good thing to have an old leather glove handy, so that you can have a look at it from time to time – this is of particular help where sticking the thumb piece into position is concerned. Gloves for big hawks must be hand-sewn, though a sewing machine with a heavy duty needle could be used for smaller gloves of thinner leather. (Of course, there are also special gloving machines on the market, but these are pro-hibitively expensive.) The corners on gloves are very difficult to sew up on a machine, and need to be sewn by hand, however. But even if you are sewing by hand, the heavy duty needle of the machine (without thread) is of great help in making your stitch holes quickly and evenly. Otherwise, you will have to use a bradawl.

The glove pattern shown is not like the pattern used by a professional glove maker, and I imagine that it would be highly disapproved of in glove-making circles. However, falconry gloves are a specialist item, and are not meant to be like ordinary gloves. I designed the 'banana' fourchettes so as to avoid as many seams as possible (most normal leather gloves have small gussets let in between the fingers), and to make the finished glove conform to the curve of the falconer's fingers when he is carrying a bird. You will have to adjust the pattern to fit your hand as you go along, trimming off the ends of fingers if they are too long,

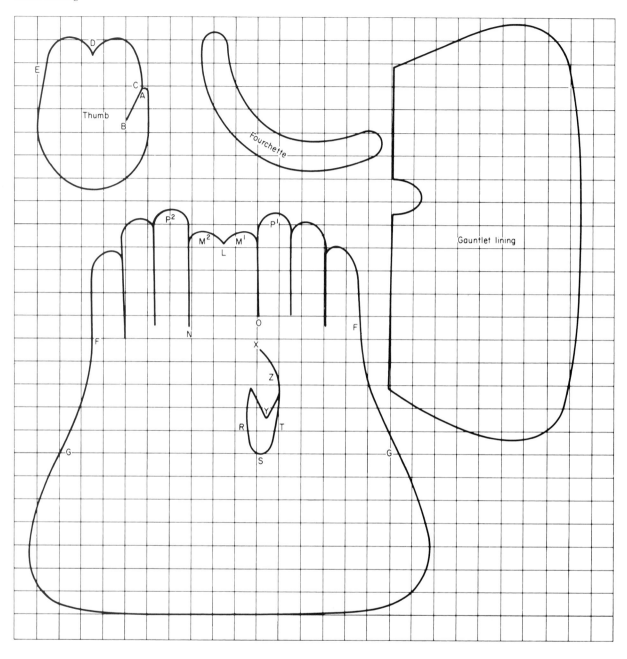

145 Glove pattern. One
square = 2 cm (¾in.)

but always allowing for your stitching in the length. The pattern is illustrated as though one were looking at the leather from the suede side (the outside of the glove), since it is from the outside that all the sewing is done.

Mark round your glove pattern on the inside, or skin side (if there is one) of the leather, as any marks will not then show on the outside of the finished glove. (Because the pattern illustrated shows the suede side uppermost, you will, if you are cutting a left-hand glove, have to turn it over so that the thumb opening is to the left of centre and not to the right. Cut out the thumb piece and the three fourchettes in the same way, with the pattern reversed. If you are making a right-hand glove, this will not be necessary.) Cut out your lining from thinner leather, and if you are making an overlay, cut it out with its thumb piece and one and a half fourchettes.

First glue the inside (skin side) of the thumb piece from D–C and from D–E, using an impact adhesive. (All gluing should be about 3 mm (⅛ in.) wide along the edges of the leather.) Stick these two edges together. Now glue round the remaining inside edges of the thumb piece, and all round the inside (skin side) edges of the thumb opening on the main body of the glove. Turn the main body of the glove over, so that the skin side is facing downwards. Pull up the glued edge of the thumb opening at point Y. Slightly turn back the glued edge of the thumb piece at CE (now stuck together), and stick it to the thumb opening at point Y.

Now stick the edges C–B and B-A (on the thumb piece) to the edges Y–Z and Z–X on the thumb opening. (The cut edges of the leather will now be side by side, standing up on the outside of the glove. If this is hard to envisage, take a look at an old leather glove and you will see what I mean.)

Continue to stick the glued edges of the thumb piece to the glued edges of the thumb opening from points X and Y round as far as points R and T. This leaves a portion R–S–T where the thumb opening is not yet stuck to the thumb pieces. Stick the two together very carefully here, as they must fit well, one into the other. You may have slightly to stretch the thumb piece or the thumb opening in order to get them fitting nicely together. If this does not correct the fault (in which case your cutting was probably incorrect to start with) you will have to enlarge the opening, or make the thumb piece smaller (or both) by cutting. If you do this, then you will obviously have to re-glue the edges. Once the thumb piece is completely stuck to the thumb opening, check that the thumb fits your hand well. If it is too long, cut it shorter (rounding it off, of course) and re-glue and stick it.

If you have a sewing machine with a heavy duty needle, you can now run it round over the edges where they are glued together, and this will make your stitch holes for you. If not, make the holes as neatly and evenly as possible, using an awl. (Some stitch markers are sharp enough to do this.) Now sew all these seams with an ordinary needle (not a glover's needle) and strong waxed thread. Make a knot in the end of the thread so that you can start sewing from the inside. Sew the seams with an ordinary running stitch – there is no need to fill in the gaps as you would do were you sewing an Anglo-Indian hood. Finish off on the inside.

When gluing and sewing the fingers it is very easy to get a finger with a slight twist if you are not careful. To avoid this, put a temporary stitch joining the front and back pieces of the fingers at their tips: M^1–M^2, P^1–P^2, and so on. Glue the inside edges of the first finger from L–M^1 and M^2, and stick them together. Try the glove on to check that the finger is the right length for you. If it is too long, cut it and re-glue it, allowing for your stitching.

Now take one of the fourchettes, and glue all round its edges on the inside. On the main body of the glove, glue the inside edges from M^1 down to O and up to P^1, and from M^2 down to Q and up to P^2. Now stick the fourchette to the fingers. It must curve inwards, to follow the shape of your hand when you are carrying a bird. Starting at the tip of the first finger, stick the tip of the fourchette into position at M^1 M^2, and continue to stick it down the edges M^1–O and M^2–N, making sure that the edges of the finger and the edges of the fourchette are aligned. From ON continue up the second finger until you reach P^1 and P^2, where you now remove your temporary stitch. You will probably have a spare piece of fourchette overlapping, and this must be cut off and the fourchette shaped so as to fit the top of the finger. Once again, check the finger for length, and trim it if necessary.

Continue with the other fourchettes in exactly the same way, until you reach the tip of the little finger. You will now see that the first and little fingers only have three sides, while the second and third fingers have four. Sew up the glued seams as you did the thumb, after checking that the glove fits well. Now glue down from the tip of the little finger as far as point F on either side. If you are not making an overlay for your glove, continue as far as point G. Stick the two edges together, sew down this seam and finish it off firmly at G. If, however, you want your glove to have an overlay, stop sewing at point F, leaving the needle and thread in position so that you will be able to sew from F to G later on. The object of temporarily stopping here is to make it easier for you to sew the overlay in position. The glove can then be sewn down to point G afterwards.

The overlay is cut slightly larger than the glove, since it is to be pulled over the top of it without constricting it in any way. It is made up as an entirely separate piece, consisting of the overlay body, the overlay thumb and one and a half fourchettes (for the first and second fingers). Many people who make falconry gloves tend to cheat here. They sew up the overlay with the glove, only using one thickness of fourchette. This has two distinct disadvantages. The back talons of any bird that needs an overlaid glove tend to rest under the first or second fingers of your hand when you are carrying it, and so this part of the glove should have a double thickness of leather. And when the overlay eventually wears out, the glove has to be partially unmade before a new overlay can be put on. (If the overlay is an entirely separate entity, it can easily be unstitched without affecting the main body of the glove at all.)

Make up the overlay in just the same way as the main body of the glove,

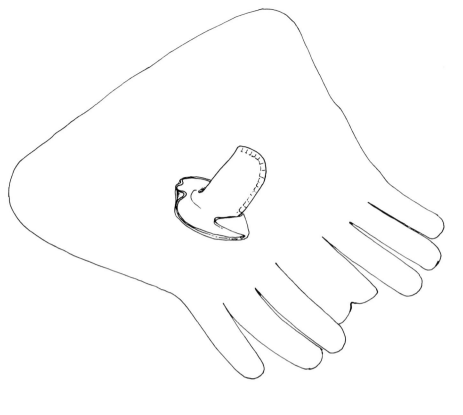

MAKING UP A GLOVE
146 The glove is cut out, with the thumb piece partly glued and in position in the thumb opening. The base of both thumb piece and thumb opening may need some adjustment to get a good fit. The marks on the thumb piece show where the glued edges have been firmly pinched together.

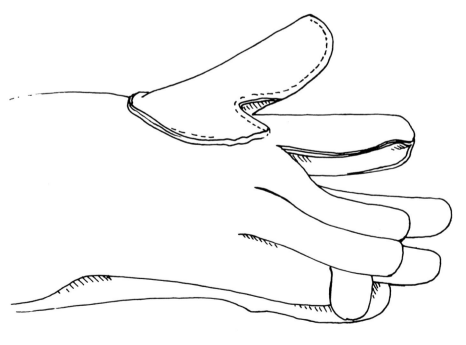

147 The first fourchette glued to the inside of the index finger.

267

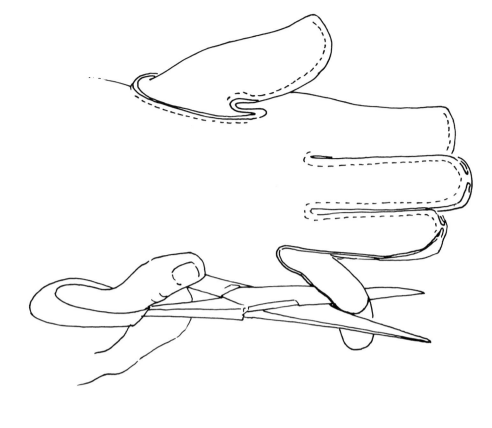

148 Trimming excess lenght from a finger to obtain a good fit.

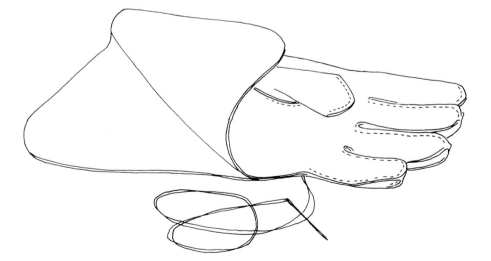

149 The lining glued into position.

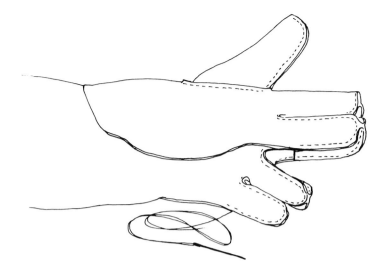

150 Pulling on the overlay.

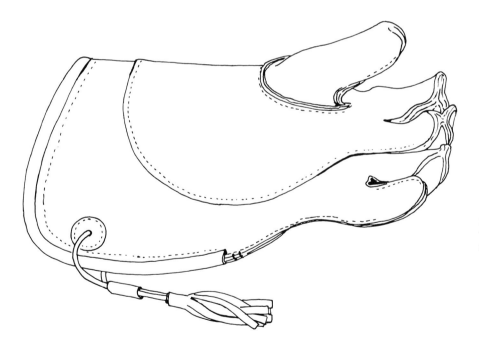

151 A completed glove with reinforcement, rolled edge and tassel.

checking constantly to see that the thumb and fingers are the correct length by trying it on, over the glove. When it is sewn up, pull it on over the main glove, so that it lies comfortably, and very faintly mark round the edge of the overlay on the main glove. (If you press the overlay well down, the nap on the main glove will sometimes lie in a slightly different way under it, and it will not be necessary to mark the glove at all.) You can glue the overlay and stick it in position before sewing if you wish, but if you do, take care that you do not leave glue marks showing.

Now sew, from the base of the second finger, right round from front to back. When a new overlay is required (many years later, if the leather is good) you simply have to unpick this stitching. If you have enough leather, now is the time to make a spare overlay for future use.

Really large eagles require very heavily padded gloves. Strips of old carpet make good reinforcement for these, but of course such gloves are terribly uncomfortable to wear. For slightly smaller eagles, such as Bonelli's eagle or Hodgson's hawk-eagle, I use a long gauntleted reinforcement with a thumb piece, which pulls on over a normal reinforced glove. (See figure 152.) The lower part of all the fingers is protected, and it works very well.

A rolled edge gives the glove a smart finish. You will need a long strip of supple, contrasting leather, about 3.5 cm (1 in.) wide. Lay this strip, suede side up, so that its edge lies parallel with the edges of the gauntlet and the lining, and then stitch it in position all the way round the glove, from G back to G. Now turn the strip of leather over to the inside of the glove, so that it covers its own edge and the edges of the gauntlet and the lining. This makes a neat roll, so that no cut edges of leather show on the outside of the glove. Once more, sew round from G to G to attach the strip inside the glove, and cut off the surplus edge of this strip.

Now cut two round pieces of the same edging leather, about 2.5 cm (1 in.) in diameter. Sew these into position on each side of the gauntlet, and punch a

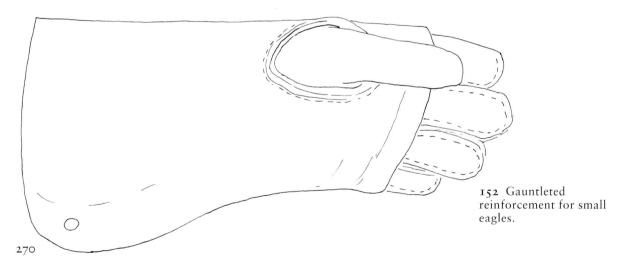

152 Gauntleted reinforcement for small eagles.

hole right through the centre of each for the tassel strap. Tassel straps have a purpose and are not merely ornamental. They are to keep your gloves hanging up when not in use. I once made up two gloves as a special order for a Danish friend, who sent me the leather for the purpose. Two weeks after he received them, he ordered two more. His dog had enjoyed both the first two!

The tassel strap is best made of strong leather; a plaited strap of 'square sennit' also looks good. (For plaited straps, see one of the many books on plaiting, knotting and splicing. These will give you all sorts of ideas for plaits.)

The tassel itself is purely ornamental, and is often overdone, in my opinion. Never have red tassels, or red leather round the edge of your glove – hawks are not colour-blind. Some people further ornament their gloves with various curlicues, flying falcons, monograms etc. It is all a matter of taste.

To make a simple tassel, take an oblong piece of leather (its size will be determined by how big you want your tassel to be). Lay it on a flat surface, and along its length, on the reverse side, mark off a strip about 1.9–2.5 cm (¾–1 in.) from the top edge. From this line, down to the bottom edge, cut the leather in strips about 3 mm (⅛ in.) wide, using a sharp knife or leather scissors. Now fold the leather along its length, and punch a hole centrally through it. Thread your tassel strap, plain or plaited, through the holes in the gauntlet. Pull the two ends down so that they are an equal length.

Now, with the aid of a winkle-pin thread each end of the strap through half the punched holes in the tassel strap, so that the ends lead down the centre of the tassel. They can now be joined, either by tying (if the strap is plaited) or by sewing (if it is plain) or by the same method as a bewit is attached. Once the tassel is pulled down, the strap ends will be hidden, and the strap will appear to run right through both tassel and gauntlet, as if it were endless. It should not be tied off each side of the gauntlet with large knots on the inside.

You will not be able to keep your glove in pristine condition for ever. It is bound to get dirty. Every so often I scrape the worst dirt off my gloves with the edge of a blunt knife, and wipe them over with a suitable disinfectant that is harmless to the bird. All hawking gear is sure to suffer from wear and tear, and inevitably gets a bit shabby from use. As my uncle used to say, 'Beware the chap who comes with a brand new bag and a clean glove. The acid test is – has he caught anything?' A few honourable scars from barbed wire and brambles are nothing to be worried about.

The Diseases of Birds of Prey

A great wealth of recent medical and surgical advances in avian veterinary medicine has made a large library of reference material available that would be difficult to summarise. Fortunately, by concentrating on the cause of disease in hawks, leaving the treatment and diagnosis of illness to the veterinary surgeon, a reasonable overview of this subject can be provided for the reader.

Active prevention of disease in birds is much more effective than treatment, if only because illness progresses rapidly and its signs are often hard to interpret. This chapter will concentrate on the symptoms of disease, assisting early recognition of illness, thus enabling the falconer to seek prompt veterinary assistance. The advice given in this book as to selection of specie, housing, diet, hygiene and falconry techniques will be repaid many times in the benefit of healthy hawks. However, the experienced falconer will inevitably encounter disease in his/her hawks at one time or another and it is important that he (or she) is equipped to deal with it. A close working relationship with your veterinary surgeon and a sound knowledge of basic first aid and nursing are important in achieving this.

Your Veterinary Surgeon

Falconers should approach a local veterinary practice to discuss whether their hawk could be accommodated and treated as a patient were it to become ill. This must be done before a crisis forces an introduction which may reveal inadequacies in treatment. Hawks often require unique medication, equipment and hospitalisation facilities and a practice anticipating work with raptors must have these on hand. Many practitioners take an active interest in avian medicine, particularly the more recent graduates who are better trained in this field. They may not have had the experience of certain recognised 'specialists', but excellent well-illustrated reference books are available, and with modern communication techniques, experienced clinicians will support and advise any colleague – if only to stabilise the patient before referral. Diagnosis and treatment of raptor diseases is undergoing rapid development and success is enhanced by modern techniques. It is important that the falconer is aware of this, as otherwise he may hesitate to seek professional advice. This will usually result in loss of the bird which reinforces the falconer's impression that treatment is futile.

Close relationship with a veterinary practice will benefit both veterinarian and falconer. Through processing samples, completing post-mortem examinations and analysing presented records, the veterinarian can help the falconer. On the other hand, falconers will assist vets by handling their hawks presented for examination, thus preserving the hawk's plumage and enabling the veterinarian to complete a thorough examination.

Post-mortem examination of dead birds is invaluable and vital if an individual dies in quarantine. Dead chicks and unhatched eggs should also be examined. Early detection of infectious diseases will help prevent the subsequent spread of disease, which may reach epidemic proportions. Pathology is a learned discipline and, even in the hands of experienced clinicians, a precise diagnosis may only be possible in 80% of examined cases. A falconer should be prepared for this and not be disheartened. Falconers should be discouraged from 'having a look' in the hope of making a quick diagnosis, but rather encouraged to contact a veterinarian as soon as possible to discuss preserving the carcass. The quality of the samples presented for post-mortem examination enhances the chances of a definitive diagnosis.

Nursing the avian patient

The correct use of fluid therapy, nutritional support and appropriate hospitalisation facilities will save more hawks than any other form of therapy.

All ill and injured hawks will be dehydrated to some extent and the importance of correcting this cannot be over emphasised. Not only will this save lives, but it will also accelerate and enhance the chances of recovery for all patients. Common methods used to correct dehydration include the oral route, sometimes referred to as crop tubing – a technique all falconers should master – and the intravenous route. Intravenous fluid therapy results in rapid fluid replacement and support of the patient's circulatory system. It is, however, complicated and time consuming with the veterinary surgeon utilising regular tests to assess the patient's progress and adjusting fluid therapy as required.

Rehydration nursing and maintenance fluid therapy (see fig. 153c) represent the initial management of raptors that are low in condition. The hawks presented are usually being trained or actively used for falconry and are often male birds in their first season. Being maintained at their 'flying weight' the hawks are motivated to progress with training and pursue quarry. Although hawks deteriorate rapidly from apparent good health, they have in fact been in a catabolic state for some time and no longer have the strength to compensate. A sudden lowering of environmental temperature often precipitates the problem. The condition is most commonly seen four to eight weeks into the birds' flying season and must be immediately recognised as they usually have only a few hours to live. Well-manned, hand-reared, steady species, like the Harris' Hawk, can usually be flown at higher weights than other individuals and are less likely develop this disease. Simple diagnostic tests employed by the veterinary surgeon will reveal the disease and treatment must begin immediately.

Sour crop (a fluid-filled, distended crop that will not empty) accompanies low condition. The condition is worsened if the falconer panics at the site of his weak hawk and forces it to take food. This only adds to the putrefaction of food in the crop and proliferation of bacteria, which together produce poisons resulting in a rapid deterioration in the hawk's condition and possible death. This disruption to the gastrointestinal function reduces digestion and absorption of nutrients in the lower bowel and the patient may succumb to bacterial infections.

If a falconer is concerned that his falcon is low in condition, his best action is to crop-tube the hawk with a warm electrolyte solution (available from all veterinary practices) administering up to 5 millilitres per pound body weight, if the bird's condition, and space in the crop allows (see photographs 153a & b). Falconers should try milking as much food as possible out of the crop or otherwise encourage the hawk to regurgitate by spraying it with warm water or driving it, unhooded, in a car. There must be no delay in getting the hawk to a veterinary clinic for immediate treatment. Stabilisation treatment may include various drugs, blood transfusions and tests in addition to the intravenous fluid therapy previously described. As soon as recovery allows the hawk may be crop-tubed a slurry consistency, complete feed (Hills a/d) available from the veterinarian. It may be several days before the hawk can be offered normal cast free food, and at this stage it is best fed small meals three to four times a day. A hawk's digestive tract functions normally without castings (few falconers in the Middle East offer their hawks any castings) and the dietary management of these hawks must progress cautiously.

In addition to fluid therapy and nutritional support, successful hospitalisation and management of avian patients includes housing in secluded and hence stress-free areas, maintaining a high ambient temperature and relative humidity, and by administering appropriate medication to correct shock and relieve pain. Treating the illness or injury with specific medication and surgery progresses alongside good hospitalisation. A capable falconer, well instructed by a veterinarian who offers appropriate support and advice, can often hospitalise and treat his recovering hawk.

Figure 153a (top)
The falcon is securely held and its mouth opened to identifY the position of the glottis (wind pipe) at the base of the tongue.

153b
A tube attached to syringe is advanced past the glottis, down into the crop and the fluid is gradually syringed into the crop.

Quarantine

There are statutory quarantine requirements for birds being imported into Britain. These are designed primarily to exclude virulent Newcastle's Disease and usually last 35 days. A valuable effect of quarantine is that many other important infectious diseases (e.g. salmonellosis) may appear during this period, often as a result of the stress experienced by the hawk being relocated.

All hawks entering a collection, including those having completed official quarantine, should be examined by a veterinary surgeon (mute and blood sample examination should be routine) and isolated for a three-week period. These hawks should be housed and cared for separately from other birds in the collection. If this is not possible, 'quarantined' individuals must be handled after the resident hawks. Clothing and falconry equipment should be changed or sterilised upon leaving the 'quarantine' area. The hawks, their mutes, feed intake and weight should be monitored daily and when necessary prophylactic (pre-emptive) aspergillosis (see infectious diseases) treatment should be given and continued for

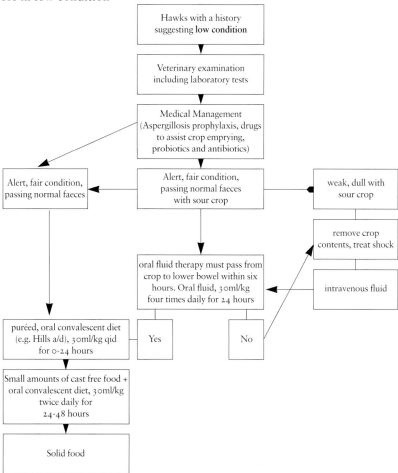

two weeks after any period of stress. Housing quarters should be thoroughly disinfected after the 'quarantine' period with the disposal of perches and other
impervious structures.

First Aid and the Management of Injured Hawks

The aim of first aid is to stabilise emergencies and provide initial treatment until
skilled help becomes available. Two common clinical conditions that frequently
require emergency treatment include injuries and seizures or fits (see later). In
both situations the hawk may be in shock or delirious and run the risk of regur-
gitating and inhaling its crop contents. Ensure the glottis (entrance to the wind
pipe-see fig. 153a) remains unobstructed until the hawk is fully conscious. At this
stage, and only if the hawks are fully conscious, should they receive oral fluids
(5ml of warm electrolyte solution per pound body weight). Fluid therapy is an
important part or first aid and veterinary treatment.

The main features of an emergency where shock may develop are severe bleeding, dehydration and pain. Severe haemorrhage can be controlled by applying pressure on the bleeding point. The pressure can be applied by hand with a clean pad at first, secured later with a tight bandage. Such an injury should receive prompt veterinary attention. Applying potassium permanganate crystals can control minor haemorrhage from claw, beak and skin injuries. Where possible wounds should be cautiously irrigated with warm saline (do not soak the bird, as this will lower its body temperature) to reduce the bacterial load on the injured tissues. Do not apply wound powder as this kills the already bruised and damaged tissue, further delaying wound recovery. Dehydration will develop if food and fluid are withheld for a period longer than twenty-four hours. Continue oral fluid administration every six hours if necessary and delay feeding if there is the possibility your veterinary surgeon will anaesthetise your bird for examination or treatment. Pain relief is difficult for a falconer to provide but may be achieved by strapping an injured wing to the body or splinting a fractured leg. This will also reduce further soft tissue damage caused by movement of the splintered bones.

Some basic principles have already been discussed (warmth, quiet and darkness) and must be provided as best as possible in the field. Birds must be dried and kept warm (wrapping in bubble pack and holding the hawk under the falconer's clothes is a good start). Hawks should be presented for veterinary examination and treatment at the earliest opportunity.

Infectious Diseases

Birds are subject to a great many infectious diseases, most being common between groups of birds. Thus all birds are susceptible to bacterial infections (for example avian tuberculosis), while most avian families have their own strain of viral infections (for example herpes virus hepatitis). Many parasites, but not all, are transmissible between avian families (for example red mite of poultry). Fungal and yeast infections can occur in any hawk, although certain conditions provoke these diseases and certain species are more susceptible to infection. Infectious diseases are rarely spread between raptors; however, disease transmission frequently occurs when the hawk's prey item is a bird harbouring an infectious disease. Disease is also commonly spread between birds through environmental contamination, where visiting wild bird's mutes contaminate a hawk's housing area.

Viral diseases

Viral infections have certain characteristic features which are important for an understanding of their control.
- Usually highly contagious, spreading rapidly between birds often without direct contact
- They are impossible to treat, with some birds surviving certain infections, conferring a strong immunity.
- Recovered, healthy birds can still infect others.
- The viruses are usually fragile and cannot survive long in the environment.

- Each virus often has various strains, some being well tolerated by certain birds but fatal to others.
-

Consequently the principles of control should include:
- Isolation of affected birds. Immunisation where possible. Disinfection of the environment, clothing and falconry furniture.
- Elimination of sensitive species from the collection.
- Offer no avian-derived food and restrict animals, birds and insects which may act as vehicles introducing infection.

Newcastle's Disease, caused by a paramyxovirus, illustrates these principles well. Outbreaks occurring in the United Kingdom have been restricted to poultry where the rapidly fatal disease spreads quickly. Fortunately hawks exhibit low or moderate susceptibility to infection. Hawks exported from the Far East and Europe may carry the disease and infected wild birds blown across the English Channel may introduce infection from Europe, where the disease is endemic in local populations. The infection can also be carried on humans or their clothing, in food and by the wind. Immunisation with vaccines is possible. The virus is killed by heat, desiccation and most disinfectants, but is protected by freezing. Signs of Newcastle's disease in falcons include nervous signs – with the head arched over towards the back and incoordination – weakness, inappetance and diarrhoea.

Unfortunately no other vaccines are available to the falconer to protect his birds from viral diseases and, although Newcastle's disease can probably affect any species, other common viruses, the pox, adeno, rota and herpes viruses generally have species or family specific strains.

Herpesvirus infections cause severe damage to the liver and other organs. They are frequently the cause of fatal infections and yet can be carried by unaffected, recovered birds for years, and spread to others. Intercurrent disease and stress have been associated with these individuals shedding virus. The falcon, owl and pigeon strain, although very similar, appear to be species specific. It is, however, inadvisable to feed pigeon to falcons and owls. Strict quarantine, especially of birds imported from the USA and separating wild (especially wild injured) owls from those held in captivity is important in disease prevention. Keepers nursing wild birds must also be cautious not to transfer infection to collections of healthy raptors. Classically falcon herpesvirus infections are typified by sudden death or a short period of weakness and diarrhoea. The disease is seen in the USA, but has rarely been recorded in the UK. Because symptoms are vague many cases may have been overlooked. Owl herpesvirus has been reported in wild and captive owls in the UK. The disease progresses more slowly in owls. They may be weak and anorexic for up to a week before dying. They exhibit numerous white spots on the roof of the mouth that may be confused with tuberculosis, frounce or capillaria lesions (see later).

Several strains of **poxvirus** exist. Although the falcon strain is not present in the UK, with movement of hawks in from the Far East, cases may soon be identified. Non-falcon strains of poxvirus do periodically affect raptors in the UK. The symptoms are similar to those caused by raptor pox (nodular encrustations on the cere, eyelids and feet), but are not as severe and usually disappear within a few days. The disease is self-limiting and individuals recover with complete immunity. Occasionally secondary bacterial infections necessitate a short antibiotic course. The infection is transmitted by mosquitos and other biting insects. Isolation of infected birds and insect control (insect netting, vapona strips, etc) will help limit infection.

Outbreaks of **adenovirus** and **rotavirus** have recently been recognised where healthy raptors fed apparently healthy, commercially reared quail, day old chicks and turkey poults succumbed to disease and in several cases died. Symptoms include lethargy, anorexia, diarrhoea and death.

Bacterial disease

Features of bacterial disease differ from viral disease, leading to different methods of prevention and control. In general they are much less contagious, spreading only by close contact between birds, animals, humans, falconry furniture or a contaminated environment. They can often be treated with antibiotics, but establish poor immunity to the recovered bird, so that reinfection is always possible. No useful vaccinations are available. The infection often originates from within the bird, where its own bacteria take over because some other stress has reduced its immunity. Infectivity is usually at its highest when the bird is ill, unlike viruses that may have high levels of infectivity before signs of illness become evident.

Prevention and control is achieved by eliminating carrier birds (through treatment and isolation or euthanasia), disinfecting the environment and equipment, good general hygiene, the use of antibiotics and good husbandry (see discussions on feeding, housing and training hawks in this chapter and elsewhere in this book).

Numerous bacterial diseases occur, and because they are less specific than viruses, they are frequently encountered in any susceptible bird. Many bacterial infections arise as the result of some other stress factor but good management will prevent most of them. Bacterial infections are common and those most important to the falconer will be discussed.

It must be emphasised that most viral, fungal and parasitic infections in birds are not a risk to normal healthy people, but bacteria are and strict hygiene is necessary when handling birds or carcasses (this includes hawk food!!). The most important of these zoonoses (diseases transmissible from animals to man) are avian tuberculosis and salmonellosis.

Avian tuberculosis is rare in raptors but common in ground living birds (for example partridge and pheasant). It occurs sporadically in other birds. Disease may enter a collection through contamination by wild birds or by feeding an infected carcass to a hawk. Unless weighed and handled daily, infected hawks will be viewed as being healthy and continue to contaminate their environment. The bacterium is very resistant, surviving in a contaminated area for several years. Treatment is protracted (as long as one year) and discouraged not least because of the zoonotic risk. It is generally accepted that all infected birds should be euthanased.

A whole host of bacteria cause **enteritis** in birds. Some bacteria, such as *Salmonella*, are acquired from outside sources, occasionally from man, but more often from wild birds or contaminated food. Others, including **Salmonella**, are normally present in the intestines of healthy hawks. Enteritis is common in raptor chicks (particularly those hand reared in captivity), as they are born with little or no gut bacteria which makes them susceptible to infection. Monitor the mutes for abnormalities in volume, colour and consistency. This may give an early indication of enteritis. Bacteria and their poisons are absorbed from the chick's inflamed gut, damaging the liver and causing septicaemia. This pattern is seen in adult birds too. The use of a probiotic (available from your veterinarian) leads to rapid colonisation of the intestines with appropriate bacteria and healthy chicks. Chicks should not be overfed and a bottom heater providing warmth will stimulate healthy digestion.

Respiratory infections can also be caused by a wide range of bacteria and are classified by veterinarians as upper (nares, nasal chamber and sinuses) and lower (trachea, airsacs and lungs) respiratory tract infections. The complicated tortouse sinuses in the hawk's head end in cul-de-sacs and commonly become infected. Birds with sinusitis present with head flicking, matted feathers around the nares, sneezing, an audible noise when breathing, a discharge from the eye that may bubble, excessive movement of the tissue below the eye when breathing and open mouth breathing. **Sinusitis** occurs sporadically and in isolation, basic hygiene together with recent treatment techniques controls its spread.

Bacterial pneumonia and air-saculitis usually occur as a result of some other initiating disease (for example *Aspergillosis* and *Syngamus trachea*) and these are discussed later.

Bacterial contamination of **wounds** commonly results in infection with abscess formation. Wounds may be an inevitable side-effect of hunting (cuts, bites and bruises), but can be associated with poor falconry management. Dry, hard, untreated aylmeri, rub and cut through tissues on the foot, introducing infections that can be very difficult to treat. Leashes tethering a hawk to a block or bow perch should be kept as short as possible. This will reduce the speed generated by a bating hawk that may result in a fractured tibiotarsal bone, distraction of the first metatarsal bone or bruising the base of the foot which may encourage bumblefoot (see later). All fresh, open wounds should be thoroughly irrigated with a warm salt solution (teaspoon of salt in a pint of water, see first aid), dressed and kept clean until fully recovered. Bite wounds from quarry often carry infection deep into bruised tissue and simple irrigation of these wounds is usually insufficient to prevent infection. When casting hawks (especially accipiters) always leave a leather gauntlet, or some similar strengthed material between the talons of the hawk's foot. This may stop the talons puncturing its foot. Not all hawks with scratches and scrapes need be presented for veterinary treatment, but it is worth remembering those skin infections that are more than a few days old are often well established may be difficult to treat. Err on the side of caution and have the bird examined within twenty-four hours if at all worried.

Bumblefoot with lesions occurring on weight-bearing parts of the foot is clinically different from other injuries and infections of the foot. Its start and progress are analogous to the slow healing bed-sore or pressure-sore seen in humans. It is still a common condition although much debate has been given to the factors which cause it. Studies show that the unrecognised and untreated disease is progressive and similar in all cases. It is mainly falcons that suffer with bumblefoot as hawks with feet infections recover rapidly. Studies show that reduced – and in some cases total – lack of blood circulation to the affected areas of the foot is responsible for the poor recovery rate of damaged tissues and the establishment of infection that responds poorly to treatment. Persistent perching with sustained pressure applied to the base of the foot causes blood vessels to collapse and the tissues, starved of nutrients, die and struggle to recover. Three main factors encourage bumblefoot: an inability to fly regularly, the falcon's weight and perches. All increase the pressure born on the base of a falcon's foot.

Most wild falcons fly more on a single day than many falconer's birds fly in a week. This is true too, of falcons kept in and flown from aviaries. Falcons and owls, unlike nervous accipiters and inquisitive hawks which move around their aviaries a lot, tend to be more sedentary. No falcon should be tethered for any time. It is better to have a falcon moult loose in an aviary where it can hop and fly about rather than be tethered. A falcon will usually moult without damaging its feathers in a well-designed aviary.

Falcons with a dense pectoral muscle mass have a higher total body weight to weight-bearing surface area of the foot than hawks (sometimes referred to as wing loading), another factor that almost excludes hawks from this disease. Weight control of falcons in aviaries, especially those in the moult, may be difficult, but in well manned, captive-bred falcons this should be possible without having to compromise their nutritional requirements for a successful moult. Overweight falcons have more pressure and consequently poorer blood supply to the base of their feet than lean birds. This principle of tissue damage is further demonstrated – perhaps the only time a hawk ever develops bumblefoot – when a painful leg is carried, transferring all the bird's weight on to the healthy limb which rapidly develops bumblefoot. For this reason amputation of a raptor's limb should never be performed.

All perching surfaces in captivity are relatively hard. The branches used for perching should be allowed to swing under the falcon's weight by suspending them from the aviary roof, much like swinging perches in a budgie's cage. The bark texture should be irregular and the perch diameter should vary to alter pressure distributed to the feet and talons. No single perching surface material suits all hawks, but vet-bed (resembles sheep fleece) which can be washed and sterilised offers buoyancy and an irregular surface. Other materials used in the past to cover perching surfaces include Astroturf (artificial turf), cork, carpets and natural stone. If the hawks are offered sufficient exercise all of these surfaces are acceptible. However, all perching surfaces in an aviary should be covered with a soft, supportive, irregular surfaced and washable material if signs of bumblefoot develop in a falcon's feet. Hawks must be flown or encouraged to fly within the aviary by changing the perches and their position in the aviary. Block perches for falcons with healthy feet can have a shallow concavity, distributing pressure away from the base of the foot towards the talons, and be covered with vet-bed. No birds with bumblefoot lesions should be tethered to a perch.

The progressive nature of bumblefoot is seen in the classification systems used to describe its symptoms. Initially the metatarsal pad (ball of foot) and occasionally those on the talons lose their rough appearance, becoming flattened, smooth, red and shiny. The skin's epithelium thins and a crust or scab forms in these areas (see photograph 153d). At this stage, with the skin's integrity broken, infection becomes a secondary problem. This would not occur without the initial pressure sore. Unless husbandry is corrected at an early stage, tissue destruction progresses with damage to tendons, ligaments, joints and bones. As the disease progresses the prognosis deteriorates and individuals with advanced diseases are incurable.

Falcons should be flown and have their feet checked daily. Strenuous exercise will encourage vigorous blood supply to the foot. The best cure and prevention of bumblefoot is 'getting the birds into the air'.

Fungal and Yeast infections

The characteristic features of fungal and yeast infections differ from those of viruses and bacteria. Both organisms are ubiquitous (continually present to a greater or lesser extent), but fungal infection of the respiratory tract occurs more commonly.

Aspergillosis is caused by a fungus that grows well on damp, rotting organic material, releasing spores into the environment. Certain species appear more sensitive to infection (Gyr Falcon, Golden Eagle, Northern Goshawk, Black Sparrowhawk and Snowy Owl), but infection may be seen in other species. Aspergillosis is a stress related disease, and any period of stress may evoke infection. Hawks housed in areas carrying a high spore load and having poor ventilation suffer a high challenge and may be susceptible to infection. Aspergillosis is a chronic wasting disease and although the organism is sensitive to certain drugs, by the time it is well established, treatment is usually ineffective. Excellent results may be achieved if the infection is detected early and treated. Falconers must be extremely vigilant as symptoms may be vague and hardly apparent at this stage. Medication can also be offered prophylactically when a stress period can be predicted (for example training, quarantine or some other infection or injury). Optimum health through good falconry management, reduced exposure to *Aspergillus* spores when transported and housed and a balanced diet will help hawks resist infection.

Infection tends to occur in the trachea or air sacs. With tracheal infections a voice change is a strong indication of infection. However, air sac infections are more vague with hawks initially showing slight exercise intolerance and a slow response to training. At this stage hawks may eat well, but loose weight. Hawks deteriorate, showing more obvious exercise intolerance and increased respiratory effort after minimal exercise or after being handled. The disease progresses slowly – often over days or weeks – with the hawks eventually becoming inappetant, with significant weight loss. Resting respiratory effort is usually obvious at this stage and the hawks are severely ill. Euthanasia at this point may be a humane option.

Yeast infections are relatively uncommon in raptors and usually occur when a hawk is receiving a lengthy course of antibiotics. All hawks receiving antibiotic treatment should be treated concurrently with probiotics obtainable from your vet. Occasionally wide, weeping, surface wounds, covered with a soft, friable, yellow, flaking exudate are found on the upper parts of a hawk's chest under the wings, or on the inner flanks. These too are thought to be caused by yeast infections.

Parasitic diseases

Parasites aim to maintain a symbiotic relationship with their host and as a result are very common in certain situations. All wild birds carry parasites. Most birds tolerate these infections and symptoms only become evident if the parasite overwhelms its host. This usually occurs with overcrowding and often affects young birds. In captivity the balance can too easily be tipped in the parasites' favour. Stress (breeding, nutritional or moulting for example) reduces the hawk's resistance and a heavy parasite challenge, perhaps through environmental contamination (see *caryospora*) or a high parasite burden in avian quarry, may also evoke disease (see *trichomoniasis*). All parasites can be killed with medication and although some survive well in the environment, strategic treatment and careful management can control all parasitic infections in falconer's hawks. Parasites may be grouped as protozoa (single celled organisms), helminths (worms) or arthropods (mites and lice).

Protozoa

Most protozoan diseases affecting raptors, apart from the blood parasites, such as malaria, which is spread by biting insects, are spread by contaminated food.

Almost all pigeons and doves carry **trichomoniasis** (frounce) without showing signs of infection and should never be offered fresh to any hawk. The organism is easily killed if frozen for a short time. Different strains of the organism exist, which together with the hawk's resistance determine the severity of the infection. Some hawks may carry the organism in their mouth or crop, with infection only developing if the bird's immunity is weakened by some other infection, injury or stress. A routine vitamin and mineral-deficient diet rapidly results in disease in nestlings. Falcons, goshawks and sparrowhawks seem particularly vulnerable to infection and the disease is most common in young birds. Clinical signs of trichomoniasis are influenced by the strain of the parasite and the hawk's own resis-

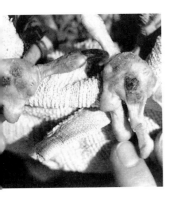

153d
Bilateral Bumblefoot lesions. The symmetrical position of the scabs illustrates the pressure-sore theory believed to initiate the disease.

tance – and are either restricted to the mouth (oropharyngeal form) or are spread to internal organs (generalised form). The oropharyngeal form is characterised by foul-smelling breath, yellow cheesy lesions in the mouth and, as the disease progresses, reduced appetite and food flicking. The generalised form is more serious and usually affects young birds.

Young falcons, particularly those being manned and trained, appear susceptible to **Caryospora** infection. Adult birds are thought to develop some immunity and these healthy yet infected hawks harbour parasites laying literally thousands of eggs daily, resulting in heavy environmental contamination. These eggs become infective after a few days, but may survive several months in the environment under warm, moist conditions. Water, perches, feeding trays, gauntlets and any food in contact with areas contaminated with faeces from these birds become a source of re-infection to these falcons and new youngsters (direct life-cycle). Earthworms (intermediate host) may also ingest the eggs and cause infection if eaten by a falcon. Adult birds can develop clinical infections if their resistance is lowered, but usually they recycle the parasite, maintaining it in the environment as described. Preventing re-infection of resistant birds, through maintainence of a clean, dry environment, eradicates the disease within two to three weeks. However, it is practically impossible to eradicate coccidial infections from a collection and doing so might be foolhardy. Falcons need to be exposed to these organisms to develop resistance. *Examination of mutes, collected into the same pot on three consecutive days, at veterinary laboratories will readily reveal these parasites.* Strategic treatment of adult birds and sensible hygiene will reduce exposure and infection in young falcons. Merlins appear particularly sensitive to infection. As with all parasite control measures, the aim is to minimise the hawk's exposure to infection and to avoid situations that might reduce the hawk's resistance to infection. *Concrete-based aviaries that can easily be disinfected, covered with a thick layer on pea gravel on a bed of lime offer a good level of hygiene and protection against infectious disease.*

Blood parasites tend to occur in warmer climes and with the exception of avian malaria, infecting Gyr Falcons that come from Arctic regions, do not tend to cause illness in hawks.

Helminths

Flukes and tapeworms are not regarded as causing clinical disease in raptors. Some roundworms (ascarids, **Capillaria** species and **Syngamus** species) however, do, but can be easily controlled. Ascarid infections are usually only clinically significant in young birds which show weight loss and depression. Infection is easily diagnosed on microscopy examination of a mute sample. The parasite's life-cycle in adult hawks (direct) is similar to that seen with **Caryospora** and control methods discussed for that parasite apply equally well here. However, because the roundworm eggs survive longer periods in the environment, the ground substrate may need replacing to reduce subsequent exposure levels.

Three forms of **Capillaria** infection occur, based on the location of the infection in the hawks body. An oral form with yellowish plaques covering tissues on the inner corners, back of the mouth and base of the tongue, an oesophageal form that may be felt as a thickening of the crop wall but is difficult to detect and may be fatal if not recognised, and finally an intestinal form where hawks may show a mild diarrhoea and occasionally weak, uneven flight with poor balance, especially on landing. As with *Caryospora* the life cycle can be direct or via an intermediate host and prevention methods are the same as described for Caryospora. Observations show hunting hawks to have contracted infections when feeding on crows and gulls.

Pheasants, partridge, thrushes, magpies, starlings and many other wild birds can be infected with **Syngamous** trachea. Although the parasite has a direct life-cycle, infection is often acquired through the hawk eating an intermediate host (for example: slug, snail, beetle or earthworm) that concentrates large numbers of infectious larvae. Infected hawks present 'crackles and kecks' and they frequently sneeze and flick their head in an attempt to rid themselves of the irritation. In advanced cases, the birds gasp for air (hence the old name 'gapeworm') and are weak. Some hawks may asphyxiate. Besides prevention principles already discussed in this section to control the intermediate hosts, raptors should not be housed in quarters that previously held any avian specie known to be suceptible to *Syngamous*.

Lice and mites

These organisms live on the outside of the bird, infesting the skin or feathers. All hawks, particularly hunting hawks and hawks to be added to a collection, should be regularly examined and treated when necessary. Only insecticide sprays and powders licensed for use in birds should be used, which will readily kill these parasites. **Dermanyssus spp**, the red mite, only attacks hawks at night, seeking refuge in cracks and crevices in the aviary during the day. To control this parasite the falconer must also treat the environment where the hawk is housed. This parasite causes dark, crusty lesions around the beak and eyes and feather loss on the inner parts of the lower limb. **Knemidocoptes spp**, the 'scaly-leg' mite is occasionally seen to infect the cere, eyelids and legs of hawks. The tissues look dry, porous and dusty. If examined closely they can be seen to be peppered with minute holes, where the parasite burrows into the skin. Its life-cycle is completed on the hawk and drugs prescribed by your veterinarian will cure affected hawks and eradicate the parasite.

Feather lice do not cause serious disease and numbers can be easily controlled with licensed insecticides. If a falconer experiences any parasite population explosion he must reconsider his falconry management and present the hawk to his veterinarian for examination, as it may have some inapparent illness or injury.

Non-Infectious Diseases

Nutrition and trauma are perhaps the most common non-infectious cause of disease in raptors. Trauma and wound management is thoroughly discussed in earlier sections of this chapter (see first aid and wounds). Nutrition is probably the most important, yet most ignored, aspect of raptor management. Ideally food that closely resembles that which a hawk would eat in the wild should be fed, but regrettably the food chosen is often determined by availability, cost and ease of handling. Day-old chicks (docs) are often the only food form offered to many raptors and can be regarded at best as a marginally balanced diet. Many birds appear to have survived being fed purely on docs for several years. Breeding and hunting performance has been shown to improve when birds are fed better quality diets that included a mixture of docs, 'grown ons', rabbit, mice, rats, squirrel, quail and beef. If avian quarry is to be fed, examine the abdomen, checking the liver. If it contains white abscess this means the carcass is likely to carry **tuberculosis** and should be discarded. All pigeons and doves should be frozen before being offered to a hawk to prevent **trichomoniasis** and remember any game birds or rabbits fed to your hawk may previously have been shot but not killed, and contain **lead** shot gun pellets that could poison your hawk.

Nutritional Disorders

Exercise restricted, overfed hawks commonly suffer with **atherosclerosis**. They have high blood cholesterol levels, and in much the same way as in man, these are deposited on the inner surfaces of blood vessels. There are no clinical symptoms evident as this disease develops and some hawks are simply found dead in their aviaries. Females are more prone to this disease as hormone changes around the breeding season are associated with high blood cholesterol levels. High dietary cholesterol levels are to be avoided. Offer lean carcasses and, if docs are fed, the yolk sac must be removed. The yolk sac does, however, contain certain important nutrients and must occasionally be left intact. Falconers should assess a hawk's weight and withhold food occasionally to prevent obesity. The disease can be detected with blood tests and corrected together with dietary management and gradual return to exercise.

Hypocalcaemia (low blood calcium levels) is a feature of several diseases, including egg binding, poor hatchability, osteodystrophy or rickets in chicks, osteoporosis in adults and fits. These conditions are discussed later. Birds should be offered diets with adequate calcium. Birds will strip muscle, which is deficient in calcium, from the food carcasses provided. Restricting food encourages the hawks to utilise the entire carcass and consequently obtain all nutrients. It is also sometimes necessary to break the bones of large quarry items, thereby releasing calcium to the hawk that ingests the splintered bones in meat. This will also prevent the occasional fatal impaction that is seen when raptors swallow large bones.

Hypoglycaemia (low blood sugar levels) is seen in hawks that are low in condition and especially in small accipiters offered frequent flights at quarry on cold days. The hawks are weak, may tremble and looked dazed. Oral administration of a glucose solution (5 millilitres per pound body weight) will help stabilise the hawk. Refer to previous notes in this chapter on feeding a hawk low in condition.

Certain breeding lines of Harris' hawks were seen to have a thiamine metabolism problem, and although sufficient thiamine was present in the diet of those hawks, their inability to utilise it resulted in fits and other neurological abnormalities.

Fits and Convulsions

Another emergency commonly presented to falconers is a fitting hawk. The most common cause in hunting hawks is **hypoglycaemia** (see hawks low in condition) which must receive immediate oral glucose administration. Hypoglycaemic fits are also thought to occur in falcons which have liver damage and are flown strenuously. The damaged liver is unable to metabolise and release glucose efficiently, hence the exercising falcon becomes hypoglycaemic. Other common causes of seizures include hypocalcaemia (see nutritional disorders) and **lead poisoning** (see poisons).

Poisoning

Falconer's hawks have never shown the vulnerability to pesticide poisoning seen in the wild. Inappropriate use of insecticides (organophosphates and carbonates) intended for use on pet mammals may result in rapid death.

Lead poisoning is relatively common in both wild and captive raptors and usually occurs through ingestion of lead shot from quarry that has been injured historically or recently killed using a shot gun. Occasionally quarry, especially waterfowl, may themselves ingest lead and be a source of poisoning. Any hawk fed such carcasses can develop lead poisoning. Lead in shot raptors, lodged in tissues outside the digestive tract, poses almost no threat to the hawk. The lead shot frequently becomes trapped in crypts in the hawk's stomach and is not expelled in castings. Small amounts of dissolved lead are absorbed and symptoms progress from weakness and inappetance with emerald green diarrhoea to recumbence with the talons rotated inwards, clutching those of the opposite foot. The problem may persist for several weeks without apparent symptoms, or progress rapidly with the hawk deteriorating to a critical condition.

Rodents, crows, gulls and pigeons are sometimes treated with alpha-chloralose to help trap these pest species. Birds feeding on these anaesthetised or killed animals will develop signs of weakness, lethargy and stupor. Owls are most commonly affected and should be kept warm. Oral administration of strong coffee seems to accelerate recovery.

Conditions of chicks

Poor incubation techniques with incorrect humidity or temperature control can cause embryonic death, poor hatchability or weak chicks that fail to thrive. Excellent texts are available describing recognition and correction of these problems. Chicks having difficulty hatching should be offered assistance as a last resort. Hatching times vary between raptor species with a Peregrine egg usually hatching within 48 hours. It is often better to let a surrogate mother assist chicks which are having difficulty hatching. These chicks frequently have non-retracted yolk sacs that should be preserved wherever possible. The yolk sacs are an important reservoir of nutrients and antibodies. These chicks should be handled with care and housed on non-adherent, absorbent material. The yolk sac will shrink, becoming dark and dry before falling off after a few days. Retaining the yolk sac in the abdomen with a single stitch usually results in the formation of an abdominal abscess.

Hand-reared chicks are denied saliva rich in digestive enzymes, healthy bacteria and calcium, which coat the food offered to parent-reared chicks. Unless steps are taken to correct this, these birds are vulnerable to bacterial enteritis (see above) and nutritional osteodystrophy. Unless the food offered to chicks has adequate available calcium levels (processed whole mice, not docs) appropriate mineral and vitamin supplements should be added. Chicks offered insufficient calcium could have deformed longbones in the wings and legs. These leg deviations are exaggerated if the chick is reared on a smooth, flat surface.

Miscellaneous conditions

Wing tip oedema and dry gangrene syndrome has been recognised for some years, but its true cause is still not clearly understood. Almost all raptor species, including owls, have developed this disease. The disease occurs almost exclusively after a period of cold weather and is commonly seen in Harris' hawks and usually in first year birds shortly after they have been taken up for training. First-year birds do not carry mature plumage and their wing tips may be more sensitive to cold weather. Certainly, historically, a bird tethered on the ground was seen to be most susceptible to the disease, but even hawks free in aviaries have developed the disease. It is, however, not inconceivable that temperatures could drop low enough in any part of an aviary to cause frostbite injuries. By placing tubular heaters underneath perching areas in aviaries, the problem of wing tip oedema can be controlled. A viral infection is another suggested cause of this disease.

The earliest clinical signs include a drooping wing, raised, clear, fluid filled vesicles at the base of primary and in severe cases the secondary feathers. The tissues become dry, thickened and dark brown before eventually falling off, taking feathers and in severe cases the wing tip too.

Hereditary conditions have been recognised (for example cataracts) and thorough record keeping will help breeders eradicate these problems. Organ failure (for example kidney failure) may be seen in some of the older captive birds of prey. **Neoplasia** (cancer) involving various parts of the body has been described in raptors.

Conclusion

The aim of this chapter has been to introduce some of the of the more common diseases that may occur in falconer's hawks. No attempt has been made to discuss medical or surgical treatment, as in this field a little knowledge is of no value. The symptoms described in each section should help the falconer recognise illness, but not empower him to make a diagnosis. The veterinarian's role and the benefits of a good working relationship with your veterinary practice are self-evident. The contents of this chapter will hopefully assist the falconer to rear fit, healthy, long-lived hawks.

24 Captive Breeding

Objects

There are two main objects of captive breeding: first, conservation; second, to meet the needs of falconers, bird gardens and the like. Unfortunately, in Britain and other countries too, captive breeding as a means of conservation has been either ignored or else regarded as a last resort. When one sees what has been done by captive breeding to increase a rare species and to save it from extinction, it seems amazing that the so-called 'conservation bodies' have been raising objections to falconers' activities through the media for some considerable time now, pressing for more legal protection; yet, when a fairly simple and efficient means to help the various species is simply waiting to be used, they turn their faces away. The red kite could easily be increased in Britain. And as for the peregrine, it is probably as common now as it is ever likely to get in Britain bearing in mind that encroachment by mankind must limit numbers. Maybe one day such bodies (the word 'authorities' would be inappropriate, implying the possession of knowledge) will realise just how valuable captive breeding, practised correctly, can be. To the falconer the demise of such birds as sparrowhawks, merlins, peregrines and so on would be far more upsetting than to those who, I believe, are now called 'twitchers'.

Partly due to the new laws regarding falconry, but also because far too many people are climbing on to the captive-breeding bandwagon, I have nevertheless somewhat altered my ideas on captive breeding. Some people, I regret to say, are using it unscrupulously to make money, regardless of the immediate consequences or the effects on falcony as a whole.

It is dishonest to breed a lot of imprinted birds for sale – one cannot tell whether the birds are imprinted or not until the new owners start training them. Only then does the wretched buyer of an imprinted bird find he has been had for a sucker. And the chances of getting his money back or having a non-imprinted bird in exchange are pretty small. In due course doubtless the breeders who do imprint birds in this way will be forced out of breeding since the buyers will learn not to go to them. But meanwhile the practice is carried on in quite a large way, and is doing a lot of harm. It is, unfortunately, very much easier and very much cheaper to breed imprinted birds.

I find it very strange that there now exists a small number of people who seem to think it is wrong to sell captive-bred birds of prey. Most of the people who are of this persuasion buy dogs, or horses, or other livestock apparently without any qualms. I can only assume that they are jealous of other people having birds that they themselves either cannot or will not afford. Moreover, these objectors do not seem to realise just how much time and money goes into a breeding project.

The falconer who would just like to breed a bird for himself and one or two for his friends should, I suggest, forget all about incubators, brooders, hand rearing, nursery aviaries indoor and out, and all the other 'essentials' that he will be tempted to get involved in.

Do not bother about incubators – just buy an ultra-violet candler such as turkey breeders use. This will ensure that when your pair of birds do eventually lay you can check that the eggs are fertile and not have your birds sitting on infertile eggs. Just let them hatch and rear their own young and be content with that. For BEWARE: once you start buying an incubator you start a chain of very expensive, time-consuming, and space-consuming affairs that you may well live to regret. Doing it this simple and natural way, your only real problem is to get a compatible pair of birds that will produce fertile eggs, hatch and rear them happily.

However, if you really want to enter the incubator game, read on – carefully – and then take time to consider before you make a decision.

The problems of incubators

Let us assume that you have decided that you want to play with incubators and by so doing breed more than one clutch of youngsters a year.

You will need, at the very least, the following:

Candler
Setting incubator
Hatching incubator (whether you will need this item will depend on the type of setting incubator you get)
Brooder, with some form of heating
Indoor nursery aviary, also may need heat
Outdoor nursery aviary, solid-walled
A really accurate weighing machine for weighing chicks and eggs
Someone to hand-feed newly hatched birds for 12 days approximately, four times a day . . . as well as look after the incubator

I am assuming that your incubator comes with an accurate means of measuring and controlling temperature and humidity. If not, you will have to have thermometers, thermostats, hygrometers etc. It may have some device for automatically turning the eggs but this is not essential and is often better dispensed with. Not many automatic turners will take more than one size of egg at a time. So this can be quite a problem if you are breeding several species.

Have a good look at the above list. Work out what it will cost you in money, time consumed putting it all together and time spent in the actual running of it, and the space needed.

If you still want to use an incubator then go ahead – but you have been warned. And you may well find that others of your household, when they find out what it all involves, will not be as keen as you. Incubators are dealt with in more detail on page 302.

Choice of species to breed

Obviously to do any breeding you must have a pair of birds. The species you choose will probably be one suitable for you yourself to fly, though you may have reason to choose some other species.

The age of the birds is the next important factor. it is possible to breed from haggards and from passage birds but you are more likely to have success from eyasses and even more likely if they themselves are captive-bred birds. Avoid inbreeding if you possibly can, as continual inbreeding can eventually raise all sorts of problems. You will have to get a licence to take or to import birds from the wild; or buy them from someone else; or if you are very fortunate succeed in persuading someone to give you a pair. Very rarely has it been known for birds to breed in immature plumage. There are records and even photographs of birds at the nest in immature plumage, it is true, obviously from the previous year, but this is not really proof that they are one of the parents.

The large rap tors tend not to breed until 3/4 years old, and the very large ones may well be a lot older than that before they breed. Sparrowhawks, merlins and similar-sized birds will generally breed in their second year but you might have to wait longer. In fact if they are not a compatible pair you might never breed from them.

So you can see from this that captive breeding can be a chancy business and you can waste a lot of time before you are successful and get any eggs. You may even get eggs only to find that none are fertile. This is where the use of a candler comes in.

Candling

Candling is very simple. In the old days a lighted candle was placed behind the egg and the light shining through would show you if the egg was fertile. Candles have, of course, long ago been overtaken by electric light which, being a lot more powerful, makes life easier. And the ultra-violet candler is best of all. An egg will have to be incubated for around 5/7 days before you can really be sure it is fertile. At first you will see very faint veins and a dark central blob; if you can only see

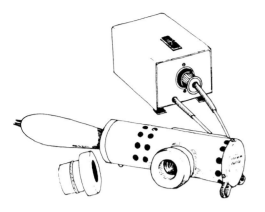

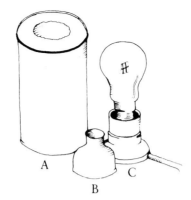

154 Ultra-violet candler

155 Tungsten-bulb candler
   A. Tin with a hole in the top.
   B. Rubber connector to a W.C. cistern. B goes on top of A.
   C. Lamp. This goes inside the tin. The egg rests on the rubber connector B.

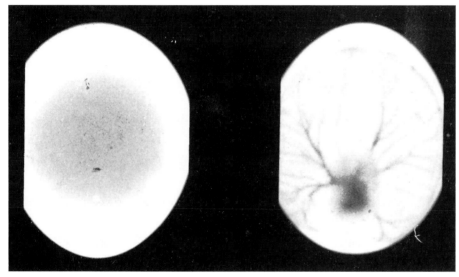

156 Left-hand side is an infertile egg, right-hand side is a fertile egg after some five days or so of incubation. How much you will be able to see of your own bird's eggs will depend on the species. If you see a nucleus and veins like this your egg is fertile. In due course the whole embryo becomes plainer to see, then much darker and the air space gets larger. Just prior to hatching the chick's beak will be seen in the air space. NEVER leave an egg for long over the candler.

the yolk then try again a few days later. Since all candlers get very hot do not keep an egg under them for more than a few seconds at a time. Cooking the embryo is not a good idea – also beware that the u.v. light does not harm your eyes.

Falcons' eggs are not as easy to see through as chickens', since the markings tend to confuse you. Like chickens' eggs, though, they can be candled with tungsten light. Hawks', buzzards', hawk-eagles', eagles', and vultures' eggs require ultra-violet light and even then some are quite impossible to see through. Some of our ferruginous rough-legged buzzards' eggs have been un-candleable; others have been no problem. The only thing you can do in the former case, as far as I know, is to float the egg in tepid water. Lower it in gently and let the water settle. If the egg is fertile you will notice it give a slight jump and cause the water to ripple. If the egg sinks it is not fertile. Just how early on in incubation this will happen I do not know. Eggs that well-advanced in incubation look very dark inside when candled except at the blunt end where the air sac is.

Once you have some fertile eggs you have got over the most formidable of the hurdles. Without fertile eggs you obviously go back to square one. Unfortunately you may already have spent a lot of money, and you will certainly have wasted a lot of time. You are now left with the big question of what best to do next. One can change partners and try a different male or female, depending on what you can get hold of. Or you can simply sit and wait another year with the pair you already have and hope for better things.

However, if you have candled your eggs within say a week or ten days of their being laid and find them all infertile do not despair quite yet. Do not on any account put the infertile eggs back under your birds, for there is no point in their sitting on eggs that will never hatch, and every point in their not so doing. Because if a bird is robbed of its first clutch of eggs it will nearly always lay a second clutch, provided that the first clutch is taken fairly early on after laying. It would not be wise to let the bird sit for longer than ten days and then take the eggs.

Extra clutches or recycling

Most birds of prey, if they lose their first clutch of eggs, will lay a second clutch (or recycle) within 12–14 days. Now, if your first clutch were all infertile you may still be fortunate and find the second clutch fertile, for this reason: very often one of the pair, more often the male, does not come into breeding condition as early as the other bird of the pair. But by the time the first clutch has been laid and incubated for, say, 10 days, and the bird has recycled a fortnight or so later, they may both be in breeding condition and your second clutch will prove to be fertile. Sometimes the last egg or two of the first clutch are fertile but those laid a day or so earlier are not. This means that the male has probably come into condition just in time to fertilize the latter part of the first clutch.

There is a theory that eggs are more likely to hatch if the bird sits on them for a few days first than if they are put into an incubator as soon as laid. My own experience is that this is not necessarily correct; I have been forced on many occasions to take eggs as soon as they are laid and have been successful with them. In fact there are times when it may be wise to take eggs as soon as they are laid. For instance some birds, particularly those from warmer climates, will often lay eggs quite early on (the time they do lay is controlled to a very large extent by the daylight hours, or 'photo-period' to become technical). But it may well be that in captivity, in a colder climate, the eggs, if not sat on at once (and birds often wait until two or three eggs are laid before commencing to sit properly) can get frosted at night. In their native country this would not have happened since they come from a warmer climate. It is possible to take eggs and store them for up to ten days or so before incubating begins. They need to be kept in an even temperature and turned every so often. The longer they are stored the greater the chances of their not hatching out. The only advantage (if indeed it is an advantage at all) is that they then tend to hatch more or less at the same time. Obviously to a chicken farmer this is a very great advantage but not in my opinion to a breeder of raptors – certainly not at the risk of some of the eggs not hatching. You must remember that raptor eggs are more valuable than chickens' eggs; the loss of one egg will mean a lot to a falconer but very little to a chicken farmer who is dealing with eggs that are much easier to produce.

So if you are going to breed from your birds in a simple way and just have one clutch a year from them, let them do all the hard work of hatching and rearing for you: once you have established, by use of your candler, that you have fertile eggs, put the eggs back and let the birds get on with it.

This is probably the simplest way to go about raptor breeding and unless you really are prepared to go to a lot more trouble, then you should stick at this, to me, happy solution.

There is an intermediate and extremely useful method that you may or may not be able to use, depending entirely on how good your breeding pair are as parents. It is possible to take the first clutch after say 7–10 days and incubate them. This will take about 28–30 days overall. Somewhere about the 21st day the parent birds will be laying their second clutch, one hopes. You leave them to sit on this and you hand-rear the first clutch for about 12 days. You then take the young you have reared and put them in the nest, at the same time removing the eggs from the second clutch. You put these to incubate. And now you watch and pray. If you are lucky the parent birds will take on the feeding of the first lot of young; and these birds will be old enough to feed themselves soon after the second clutch have hatched. So you perform the same trick again, and while the first clutch are feeding away in a nursery aviary on their own, the second lot are taken over by the parents. BUT it may not work – in which case you will have to rescue the first young, replace the second clutch of eggs, and just hope you have not upset the parents too much. You may even be able to use foster parents; they do not necessarily have to be the same species as the young. In fact you can even mix species and get away with it. I have had Redtails rear their young and young from a Harris. And of course you do not require any nursery aviaries if you are able to persuade your birds to help you by fostering in this manner.

Some people, instead of waiting for the full clutch to be laid and then taking it, go in for 'pulling' the eggs. This mayor may not increase the size of the clutch. This pulling consists of taking the first egg once the second egg is laid, then the second egg is taken when the third is laid and so on. Some birds will go on to lay a very large number of eggs but others may well be put off by this method and cease to co-operate (and who can blame them!).

The decision is up to you. I have had Harris' hawks lay five clutches in a year, and with this species three clutches is quite common. But do be reasonable and don't push your birds too far by being greedy.

157 Red-tailed buzzards
in a wire mesh aviary.

Food and minerals

Breeding birds should of course have extra calcium given with their food in order to assist the formation of the egg shells. Failure to do this can result in the bird trying to supply sufficient calcium from its own body and ending up unable to stand. Young birds too must be given plenty of calcium to form good sound bones. When one considers how quickly a bird the size of a goshawk reaches the age of flying from a comparatively small egg then one is made to realise how important it is to give it a good start in life. Of course this applies also to puppies, kittens and horses etc. Rickets is usually caused by insufficient calcium when young. Although SA37 has calcium in it I add more for breeding birds.

Aviaries

This is a really difficult subject; I do not think anyone can lay down any strict rules and regulations about size, type, etc. The best thing an author can do is to give as much information as possible and leave the reader to decide what suits him and his birds best. Obviously there are a number of factors to be taken into consideration and each breeder will have different problems to overcome.

Size of aviary
I doubt if one could ever have an aviary too big. Too small an aviary, however, will not help matters, though birds have been known to breed in aviaries that many people would consider not only too small, but small almost to the point of cruelty. The bigger the bird the bigger the aviary should be, and it should give the birds room to fly around and to take exercise. Exercise is most important to breeding, and you will notice that a pair of birds will take a lot more exercise several weeks before breeding.

Types and construction of aviaries
The type and construction of your aviary can vary a great deal. One can have entirely indoor aviaries, though these must have adequate ventilation and preferably a great deal of it when the weather is suitable; in some countries the ventilation may have to be such that it can be almost totally shut off to counter either very cold or very hot weather. In very hot countries indoor aviaries with air conditioning may well prove to be essential.

Outdoor aviaries can be of two types. *Solid-walled aviaries* give the birds an immense amount of privacy but plenty of air, as the top will be of some sort of mesh.

Open aviaries have at least one side and the whole top (apart from shelters) of mesh and therefore offer considerably less privacy. I am not in favour of all the sides being open; if they are, then it is hest to make sure that there is at least one side from which no people or animals can ever approach the birds.

The shape of an aviary is important, and the height too. The higher it is the better. Birds that can fly up above onlookers will probably not bother about them. But do not expect your birds to go up like a lift to get height. They need perches to help them 'ladder' their way up.

The more room they have for flying the better. From a point of view of using the least amount of material to enclose the greatest amount of space, then a circular form wins until you come to roofing it in. You will then generally find that there is an immense amount of waste. Building anything in a circle, certainly a solid-walled aviary, is usually not easy. Of course the shape of your aviary may well be dictated by the position you choose, and there may well be certain limitations of space which will define its shape. So having dismissed circular aviaries let's look at a more practical alternative: the hexagon. If you are intending to build a block of four or more aviaries then undoubtedly the hexagon has a great many advantages. Building a block of four saves five sides or nearly one whole aviary. A block of seven saves 12 sides or two complete aviaries. The number of sides you save are sides that are common to two aviaries. Of course these hexagonal aviaries do not have to be solid-walled all round, in zoos and bird gardens the provision of just one wall of mesh makes a very nice viewing point for visitors but at the same time gives the birds in each aviary a lot of privacy not only from visitors but also from birds in the neighbouring aviaries. (see p. 158).

One of the main advantages of the hexagonal aviary is that, if the particular species in the aviary has a turning circle smaller than the area enclosed, the birds can go on flying in circles for a considerable time, whereas in rectangular aviaries that are narrower than the birds' turning circle the birds can only fly to and fro the length of the aviary and must stop and turn round at each end. The turning circle of hawks is smaller than that of falcons, size for size. You need a hexagon about 60 feet across for a gyr falcon to be able to fly round in this manner but a bird like a merlin would be able to do so in about a third that size.

This hexagonal design is extremely strong and can be added to fairly easily, though adding to existing aviaries very often involves moving the birds in the neighbouring aviary before work on the addition disturbs them. This of course applies to additions to any type of aviary.

Visitors to aviaries

Birds that are constantly exposed to people such as in bird gardens or zoos soon get used to visitors and do not worry about their privacy at all. Similarly if only a few people go to see them, people who look after the birds and whom the birds get used to seeing every day, then once again the open aviary will do very well. But sudden invasions by crowds of strange people can be most upsetting, especially people who may act in a stupid way, try to make the birds fly, bang against the aviary side or commit some other similar idiocy.

Photographers can be extraordinarily stupid in this way, causing your birds to damage themselves and stopping any chance of breeding. Incidentally, one of the

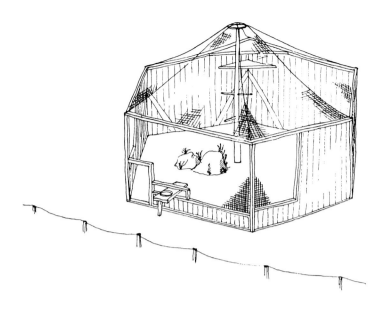

best barriers to stop visitors going into places you do not want them is the common stinging nettle. A good nettle bed will keep people out very efficiently, though I did once have a party of visitors who unwittingly decided that a nettle bed would be a good place to sit down and have a picnic!

Some establishments close during the winter months and open around Easter time or thereabouts. Towards the end of this closed period the birds will certainly be thinking of nesting and when the place reopens any large influx of visitors may well do no good at all to your breeding hopes that season.

Shelters, Ledges, Water, Baths etc.

Other matters to be considered in aviaries include food ledges, with easy access not only for putting the food on but also for cleaning. You can of course just throw food in onto the ground but this is a great encouragement for rats and the like; local cats will even try to put a paw through and pull out some food. Ledges lessen this problem but unless they are made rat-proof (which is almost impossible) then one must do one's best to avoid over-feeding and so avoid having food left lying about. This is fairly simple until your pair have young to feed and then you will have to put in plenty of food to ensure the young get all they need.

Aviary floors in most zoos and bird gardens are concrete and this is something that I think should be avoided at all costs, for concrete floors must be washed down nearly every day and swept with a stable broom. All of this is going to disturb the birds a great deal and will also increase the humidity greatly, which will of course tend to affect the eggs, especially in species that lay on the ground.

297

And ground nesters do not think much of concrete floors, as they cannot make a scrape in concrete. I prefer plain earth floors; shrubs or even trees not only improve the looks of the aviary but give cover to the birds. Earth floors are almost self-cleaning but in certain places will need to be dug over every so often (not while the birds are breeding) and some grass seed sown. Gravel is used by some people in their aviaries but this is not easy to clean. Polythene sheeting on both floors and walls of indoor aviaries keep them clean very simply. A staple gun will fix the sheeting to the walls very quickly and the sheeting can be ripped out and burnt every so often and easily replaced.

Water is another problem that has to be tackled. Birds of prey do not drink much except in very hot weather. In fact a bird seen drinking in cold weather must be suspected of being ill and a close watch kept on it for the next few days. But most of them like bathing and so baths of suitable size for the species concerned must be provided and some means of getting them in and out of the aviary to empty and to clean them. In warm weather algae grow quickly and baths get very nasty in a couple of days or so. The normal type of hawk's bath is fine but it may be possible to do even better in an aviary and to devise a bath which has a sloping bottom so that the birds can wade in as deep or as shallow as they like. And some birds will wade in up to their necks. Other birds will go for weeks or even months without ever bathing. Some goshawks are reluctant to bathe and others may bathe nearly every day. Falcons usually have a bath every day and some birds also like a dust bath. This is fairly easy to arrange. Either sand or sawdust (the sawdust must be free from any toxic contamination – some wood is treated at times with toxic chemicals which can have a disastrous effect) is placed fairly thickly (6 inches or so) under a low shelter roof to prevent it getting too wet. This is the sort of thing that gamekeepers make for pheasants and partridges.

Full baths are not easy to empty when on the ground unless you don't mind the ground getting soaked so I suggest a similar arrangement to that shown in Chapter 4 in the diagram on p. 54.

Concrete baths can be constructed sunk into the ground and with a drain hole like a sink. Or fibre-glass with a built-in drain.

Obviously (though it is amazing how what should be obvious is often not so), all aviaries should have shelters for the birds, water, food ledges, perches in both sun or shade, and alternative nesting sites from which the birds can make their own choice. And if they build their own nests then nesting materials must be put in for them. Sometimes it can be a help wholly or partially to construct a nest, though it is amazing how difficult it is for man with two hands and a better-than-bird-brain to make a nest that is remotely as good as the one a bird itself will build. Man-built nests may well be pulled to pieces by the birds with great disdain for your clumsy efforts. Nest ledges should have drainage holes to prevent a nest being drowned out.

Birds that nest in holes, hollow trees, etc. will require similar accommodation with suitable lining material such as chips of soft rotten wood, sawdust, etc.

Photography

If you want to photograph your birds then make suitable photographic positions for your camera and yourself at the time the aviaries are being built; make sure you get the proposed camera position correct for the light at the time of day when you are most likely to be filming.

One-way Glass and Background Music

Some people with indoor or solid-walled aviaries put in one-way-vision glass in order to view the birds without disturbing them. This can be quite expensive and in outdoor solid walled aviaries is, in my opinion, a complete waste of money. Falconers' birds have no sense of smell but to make up for this loss they have the proverbial hawk eye and also an extremely acute sense of hearing; and although in an indoor aviary one can nullify this sense by playing radio programmes or taped music loud enough to prevent the birds hearing your approach, this seems to me to involve a lot of money and an added irritation to oneself. Personally I dislike having background music imposed upon me by shops, restaurants and pubs, and I cannot believe that anyone chooses to frequent these places because they are equipped with such 'decibeliache' devices. Once again I would say, consider the birds in the wild and the way they act.

Netting and mesh

Mesh, where it is used, must not be of the chicken-wire type. This material is a disaster to birds. If they fly against it, the mesh acts like cheese wire and cuts their ceres to bits. A slight cut will heal in due course but continued damage will not only spoil the looks of your birds but can also affect their breathing to the extent that they become useless for flying. Chicken wire may be used sometimes for the roofing of aviaries but it should be well supported either by extra wires or by extra supports in order to avoid disaster caused by snow, which can build up to a vast thickness and becomes so heavy that even supports can break under the weight. It is most important when building any aviary to think ahead of what extremes of climate etc. can do. Overhanging trees can fall on your aviary; very high winds will catch a solid-walled aviary that is not solid enough and carry it away in a sadly demolished state. One can hardly guard against earthquakes and such but you will do well to think ahead. Always make exterior aviary doors open outwards. Deep snow will stop you pushing open an inwards-opening door. Remember that in winter your aviary will not get as much sun as in summer and maybe none at all if you place it wrongly.

Low-flying aircraft can be a disaster and there is very little you can do against them. Low-flying helicopters can wreck a whole breeding season and it is surprising how many helicopter pilots seem to think that frightening animals just does not matter. There are numbers of 'Safari'-type films showing herds of antelope or buffalo or whatever streaming across the ground in obvious panic, often to the background voice of a commentator who knows little or nothing of the animals!

The alternative to chicken wire for .any meshed side or roof may be netting such as nylon or Terylene of a fairly thick gauge, since thin twine cuts the cere just as badly as wire. Mesh of this sort needs to be kept fairly taut otherwise a bird may cling to it and then twist round and catch a toe in it. The hexagon aviaries usually have a pole in the centre with a motor tyre or something similar at the top to spread the load. Rubber or heavy plastic dustbin lids are also good for this purpose. The pole can push up the netting to a height above the surrounding walls and if perches are put across the pole high up the birds can get sun and air whenever they wish just as much as if they were in a fully open aviary. Weld mesh or Twilweld is good for the sides of aviaries but if used for the roof will need a lot of support as it is very heavy. It can come in rolls or in cut sheets and in mesh of various sizes. It is best bought hot-dip galvanized as otherwise it soon rusts and deteriorates very quickly then. If the Weldmesh is painted with a black bitumen paint (best applied with a roller type of brush) then this adds to its life and makes it very much easier to see through.

Perches, nest sites etc.
Perches are of course necessary but it is not always easy to place them in the best situations. They should be at various heights of course, and of various diameters with no sharp edges; they should not be like broom sticks, the same diameter throughout, which can lead to foot troubles. Perches with the bark still on are good and if obtainable cork oak is perhaps by far the best. Alternatively cork bark can be attached to other types of wood. Avoid padded perches unless the padding is waterproof or in a rainproof area.

Try to avoid putting perches where the birds' droppings will go onto a nest site or onto a wall which will be hard to keep clean. Have a choice of perches in sun or shade and in shelter from varying winds.

Rocks placed in strategic positions are not only good for perching places but help to keep talons from overgrowing. Quite small rocks placed on top of a wooden stump in order to get them higher up are useful.

Nest sites should be sheltered too and if the site is high up out of your reach then it should be accessible from outside the aviary by means of a ladder and some sort of doorway which needs to be safely fastened.

Security
Security is also a consideration these days. There are thieves around and they can do a great deal of damage by stealing birds. In fact I had two pairs of peregrines stolen from aviaries just after both pairs had made scrapes and were about to lay. These could have produced the first captive-bred peregrines in the world, had they not been stolen and I have no doubt whatsoever that the thieves did no good with any of the birds. For peregrines are one of the least suitable birds for the average falconer in Britain today. I doubt whether more than 5 per cent of the big falcons in captivity in Britain are ever flown regularly and consistently take quarry. In fact I only know of two falconers at the time of

writing who have the time, the place, the money, and the ability and who fly their birds throughout the season. There may be more whom I do not know, but most certainly very few indeed. Sadly most of the books tend to say that the peregrine is the best bird for falconers, and the beginners and the 'cowboys' believe this. Some of the so-called 'conservation' bodies even tend to encourage this idea by stating that peregrines are the favourite bird, that they fetch quite unbelievable sums of money and so on. By doing this they do harm to both conservation and falconry, by encouraging theft both from the wild and from falconers. And the eternal cry that is now trotted out by such bodies, 'falcons fetch fantastically high prices from Arab sheiks', is really one of the most stupid statements they could make. Arab falconers far prefer to fly sakers and even those few that do fly peregrines do not like either captive-bred birds or eyasses taken from the nest in the wild. They do not understand the training of eyasses and use passage birds. Those that may have been silly enough to buy eyasses (but not at the prices suggested) would be extremely disappointed in their performance simply because their falconers have never been taught the difference in training between the eyass and the passager or the haggard. Any breeder who starts selling birds that are not of use to a falconer will very soon find he is extremely unpopular and in due course no-one is going to buy from him.

Breeding some species in captivity is not easy. When I first tried I would most certainly have guessed that sparrowhawks, notorious for their temperamental manner, would be the hardest of all. In fact I have found that goshawks are far more difficult and the females only too often kill the males, even after several months or even years in an aviary together. But sparrowhawks seem to settle down remarkably quickly and are not after all difficult to breed.

But there is always a certain amount of luck. For years I had a very beautiful saker who year after year laid clutch after clutch of infertile eggs and had quite a number of different mates offered to her to choose from. One year my assistant Ray Shatwell spent a lot of time giving more attention to her and feeding both her and her mate a special diet; and still after what seemed a very promising start the pair failed to mate. The year after I again changed males for a bird that had already bred with another saker. And at long last, success!!!

When your efforts go wrong year after year, especially with a bird that you want to breed from for some particular reason, and then at long last it all goes right, you really feel you are winning. Some species are very easy to breed and are almost as bad as rabbits or guinea pigs. My first pair of kestrels, both injured birds, the male, a haggard, bred 96 young before the female (a passage bird) died.

Birds in captivity should live longer and their offspring should have a higher survival rate than those in the wild. In captivity they are not only protected far more from other predators, but provided you have a good vet then you can avoid a lot of disease and cure some if disaster should strike.

It is my theory that the better your birds like their aviary and the conditions you give them then the more likely they are to enjoy life and to breed well.

I also think that birds that have been trained and flown make better breeding birds. And of course in many cases there is no reason why you should not have the best of both worlds. Fly your birds and breed from them – but don't forget you can lose a bird whilst flying and so break up your breeding pair.

Incubators

A great deal of information has been written about incubators and incubating. I would thoroughly recommend *The Incubator Book* by Anderson Brown, but with the reservation that it is not written from the point of view of raptors but rather of domesticated fowls and also of wildfowl. And I think there is quite a difference which should be considered. The book tends to deal with large quantities of eggs rather than a few eggs that may well be far more valuable egg for egg; and so a somewhat different attitude is necessary.

Provided the parent birds are good parents (and as with the human race this is by no means always the case), then they are most likely to be better at incubating than any artificial methods. Next to them I would put foster parents of the same or very similar species and also of similar size. Other species of raptor may work happily but one would have to do quite a lot of experimenting to come to any satisfactory conclusion. I have hatched raptors' eggs under domestic fowl, chicken, bantams etc. I have also hatched both kestrel and lanner eggs under house pigeons but here one must be very careful as the hatching time for pigeons is about half that of raptors, and so you may have to move the eggs from one pair of pigeons to another midway through incubation. Using any foster parent other than a raptor of a similar species obviously brings problems. But foster parents both for hatching and for subsequent rearing can be of great use. The main difficulty is in finding foster parents at exactly or very nearly exactly the right time. And certainly one would have to keep a number of chicken, bantams or pigeons to be able to have a broody bird ready when you need it. Of course you are not going to expect the bantams or the pigeons to feed the young raptors, I hope. And some foster parents, particularly bantams, can be very clumsy with their feet when getting on and off the eggs, and can only too easily break an egg.

Having tried all these different ideas I would be very disinclined to use any non-raptors as foster parents for incubating.

So we come to artificial incubators. Basically all that an incubator consists of is a box with heat and humidity that is as near as possible to that provided by the parent birds. There are so many varieties of these on the market that you can become very bewildered. But obviously you are not going to want any that hold more than say a couple of dozen eggs at a time unless you are running a very large raptor establishment. And even then you may well prefer to have several small incubators rather than one large one. Certainly the phrase 'Divide and Conquer' is often very applicable here. An incubator can go wrong in many ways only too easily and if you divide your clutches into two and use two

incubators you have an extra safeguard. However this means more expense and with a well-made, reliable incubator you should not have to go to these extremes. Incubators can be run by gas, paraffin, or electricity; the last of these is generally the most convenient.

Incubators can be divided into two types, still-air or forced-air. Still-air incubators work by convection and so are often used as hatching incubators rather than as setting incubators. However some setting incubators can also be used for hatching, though few people seem to do so. Setting is the period of incubation before the chick starts to 'pip' or break out of the egg – hatching in other words.

Forced-air incubators have a fan (sometimes more than one) which helps to keep the temperature even throughout the whole area of the machine. Still-air incubators having no fan, have a horizontal stratum, usually about central, where the temperature is correct.

Most raptor eggs require a temperature of 98.5°F (36.9°C) approximately. Both types of incubators will have some means of varying the temperature and setting it to whatever you require. The thermostatic controls must be good enough to keep the temperature within a quarter of a degree Celsius all the time once the machine has been started up and had time to reach the maximum heat required, and settle down and become balanced.

It must be realised that excessive heat from outside the incubator, cannot be

303

160 My own home-made incubator based on one made by Egan Muller. The thermometer on the outside (top left) gives me room temperature. The one half way down on the right is a right-angle thermometer that can be read without opening up the incubator. It reads just about egg level. The contact thermometer is on the right-hand side and reads the temperature inside but the main works of it are outside on the right out of sight. It can be altered by turning a magnet on top of it. The two hair-line hygrometers measure humidity that can be viewed through the little port holes in the door flap. There are two fans and two ring heaters but the top lot are in the ceiling and not visible. The humidity dishes are glass dishes either side of the lower ring-heater. There is an extra thermometer in the door flap and on top an egg timer which can be set and put in your pocket to remind you when to turn the eggs next. The eggs are sitting on plastic-coated dowel rods. By placing the rods with varied spaces between them it can take different sized eggs. You can see the arrows that tell you which way to turn the eggs. The egg shelf slides out and there are six vent holes, three each side (only three are visible). 35mm film cases serve as vent hole blocks in case of a power cut. There is a dimmer switch just showing top right exterior. The wiring from the ring-heaters and fans runs through a false top and bottom to the switches on the right hand side. There are two switches: one for the light inside the incubator (a 15-watt bulb in the ceiling), and one for the fans and ring-heaters. There is also a relay box here that connects the contact thermometer to the heaters. The dimmer switch is an added extra for boosting the heaters when the room temperature is very cold or for reducing the output from them when the room is a lot warmer. If I had an air-conditioned thermostatically controlled room this would be unnecessary as would be the insulating layers between the inner and outer walls. But insulation is often poor on cheap incubators although this is something which is easy to improve. The little box at the back with the thick lid is where the eggs are put as soon as they start to chip. This box then becomes a still-air incubator inside a forced-air incubator. A small container of water inside this hatching box will increase the humidity and conversely a packet of silica gel should decrease it.

My smaller incubator is similar to this model but with only one ring-heater and one fan in the base.

controlled by such thermostats. Strong sun falling on an incubator, especially if it has a perspex top, can cook your eggs in a very short time. It is possible to build in a cooling system but this would be quite unnecessary in Britain. Personally I regard any incubator that has a perspex top as being a thing definitely to avoid, even more so if it opens from the top. Yet a great many makers produce this sort of thing. They will hatch eggs up to a point but can hardly be regarded as serious machines for use with valuable eggs. They are more of a toy: good for showing school children how eggs hatch. You would be very lucky to get as high a success rate from such machines. The insulation of the body of many of these is extremely poor. Control of both temperature and humidity is far easier if your incubating room is air conditioned and temperature controlled; which in Britain is extremely unlikely except for commercial breeders. The number of private houses in Britain which have air conditioning must be tiny. But if you can keep your incubator in a room where the temperature does not vary a great deal it will probably help, though at the Falconry Centre where we often had eggs in December and the room temperature would be down to below 8 degrees Celsius during a really cold night and up to 20 degrees or more in midsummer, I did not find any real problem except that the contact thermometers had to work hard in cold weather. I did in fact put in a 'dimmer' switch to my heaters so that in very cold weather they would heat up more quickly after the incubator had been opened up. In hot weather the heaters were run at half the full rate so that one got less overshoot. Overshoot is quite simple. The incubator reaches the required temperature and the heaters are then switched off by the contact thermometer. But of course there is still heat being emitted from them so the temperature will go on rising for a variable length of time depending on how hot the heaters were and how long they take to cool down. This rise in temperature is known as overshoot. Similarly one gets undershoot, i.e. the temperature drops, the heaters come on but they take time to get hot so there is a time lag or undershoot. So heaters working at half power will give you longer undershoot and shorter overshoot, whilst at full power the reverse happens.

Most people put their eggs in a forced-air incubator and they stay in there until they start to 'pip' – i.e. until the chick makes a small bulge or even a crack. The egg is then put in a still-air incubator and is no longer turned.

Turning is essential to eggs hatching and the birds themselves shuffle their eggs around every so often; but of course they do not turn then by 180 degrees at set intervals, which is what most people do. The number of times an egg should be turned is still a matter of great argument. I would recommend a minimum of three times every 24 hours but preferably more. Personally I dislike intensely those incubators that turn the eggs automatically, though most people use them and commercial producers are more or less forced to do so. Eggs can and do go wrong, only too often. If they are in an automatic turner then the person who is looking after the machine tends to say, 'Well the machine will turn them for me so I don't have to worry.' Correct. He doesn't have to worry about the turning (unless the machine goes wrong). BUT the breeder who hand-turns his eggs will have to open up his machine and handle the eggs and this is where he has a great advantage. For eggs that go wrong usually smell before they actually burst, and so the manual turner will spot this sooner and avoid the disaster. When the contents of a burst egg hit the fan, every egg in the incubator will have to be cleaned and if possible moved into another incubator while the first is being disinfected. In addition to this the breeder will all the sooner spot if a heater or a fan has stopped working. Safety devices to warn you of such troubles can be introduced and it is a wise precaution to do so.

Incubator cleaning

Every so often (and immediately if you should have an egg explode), your incubator should be cleaned and fumigated. This is quite a simple job but the fumigating is done by a toxic gas and care must be taken to avoid inhaling the fumes. Firstly vacuum the incubator thoroughly to remove dust, fluff etc. Then wipe over all the surfaces with a damp cloth impregnated with a solution of Dettol or a similar disinfectant. Then warm the incubator up and switch off. Block off all air vents. You will need 0.5 g of Potassium Permanganate to 0.8 cc of formalin per cubic foot of incubator interior. Pour the Potassium Permanganate into your glass water dish or some other suitable container. It is best to do this with the container in place on the floor of the incubator. Then add the formalin and close up the incubator. Leave for at least 30 minutes and then open all windows in your incubator room and unstop the vents and open the door. Remove the dish. Switch on the fan and leave the incubator and the room until the toxic gas has dispersed. Clean the dish. Do not get any electrical components damp when cleaning.

In an experiment one year I decided I would try to emulate the birds' method of turning and so I bought some shallow bowl-shaped nylon sieves, such as cooks use for sifting flour. I put these into a forced-air incubator and when turning time came (which was very roughly once every two hours starting at 8.30 in the morning and going on till around midnight) I simply shuffled the eggs around in the sieves with a gentle stir of the finger. It worked perfectly well. And why not? After all the nearer you can get to doing what the birds do the better it should be. Certainly I got some very high hatch rates by these methods and if you get over 90 per cent hatch of fertile eggs you are doing very well. I have done better than 90 per cent at times but no-one can ever expect to get 100 per cent success rate more than once in a blue moon, no matter what he is breeding.

I try to turn my raptor eggs at least 11 times in 24 hours at roughly two-hourly intervals. But they do have a longer interval during the night when I too am having a rest. I try to turn them an odd number of times per day so that during the longer interval they are resting on one side one night and on the other side the following night.

I mark my eggs with two arrows, one each side of the egg to show which way the egg must be turned. And if you put any additional eggs into the machine then put them so that all the arrows face the same way as this will help you to check that you have not missed out an egg when turning time comes round.

There are many disasters lying in wait for you: infertile eggs, disease, careless handling of eggs and that dread of many people in many walks of life – a power cut. You need not get too fussed about power cuts the moment they happen. Just do not open your incubator (this avoids loss of residual heat). Block all vent holes. You can cover it up with some form of insulation such as blankets etc., but if the machine has been decently insulated this should hardly make any difference and personally I would not bother. However, the perspex-top machines are often very badly insulated. Try to get a standby generator set up and if you haven't got one available then think about things like hot water bottles. A cut of several hours will probably not have any effect – after all, look how long wild birds can be off the nest, often deliberately, though sometimes through interference of some sort: for hours may be and still nothing goes wrong. Power cuts are far more likely to affect your brooders to a very considerable extent in quite a short time and this is where a standby generator comes in to rescue you, and to add to the expense too of course. Here again a warning device for power cuts is helpful but remember it won't work if it is on the mains supply! And when it's over, remember to open the vents.

Cleaning of eggs
Some eggs get very dirty in the nest and it is best to clean them before they go into an incubator. You can do this with a soft damp cloth though not all people approve of this idea. Or you can use a very fine sandpaper.

Humidity
Humidity is also important. Here again many incubator producers seem to assume that their buyers are remarkably stupid: they avoid giving any sort of hygrometer and just tell you to keep the water compartment in the machine topped up to a certain level. This seems to me to be a very hit-and-miss approach; one American firm had an upturned bottle affair arranged to keep the water level up but which made it quite impossible either to put this reservoir back or to lift the perspex top to see to the eggs without spilling water – not a very accurate way to go about things. It required only two small saw cuts in the perspex top and a couple of small nuts and bolts to avoid all this!

When I first became interested in incubators I happened to be flying some birds at the Game Fair, so I took the opportunity to go round the stands which were selling incubators and have a talk with the makers' representatives. After all, I reckoned they should be clued up about incubation. I was soon disillusioned, especially when it came to talking about humidity. Not only were they ignorant of the subject but they seemed to think that so long as their machines hatched around 75 per cent of fertile eggs then that was fine.

I would consider any incubator hatching less than 85 per cent of fertile eggs to be a poor machine, subject of course to proper handling. Not all hatching failures can be blamed on the incubator of course.

Humidity

There are two main ways to measure humidity. Firstly you can use a hygrometer, preferably a hairline hygrometer; this is quite expensive and it is best to have two in order to check that they are correct. Secondly you can use an ordinary thermometer which is put inside the incubator and has a small wick wrapped round the bulb end (hence it is called a wet-bulb thermometer). This wick runs down into the water reservoir or into one of its own, also inside the machine. This is a very cheap and accurate way of measuring humidity, but if the water going to the wick is hard then the wick calcifies and you will not get accurate readings. This problem can be overcome by using distilled water.

I like my hairline hygrometers to read around 50 to 55 per cent humidity. Wet bulb thermometers give you a similar percentage humidity at 85° farenheit when incubating at 98.5° F (36.9°C). You can test a hairline hygrometer by throwing a saturated cloth over it; it should then in a very short time read 100 per cent. Most hairline hygrometers are adjustable.

If you have removable water dishes that calcify with hard water just clean them by leaving watered down vinegar in them for a day. You will need spare dishes of course.

Some breeders advise increasing the humidity at or near the hatching date. This sounds all very fine, but I simply cannot see how an owl, for instance, sitting on say five eggs, sharing the sitting with her mate, can possibly increase the humidity to the egg which is nearest to hatching without increasing it to the whole clutch; and in any case, how could she know which egg requires this increase? Owls may be wise birds but not to this extent. So I rather question whether this increase in humidity is necessary. Certainly the level to which some people increase it means the chicks are hatching into a sauna-type atmosphere and must surely be gasping for breath. The theory that ducks need more because a duck near to hatching goes back onto its nest wet from a swim I find very odd. How do you get a duck wet? Do ducks have some miracle way of de-waterproofing their feathers?

Obviously eggs must be treated with care. Too much shaking or turning the wrong way can do a lot of harm. In the wild, eggs must stand quite a lot of moving around when they are in nests high up in a tree and a gale of wind is blowing. So I do not believe it is necessary to bolt incubators to the floor, as has been suggested.

There is no reason why you shouldn't make your own incubator. It would certainly save a lot of money and you could put in more reliable thermostats and hygrometers than some of the cheap rubbish that is often to be found in some of the smaller incubators. I made mine from a design by Egon Muller; this in turn was partly based on the small German Schumacher incubator, a machine I would recommend for setting and hatching small numbers of raptor eggs – up to say 30 or so. In cases where such a machine does not have automatic turning, it would be comparatively easy to fit such a device. I used a similar machine for a number of years after trying out various other makes and discarding them for one reason or another (see p. 304).

Most people would call this a setting incubator but Herr Muller devised a method of using this type as a hatcher too. Once the eggs started to pip they were transferred as they did so into a small box of wire mesh lined with tissues and with a lid which (after various trials) was of two sheets of ply spaced about an inch apart and with four holes in each sheet about an inch in diameter, drilled so that the passage of air was indirect, i.e. the holes were placed, not one directly above the other, but staggered. The eggs in the container were no longer turned.

The humidity was controlled by pushing the glass water dishes nearer to the fan to increase or further away to decrease.

As incubation proceeds so the egg loses weight and the air sac at the blunt end of the egg becomes quite obviously larger.

Some breeders weigh their eggs every day to see how much weight they have lost and they have worked out what the correct percentage of loss should be. One should know the weight of the egg the day it was laid, which is by no means easy since one is disinclined to disturb one's birds any more than absolutely necessary. There is a formula for estimating the initial weight but it is a quite a complicated affair. If the weight loss is incorrect then they will move the egg concerned either into an incubator with a higher humidity or into one with a lower humidity – or even one that has zero humidity produced by introducing silica-gel into the machine.

Obviously this involves having a number of incubators and the whole affair becomes extremely complicated and very very expensive. I have to confess that although I have toyed with this idea I finally washed it out simply because I had birds laying eggs sometimes in December and eggs still being laid as late as November the next year, from different species, requiring different incubating times and varying in size from those of tiny American kestrels to large eagles; with a very limited purse and not half as many staff as I should have liked the method was a non-starter.

Raptors take quite a long time to hatch from the time they first pip. You may well hear the young cheeping inside the egg and a quick examination under the candler will generally show that the chick has broken through into the air sac. Forty-eight hours is quite a normal time though some are quicker. One should not get too worried until at least 48 hours have elapsed. Then it is helpful to use the ultra-violet candler again to ascertain exactly where the bird is in the egg. Helping a bird out is something to be avoided if possible, and definitely not an action to be taken lightly. It is very easy to act too soon and if blood vessels are broken then the chick can only too easily bleed to death. The chick should turn round as it pips and so chip the top off the egg and then push its way out. This is not done in a steady progression but with intervals during which the chick rests

161 Young birds a few
days after hatching in the
incubator – three
goshawks, two Harris'
hawks and a common
caracara.

before having another crack at it. The turning is clockwise looking from the
sharper end of the egg. But some chicks will stop turning, and turn the other
way, or actually be stopped by reason of the membrane sticking to the inner wall
of the shell. This can be caused by too much air getting into the hole the chick
has already made and some chicks make a very large hole. A chick that is stuck
can be helped by very very gentle application of tepid water on a soft brush
through the hole.

You can help keep this area moist by placing a half eggshell of a slightly larger
size over the end of the egg. In addition, by using a very small torch of the type
used by fishermen for tying on their flies in a bad light, one can see whether or
not the veins in the membrane have emptied of blood. If they have, one can
proceed by gently removing more of the shell. A small pair of eyebrow tweezers
are a help.

A chick may hatch out with the yolk sac still protruding. For the average
breeder of little experience I would now suggest you turn to a really good raptor
vet. But it is possible to tie off the yolk sac and cut it away or even to make an
incision in the bird, put the yolk sac into position, and stitch up the chick. I am
none too keen on inexperienced people trying either of these solutions on their
own.

Hatched chicks should be left in the hatching department, whether it be in a
separate incubator or in the micro-type hatcher I use, until they are dried off.

They can then be removed to a previously warmed brooder.

There are many different ideas on brooders: small electrically heated pads, and brooder floors heated from below by various means ranging from light bulbs or electrical elements to just plain hot water bottles. Basically these types are all heated from below; I have tried several of them but have come to prefer the sort of heat the bird gets in the wild, i.e. heat from above. Place the heater off-centre so that one end of the brooder is warmer than the other. In this case the bird may move away from the heat source if it gets too hot, or move nearer if too cold. And very small recently hatched raptor chicks, though nothing like as mobile as quail or chickens, will manage to move themselves around as they require more or less heat. I ended up with large plastic cold-water header tanks in which, at the start, the chicks were contained in a plastic ice-cream container lined with tissues. These containers need to be large enough for the birds to move around in. It helps to have a bowl-shaped depression for the chicks and if they appear to slip around on the tissues then fine gravel such as is often used in aquariums will help to avoid the problem of splayed legs. These are quite obvious and if a bird does get splayed legs then a light rubber band to help keep them close, but not too close, will cure the trouble. It need not be on for long as a rule.

The heat is provided by dull emitters suspended on chains from above. As the birds grow older so the heat can be lessened either by dimmer switches or by moving the heater higher up. This has proved to be quite a satisfactory method. By 12 days most raptors are old enough to do with no heat whatsoever unless it suddenly gets very cold indeed (I am talking about the average climate in the South of England; obviously it will differ for those breeders in more extreme conditions, whether hotter or colder).

Feeding

Chicks do not usually require food for up to 24 hours after hatching. But the period does vary with different species and some will be asking for food 4–6 hours after hatching. We weigh our birds eight times a day before and after each of the four daily feeds. The first feed of the day compared with the first feed of the previous day tells you whether your bird is gaining or losing weight. You may get a slight drop of a few grams between the weight at hatching and the first feed. But this is normal. Later on a weight drop must be regarded as an indication of something wrong. Obviously the difference in a before and after weight gives you the amount of food consumed.

Never feed a chick if it still has food in its crop from the previous meal. This will nearly always cause trouble. It tends to make the food in the crop ferment. Do not worry about one meal missed; you will almost certainly find the chick will make up at the next meal. But remember owls do not have a crop.

Meals do not have to be evenly spaced; chicks certainly do not get fed on the dot in the wild. So you don't have to make feeding as inconvenient as with

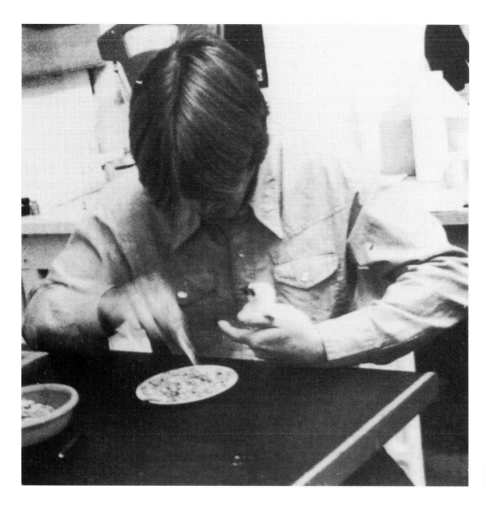

162 Hand feeding a young Blyth's Hawk Eagle just a few days old.

human children who get into the habit of regular feeds and scream the place down if you're late. Just be reasonably up to time.

As regards the sort of meat to give your birds we again run into all sorts of differing opinions and once again it depends a great deal on the individual breeder's circumstances, what food is easily available and so on. The choice is pretty considerable – from day-old cockerels to older chickens, quail, sparrows, starlings, pigeon, mice etc. Although it is best to get as near to their natural diet as possible, it is obviously very difficult to do so and when one is dealing with large numbers of birds it becomes quite impossible. The choice is yours.

Most people have seen films of raptors feeding their young and realise that they are very much more gentle than blackbirds or warblers or such. Small pieces are torn off the prey and offered and if the chick has difficulty in swallowing then the piece may be removed and a smaller one given in place. At first the size of each piece should be about that of half a peanut or smaller, and little or no castings should be given. In the early stages it is best to skin the food and remove legs, head, crop, gizzard and guts. Some people then grind the whole

313

thing up in a mincer and put the resultant mush in a polythene bag; they clip off a corner and squeeze the food into the chick's open beak rather like icing a cake. I have never liked this scheme myself; sharp bones can still get through and be dangerous in that they may perforate the chick's crop or stomach. Also, feeding this way tends to be over too quickly and this is not natural. The parent birds would be taking quite a time at this stage. If the meat is sticky it helps to dip it into water before offering it to the bird.

As the chicks grow up, which most species do at an amazing rate, so they get bigger lumps at each meal, and more castings, and in a very short time they will pull for themselves. Where captive-bred birds are concerned they will learn to pick up suitably sized chopped-up meat from a bowl in a very short time. In 12 days or so the tweezers may be discarded. However some species are very slow growing up. I had a Blyth's hawk-eagle chick that took far longer than a ferruginous buzzard, though the buzzard would have been a heavier bird when fully grown. Whether this applies to all the hawk-eagles I have no idea.

This is the stage when the chicks should go into a small, possibly heated, brooder where they cannot see humans and where the food is put into the brooder through a slot to prevent any more imprinting. If you have their parents or foster parents available to look after them then they may go to them even earlier. But a close eye should be kept on the reactions of the old birds when this is done. They do not always approve of the idea and you may have to act very quickly if they start to attack the newly introduced young.

Extra calcium and extra vitamins are essential and we use S.A.37 plus extra calcium. This is sprinkled on the food at each meal. Soon they will be strong enough to pull for themselves and can be put into a large indoor aviary until they are well feathered and able to go into an outdoor nursery aviary with solid walls. The less they see of humans the better; this helps to remove any imprinting.

Imprinting is the process whereby you take the place of the parent birds in the mind of the chick. In the wild when the young see one of the old birds coming to the nest they all start to scream for food. In due course they learn to fly and to fend for themselves and the parent birds go their own ways and pay no more attention to the young. So there is no longer anyone to scream at. But in captivity the human on whom the bird becomes imprinted does not go away, and so the bird will scream endlessly at humans. An imprinted bird is not a bird you want for falconry purposes, for it will scream at you without stopping; this is extrememely hard to cure and often impossible. Now if the bird is very well fed you may only too easily be fooled into thinking that, as the bird is not screaming at you, it is not imprinted. Once it is hungry you will soon find out. And by then it may be too late.

Artificial insemination

Imprints are useful for breeding by artificial insemination. It must be quite clear that A.I. can be of great use. The method can certainly enable one to breed from

a bird which would otherwise be impossible. However in my opinion, A.I. has in certain cases been misused to the point of being ridiculous, indeed downright stupid. There have been hybrids between birds that just do not make any sense at all. But we are being forced to breed some hybrids simply because we are not being allowed to obtain the correct mate for certain of our birds. I have myself been forced to breed gyr prairie hybrids and I shall be forced to continue to breed similar birds because I have been unable to obtain an import licence for a mate for my gyr.

However, I do think that the indiscriminate crossing of species which has been done is pointless. Often the breeder hopes he will breed the best characteristics from each species and so breed a super-bird. Personally I feel this is not a good thing. The natural species have and still do provide man with all that he needs and a super-bird that is going to outdo all the natural species would very rapidly become a bore. If your bird always caught the quarry; if your racing car always won; if you never backed a loser the fun would depart.

I do not propose to go into A.I. here simply because I have not anything like sufficient experience; others who are experienced should write about it.

However, those who say that A.I. should not be used had better not eat turkey at Christmas or Thanksgiving – nearly all, if not quite all, turkeys are produced by A.I.

Appendix 2 gives records of the weight of young birds when hatched and before and after feeding are, the period they are still in the first brooder. Since the Falconry Centre has now (1985) bred over 42 different species of raptor, I have selected a cross-section of species that I hope will prove useful to other breeders.

163 Gyr falcon (grey phase) feeding home-bred eyass gyrs and peregrines. Using other birds as foster-parents can be very helpful to captive breeding.

315

164 Goshawk from *The Mirror of Hawks*.

25 Hawking houbara with sakers

A few years ago I was most kindly invited by two Saudi Arabian princes to go to Morocco and watch their sakers flying at McQueen's bustard, or 'houbara' as the Arabs call them.

There are a few records of McQueen's bustard visiting Britain. Lodge and Bannerman's *The Birds of the British Isles* has quite a bit of interesting information about them in Volume XI. But this information did not in one respect coincide with what I found in Morocco. That is that some of the birds the falcons caught had only three bars on the tail and others had four. Like capercaillie they have 24 tail feathers instead of the more normal 12 of most birds. But they are strange birds and since the only one we ever had in Britain (the great bustard) is now extinct the best way to describe one is that they look like a very large Norfolk plover or stone curlew. They have more of a heel than a hind toe, quite long necks when they are stretched out, and the very bright yellow eye also.

I flew out to Marrakesh and from there we drove via Ouazazarte and Figuig to the camp on the Eastern borders to Algeria. It was December and we were at quite a high altitude so at night it was frosty.

I arrived in the dark and the falcons were sitting very close to each other on their blocks at the back of an enormous marquee type of tent. One could not have left peregrines as close to each other as this without their fighting. Apart from a Lanner which they had trapped whilst there all the birds were female sakers, 28 in all. They were of varying markings and colorations and I enquired about the reason for favouring the paler birds. I was told that although they liked the looks of the paler variety, colour most certainly had nothing to do with performance in the field.

All the birds were very well manned and rarely bated. Always there was someone close-by to attend to them. In front of them was a low barrier which one could lean against, sitting on the cushions placed on enormous carpets spread out on the ground. Mint tea was constantly being served.

The following morning I was able to examine the set-up more closely. The camp was nowhere near any villages or houses and was a self-contained unit of some 150 personnel. Petrol tankers, water bowsers, a large generator and most other mod. cons. were available.

Soon after breakfast each falconer hooded up his bird and the party set off in various vehicles. Those for the falcons were custom-built. They were large pick-up type trucks, but with a number of specialised extras. The cab had a bench

165 Trained Sakers back at camp.

seat; the roof was able to be opened wide; and there was a seat at the back of the bench seat but higher up, so one could see out over the top and one's legs rested against the back of the bench seat. All the edges of the truck were heavily padded so that one did not hurt oneself when travelling at speed over rough terram. There were seats for the falconers behind and perches for those falcons not already on the fist. Small runged ladders on the sides of the trucks made it easy to climb aboard. All the vehicles had intercom radios.

The whole party travelled quite a distance together and then, when they had reached the agreed hunting ground for the day, split into three. There were two hawking groups of three vehicles, one for each of the two Princes. The third group was there to arrange the luncheon area, light a fire and do all the necessary chores.

I went with one of the hawking groups. We drove across country quite slowly in line abreast with the falcon truck in the centre. The other two vehicles were several hundred yards away on either side. I suppose some people would call this a desert (I've even heard a member of Parliament call the Scottish moorland a desert!) but there were many varieties of plants, some very prickly and some quite tall, plenty of cover for animal and bird life. Every so often we came across

a 'ouadi', a dried-up river bed lined with green bushes several feet high looking rather like a broom. These ouadis were not very wide but had quite steep banks and only in a few places was it possible to get across them in the trucks.

As we drove slowly along over the gently rolling plateau everyone kept a look-out for any signs of houbara. And the Arabs were extremely sharp-eyed. They would spot the tracks of the birds in the sandy soil and seemed to know if they were fresh or not. Every so often we would stop and one of the falcons would be unhooded and raised up so it could see more easily in front of us. They chose falcons that were good at spotting the quarry in the distance and I was informed that a good spotter was invaluable. One of the falconers would call out (a camel call I was told) and this might have the effect of making any houbara move if heard. Once one of the falconers spotted a houbara not far from the truck. I managed to photograph this bird before it was flushed and I had quite a job to see it even when it was pointed out to me; it was superbly camouflaged. But of course my hosts knew what they were looking for and I didn't and that makes a lot of difference. Gamekeepers can spot sitting pheasants better than stockbrokers because they are used to it.

Once the spotter falcon saw a houbara she would leave the fist and head off

166 The specially built truck for desert hawking. Once on board the truck when a likely place is reached the best falcons at spotting are unhooded and have a look around. The convoy moves on if nothing is found. If they spot a Houbara off they go with the truck following in hot pursuit.

319

167 McQueen's Bustard
or Houbara are well
camouflaged.

168 When threatened by
a falcon they have a
curious display similar to
that of the owl family.
They try to look twice as
big to frighten the falcon
away.

towards it. Generally it was too far off for us to see but the moment the falcon was in the air we were off and one had to hang on tight for there was no question of going slowly because of the bumps. And there was at times some very rough and rocky terrain and bumps aplenty. I was very glad of all the padding arrangements around the truck especially as I was trying to take photographs and had only one hand to spare.

In fact photography proved exceedingly difficult. The light was very good and I could use quite a fast shutter speed but the moment the truck slowed down or stopped it was enveloped by its own dust cloud which made it very hard to focus and did not help the quality of the photograph.

Sometimes we found just a single houbara; at other times there might be a small party of five or more. Most of them were very much disinclined to fly. Any wild falcons around were probably too small to attack so big a bird – the males weigh 5–7lbs and the females a pound or so lighter. Also they had another method of approach to any such attack. They would spread their wings and tail and make themselves look even bigger, rather like an eagle-owl displaying, and then would turn round and squirt out for a distance of two or three feet some very slimy faeces which can partially blind the falcon and gum its feathers up until washed. The sakers however usually just piled in on any houbara and rather too easily overwhelmed it. The falconers of course wanted to see some good flying and tried hard to get to the houbara before the falcon, or at least by making a lot of noise and banging on the sides of the truck tried to make the houbara take to the wing.

From what I saw of it, the houbara needs at least 50–100yds before he has picked up speed. Once he has done so, though, he goes along quite fast and can climb well and will sometimes ring up just like a rook or a crow with the saker ringing up after him. If that happens he will then take a lot of catching and the flight may well cover a very considerable distance. The saker may consider she is outflown and will then give up.

At lunchtime we all gathered together by a ouadi where a fire had been lit and carpets laid out and lunch ready once we had washed. The morning flights were discussed over the meal. Another wash and off we set again.

Sometimes one of the accompanying trucks would spot some houbara and the intercom would burst into excited action.

I watched one flight where the houbara went ringing up and then when the saker was at the same level he set off in a straight line with the falcon in hot pursuit. We followed in the truck with a lot of very excited talk going on. As it was in Arabic I understood not one word of it but the gist was plain enough. Just how far we went I don't know but we were finally stopped by a steep-sided ouadi and there we stayed and watched through binoculars. Both birds went out of sight finally and we never knew the end. As far as I know the saker was lost. It had not been found when I left a few days later. That was by far the best flight I saw.

Most of the others were of course interesting to someone who had never seen this type of hawking done before but it was a very small percentage that really got going and got up several hundred feet. There certainly seemed to be plenty of houbara about in that particular area but I was told that every so often they would move the whole camp several miles further on and hawk a fresh area.

Just before dusk the whole party would come together again and the falcons would be fed up; then as the sun was setting the party would turn to Mecca and evening prayers would be said before the return to camp. There followed more discussion over the evening meal and sometimes a video film, taken of some the previous year's hawking, would be shown.

A lot of houbara were killed; exactly how many I don't know but it seemed to me that, with all due respect to my Arab hosts, there would soon be an end to houbara hawking if it went on in this way.

I have, like many others, given considerable thought to this problem and it seems to me there are two possible solutions.

1. It would be quite possible for those houbara caught close to the truck, which the majority were, to be rescued and later released with little or no harm done to them. In much the same way a fisherman releases a fish that is too small. Furthermore I am of the opinion that it would be possible to get far more really good flights by using a dog to flush the houbara and then, as in coursing with greyhounds, to give the houbara a fair amount of 'law' before slipping the falcon. It is of course extremely difficult to alter any tradition and often quite wrong to do so; but in this easel feel a change would be worthwhile, a feasible and not-too-difficult means of preserving both the houbara and the houbara hawking.

2. Whether it would be possible to increase the number of houbara by captive breeding I rather doubt. Unlike wildfowl and game birds houbara do not lay many eggs. A lot of its breeding grounds are beyond the Iron Curtain and captive-bred birds should be released in their breeding grounds, not in their wintering quarters. A great many used to be shot on migration; this may still happen and would be difficult if not impossible to control. Young houbara would probably not be at all easy to rear. This latter solution would be more difficult, but perhaps both could be tried out. After all the hunter has always looked after the hunted once it is realized that there will soon be no hunting otherwise.

It may well be that with so brief an experience of houbara hawking my views are not really justified. But sometimes the spectator sees more of the game.

I shall always be grateful to my Arab hosts for their hospitality and for showing me sakers flying in top style. I only hope that they will find some way of continuing this branch of falconry. But I do wish I had seen it as it used to be, not from a truck with intercom radios but from camel back.

I once went stalking in a 'Snowtrack', which saved a lot of hard walking and even harder climbing but took all the gilt off the gingerbread. One simply did not feel one had worked for one's beast – what a lot one misses if one goes about the countryside in such an easy way.

Glossary

Many of the following technical terms have now fallen into disuse.

Arms The legs of a hawk from the thigh to the foot.
Austringer (Fr. *autoursier*) a trainer of short-winged hawks, as against a falconer, who trains falcons.
Aylmeri Leather anklets, taking the place of jesses (an invention of the late Guy Aylmer).

Bate, to (Fr. battre) to beat the air with the wings.
Beam feathers The primaries.
Bechins (Fr. bechée, beccade) Morsels, beakfuls.
Bewits Strips of soft leather fastening the leg bells round the hawk's feet.
Bind to, to To catch and hold the quarry in the air.
Block A perch for falcons.
Blood feathers Feathers still growing.
Bolt, to fly at To fly straight from the fist at quarry (used of an *accipiter*).
Bowiser A young raptor that has reached the stage of being able to fly from bough to bough. Also called a 'brancher'.
Bow perch A perch for *accipiters*, buzzards and their like.
Bowse, to (Dutch – *buisen*, or Fr. *boire*) to drink, (Also bouse, boose, bouze, booze.)
Brail A soft, pliable leather thong with a slit in it, used to stop an unruly bird from bating, by preventing the wing from opening. Rarely if ever used nowadays, except for sick birds.
Brancher See Bowiser.
Break into, to Begin to eat.

Cadge A means whereby several birds can be carried at once.
Cadger, cadge-man, cadge-boy The person carrying the cadge. The word 'cad' is supposed to derive from this; also 'cadger' – someone who gets something for nothing. The cadgeman used to be given tips by onlookers for telling them about his charges.
Call off To lure a bird from a perch, or from someone else's fist. One would call or whistle while doing so.
Carry, to To fly away carrying the lure or the quarry.
Carry, to To tame a bird by carrying it.
Cast, to To hold a hawk round the body, so as to immobilize her while she is being coped, having a tail bell put on, etc.
Cast, to To throw up a casting, or pellet.
Cast Two hawks (not necessarily a pair).
Cast gorge, to To bring up the contents of the crop.
Casting The pellet containing fur, feathers, etc. which are not digested.
Cast off, to To let the bird fly from the fist.
Cawking time Pairing, mating time.
Cere (Fr. cere, Lat. cera) the waxlike part above the beak, where the nostrils are situated.
Chanceleer, to (Fr. *chanceler*) to make two or three sharp turns while stooping.
Check, to fly at To leave one quarry and pursue another.

Cope, to To cut or file overgrown talons or beaks; sometimes to blunt talons.
Cowering Quivering or shaking of the wings, seen in young hawks.
Craye, cray A form of constipation.
Creance, cranes The long line on which a bird is flown during flight before it can be trusted loose.
Crines Short, hair-like feathers round the cere.
Croaks A respiratory disease which causes the bird to croak.

Deck feathers The two centre feathers of the tail.
Draw the hood, to To pull the closing braces of the hood.

Endew, to To put over the crop.
Enew, inew To put in, to go into cover.
Enseam, to To bring a hawk into flying condition after the moult.
Enter, to To introduce (enter at quarry, enter to the hood).
Eyass, eyas Young bird in the nest, not yet able to fly.
Eyrie, eyre, ayre (Fr. *aire*) the nesting place of a bird of prey.

Falcon The female peregrine; now used to denote females of other species of long-wings, but not merlins, kestrels or hobbies.
Fall at mark, to To put the quarry into cover, and then alight on the ground.

Feak, feake, to To clean the beak by wiping it on the perch.

Fetch, to To reach the quarry and turn it.

Filanders (Lat. *filaria*) intestinal worms.

Flags Secondary feathers.

Fly on head, to To miss the quarry and check.

Foot, to To strike or clutch with the foot. (A good footer is a bird which is clever with her feet.)

Fret marks Lines appearing across the webbing of feathers which are still growing, caused by shock to the bird.

Frounce A disease of the mouth and throat, once thought fatal, but now fairly easily cured.

Full-summed All new feathers are full length and the quills have hardened off.

Get in, to To go to the hawk as soon as she has killed or is on the lure.

Gleam To throw up slime after casting.

Gorge To eat to repletion.

Hack A period of liberty allowed to young eyasses before training begins.

Hack back, to To hack, and by doing so, release birds to the wild.

Hack bells heavy bells, formerly used to slow up hack hawks.

Haggard A bird taken from the wild in mature plumage.

Halsband (Ger. also called *Jangaoli* in the East) a neck-band used in some Eastern countries to give a hawk more impetus when leaving the fist.

Hard-penned or hard-down See Full-summed.

High Generally used to mean that a bird is overweight.

Hood-shy Describes a bird that has been spoilt by incorrect hooding and consequently dislikes the hood.

Hunger trace See Fret marks.

Indue, to See Endew.

Imp, to To repair broken feathers (Lat. *imponere*).

Inke The neck of the quarry (obsolete).

Intermewed A bird that has moulted in the mews. (An eyass then becomes an intermewed eyass, a passager an intermewed passager, and so on.)

Jack A male merlin.

Jangaoli See *Halsband*.

Jerkin A male jer (gyr).

Jesses Leather leg straps.

Jakin Sleeping.

Kecks See Croaks.

Leash The leather or braided thong by which a bird is tied to its perch.

Lines, lunes, lewnes, loynes A term whose meaning is obscure; it was possibly the jesses, or an extension of the jesses, or the creance.

Lure An imitation quarry, swung on a line, used to tempt the hawk back to the falconer.

Mail A hawk's breast feathers.

Make, to Completely to train a hawk, when she is said to be 'made'. To make to the lure or make to the hood mean to train the bird to come to the lure or to wear a hood.

Make-hawk An old experienced bird, used to teach, or at least to encourage, younger birds.

Make in, to To move in towards the hawk when she is on the lure, or on her quarry.

Make point, to To throw up into the air over the spot where quarry has put into cover.

Man, to To tame.

Mantle, to To spread the wings like a cloak when feeding, to hide the food. Most often seen in eyasses.

Mar-hawk An inept falconer who spoils a hawk by clumsy handling.

Mark, to fly at To take stand, marking the spot where quarry has put into cover.

Mew To put a hawk down to moult.

Mews Formerly, the place where hawks were put to moult. Now more generally used to denote a place where hawks are kept. (Fr. *muer.*)

Musket A male sparrowhawk.

Mutes Droppings of falcons.

Nares Nostrils.

Pannel The hawk's stomach.

Pantas An old name for respiratory disease.

Passage hawk A bird taken from the wild after it has left the nest, but while still in immature plumage.

Pelt The dead body of any bird which the hawk has killed.

Petty single The toe of a hawk.

Pitch The height at which a falcon waits-on.

Plume, to To pluck.

Put in, to Either to drive quarry into cover, or the action of the quarry of going into cover.

Put out, to To drive quarry out of cover.

Put over the crop To empty the crop of food, which then passes into the bird's stomach.

Pounces The claws of a short-winged hawk.

Quarry Any game flown at.

Rake away, to (Usually of falcons) to drift away too far while waiting-on; sometimes used to mean that a falcon has given up the flight and has gone off down-wind.

Ramage-hawk See Bowiser.

Rangle Small smooth stones, left by a hawk's perch in case she should want to take one. Swallowing rangle is thought by some to aid the hawk's digestion.

Reclaim, to (Fr. *réclamer*) to tame a hawk. Often used to mean re-manning of a hawk after the moult.

Red hawk Bird in immature plumage (usually applied only to peregrines).

Refuse, to Sometimes used in the same sense as to turn tail, i.e. to give up a flight at quarry after a short time. Can also mean that the hawk will not fly the quarry at all.

Ring up, to To climb in spirals.

Ringer Used to describe a quarry that rings up.

Robin A male hobby.

Rouse, to To shake the feathers.

Rufter hood A simple hood used more by hawk-trappers than by falconers (Fr. *chapon de rust*).

Sails A hawk's wings.

Sarcel The outermost primary in the wing.

Seel, to The eastern practice of sewing a newly-trapped hawk's eyelids together with silk thread, to save using a hood. Never done in the West.

Serve, to To put the quarry out of cover for the hawk.

Sharp set Keen.

Slice, slicings Droppings of short-winged hawks, buzzards, eagles etc.

Snite, to To sneeze.

Sock A kind of jacket into which newly-caught hawks were put, in order to stop them hurting themselves. Nowadays, a section of a nylon stocking can be used.

Screen perch An obsolete and dangerous perch still used by some falconers.

Sore-hawk (Fr. *sore – sorrel*) a bird in immature plumage (see red hawk).

Spring, to To flush the quarry.

Stoop, to To dive from a height.

Strike the hood, to To pull the opening braces of the hood so that it is ready to be removed.

Shift, to To swerve (of quarry).

Swivel Means of attaching the jesses and leash to one another, so that they do not get twisted.

Take stand, to To perch in a tree.

Throw up, to To swing up into the air, usually after a stoop.

Tiercel, tercel, tassel, tarsell Used on its own, this means the male peregrine. Qualified with the word 'goshawk', it means a male goshawk. Now often improperly used for male prairie falcons, luggers etc.

Tirings Tough or bony pieces of meat given to a hawk to prolong her meal, exercise her back and neck muscles, and also to keep her beak in good trim and to stop her getting bored.

Tower, to To ring up.

Train The tail of a hawk.

Truss, to To bind to the quarry in mid-air.

Tyrrit (Fr. *touret*) the old name for a swivel.

Turn tail, to To give up chasing the quarry in mid-flight.

Unreclaimed Wild.

Unsummed A bird which has not yet finished moulting.

Varvels Used in place of a swivel in the old days. These were small flat silver rings, with the owner's name or coat-of-arms engraved on them. They were fastened to the ends of the jesses, and the leash was passed through them.

Wait-on, to To circle round in the air at a good height, until the game is flushed below.

Wake, to To man a bird by preventing it from sleeping.

Warble, to To stretch both wings up over the back until they nearly touch each other, and at the same time to spread the tail.

Washed meat Meat that has been soaked in water, and then had the goodness wrung out of it by being squeezed hard.

Weather, to To put hawks out in their weathering-ground.

Weathering-ground A place in the open air, sometimes with shelters against bad weather, where hawks are put when not in the mews,

Yarak An Eastern term describing a hawk in fit, keen flying condition.

Appendix 1: Some Useful Addresses

The following appendix comprises a list of names and addresses of Clubs and Associations which may be of help to anyone interested in falconry. The information has been updated since the first edition but as the addresses and officials change so frequently their accuracy cannot he guaranteed subsequent to publication. When writing to any of these bodies, it is always advisable to enclose a stamped, addressed envelope; if writing to an address overseas, it is best to send an international reply paid form, obtainable from the Post Office.

Clubs and associations
Association Nationale des Fauconniers et Autoursiers Français

The British Falconers Club
c/o Mr J Chick
Moonrakers
Allington
Salisbury
Wilts

Circolo dei Falconieri d'Italia

Deutscher Falkenorden, West Germany

North American Falconers Association
Correspondence Secretary
Brian James Walton
The Predatory Birds Research Group
Lower Quarry
University of California
Santa Cruz
California, USA

Raptor Breeders Association
David Mould
Merryfield
Emery Acres
Upper Basildon
Nr Reading

Welsh Hawking Club
The Secretary
Mike Shuttleworth
21 North Close
Blackfordby
Burton-on-Trent
Staffs

British Field Sports Society
59 Kennington Road
London SE1   Tel: 01 978-4742

The Hawk Board
K.J. Wood Esq
30 Linwood Road
Redhill
Surrey

The Hawk Trust
The Secretary
c/o Birds of Prey Department
London Zoo
Regent Park
London NW1

For any further information on the above contact the British Field Sports Society.

Breeding and conservations establishments
Now that the author has retired from The Falconry Centre please address him do the Publishers Messrs Batsford

Mr and Mrs J. Parry-Jones
The Birds of Prey and Falconry
Conservation Centre
Newent
Glos. GL18 1JJ
Tel: 0531-820286

The Hawk Conservancy
Weyhill
Nr Andover
Hants   Tel: 0264-772252

Birds of Prey Trust
Boulesdon House
Newent
Glos

Transmitters

Equipment
The Birds of Prey and Falconry
Conservation Centre
Newent
Glos
GL18 1JJ (counter service only)

Martin Jones
The Lodge
Huntley Manor
Huntley
Glos (mail order only)

Bells
Martin Jones (address above)

P. Asborno, 4530 West 31st Avenue,
Denver, Colorado 80212, USA

Transmitters
Martin Jones (address above)

Custom Electronics
2009 Silver Court West
Urbana, 111, 61801, USA

Aviary nets
Bridport Grundy
Bridport
Dorset

Braided cotton lure line
Young and Sons
Enterprise Works
Misterton
Crewkerne
Somerset

Hygrometers
(hairline type)
Messrs Ferris
Scientific Supplies
Kenn Road
St George's
Bristol 5
Avon

Gallenkamp Ltd
Technico House
Christopher Street
London EC2P 2ER

Contact thermometers and relays
Jumo Instrument Co
Hysol
Harlow
Essex

Knives (Opinel)
Malcberry Ltd
366 Croydon Road
Beckenham
Kent

Weighing scales
Avery scales

Books
Martin Jones (address above)

The Birds of Prey and Falconry
Conservation Centre (address above)

Licences (and questions regarding the
law as regards raptors in Britain)

The Department of the Environment
Tollgate House
Houlton Street
Bristol

Appendix 2: Food and weight charts

Day	Feed	Weight before feed	Weight after feed	Notes
TAWNEY EAGLE				
1.	1	58.8	61.6	
	2	60.5	64.2	
	3	63.6	67.4	
	4	65.4	69.1	
2.	1	65.2	69.6	
	2	68.4	73.0	
	3	71.9	76.5	
	4	74.0	78.1	
3.	1	74.3	78.1	
	2			fed, but not weighed
	3	80.9	86.6	
	4			electricity cut, therefore, fed in house – not weighed
4.	1	89.3	96.8	
	2	94.6	102.4	
	3	100.4	107.1	
	4	102.7	112.1	
5.	1	104.2	114.6	
	2	111.2	120.0	
	3	115.9	125.3	
	4	121.5	129.6	
6.	1	121.4	131.3	
	2	128.1	138.5	
	3	136.0	146.0	
	4	141.5	152.7	
7.	1	146.0	161.6	
	2	157.7	175.2	
	3	171.4	183.8	
	4	178.0	190.5	
8.	1	174.5	185.0	
	2	180.9	193.5	
	3	189.3	206.9	
	4	202.4	221.1	
9.	1	211.5	231.9	
	2	226.2	236.0	not feeding well – too hot?
	3	229.8	244.8	
	4	236.8	250.9	

Day	Feed	Weight before feed	Weight after feed	Notes
10.	1	241.6	258.6	
	2	252.0	261.0	
	3	256.6	279.0	
	4	273.7	291.8	
11.	1	276.5	293.1	
	2	289.0	307.5	
	3	301.0	323.0	
	4	313.0	334.5	
12.	1	321.0	337.4	
	2	333.0	356.2	
	3	349.7	369.0	
	4	361.6	382.0	
13.	1	363.0	387.4	
	2			tried back with parents – not interested. Took away
	3	377.7		
	4			ready to feed itself
14.	1	412.5		weighing once in a.m. only
15.	1	488.0		
16.	1	529.0		

Tawny eagle put in nursery aviary at this point

BLYTH'S HAWK EAGLE

Day	Feed	Weight before feed	Weight after feed	Notes
1.	4	53.6	54.3	
2.	1	53.6	54.8	
	2	53.8	55.7	force fed second feed
	3	54.9	55.8	
	4	54.6	57.1	
3.	1	56.0	57.4	
	2	56.1	58.5	
	3	57.8	60.0	still had crop
4.	1	56.4	59.2	
	2	57.8	62.0	
	3	61.3	66.3	
	4	65.0	69.6	
5.	1	67.0	71.2	
	2	70.0	74.8	
	3	73.4	77.5	
	4	75.2	82.9	
6.	1	78.1	84.3	
	2	82.2	88.6	
	3	86.3	92.8	
	4	90.2	100.0	
7.	1	93.1	99.3	
	2	90.6	94.4	brought up crop. Gave amoxyl
	3	92.2	98.2	
	4	94.8	101.7	
8.	1	95.2	105.7	
	2	102.7	109.8	
	3	104.6	111.8	
	4	107.6	116.6	

Day	Feed	Weight before feed	Weight after feed	Notes
9.	1	112.7	122.3	
	2	115.2	124.0	
	3	120.2	130.3	
	4	125.7	138.4	
10.	1	128.3	138.9	
	2	135.8	152.0	
	3	147.3	156.4	
	4	150.2	158.7	
11.	1	148.6	158.0	
	2	151.9	166.6	
	3	160.5	175.8	
	4	166.0	180.0	
12.	1	165.0	175.4	
	2	169.0	182.5	
	3	176.6	188.0	
	4	181.5	201.8	
13.	1	184.8	198.0	
	2	190.1	213.5	
	3	206.2	210.0	still had crop
	4	199.3	217.3	
14.	1	202.4	225.3	
	2	217.0	234.1	
	3	224.5	243.2	
	4	229.4	255.6	
15.	1	230.2	243.0	
	2	234.8	256.7	
	3	248.5	253.8	
	4	244.6	276.3	
16.	1	256.2	287.3	
	2	279.0	286.4	
	3	281.5	312.0	
	4	296.0	304.1	
17.	1	274.9	289.5	
	2	284.0	316.6	
	3	307.6	310.0	still had crop
	4	298.2	315.6	
18.	1	295.7	322.5	
	2	310.9	318.4	
	3	308.5	329.3	
	4	322.3	330.0	
19.	1	314.1	343.2	
	2	323.4	343.2	
	3	340.3	369.1	
	4	347.3	378.6	
20.	1	365.4	383.6	
	2	362.8	391.0	
	3	390.0	400.0	
	4	397.7	409.4	

Note: Growth rate of this species is remarkably slow.

Day	Feed	Weight before feed	Weight after feed	Notes
COMMON BUZZARD				
1.	4	38.5	40.6	
2.	1	40.8	43.8	
	2	43.2	45.5	
	3	44.5	48.6	
	4	48.2	50.9	
3.	1	49.5	53.5	
	2	51.8	55.2	
	3	54.5	59.5	
	4	58.7	64.0	
4.	1	62.2	69.0	
	2	66.5	73.3	
	3	72.5	76.4	
	4	75.3	81.0	
5.	1	78.4	82.7	
	2	79.4	84.9	
	3	82.6	88.9	
	4	87.0	95.9	
6.	1	92.1	97.2	
	2	94.5	102.5	
	3	99.8	109.8	
	4	107.7	118.5	
7.	1	114.7	123.1	
	2	119.2	128.0	
	3	125.8	136.6	
	4	133.5	145.0	
8.	1	138.5	153.3	
	2	151.5	170.2	
	3	168.0	185.0	
	4	180.2	195.5	
9.	1	175.5	190.0	
	2	185.0	199.0	
	3	193.0	217.0	
	4	290.5	225.5	
10.	1	212.0	233.5	
	2	220.2	239.0	
	3	236.0	256.0	
	4	246.5	262.0	
11.	1	232.8		weighing once in a.m. only
12.	1	274.0		
13.	1	322.0		
14.				put in non-imprint brooder
RED-TAILED BUZZARD				
1	2	47.7	50.3	
	3	49.1	52.2	
	4	50.4	56.6	
2.	1	52.2	56.4	
	2	54.7	60.5	
	3	58.9	62.7	
	4	60.5	54.4	

Day	Feed	Weight before feed	Weight after feed	Notes
3.	1	60.2	66.7	
	2	63.2	68.4	
	3	65.0	70.4	
	4	69.2	75.4	
4.	1	67.9	74.8	
	2	72.5	78.9	
	3	76.8	85.4	
	4	82.1	87.8	
5.	1	78.9	83.8	
	2	81.0	90.8	
	3	88.4	101.5	
	4	98.8	107.2	
6.	1	95.3	110.5	
	2	108.2	120.6	
	3	118.1	132.1	
	4	126.8	134.4	
7.	1	127.0	145.5	
	2	142.5	157.7	
	3	153.0	166.8	
	4	161.3	172.8	
8.	1	151.9	165.6	
	2	163.1	178.2	
	3	172.9	183.3	
	4	177.0	184.7	
9.	1	171.1	187.1	
	2	183.2	194.7	
	3	189.9	214.5	
	4	210.2	228.0	
10	1	207.7	231.1	put a close ring on
	2	229.5	242.5	
	3	234.0	256.8	
	4	251.3	270.5	
11.	1	248.0		weighing once in a.m. only
12.	1	277.5		
13.				back with parents

HARRIS HAWK (*Buteo Unicinctus*)

Day	Feed	Weight before feed	Weight after feed	Notes
1.	2	32.2	34.2	
	3	33.9	37.3	
	4	36.5	38.7	
2.	1	37.0	40.8	
	2	39.6	43.1	
	3	42.2	46.4	
	4	45.8	48.3	
3.	1	46.2	50.3	
	2	49.1	55.5	
	3	54.4	60.5	
	4	59.1	64.8	
4.	1	62.1	69.6	
	2	68.0	75.3	
	3	73.0	79.7	
	4	77.5	85.6	

Day	Feed	Weight before feed	Weight after feed	Notes
5.	1	80.4	88.8	
	2	85.0	92.4	
	3	88.9	99.2	
	4	96.8	105.5	
6.	1	98.5	106.8	
	2	103.2	112.4	
	3	109.5	120.5	
	4	118.0	129.8	
7.	1	122.0	129.0	
	2	124.4	137.5	
	3	133.8	141.3	
	4	137.3	146.7	
8.	1	138.5	151.8	
	2	145.7	158.9	
	3	154.4	159.2	
	4	163.7	175.6	
9.	1	166.1	181.9	
	2	176.8	185.5	
	3	179.0	192.7	
	4	186.1	205.0	
10.	1	194.4	208.1	
	2	200.7	214.2	
	3	208.0	224.5	
	4	213.5	227.5	
11.	1	210.5	230.3	
	2	226.5	250.0	
	3	241.5	269.0	
	4	256.5	273.2	
12.	1	251.0	273.6	
	2	266.0	283.2	
	3	272.0	280.1	
	4	268.5	302.0	
13.	1	285.5	316.0	
	2	298.8	323.7	
	3	311.0	341.0	
	4	327.5	356.5	
14.	1	310.5		weighing once in a.m. only
15.	1	327.0		
16.	1	350.0		into nursery aviary at this point

N.B. This bird was almost certainly a female

HARRIS HAWK

Day	Feed	Weight before feed	Weight after feed	Notes
1.	3	30.2	31.1	
	4	30.4	31.5	
2.	1	30.0	31.4	
	2	30.7	33.2	
	3	32.3	36.2	
	4	34.7	37.0	
3.	1	34.5	37.4	
	2	36.3	40.7	
	3	39.7	43.5	

Day	Feed	Weight before feed	Weight after feed	Notes
	4	41.8	45.5	
4.	1	42.0	45.0	
	2	43.6	46.3	
	3	45.1	49.0	
	4	46.9	50.3	
5.	1	46.6	51.5	
	2	49.5	55.0	
	3	53.6	57.9	
	4	55.5	61.4	
6.	1	57.9	63.7	
	2	60.7	68.0	
	3	66.6	72.4	
	4	70.0	72.0	not very hungry
7.	1	66.3	72.5	starting to feed itself
	2	70.3	78.4	
	3	76.2	82.8	
	4	80.6	88.2	
8.	1	83.0	91.4	
	2	88.7	98.7	
	3	96.0	—	feeding itself now
	4	—	—	
9.	1	108.0		weighing at first feed only now
10.	1	129.5		
11.	1	157.5		
12.	1	180.0		
13.	1	207.3		
14.				into nursery aviaries now

N.B. This bird is almost certainly a male. See comparison with female chart

ROUGH-LEGGED FERRUGINOUS BUZZARD

Day	Feed	Weight before feed	Weight after feed
1.	1	56.3	60.2
	2	58.9	63.9
	3	62.7	68.0
	4	67.0	73.7
2.	1	70.5	75.2
	2	73.6	80.8
	3	78.7	84.5
	4	80.8	85.4
3.	1	81.1	88.2
	2	85.5	96.3
	3	93.7	100.2
	4	97.6	105.9
4.	1	99.7	103.8
	2	100.8	109.4
	3	106.2	116.3
	4	114.1	126.7
5.	1	120.4	126.9
	2	124.7	133.1
	3	131.2	142.8
	4	141.0	157.0
6.	1	148.3	166.0
	2	163.2	182.0

Day	Feed	Weight before feed	Weight after feed	Notes
	3	176.0	191.4	
	4	184.5	200.5	
7.	1	187.5	198.2	
	2	191.8	202.8	
	3	198.8	220.5	
	4	213.5	236.6	
8.	1	223.4	247.3	
	2	238.9	250.7	
	3	241.2	269.1	
	4	261.7	274.4	
9.	1	259.7	279.5	
	2	271.2	288.0	
	3	279.8	313.7	
	4	305.5	328.5	
10.	1	307.7		weighing once in a.m. only
11.	1	363.5		
12.	1	392.5		

AMERICAN KESTRELS

Day	Feed	Weight before feed	Weight after feed	Notes
1.	3	14.0	15.7	
	4	15.1	16.6	
2.	1	15.7	17.1	
	2	16.4	18.2	
	3	17.0	20.0	
	4	19.2	21.4	
3.	1	20.3	22.3	
	2	21.2	24.0	
	3	23.2	26.7	
	4	25.7	28.4	
4.	1	26.3	30.0	
	2	29.0	31.5	
	3	30.3	33.9	
	4	32.0	36.4	
5.	1	33.4	36.3	
	2	35.0	40.7	
	3	39.0	43.6	
	4	41.0	47.0	
6.	1	42.5	50.0	
	2	47.8	54.4	
	3	51.0	56.5	
	4	52.2	58.9	
7.	1	51.7	55.9	
	2	55.8	60.4	
	3	56.2	64.6	
	4	61.6	68.7	
8.				back with parents

LANNERS

Day	Feed	Weight before feed	Weight after feed	Notes
1.	4	26.7	28.9	
2.	1	27.6	29.5	
	2	29.1	31.4	
	3	30.7	33.2	
	4	32.7	35.1	

Day	Feed	Weight before feed	Weight after feed	Notes
3.	1	33.4	36.4	
	2	34.8	37.8	
	3	36.5	41.1	
	4	39.9	42.9	
4.	1	40.6	44.4	
	2	43.1	48.4	
	3	47.6	53.0	
	4	51.3	57.6	
5.	1	52.4	57.5	
	2	55.8	61.9	
	3	59.7	65.9	
	4	63.8	70.7	
6.	1	62.4	68.1	
	2	66.2	72.6	
	3	70.6	80.2	
	4	76.9	84.1	
7.	1	76.7	85.7	
	2	84.0	93.4	
	3	90.7	103.5	
	4	101.0	109.6	
8.	1	101.6	112.2	
	2	108.7	117.4	
	3	114.3	128.8	
	4	104.9	133.3	
9.	1	124.1	137.2	
	2	133.9	149.7	
	3	145.2	158.1	
	4	152.9	165.9	
10.	1	152.3	161.3	
	2	155.8	169.8	put a close ring on
	3	164.0	174.7	
	4	168.2	188.3	
11.	1	172.8	192.5	
	2	185.6	206.1	
	3	194.8	218.1	
	4	206.1	211.5	
12.	1	194.5	219.4	
	2	210.5	234.2	
	3	221.2	247.0	
	4	236.5	262.2	
13.	1	232.6	257.0	
	2	245.2	275.0	
	3	262.7	285.4	
	4	272.6	296.0	
14.	1	265.5		tried with parents refused. Brought back
15.	1	291.2		weighing once in a.m. only
16.	1	322.0		

Lanner now in nursery aviary

PEREGRINE/BARBARY

1.	2	22.8		not hungry yet
	3	22.6	23.7	
	4	23.2	23.9	

Day	Feed	Weight before feed	Weight after feed	Notes
2.	1	23.2	24.3	
	2	23.7	25.3	
	3	24.5	26.9	
	4	26.4	28.9	
3.	1	27.0	29.0	
	2	28.1	31.0	
	3	30.2	32.5	
	4	31.3	34.5	
4.	1	32.1	35.3	
	2	34.4	37.3	
	3	35.9	40.0	
	4	38.0	42.2	
5.	1	38.5	41.5	
	2	39.8	44.3	
	3	43.0	47.0	
	4	45.1	50.0	
6.	1	44.7	49.4	
	2	48.0	53.0	
	3	51.3	55.1	
	4	53.2	59.0	
7.	1	55.0	59.0	
	2	57.5	63.2	
	3	61.5	66.8	
	4	65.1	72.7	
8.	1	68.4	74.1	
	2	72.2	77.9	
	3	75.9	82.1	
	4	79.1	83.3	
9.	1	78.9	84.0	
	2	81.0	86.2	
	3	83.3	89.7	
	4	87.5	95.0	
10.	1	88.7	94.5	
	2	91.8	99.4	
	3	95.6	104.7	
	4	101.0	110.2	
11.	1	102.2	111.0	
	2	109.5	126.1	
	3	120.8	129.4	
	4	124.6	134.5	
12.	1	123.0	136.1	
	2	132.5	153.0	
	3	148.5	164.6	
	4	158.5	174.6	
13.	1	161.0	177.7	
	2	168.9	190.0	
	3	181.0	197.7	
	4	189.0	200.6	
14.	1	186.4	205.1	
	2	197.4	211.7	
	3	203.3	223.3	
	4			fed, but not weighed
15.	1	213.6		weighed once in a.m. only
16.	1	233.5		

Day	Feed	Weight before feed	Weight after feed	Notes
17.	1	256.0		

SAKERS

Day	Feed	Weight before feed	Weight after feed	Notes
1.	4	32	33	
2.	1	31.8	33.5	
3.	2	32.7	34.8	
	3	33.7	37	
	4	36.4	38.6	
2.	1	36.2	39.2	
	2	37.9	40.3	
	3	39.2	41.9	
	4	40.2	43.3	
3.	1	41.0	46.5	
	2	44.5	47.1	
	3	45.5	51.0	
	4	48.4	52.9	
4.	1	50.0	55.7	
	2	52.8	58.5	
	3	55.9	63.0	
	4	60.2	65.3	
5.	1	61.5	68.6	
	2	64.9	71.5	
	3	67.7	76.2	
	4	74.7	83.0	
6.	1	77.4	86.5	
	2	84.6	94. 5	
	3	91.3	102.1	
	4	98.9	108.2	
7.	1	98.1	108.1	
	2	104.2	116.7	
	3	112.7	122.7	
	4	118.2	125.6	
8.	1	116.8	126.4	
	2	124.1	135.3	
	3	131.0	143.1	
	4	138.0	151.4	
9.	1	140.4	150.4	
	2	144.4	161.5	
	3	154.6	175.0	
	4	169.8	183.8	
10.	1	165.2	187.3	
	2	180.7	198.0	
	3	184.7	204.2	
	4	195.8	212.0	
11.	1	194.5	214.7	
	2	206.1	227.4	
	3	214.6	238.8	
	4	228.5	251.4	
12.	1	224.0	243.2	
	2	236.0	256.2	
	3	240.4	262.8	
	4	258.8	280.0	

Pur back the following morning with its parents and reared by them to flying age

Day	Feed	Weight before feed	Weight after feed	Notes
GOSHAWKS (*European*)				
1.	4	40.9	42.9	
2.	1	40.7	44.9	
	2	43.5	45.8	
	3	44.2	46.7	
	4	43.8	47.3	
3.	1	45.6	49.2	
	2	47.6	51.4	
	3	49.6	55.0	
	4	67.0	73.7	
4.	1	55.4	61.2	
	2	59.5	63.4	
	3	60.6	62.1	
	4	59.2	67.7	
5	1	63.5	70.7	
	2	68.1	73.7	
	3	71.1	76.9	
	4	74.4	83.6	
6.	1	78.7	83.8	
	2	81.9	91.6	
	3	87.2	100.9	
	4	97.8	105.7	
7.	1	100.0	109.0	
	2	105.6	120.1	
	3	116.6	131.2	
	4	127.3	137.0	
8.	1	125.5	139.7	
	2	134.9	143.5	
	3	138.6	156.0	
	4	149.6	164.9	
9.	1	151.5	162.3	
	2	154.9	174.0	
	3	170.5	185.1	
	4	176.8	195.7	
10.	1	181.0	196.5	
	2	189.0	213.5	
	3	205.0	215.5	
	4	204.3	218.6	
11.	1	200.4	223.9	
	2	216.2	238.0	
	3	226.7	245.8	
	4	235.6	254.4	
12.	1	230.0		feeding itself, weighing only in morning
13.	1	267.0		
14.	1	291.3		
SPARROW-HAWK (*Accipiter Nisus*)				
1.	1	14.8	15.2	
	2	15.1	15.6	
	3	15.4	16.3	
	4	16.0	16.6	
2.	1	15.5	16.8	
	2	16.2	17.5	

339

Day	Feed	Weight before feed	Weight after feed	Notes
	3	16.4	18.2	
	4	17.0	18.4	
3.	1	16.7	19.0	
	2	18.5	20.5	
	3	19.2	21.0	
	4	20.0	21.4	
4.	1	19.6	20.5	
	2	19.3	20.4	
	3	20.1	21.5	
	4	20.3	22.7	
5.	1	20.9	23.2	
	2	22.5	24.4	
	3	23.7	25.9	
	4	25.1	27.9	
6.	1	26.0	28.7	
	2	27.5	31.0	
	3	29.9	33.2	
	4	32.2	36.0	
7.	1	33.1	36.5	
	2	34.9	39.9	
	3	38.5	42.1	
	4	39.8	45.0	
8.	1	35.0	38.5	
	2	36.6	40.0	
	3	38.0	44.3	
	4	42.0	47.7	
9.	1	42.8	49.0	
	2	47.0	54.4	
	3	51.4	60.4	
	4	56.7	63.0	
10.	1	53.7	60.5	
	2	56.5	64.5	
	3	60.5	66.7	
	4	63.6	68.1	
11.	1	61.5	71.0	
	2	67.6	75.7	
	3	67.6	77.6	
	4	74.1	84.7	
12.	1	74.3	81.0	
	2	77.1	87.2	
	3	78.8	87.2	
	4	84.4	94.5	
13.	1	84.5	93.2	
	2	84.6	97.0	
	3	89.2	103.4	
	4	96.6	107.0	
14.	1	92.2	102.0	
	2	97.5	111.0	
	3	104.6	113.7	
	4	108.0	122.0	
15.	1	103.0	115.2	
	2	112.2	129.9	
	3	122.2	127.9	
	4	118.1	127.2	

Day	Feed	Weight before feed	Weight after feed	Notes
16.	1	111.2	125.0	
	2	122.0	137.9	
	3	132.2	140.6	
	4	128.6	139.0	
17.	1	122.5		weighing once in the morning only 7.
18.	1	131.0		
19.	1	135.5		
20.	1	136.0		
21.				stopped weighing

Appendix 3: Observations

Some intermittent observations made by
R. Shatwell of Captive Blyth's hawk eagles
breeding at the Falconry Centre
Date

Jan. 1st   Male flying back and forth, female calling from nest. Both birds feeding together on lower ledge.

7th   Female feeding male at lower nest ledge.

13th   Both birds roosting at nest.

17th   Female calling at nest, male then flying to nest. Both birds calling to one another.

19th   Female calling at nest, male flying back and forth from ledge to front perch. Both birds roosting at front perch. Female calling again at nest at 4:30, male was at front perch, calling back.

22nd   Pair feeding together on ground. Some calling by the female later on in the afternoon at the nest. She started again at dark.

23rd   Female calling at nest, male flying back and forth doing a circle display and returning to front perch.

24th   Male doing a circle display and returning to front perch. Pair roosting together at far perch.

29th   Female feeding male at lower ledge.

31st   Pair feeding together at front ledge. Later on in the day, male was doing the circle display, female calling at nest throughout the whole display.

Brief Summary: From October until the end of December, the pair stayed separated for most of the time. They generally fed at different times throughout the day.

Early January courtship begins. This will usually commence with the female calling to the male, usually in the vicinity of the nest. Mid-January, the male starts a flying display which usually starts later on in the afternoon. The display consists of flights from the back of the aviary to the front, calling as he returns to each perch. The female is usually at the nest when this happens.

End of January – beginning of March, the male starts to fly a circular flight, returning to the perch which he started from. This flight pattern is different from the back and forth flight pattern and he will alternate them at different times throughout the day often returning to the nest rather than his own perch, but only in instances when the female was also on the nest. Then both birds would call to one another. Sometimes the male would rearrange the nest.

Beginning of March to the beginning of April courtship feeding begins. Usually the male will bring the food to the female early in the morning if they want to eat in the morning. This consists of the male picking up the food and bringing the food to the female at the front ledge. The female will call first when taking the food. Both birds then feeding together with the same food. But, most of the time in the afternoon when the birds are feeding, it has always been the female picking up the food and bringing it to the male at the back ledge. There, the female will feed first, call the male over, and proceed to feed the male. She will sometimes leave him with the food and return to the nest.

Mid-March through April – copulation occurs. It usually starts in the late afternoon early in the season at about 4:30. This involves the female standing on the lower ledge and calling the male over. The male will then fly next to the female, both birds standing upright and calling to one another. This goes on until the female goes into copulation posture. Both birds calling while copulating. Copulation occurs more frequently throughout the day, becoming most frequent two weeks before egg laying. Not much nest building by this pair of birds and when it was done the male always brought evergreen twigs.

*Although certain types of courtship display occur early on in the year, such as the female feeding the male and the circular flight display by the male, these actions occur much more frequently at the times of the year stated above.

Some intermittent observations on sakers 1982

Feb. 7th 5.40   Old male introduced back again with female. This bird has been with the female for the last 2 years but produced infertile eggs only. 2 clutches of 5 each year. Hormone implants had been tried previously. On reintroductin both birds flew to the nest calling and bowing.

17th 5.45 Cold, cloudy. Snow previous night.   12.30 male making scrape at nest.

18th 5.40 Cold, cloudy.   Female passing food to male at the nest.

25th 6.15 Sunny, cool.   Not roosting at nest. Some calling in morning. Food present but none passed. Pair feeding at nest calling while feeding.

Mar. 2nd. 6.30 Rain. a.m. cold all day   Both birds feeding at nest. No food passing. Male making scrape and calling while making scrape display. Female standing next to him 6.15 p.m. both roosting together on far perch away from nest.

4th 6.30 Sunny, cold   Male fed first. Female called for food. Not passed. 4.00 p.m. fed quail. Female took it first, then male took his. Both fed at nest. Male: 2 quail, female: 1. total 270 gms.

5th Sunny, cold   2 quail, 2 chicks (day olds), total 260 gms.

6th 6.30 Cold, rain   3 quail. 2 chicks, 350 gms.

7th 6.30. Cold, cloudy   4 quail 2 each 360gms.

8th 6.45 Rain a.m. sunny later, cold.   1.00 p.m. Male making long call at nest ledge. 4.00 p.m.

Male making scrape display. 10 chicks, 400 gms.

9th 6.30. Sunny a.m. rain p.m.   Male flying to nest just before dark to join female. Male calling and scrape displaying. Female calling and bowing then flying to far perch to roost at 6.20. Female ate 2 quail & 3 chicks. Male only I chick. Total. 290 gms.

10th 6.40. Sunny a.m. rain. p.m.   Male scrape display and calling. Female disinterested on far perch. (a.m.). Similar p.m. when female at nest but still disinterested. 6.30 p.m. Male lying in nest. Female on centre perch. Male calling. Female not interested. 2 quail, 4 chicks, 440gms.

11th 6.40 Cloudy, cool   Male scrape display 8.45 a.m. Male feeding and calling. No interest from female. 4.30 scrape display by male. 11 chicks, I quail, 520 gms.

12th 6.40. Sunny a.m., cloudy p.m. cool   Male lying in nest a.m. Male scrape display in evening. 1 quail 3 chicks, 320 gms.

13th Sunny, cool   Male taking food first to nest. Female flying off nest away from male. Male calling a lot and scrape displaying. Female back to nest. Male calling again. 9.30 both feeding at nest. Male then flying to ground and feeding there. 4.00 male passing food to female at centre perch. 5.30 exactly the same but female calling for food now. Food passing from beak to beak. Male at nest sitting low down at sundown. 3 quail 300 gms.

14th 6.40 Sunny, cool   Male passed food to female at far perch. 12.30 male scrape display. Female at pole perch disinterested.

15th 6.20 Rainy, cloudy   Male passing food at far perch. Female taking it to nest to eat. Male passed more food to female at nest. 3 chicks 1 quail, 380 gms.

16th 6.45. Partly sunny   Male called female to far perch and passed food. 11.45 scrape display

17 6.45 Sunny a.m. cloudy p.m. cool.   Food passing at nest in morning. At far perch in afternoon and after at pole perch. 6 chick poults, 420 gms.

Mar. 18th 6.50 Sunny, cool.   Saker male passing food to female at pole perch. Female feeding at nest. Male passing food to female at far perch then returning to nest. 3 chick poults, 240 gms.

19th 6.40 Rainy, cold. In a.m. male saker trying to pass food to female and she is not interested. Afternoon Male passes food to female on the ground. Male doing scrape display at 6.00. 2 chick poults, 160 gms.

20th 6.50 Cloudy a.m. Sunny p.m. Male passing food to female at far perch. Then passing again at pole perch. Food passing again at pole perch in afternoon. Male doing scrape display at 3.30. 2 chicks and 1 quail, 280 gms.

21st 6.50 Cloudy, rain Male passing food 3 times each time at the nest in the morning. Twice in afternoon at far perch. Male doing scrape display at night. 4 chick poults, 360 gms.

22nd 7.00 Sunny, warm Female in nest in morning. Sitting. Male calling female over for food. Female dropping it, he picks it up and passes it on to her again. Male does scrape display at 10.45 and again at 11.30 a.m. Passing food at far perch. 3 chick poults 1 quail 500 gms.

23rd 7.00 Sunny, warm Male passing food at far perch. Male in nest calling (12.00). 1.00 – male coming down to food, calling to female. She is not interested in food. Male going back to nest and doing scrape display. 3.00 – female is lying down in nest, then flying off to pole perch and joining male. 2 chick poults 1 quail, 400 gms.

24th 7.00 Sunny, warm 7.30 a.m. male is passing food to female, female dropping it. 9.00 a.m. male in nest is calling, short calls. 3.00 p.m. male is starting to store food on ground in aviary. Picking up stored quail at 3.00 and passing it on to female at far perch. 4.00 p.m. male is passing food to female, bringing it to her at pole perch. 4.30 p.m. male doing scrape display. 1 quail 1 chick, 240 gms.

25th 7.00 Sunny, warm Male passing food at far perch. Passing food again at far perch. In afternoon passing food at far perch. Female in nest, male calling. Passing food to her at far perch. 4 chicks 1 quail, 410 gms.

26th 7.00 Sunny, warm Food passing at pole perch. And again and at far perch. Continuous passing. 3 chicks, 3 quail, 300 gms.

27th 7.00 Sunny, warm Food passing at far perch. Male calling in nest. Also scrape display. Female behind him calling a little. (11.00) Food passing at far perch. 4 chicks 2 quail, 380 gms.

28th 7.00 Sunny warm No passing a.m. Scrape display by male. Less food being eaten past few days. 4.00 food passing pole perch. 3 chicks, 150 gms.

29th 7.00 Partly sunny, very cool Food passing far perch. And again. Female taking it to ground and leaving it. Male picking it up and giving it to her on far perch. Male feeding next to female, eating half then passing rest to her at pole perch. 5 chicks, 70 gms beef, 320 gms in all.

30th 7.10 As yesterday 3 chicks, 150 gms.

31st 7.10 Cool, partly sunny Food passing at far perch. Also on ground. Male in nest 6.30 Still there 7.20. Female on nest ledge. 5 chicks, 2 quail. 510 gms.

Some intermittent observations of captive redtailed buzzards 1982

Date

Jan. 4th Male redtail picking at straw on ground.

6th. 10.30 a.m. Male in nest, then on ground picking up things but not putting them into nest.

11th. (heavy snow last 3 days) feeding at nest today.

12th (cloudy, fog, cold.) Pair roosting close together on perch.

17th (warm weather past three days) female feeding in nest.

19th. Female in nest in afternoon. Not roosting at nest.

20th. Little activity. Female spending some time at nest but doing nothing.

23rd. Both birds at nest during afternoon. Roosting together at perch.

24th. Male calling a little and flying, feet first into front barrier mesh, at 3.30. Pair roosting together at back perch, very close.

29th. Male picking up nesting material and taking it to nest. Female arranging it.

30th. Male in nest arranging material. Not seen to be picking it up.

31st. 4.45 Male flying to and fro a lot.

Feb. 1st. A lot of nest building going on by both birds.

4th. A lot more nest building. Male food passing at stump 3.30 Attempted mating at centre perch.

18th. Not much progress since 4th Feb. Some nest building. Bad weather for the past week.

20th. Attempting mating in morning.

23rd. Mating.

24th. Mating 12.00 and 3.30

25th. Mating 11.00 and 3.00 Female settling in nest for about 10 minutes. Roosting with male on back perch.

26th. Mating at 11.00, 2.00 and 4.00.

27th. Mating at 11.00 and 3.00.

28th. Female on nest at night. Male roosting at back perch.

March 2nd. Mating twice in morning.

3rd. Mating 8.00 a.m. and 5.45 .m.

4th. Mating 8.40. 10.15.

20th. 1st egg laid.

April 2nd. Three eggs taken and put into incubator.

Index

Page numbers in bold (thus **24**) refer to pages on which illustrations appear
G indicates entry in Glossary on pp. 323–5

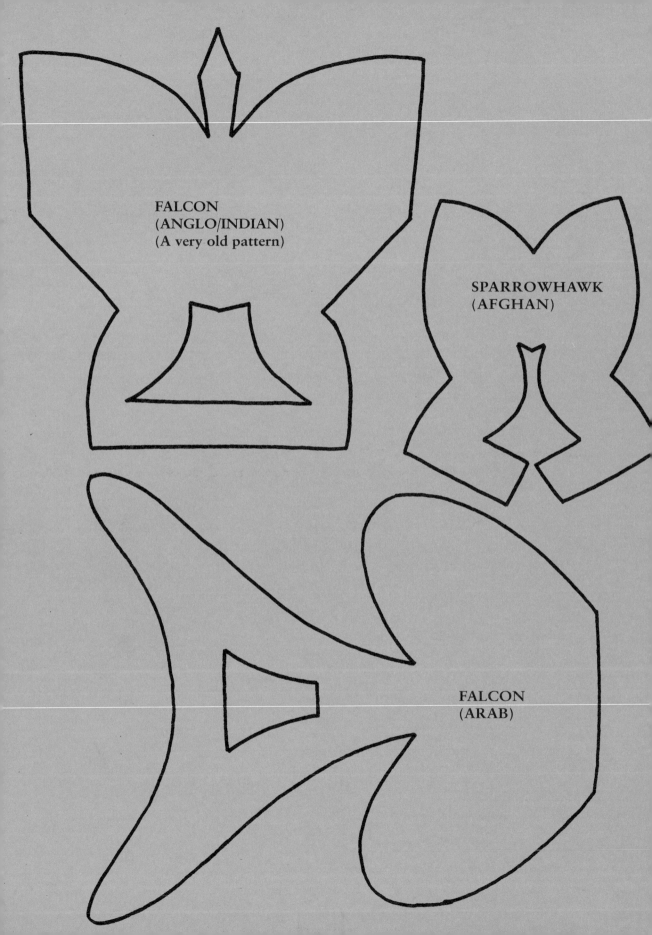

FALCON
(ANGLO/INDIAN)
(A very old pattern)

SPARROWHAWK
(AFGHAN)

FALCON
(ARAB)